LARRY BIRNBAUM

On Raising

Current Studies in Linguistics Series
Samuel Jay Keyser, general editor

On Raising:
One Rule of English Grammar
and Its Theoretical
Implications

Paul M. Postal

The MIT Press Cambridge, Massachusetts, and London, England

This book was set in Linotype Baskerville,
printed on Mohawk Neotext Offset
and bound in Whitman P.O.C. "Emerald Green"
by Halliday Lithograph Corporation
in the United States of America.

Library of Congress Cataloging in Publication Data

Postal, Paul Martin, 1936-
    On raising: one rule of English grammar and its theoretical implications.

    (Current studies in linguistics series, 5)
    Bibliography: p.
    1. English language—Sentences.   2. English language—Grammar, Generative.
I. Title.
PE1380.P6   425   73-16482
ISBN 0-262-16057-9

I should like to dedicate this study to Noam Chomsky. The present work is highly critical of some of his more recent grammatical proposals, as several other post-1968 works of mine have been, and as future works will in all likelihood be. But no matter how the issues are ultimately resolved, it is clear that none of this kind of work would ever have been possible without the many fundamental, ground-breaking insights and the radical reorientation of the goals and methods of linguistic inquiry which he has played such an enormous role in bringing about. While he and I have many important, some quite profound, disagreements about the nature of grammatical structure (in particular, about the role of meaning in this structure, about the role of global rules, about the existence of deep structure, and about the existence of syntactic features), these disagreements exist within a context of accepted questions and premises that his earlier work created. Thus, while the present work stresses disagreements, a certain framework containing many underlying agreements is implicit in most contexts. Finally, it is also true that his recent proposals have been among the chief stimuli leading to the preparation of this volume.

Contents

Foreword

We are pleased to present this book as the fifth volume in the series Current Studies in Linguistics.

As we have defined it, the series will offer book-length studies in linguistics and neighboring fields that further the exploration of man's ability to manipulate symbols. It will pursue the same editorial goals as its companion journal, *Linguistic Inquiry,* and will complement it by providing a format for in-depth studies beyond the scope of the professional article.

By publishing such studies, we hope the series will answer a need for intensive and detailed research that sheds new light on current theoretical issues and provides a new dimension for their resolution. Toward this end it will present books dealing with the widest range of languages and addressing the widest range of theoretical topics. From time to time and with the same ends in view, the series will include collections of significant articles covering single and selected subject areas and works primarily for use as textbooks.

Like *Linguistic Inquiry,* Current Studies in Linguistics will seek to present work of theoretical interest and excellence.

Samuel Jay Keyser

Preface

This study is devoted in considerable part to showing that English sentences like (i) have surface structures in which *Melvin* is an object of the main verb, though they have underlying structures in which *Melvin* is a subject of the complement clause, these stages being mediated by a rule of grammar called Raising.

(i) Max $\left\{ \begin{array}{l} \text{believed} \\ \text{proved} \\ \text{found} \end{array} \right\}$ Melvin to be immortal.

In a way it is somewhat ridiculous to devote the extensive space taken here to the narrow range of questions involved in this matter, for reasons independent of the fact that until very recently the claims just made about (i) would not have been regarded as controversial. Several hundred pages are taken up to show little more than the existence of one rule in the derivations of sentences with at most a few hundred English verbal elements. While I am not unsympathetic to the view that this is overkill, there is another point of view, one which would criticize a work like this, not for its depth, but for its superficiality. For, despite the fact that this work hardly suffers from brevity, few of the matters dealt with have really been adequately treated, and the empirical ramifications of claim after claim have in general been only superficially investigated, if at all. This is, I think, due more to the vast extent of English grammar, the incredible number of interactions between diverse grammatical properties, and the fact that even in 1972 most of English grammar remains uncharted than to research defects.

An important related point is that among the many limitations of current grammatical description and theory, even for an extensively studied language like English, there appear to be few, if any, really solidly supported analyses. Consequently, as one begins the study of any particular domain, there are no strong empirical constraints on work derivable from deeply justified analyses of other parts of the grammar, analyses that must be taken as givens. The whole system is so little understood that every part of any proposed structure is somewhat shaky. If this judgment is correct, it is highly worthwhile to seek to justify in depth certain points to serve, among other things, as beginnings of a basis for other studies.

One may disagree with the extent to which the present work succeeds in providing such a relatively well justified analysis of an element of

English grammar in the case of Raising. But if the general principle is acceptable, the combination of the length of this work with the narrow range of questions considered may be agreed to be a function of more than pedantry.

If I am correct, not only is the present study not a definitive treatment of the topic of Raising in English, it is hardly more than an introduction to the investigation of what still remains little-studied territory. I shall be pleased if others are stimulated to investigate it in greater depth than I have been able to. In particular, what emerges as a clear necessity is the large-scale study of each of the individual verbal items that interact directly with the Raising rule. In Chapter 9, I give a relatively extensive, though unquestionably incomplete, listing of what I take to be the major members of this set.

A word is in order about the descriptive framework implicit in most of the following discussion. I believe that one should make every effort at this primitive stage of grammatical understanding to describe the sentences of particular languages in what I shall call *natural* grammatical terms. This means, among other things, that one should assume the existence of no elements of structure, no levels of structure, and no kinds of representations whose existence is not absolutely necessary. I therefore assume, with work called "generative semantics," that underlying grammatical structures are subparts of the logical structures of sentences, for it is known independently that these must exist. I also assume that the devices available for describing sentence structure are constrained so that the only symbols usable (ignoring the "neutral" elements of the underlying mathematical system, the concatenation operator, etc.) are the set of symbols necessary for the formation of surface structures and the set of symbols required to describe logical structures. Thus I reject all so-called syntactic features, doom markers, other abstract syntactic markers, coding devices, "empty nodes," "doubly filled nodes," and, in short, the entire a priori unlimited set of symbolic elements available in an unconstrained system. I claim that the symbols needed to describe particular sentences beyond those required to describe the surface structures of those sentences are the symbols for describing the logical structures of the relevant sentences, and the direct reflections of these in derived structures distinct from surface structures. The one relaxation I shall accept is to allow also a set of universally specified symbols that can be mechanically defined in terms of the two sets of logical and surface symbols—a set of derivative categories like *subject (of)* and Reflexive. This restriction to natural symbols is a strong constraint on grammars but still, undoubtedly, too weak. Nonetheless, it provides an important demarcation between the general approach underlying this study and that of much past and present work within generative studies in which it is assumed, apparently, that grammatical structure involves a host of symbolic devices justified neither by the nature of logical structures nor by the nature of surface structures.

In addition, I assume the availability of "global" statements in grammar, rules that range over more than one (not necessarily contiguous) tree in derivations. While reference to globality is not crucial to the argument in general, it is appealed to in several places as providing the best descriptive account of some range of phenomena.

Finally, even more peripherally, I appeal to "transderivational" rules, principles defined over sets of derivations. This also is not typically crucial to the argument, with the exception of the discussion in Section 12.5.

The present study involves hundreds of judgments about English sentences and nonsentences, grammaticality judgments, ambiguity judgments, constituent structure judgments, truth-functional equivalence judgments, etc. Many of these judgments are of varying degrees of subtlety. I have no doubt that many readers will disagree with a substantial number of them. Some of the disagreement may be due simply to error on one side or the other, but part of it is unquestionably an irresolvable matter of idiolect difference. Such differences may render certain arguments inapplicable for certain speakers. Nor can one rule out the possibility, though I think it is less likely, that certain disagreements might reverse the conclusions of some arguments. While it has been impossible to make any serious study of idiolectal variation for the phenomena considered in this study, I think I have received enough feedback from readers to suggest that the general trend of judgments is widely shared, enough so that I believe the viability of the conclusions reached depends more on the logical structure of the arguments, hidden premises, and relations to still unstudied matters than it does on the solidity of the judgments. But this is ultimately for others to decide. Furthermore, within the range of speakers with whom I have communicated over many years, my own judgments of grammaticality tend to be far on the restrictive side. That is, I tend to reject as ill-formed certain structures that many others accept, indicating that I have various constraints in my grammar which others do not. Thus, for the most part, I expect that grammaticality disagreements on the reader's part will involve acceptance of structures that I regard as ill-formed.

Of course, judgments differ in their clarity or firmness, but it has not been possible, by and large, to indicate degrees of certainty or degrees of grammaticality, although this sort of a gradient of acceptability and indeterminateness is everywhere experientially the rule. The use of the familiar notational system of starred versus unstarred examples, modified only by an occasional question mark, tends to give a misleading, largely binary appearance to a system of judgments which is in fact far murkier and more complicated. I hope, though, the effects of this are not critical for the issues under investigation here.

I should like to express great appreciation to Georgia Green, Maurice Gross, Jorge Hankamer, S.-Y. Kuroda, George Lakoff, Ronald Langacker, Howard Lasnik, and Emily Pope, for the large number of helpful criticisms and suggestions they have provided. Special thanks are due to C. L. Baker, Richard Kayne, Susumu Kuno, James D. McCawley, David Perlmutter, Warren Plath, and John R. Ross, who have gone over earlier versions of this work in great detail. The enormous contribution they have jointly made to the quality of the present version of this study far exceeds that indicated by the too few explicit credits in the text. Altogether these critics have saved me from many errors, provided a host of insights, and clarified the line of argument at many points. Naturally, they are to be absolved of any responsibility for remaining inadequacies. Those deficiencies of this final version which are not attributable to sunspots are to be blamed entirely on the author. Last, but not least, I should like to thank Nancy Perry for nearly endless help with the manuscript.

1
A Bit of History

1.1 Introduction
In this study I shall consider the rule of English grammar which has variously been called Pronoun Replacement, *It* Replacement, and Subject Raising, and which, following Kiparsky and Kiparsky (1970), I shall call simply Raising.

From the narrowest point of view, my goals are to review the traditional arguments for such an operation, to add many new ones, and to show that an account along the lines briefly given in McCawley (1970a) is essentially correct, as opposed to a recent proposal by Chomsky (to appear), which claims in effect that the scope of Raising is limited to a restricted subset of the cases previously thought to involve Raising. McCawley assumes, following the generally accepted position in generative studies since at least the time of Rosenbaum's 1965 dissertation (see Rosenbaum, 1967), that Raising operates to form both derived main clause subjects and derived main clause objects. He argues further that these two distinct functions can be combined in a single rule only under conditions requiring underlying structures of a sort rather different from those previously widely accepted. In particular, McCawley argues that the proper combination of these rules requires the assumption that English has verb-initial underlying clause structures. Chomsky (to appear), on the other hand, rejects the view that Raising operates to derive main clause objects, and he also rejects the verb-initial assumption.

Although one result of this discussion is that McCawley's line of argument in favor of the verb-initial assumption is considerably strengthened in several respects, the validity of this conception is nonetheless far from established. What does result, I think, is only the conclusion that the verb-initial view is superior to the approach initiated in Chomsky (1957), according to which the basic structure of English clauses is of the form NP + VP. But there are other possibilities, including underlying verb-final structures and underlying structures in which the order of the verb and nominal constituents is not fixed.

The central core of this work is thus directed toward validating the claim, not hitherto controversial, that Raising generates derived objects.

In later chapters, I survey some of the properties of Raising: its cyclicity, its relation to extrinsic rule ordering, and the possibility that, in contrast to all previous treatments, the proper formulation of this rule inherently involves grammatical relations. I also consider the idea that many of the fundamental properties of Raising might not have to be stated in English grammar but are instead lawful functions of general principles of universal grammar. I further investigate briefly the idea that Raising is not, in fact, a particular element of English grammar but is rather only the English instantiation of an operation of universal grammar. This idea is elaborated in connection with a brief exploration of the analogue of Raising in Japanese, based on work of Susumu Kuno. In another chapter, I discuss the role of Raising in nominalizations, considering how this phenomenon bears on the so-called lexicalist hypothesis about nominalizations suggested by Chomsky (1970). I also provide an extensive, though incomplete, categorization and listing of those verbal elements which trigger Raising operation, and I consider some difficult and unresolved problems involving constraints on Raising, especially cases where Raising operation seems to be linked with particular semantic assumptions.

Although descriptive and theoretical questions form the chief elements of interest in what follows, this monograph can also be regarded in part as a reference work in which a rather large number of restrictions involving Raising constructions and related areas are documented, even if they are not explained or even adequately described.

1.2 Lees's Account

Problems involving Raising seem to have been considered first within generative studies by Lees (1960: 62–63). Lees noticed such sentences as the following, all of which are, of course, passives:

(1) a. He is known to have gone there.

   b. They were believed to have seen him.

   c. She is said to be educated.

He believed, in fact, that the descriptive problems posed by sentences like (1) were essentially a matter of passivization and proposed that such examples were a kind of "second passive" of *that*-clause complements. Lees thus provided the paradigm given here:

(2) a. I think that he is rich. (*that* clause)

   b. That he is rich is thought by me. (?) (1st passive)

   c. He is thought to be rich by me. (2nd passive)

   d. But not: *I think him to be rich. (complement)

Under the assumption that sentences like (1) were limited to passive cases, Lees proposed a Second Passive rule, which gave the option of operating on structures like (2)a to yield (2)c, where the standard rule Passive would yield (2)b.[1] Hence, where Passive would operate on the whole object of *think,* as on the objects of other verbs, Second Passive, the new rule proposed by Lees, would operate on the subject NP of the embedded clausal objects of verbs like *think.*

However, Lees's assumption that the problems of describing (1) involved essentially exceptional passivization rested largely on the fact that his (2)d was ill-formed. For if (2)d were well-formed, and if *him* were taken to be the object of *think* at the point when Passive applied in the main clause, then (2)c would have a natural derivation from (2)d by Passive, with no need for an additional rule Second Passive. And, in fact, the ill-formedness of (2)d can be seen to be basically fortuitous,[2] since other verbs that fit into paradigms like (2), including *believe, find, prove,* and *show,* have well-formed analogues of (2)d. Hence, Lees's evidently generalization-missing postulation of a Second Passive rule[3] can be seen to have rested on an accidental feature of some of the relevant

1 Lees made a poor choice in picking underlying first person subject NPs since, at least for many speakers, these are ill-formed when occurring in passive *by* phrases (see Ross, 1970a). This consequently introduced an irrelevant and possibly confusing factor into the examples. That is, (2)b, c are deviant sentences because of this constraint.

2 Such claims are always somewhat risky since, in claiming that certain facts are fortuitous, one may only be illustrating ignorance of underlying regularities. In fact, in Section 9.3, a constraint (DOC) is uncovered which predicts many facts similar to those like (2)d. The subcategorization of verbs with respect to paradigms like (2) is discussed in limited detail in Chapter 9.

3 An argument that there is, in fact, no Second Passive rule distinct from ordinary Passive can be based on the verbal stem *rumor.* This occurs only in passive clauses:

(i) a. It is rumored that Spiro is nervous.

   b. Spiro is rumored to be nervous.

(ii) a. *I rumored that Spiro was nervous.

   b. *I rumored Spiro to be nervous.

   c. *What they rumored was that Spiro was nervous.

complement-taking verbs, particularly *think* and *say*, for which the analogues of (2)d are ill-formed.[4]

Once it is recognized, however, that this feature is not a systematic property of paradigms like (2), the descriptive problems of sentences like (1) are seen to involve essentially, not unmotivated passivization, but rather the question of the relations between sentence pairs like those in (3):

(3) a. Jack believes (that) Bill is foolish; Jack believes Bill to be foolish.

 b. Joan proved (that) Melvin was a spy; Joan proved Melvin to be a spy.

 c. I showed (that) his proposal was inconsistent; I showed his proposal to be inconsistent.

Moreover, there is every likelihood that a proper specification of these relations will automatically predict, by means of the standard rule Pas-

---

This can be accounted for under the analysis to be adopted here by adding to the grammar statements to the effect that verbal *rumor* can be only the verb of a clause that has undergone Passive. But in Lees's system, with its rule Second Passive, this generalization must be replaced by a disjunctive claim to the effect that verbal *rumor* must undergo either Passive or Second Passive, since (i)a would involve the former, (i)b the latter.

Observe, incidentally, that this argument cannot be overthrown by claiming that the constraint on *rumor* is really that it takes an underlying unspecified agent NP, and that this agent NP must be deleted, therefore requiring the agent NP to occur in contexts in which such deletion is possible. This approach would make it a derivative fact that *rumor* occurs verbally only in contexts like (i), and not (ii), since agent deletion is possible in the former but not the latter. However, this argument cannot be correct, since it fails to explain why *rumor* cannot occur in active form in various embedded contexts in which agent NP deletion is possible for unspecified NP (see Postal, 1970: 478–482). For instance, (iii) is possible, but (iv) is not:

(iii) a. Inviting their ambassador was proposed by the secretary.
 b. Selling them nuclear weapons was discussed by the committee.

(iv) a. *Rumoring that the president was a vampire was proposed by the secretary.
 b. *Rumoring that they had nuclear weapons was discussed by the committee.

It thus seems that it is necessary to restrict verbal *rumor* to Passive contexts independently of matters of unspecified agent deletion.

[4] A conclusion already reached by Rosenbaum (1967: 115):

One of the most interesting aspects of Lees' analysis concerns the formulation of a "second passive" transformation to handle the derivation of sentences like (3).

(3) a. they were believed to have seen him.
 b. he was thought to be rich.

sive, the passive sentences that first attracted Lees's attention. In short, what needs to be clarified is the relation between infinitival and *that*-clause complements for verbs of the *believe, prove*, etc., class (henceforth: B-verbs).

1.3 Rosenbaum's Analysis

Following Lees's discussion, these matters seem to have been largely ignored[5] until Rosenbaum's 1965 thesis on complementation (Rosenbaum, 1967), which made, in my opinion, a fundamental contribution to the understanding of the problems raised by Lees in the context of a wider analysis of many other constructions. Although formulated in terms of several assumptions that do not now seem acceptable,[6] Rosenbaum's chief insight was that sentence relations like those in (3) are a function of a rule, which he called Pronoun Replacement (here Raising), which lifts the subject NP of the *that* complements of B-verbs out of the subordinate clause, making the former subordinate subject NP a derived superordinate object NP. This is shown schematically in (4).[7]

In Lees' analysis, the second passive transformation operates on a string like "I think that he is rich" to generate the string "he is thought to be rich by me." Lees was forced to postulate this additional transformation since the "regular" passive must apply to the highest level NP to the right of the verb in the phrase structure. Thus, the regular passive would always yield the string "that he is rich is thought by me" and never "he is thought to be rich by me" since the pronoun "he" is necessarily dominated by a higher NP. We now know that the passive sentence "he is thought to be rich by me" does arise through the application of the regular passive transformation, at least in part. The passive transformation produces the string "it for he to be rich is thought by me." Through the application of two independently motivated transformations, the extraposition transformation and the pronoun replacement transformation, we generate first "it is thought by me for he to be rich" and second "he is thought by me for to be rich." Applying the second complementizer deletion transformation, we derive the string "he is thought by me to be rich." It thus appears probable that Lees' second passive transformation is unnecessary.

5 Although important observations amounting to the principle of cyclic application of transformational rules (see Chomsky, 1965) were made by Fillmore (1963) in a pivotal and overly neglected study of complement constructions.

6 In particular, Rosenbaum assumed (i) an underlying NP + VP structure for clauses; (ii) that Raising operated on the output of Extraposition; (iii) that Raising was a rule that replaced a pronoun; and hence (iv) that underlying complement NPs had the structure $[_{NP}$ it $[S]$ $_{NP}]$. Reasons for rejecting these assumptions are found implicitly or explicitly throughout the body of this study. Rosenbaum also assumed that various rules, like Passive, Raising, and Extraposition, had to be crucially ordered by extrinsic rule-ordering statements. But, in fact, given the principle of the cycle, there is no evidence for this. More generally, it is not hard to doubt the existence of any ad hoc ordering statements for grammatical rules. See Section 8.3.

7 Notice that (4) does not embody the final three assumptions of footnote 6.

(4)

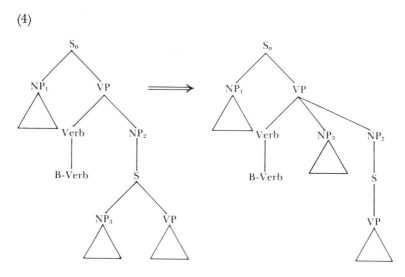

    This account ignores any question of the operation pruning the S node dominated by NP_2 (see Ross, 1967, 1969a; Perlmutter, 1971; and Section 6.5). If Raising is supplemented by operations that guarantee in some way[8] that application of Raising with B-verbs triggers modification of *that* clause + finite verbal form to infinitival form, the relations between pairs like those in (3) are naturally described[9] in a system that claims that such pairs have the same underlying (transformational input) structure. Under reasonable assumptions, in particular, under the

---

[8] I shall take no position in this study on *how* this deformation is to be characterized, insisting only that infinitival form in B-verb complements is induced *during* derivations, rather than being a function of distinctions drawn in the maximally underlying structures (as in Bresnan, 1970, and Chomsky, to appear). See Kiparsky and Kiparsky (1970).

[9] This ignores, of course, the fact that many *that* clauses have no infinitival counterparts. For instance, this is true of all those *that* clauses that have presubject (adverbial) constituents and of those containing modals or special sequences like *had better* and *supposed to,* since these elements just cannot occur in infinitives (see Langendoen, 1969, 1970). It also ignores the fact that there are other concomitants of the switch to infinitival form. For example, past tense shows up in B-verb infinitival complements as the verb *have*:

(i) a. I proved that she lied yesterday.
    b. I proved her to have lied yesterday.

I assume that all facts like those mentioned in this paragraph are a function of rules and constraints distinct from Raising, though obviously related to it.

assumption that sentences with the same meaning have the same underlying structures, the latter conclusion is supported by the lack of semantic contrast between such pairs.[10] In addition, an analysis of B-verbs like (4) means that such elements must be said to occur in only one kind of underlying structure.[11]

Rosenbaum argued that the analysis of B-verbs in terms of Raising was supported by the fact that Raising had much independent basis in other constructions, particularly in relating pairs such as the following:

(5) a. It turned out that Melvin was insane; Melvin turned out to be insane.

  b. It happens that Max is going to Tunisia; Max happens to be going to Tunisia.

  c. It seems that Mitchell is a cretin; Mitchell seems to be a cretin.

  d. It appears that you have an embarrassing disease; you appear to have an embarrassing disease.

Rosenbaum suggested that his rule of Pronoun Replacement was also operative with these verbs (henceforth: A-verbs), moving the complement subject NP into the position of the superordinate clause subject. I shall not go over here any of Rosenbaum's arguments for the operation of this rule in the second member of pairs like (5). Suffice it to say that the arguments he did give are only a subset of the grounds that can be given today (see Section 12.1).

Although intuitively it seems that Rosenbaum's idea that the same

10 Ultimately, in Chapter 11, I shall consider cases where application of Raising is associated with certain types of semantic contrast.

11 As opposed, for instance, to an analysis of sentences like (i) of the form [NP Verb NP S], which, in conjunction with sentences like (ii), means that *show* must occur in two distinct types of configuration.

(i) Bob showed Mary to be incompetent.

(ii) Bob showed that . . .

A crucial point, I believe, is that the structure [. . . Verb + NP + S] for sentences like (i) is *logically* inexplicable, since it seems that *show* (and other B-verbs) represent transitive predicates that relate an individual and a proposition in sentences like both (i) and (ii). This logical structure thus predicts, within a natural system of grammar, the structure [. . . Verb + NP] for both (i) and (ii), while [. . . Verb + NP + S] is without independent motivation.

rule is functioning in both (3) and (5) is correct, it was not easy within the framework of assumptions made in 1965 to formulate a single operation to do the job. What was required, apparently, was a single rule that could do both, as shown in (6). Within anything like a standard transformational framework, it was (and is) impossible to formulate a single rule to accomplish both of these mappings. Rosenbaum's approach to this problem was to argue that his Pronoun Replacement operated, not on structures like (6)a(i), b(i), but rather on the result of applying the rule of Extraposition to them. The latter is the rule that

(6) a. (i)

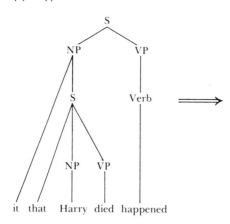

a. (ii)

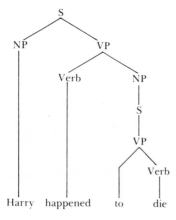

b. (i)

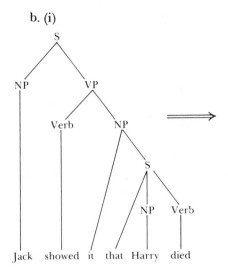

Jack showed it that Harry died

b. (ii)

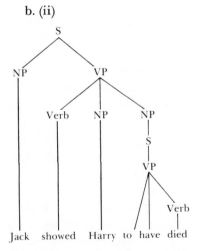

Jack showed Harry to have died

throws embedded clauses to the end of the immediately superordinate clause, deriving (7)b and (8)b from structures like (7)a and (8)a, respectively:

(7) a. That Bill is clever is obvious.

  b. It is obvious that Bill is clever.

(8) a. For Bill to do that would be unwise.

  b. It would be unwise for Bill to do that.

Hence, in the derivation of (6)a(ii), Pronoun Replacement in these terms would operate, not on a structure like (6)a(i), but rather on one like (9):

(9) It happened that Harry died.

Similarly, in the derivation of (6)b(ii), Pronoun Replacement would operate, not on (6)b(i), but rather on the result of applying Extraposition "vacuously" to this tree, which has the effect of leaving the terminal string unchanged but of taking the complement S out from under the NP node and attaching it higher up in the tree. A consequence of the assumption that Pronoun Replacement operated on the output of Extraposition was that in all cases Pronoun Replacement would be moving an NP to the left, permitting a single statement for both A-verbs and B-verbs.

1.4 The Lakoff-Ross Critique
Although they accepted as correct Rosenbaum's view that the same rule functions to determine both the derived subjects of A-verbs and the derived objects of B-verbs, Lakoff (1967) and Ross (1967) together developed a series of objections to Rosenbaum's claim that the relevant rule could operate on the output of Extraposition. One argument took the form of a purported demonstration that Extraposition was a postcyclical rule, while Pronoun Replacement was cyclical, hence precluding the possibility of the latter operating on the output of the former. The view that Extraposition is postcyclical has in general persisted up to the present (see McCawley, 1970a). It is, however, by no means a certain conclusion, and some recent evidence argues for its cyclicity (Grinder, 1970). If it is a cyclical rule, the objection to Rosenbaum's proposal based on the postcyclical assumption does not stand up.

A second objection was that Rosenbaum's formulation required, in the case of B-verbs, the possibility of "vacuous" applications of Extraposition, that is, applications that rearranged tree structure without altering the terminal string, as would be the case if Extraposition applied to (6)b(i). Lakoff and Ross argued that such operations were not well defined, in particular, that the proper derived constituent structure was not uniquely specified. But this objection does not seem fatal, since there are various algorithms that would deal with this problem.

It is argued later, in Section 4.11, that the rule Complex NP Shift operates in certain cases "vacuously." [12]

A third objection was based on ordering arguments involving the rule Reflexivization with reference to the rather unique reflexive forms found in sentences like (10):

(10) It suggests itself to me that Harry is a liar.

The argument had the following form: if Extraposition precedes Pronoun Replacement, it must also precede Reflexivization, since Pronoun Replacement precedes Reflexivization, as sentences like (11) show:

(11) Jane believes herself to be incompetent.

But with this ordering, it was claimed, (10) cannot be derived, presumably because the "antecedent" structure would be to the right at the point of Reflexivization application. However, this argument seems to have no force today, since it depends totally on the assumption that Reflexivization is an ordinary replacement transformation requiring full constituent identity between two NPs, so that underlying (10) would be as follows:

(12) [that Harry is a liar suggests that Harry is a liar to me]

But hardly anyone takes such a view seriously today, for a variety of reasons. Moreover, even if such a view were adequate for reflexives in general, it would be dubious for those in sentences like (10), since the reflexive in (10) does not seem to correspond to any argument in logical structure. Therefore, I suggest that the pronoun in sentences like (10) arises through a doubling rule.

Another objection[13] of an ingenious sort claimed that Rosenbaum's Extraposition approach to Pronoun Replacement could deal only with the correlation between the anomalies in sentences like (13) by way of a rule ordering like (14):

---

[12] Kayne (personal communication) suggests that there is an argument that the rule of French he calls L-Tous (Kayne, 1969) must be allowed to apply "vacuously" to capture certain generalizations. Chomsky (to appear) suggests without detailed discussion a ban on cyclical rules all of whose applications are "vacuous". It is not clear that even this weaker principle can be sustained. See Chapter 7 for some brief discussion.

[13] This argument is given in detail in Postal (1971: 255–259).

(13) a. *Jane was criticized by herself. (weak stress on *herself*)

    b. *Jane was believed by herself to be rich. (weak stress on *herself*)

(14) Passive———→Extraposition———→Pronoun Replacement———→
Reflexivization

But if this is the case, Passive applies to the putative underlying structure of (13)b, that is, roughly as shown in (15). In this case, Passive actually interchanges the positions of the NP *Jane* and *that Jane is rich*. Here Lakoff and Ross assumed essentially the crossover principle (Postal, 1971) as an explanation for violations like that in (13). The trouble is that, given the derivation required by the theory that Pronoun Replacement operates on the output of Extraposition, the explanation in terms of this principle predicts wrongly that (13)b is well-formed, since Passive does not "cross" one NP over another with which it is coreferential in the appropriate way. Lakoff and Ross thus argued that the derivation of sentences like (13)b must be such that Passive applies only after Pronoun Replacement, so that Passive will actually interchange the two coreferential occurrences of *Jane*. But this is incompatible with the view that Pronoun Replacement operates on the output of Extraposition.

Although this argument seemed strong when given, it depends totally on the crossover type of explanation for the deviances in (13). Unfortu-

(15)

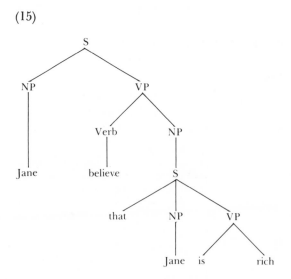

nately, today, given the possibility of global rules (Andrews, 1971; Lakoff, 1969, 1970, 1972a, 1972b; Perlmutter, to appear; Postal, 1972; Ross, 1972a), there are several ways to state the restrictions in (13) which would be perfectly neutral between the alternatives discussed by Lakoff and Ross.[14] Hence, at the moment, I fear that this formally appealing line of reasoning also has no real force.

It seems to me then that of these five arguments, none has much force today. However, Lakoff and Ross gave two other arguments, and these are, I believe, still essentially unimpeachable.

First, Rosenbaum had pointed out that a verb like *begin* in its uses in sentences like (16) is parallel in behavior to A-verbs:

(16) Arthur began to run.

If so, it should be analyzed parallel to other A-verbs in sentences like (17):

(17) Arthur seemed to run.

Given the ill-formedness of (18), it is necessary to say only that Raising is obligatory for *begin* (though optional for *seem*, for example).

(18) *It began that Arthur ran.

Next, it can be noted that *begin* (also *start, stop, continue, keep on, end up, persist in,* and *start out*) also occurs in structures parallel to (16), except that the complement is gerundive rather than infinitival:

(19) a. Arthur began running.

   b. Arthur started running.

   c. Arthur ended up winning.

   d. Arthur started out supporting the communists.

Notice the possible occurrence of existential *there,* a typical indicator

---

[14] One formulation might say that the total effect of cyclic rules cannot be such as to "reverse" asymmetrical antecedent relationships. Hence a derivation would be ill-formed if at one stage there are two coreferential NPs, NP_a and NP_b, such that NP_a precedes and commands NP_b, and a later stage in which the correspondents of these, call them NP_a' and NP_b', are aligned such that NP_b' precedes and commands NP_a'. Such a formulation, appropriately constrained (for example, to eliminate Topicalization from the scope of the constraint), models the effect of previous constraints described in terms of crossing.

of Raising application (see Section 12.1) in both (16) and (19) type structures:

(20) a. There began to be riots in the Sudan.

　　b. ?(When) there began being riots in the Sudan, (I fled).

　　c. There kept on being riots in the Sudan.

　　d. There ended up being riots in the Sudan.

　　e. There started out being seven candidates.

Thus Lakoff and Ross concluded that *begin* sentences with infinitival and gerundive complements should have parallel derivations. But this is incompatible with the view that both involve the operation of Raising on the output of Extraposition, since, as Rosenbaum stressed throughout his work, gerundive complements do not in general undergo Extraposition.[15] Hence, the Extraposition solution proposed by Rosenbaum to the problem of formulating a unitary version of Raising is incompatible with the fact that Raising operates in certain cases for what show up as gerundive as well as infinitival complements, in particular, for the *begin* class of verbs.

There is, however, one possible flaw in this argument, namely, the problems raised by the sentences in footnote 15. Because the matter is of some importance, it is worth considering in detail. It is clear that sentences like (21) exist and are evidently related to those like (22):

(21) a. It is fun calling Sally.

　　b. It is hard working for RCA.

　　c. It is useless talking to him.

(22) a. Calling Sally is fun.

　　b. Working for RCA is hard.

　　c. Talking to him is useless.

This indicates the existence of some rule that can extrapose at least

---

[15] Rosenbaum (1967: 124) did point out, however, as Kayne has reminded me, that extraposition of gerundive complements is apparently possible in a few cases:

(i) a. It is useless calling Sally.
　　b. It is more fun talking to her than kissing her.

Such sentences will be discussed later in the text.

some gerundive clauses.[16] Thus the question arises as to what precludes the claim that gerundive Raising sentences like (23) are derived by operation of Raising on the output of the rule relevant for (21), and, even further, the identification of that rule with Extraposition, operative for *that* and infinitival clauses.

(23) a. Melvin began screaming.

b. I ended up supporting the socialist candidate.

Unless such claims can be disproved, the argument given originally by Lakoff and Ross that sentences like (23) show that Raising cannot operate on the output of Extraposition falls apart.

There are, however, a variety of factors strongly suggesting that it is mistaken to assume that sentences like (23) could be derived from the operation of Raising on shifted clauses like those in (21). *First,* the process shown in (21)—henceforth called Shift—can reorder only *subjectless* gerund phrases:

(24) a.   My talking to Melvin would be useless.

b. *It would be useless my talking to Melvin.

(25) a.   Jim's doing that was wrong.

b.   Doing that was wrong.

c. *It was wrong Jim's doing that.

d.   It was wrong doing that.

---

16 Crucially, we are concerned here with reordered clauses *not* separated from preceding structure by a sharp intonational break. With the latter marking, of course, postposed clauses are found much more widely:

(i)   It bothers me, having to live in this slum.

(ii) Harry hates it, his wife being away.

(iii) I discussed it with George, your leaving early.

This phenomenon, however, is related, not to the sentences clearly generated by Extraposition, but rather to sentences produced by Right Dislocation (see Ross, 1967). This rule is operative in such cases as the following:

(iv) He's a communist, Charley.

(v) I told him to leave, your brother.

Note that sentences like (i)–(iii) are matched by sentences in which the postposed phrase is not sentential:

However, in order to derive (23) from the output of Shift, it would be necessary to say that Shift also worked on full gerundive clauses.

Second, for many speakers at least, the clear cases of Shift output, like (21), are weak "islands." Elements can be extracted from them only with a certain degree of violation:

(26) a.   It is fun kissing Gladys.

    b.   It is fun to kiss Gladys.

(vi) It bothers me, that pile of garbage.

(vii) Harry hates it, the Red Cross Official Song.

(viii) I discussed it with George, your attempt to make me seem foolish.

A crucial property of Right Dislocation, in contrast to Extraposition, is that it cannot apply in subordinate clauses:

(ix) a. *The fact that he is a communist, your brother, is well known.
    b. *If he comes, your brother, I am going to leave.
    c. *I proved that he was insane, your brother.
    d. *I regret that you gave him a book, your brother.

Compare embedded Extraposition application in (x) with the results of embedding clauses like (i)–(iii):

(x) a. The fact that it is obvious he is insane is well known.
    b. If it is obvious that he is insane, then Melvin must be aware of it.
    c. That it is obvious he is insane is generally recognized.

(xi) a. *The fact that it bothers me, having to live in this slum, is obvious.
    b. *That Harry hates it, his wife being away, is unfortunate.
    c. *I regret that you discussed it with George, my leaving early.

This indicates that the rule operative in (i)–(iii) is Right Dislocation. Further evidence is the fact that structures postposed by this rule are "islands," and nothing can be extracted from them. This is not, in general, the case with those reordered by Extraposition:

(xii) a.   Charley, it is obvious that Mary does not love.
    b. *Charley, I discussed it with Melvin, that obscene picture of.

But note the following:

(xiii) a. *Charley, it bothers me, Mary's loving.
    b. *This slum, it annoys me, having to live in.

These facts strongly indicate that examples like (i)–(iii) must be distinguished from intonationally unmarked postposed gerundive clauses like those in (21) in the text. We shall see, however, that the latter share, at least partly, some of the properties of (i)–(iii) in contrast, for example, to postposed subjectless infinitival clauses, which display typical Extraposition properties.

    c. ?*I believe it to be fun kissing Gladys.[17]

    d.   I believe it to be fun to kiss Gladys.

    e. *Who is it fun kissing?

    f.   Who is it fun to kiss?

    g. *Who do you believe it to be fun kissing?

    h.   Who do you believe it to be fun to kiss?

(27) a.   It is useless talking to him.

    b.   It is useless to talk to him.

    c. *Who is it useless talking to?

    d.   Who is it useless to talk to?

(28) a.   It is hard living with witches.

    b.   It is hard to live with witches.

    c. *Witches, it is hard living with.

    d.   Witches, it is hard to live with.

It can be seen that the output of Shift contrasts in these cases with in-finitival clauses in the same position,[18] the latter being presumably a function of the operation of Extraposition. This is supported by the correlation between the island facts in (26)–(28) and the possibility of having subjects in the reordered clauses:

(29) a. *It is fun my kissing Gladys.

    b.   It is fun for me to kiss Gladys.

    c. *It is useless my talking to him.

    d.   It is useless for me to talk to him.

---

[17] We shall see later that deviations like that in (26)c are a special case of more general limitations on embedding such clauses.

[18] The following extraction restrictions are also worth noting:

(i) a.   It was hard to live in this city.
    b.   It was hard to get Betty to live in this city.
    c.   It was hard living in this city.
    d.   It was hard getting Betty to live in this city.
    e.   This city was hard to live in.
    f.   This city was hard to get Betty to live in.
    g. *This city was hard living in.
    h. *This city was hard getting Betty to live in.

e. *It is hard my living with witches.

f. It is hard for me to live with witches.

In contrast to clear cases of Shift, the gerundive clauses involved with Raising in cases like (19) are *not* islands:

(30) a. Melvin began screaming at Louise.

b. Who did Melvin begin screaming at?

c. The girl who Melvin began screaming at was Persian.

d. Sally, Melvin suddenly began screaming at.

(31) a. Ed ended up supporting that candidate.

b. Which candidate did Ed end up supporting?

c. The candidate that Ed ended up supporting was a communist.

d. Melvin, Ed ended up supporting only perfunctorily.

Thus the claim that sentences like (23), (30), and (31) are derived by the operation of Raising on the output of Shift would mean that Raising operation in this case somehow has the power to turn islands into non-islands.[19]

Third, for many speakers again, operation of Shift is mysteriously not permitted in many kinds of subordinate clauses. We saw this initially in (26)c.

(32) a. It seems that it is useless talking to him.

b. It seems that it is useless to talk to him.

c. *It seems to be useless talking to him.

d. It seems to be useless to talk to him.

---

[19] Note that it is not generally the case that subjectless gerundive complements are islands:

(i) a. I approve of tearing down slums.
   b. Slums, I approve of tearing down.

(ii) a. We $\begin{Bmatrix} \text{considered} \\ \text{discussed} \end{Bmatrix}$ bombing that town.

b. The town which we $\begin{Bmatrix} \text{considered} \\ \text{discussed} \end{Bmatrix}$ bombing

(iii) a. I like dating Sally.
    b. Sally, I like dating.

(33) a. I proved that it was fun dating Sally.

    b. I proved that it was fun to date Sally.

    c. *I proved it to be fun dating Sally.

    d. I proved it to be fun to date Sally.

(34) a. *I regret that it wasn't fun dating Sally.

    b. I regret that it wasn't fun to date Sally.

The violations in (32)–(34) are rather subtle but clear in comparison with the quality of the infinitival examples, which are perfect. Again, however, sentences like (23) can occur in these environments with no trace of ill-formedness:

(35) a. It seems that Jack began screaming at his wife.

    b. Jack seems to have begun screaming at his wife.

    c. I proved Jack to have ended up supporting a communist candidate.

    d. I regret that Jack ended up supporting a communist.

Compare also the following sets of examples:

(36) a. I tried to arrange for it to be easy to work with Bob.

    b. *I tried to arrange for it to be easy working with Bob.

    c. I tried to arrange for Bob to begin screaming at ten.

(37) a. This letter proves it to be useless to talk to Max.

    b. *This letter proves it to be useless talking to Max.

    c. This letter proves Max ended up supporting the communists.

Therefore, if sentences like (23) are derived from the output of Shift, the application of Raising must also have the effect of canceling violations like those in (32)–(37).

Fourth, the idea that Raising derives sentences like (23) by operating on the output of Shift means that Shift must be triggered not only by elements like *useless* or *nice* but also by those like *begin.* However, unlike Extraposition, which is extremely free, Shift is a highly restricted operation. In all clear cases of its operation, it is triggered by a main verbal element that is either an adjective (*useless, nice, . . .*) or a predicate nominal (*fun, a drag, . . .*). In fact, Shift does not even work for all predicational cases:

(38) a.   Shaving birds is illegal.

  b. *It is illegal shaving birds.

(39) a.   Saving money is important.

  b. *It is important saving money.

This strongly suggests that only an ad hoc and unmotivated statement could guarantee that Shift would operate for the class of elements like *begin*.

I shall take no position on whether Shift can, in fact, be identified with Extraposition, although this seems extremely doubtful. In any event, it is evident that Shift is subject to a variety of special constraints that are not typical of Extraposition and that, more importantly, are not associated with the class of verbs, such as *begin* and *end up,* which trigger Raising with gerundive complements. For this reason a grammar that claims that Raising in these cases operates on the output of Shift requires a maze of peculiar statements to cancel in some way the atypical restrictions associated with Shift but not with the relevant gerundive Raising cases. But this counts as strong evidence that the Raising derivations are independent of Shift. I conclude, therefore, that the Lakoff-Ross argument against Rosenbaum's claim that Raising operates on the output of Extraposition based on sentences where Raising is associated with gerundive complements is valid, in spite of sentences like (21). It seems that such sentences are not derived by Extraposition, but, even if they are, this class of Extraposition derivations is associated with a variety of constraints that do not show up in the Raising cases.[20]

I have suggested that Raising is operative for certain intransitive verbs like *begin* and *turn out* with gerundive complements. I shall argue

[20] In the text it has been argued on empirical grounds that Raising does not operate on the output of Extraposition. In Perlmutter and Postal (to appear a) a general theory of a class of rules, called "Promotional Rules," is presented. It is argued that such rules, which include Raising, apply only to NP constituents that bear particular grammatical relations to other elements, that is, to subjects and objects. If this restrictive theory can be upheld, it follows on quite independent theoretical grounds that Raising cannot operate on the output of Extraposition. For the latter rule places constituents in configurations over which the basic relations are no longer defined.

later that Raising is also operative for gerundive complements with transitive verbs like *prevent* and *keep* in sentences like those in (40):

(40) a. I prevented Bob from doing that.

 b. The accident kept Tom from winning.

 c. They stopped her from boarding the plane.

In discussing arguments given by Lakoff and Ross that Raising does not operate on the output of Extraposition, I gave five arguments that seem today to have little force, but I have just elaborated one argument that still seems valid. A second argument of this type is based on Lakoff and Ross's observation that Rosenbaum's proposal to have Raising operate on the output of Extraposition yields the wrong derived constituent structure for many sentences. Thus, for example, if (41)b is derived from (41)a, and (42)b from (42)a, there is no accounting for the fact that, while in the *a* examples there are main constituent breaks after *believed* and *me*, there are no such breaks in the *b* examples.

(41) a. It is widely believed that Melvin is an ex-priest.

 b. Melvin is widely believed to be an ex-priest.

(42) a. It seems to me that Marilyn has a chance.

 b. Marilyn seems to me to have a chance.

Thus the superficial constituents of (41)a are *it is widely believed* and *that + S*. In (41)b, however, *is widely believed to be an ex-priest* is a superficial constituent. Rosenbaum's original analysis, unless expanded to include special, ad hoc "readjustment" statements, predicts that the *b* examples should have derived bracketings like the *a* examples, that is, with a main break before the infinitival *to*, which is wrong. These observations of Lakoff and Ross appear as valid today as when originally made.

It seems, then, that while the negative arguments are not as overwhelming as seemed to be the case in 1967, there are serious objections to an attempt to formulate a unitary rule of Raising which operates on the output of Extraposition. Lakoff (1967) proposed an alternative, namely, a way of directly formalizing a unitary mapping that operates essentially as in example (6). In order to do this, however, he was forced, first, to go far beyond the ordinary framework for rule statements; second, to do so in a unique and subsequently unparalleled fashion; and, third, to utilize a statement that was incredibly complicated and unnatural. The solution was thus highly implausible, and this, combined with the fact that the work was never published, led to its being by and large ignored.

This was apparently how matters stood until the summer of 1968. Most investigators seemed in agreement that there was a unitary rule of Raising operating at least for B-verbs and A-verbs, but both attempts (by Rosenbaum and by Lakoff) to formulate such a unitary operation seemed unsuccessful.[21]

1.5 McCawley's Proposal

In lectures at the Summer Institute of the Linguistic Society of America in 1968, McCawley offered arguments that the underlying structures of English clauses are of the form shown in (43), that is, that English is a verb-initial language.

These arguments were presented in explicit form in McCawley

(43)

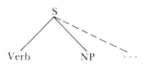

---

[21] Stockwell, Schachter, and Partee (1968: Volume II, Chapter IX) consider the questions raised here so far and adopt a different analysis. They reject Rosenbaum's claim that the raising mappings operate on the output of Extraposition. Moreover, instead of trying to solve the problem of how to formulate the mappings uniformly for A-verbs and B-verbs, they simply assume there is no uniformity and state them as two separate rules, their Rais-Subj (essentially Raising for A-verb cases) and Rais-Obj (essentially Raising for B-verb cases).

It seems to me, incidentally, that these authors at one point somewhat wrongly describe their own analysis in saying (1968: 25): "Our analysis of such sentences . . . is essentially the same as Lees' . . . ." But this is not the case, for the correspondent in their system of Lees's Second Passive rule is Rais-Obj, which is not uniquely linked to the generation of so-called second passive sentences like (i) but functions also in nonpassives like (ii):

(i) He is believed to know Spanish.

(ii) They believed him to know Spanish.

In any event, these authors apparently abandoned the goal of finding a uniform characterization for A-verb and B-verb subject raisings.

(1970a).[22] In particular, one of McCawley's most telling arguments is that the verb-initial assumption provides a trivial way of stating Raising in a unitary fashion.[23] Recall that from Chomsky's (1957) *Syntactic Structures* on, almost every generative work on English grammar had assumed an underlying clause structure of essentially the following form (ignoring questions of those elements generally assigned to a so-called Auxiliary constituent), that is, a subject-NP-initial structure, containing a VP constituent:

(44)

In particular, this was assumed by Rosenbaum in his dissertation work and by Lakoff and Ross in their critique of Rosenbaum's analysis. The latter led, as we saw earlier, to the paradox that, although there is intuitively a unitary operation of Raising operative for both A-verbs and B-verbs, no acceptable way of stating such an operation formally had been proposed. McCawley showed, however, that it is simple to state such an operation under the assumption of clause structures like (43). For under this assumption, both subject and objects *follow* their verbs. Consequently, sentences like (45) and (46) will have the underlying representations shown in (47) and (48).

(45) a. Joan believes (that) Bob loves Sylvia.

    b. Joan believes Bob to love Sylvia.

---

[22] A revised version is found in McCawley (to appear b), which includes replies to certain criticisms.

[23] The argument for verb-initial underlying clause structure as against NP + VP structure based on Raising is somewhat stronger than McCawley's discussion indicates. McCawley gives the argument purely in terms of simplicity: Verb-initial order makes a uniform account of Raising easier to state than underlying NP + VP structures. But, as indicated earlier, with NP + VP structure, there is no known way to formulate a uniform rule within the normal constraints on rule structures; thus the advantages that verb-initial structures provide for the description of Raising are more fundamental. This assumes, of course, the correctness of the arguments showing that Raising cannot operate on the output of Extraposition. The latter possibility also permits a uniform account under the NP + VP assumption within the generally accepted constraints on rule formulation.

(46) a. It happens that Bob loves Sylvia.

b. Bob happens to love Sylvia.

(47)

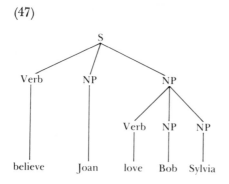

(48)

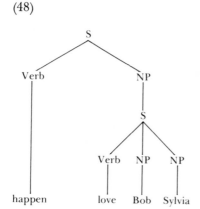

Given such underlying structures (together with the assumption that Subject Formation, the rule that turns underlying verb-initial structures into the typical English declarative order of NP + Verb, is *postcyclic*),[24] Raising can be naturally formulated as a cyclical rule op-

[24] Having Subject Formation *last cyclical* instead of postcyclical works correctly only if there are rule-ordering statements, so that it can be guaranteed that Subject Formation follows Raising on the last cycle. Since I know of no strong evidence for syntactic rule ordering, I take this to be simply an argument for having the rule be postcyclical. If Subject Formation is postcyclical, it must, on various grounds, be a global rule in the sense of Lakoff (1970a), defined in terms of the same notion of "cyclical subject" needed to state Classical Greek case agreement (see Andrews, 1971; Lakoff, 1970a). This is necessary, among other things, to prevent erroneous application

erative for both B-verb cases like (47), where the raised NP becomes a derived object, and for A-verb cases like (48), where the raised NP becomes a derived subject, in terms of the following structural condition:[25]

(49) Raising

$$X, \text{Verb}, (\text{NP}), [_{NP} [_{S} \text{Verb}, \text{NP}, Y_{S}]_{NP}] Z$$
$$\quad 1 \quad 2 \quad 3 \qquad 4 \quad 5 \quad 6 \qquad 7$$

Thus the rule detaches the NP meeting the condition on the fifth term of (49) from the complement S and reattaches it to the superordinate S directly to the left of the complement S-containing NP. This is shown schematically in (50). In the case of A-verbs, the optional NP in (50) is not present, and the raised NP is removed from the superordinate sentential subject. In the case of B-verbs, the optional NP is there, and the raised NP is removed from the superordinate sentential object.

It is thus elementary that verb-first order permits an elegant solution to the problem raised by Rosenbaum's hitherto effectively unstatable insight that English contains a unitary rule of Raising, operative at least for both B-verb and A-verb structures. The difficulties in the way

---

of Subject Formation to objects in cases where the subject has undergone Raising, that is, to prevent (i) from forming (ii) instead of the correct sentence (iii), where Subject Formation is blocked on the lower clause because the postverbal NP is not the correspondent of the cyclic subject of that clause.

Subject Formation

(i) [believes Melvin Joan to know French]

(ii) *Melvin believes Joan French to know.

(iii) Melvin believes Joan to know French.

[25] This account ignores, of course, all restrictions on the superordinate and subordinate verbs, that is, what main verbs can trigger application of Raising and with what complement verbs. Thus nothing is said here about the problem of distinguishing pairs like the following:

(i) a. I believe Bill to know French.
 b. *I assert Bill to know French.

(ii) a. It is certain that Bill will go; Bill is certain to go.
 b. It is probable that Bill will go; *Bill is probable to go.
 c. I believe that Bill will win tomorrow.
 d. *I believe Bill to win tomorrow.
 e. I expect that Bill will win tomorrow.
 f. I expect Bill to win tomorrow.

(50) a.

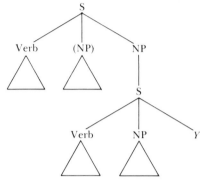

Raising
⟹

b.

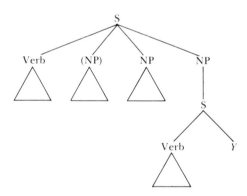

of a unitary formulation of such an operation seem to lie in the assumption of underlying NP + VP structures for English clauses, because this
places sentential subjects and sentential objects, which determine Raising, on opposite sides of the verb. The verb-initial assumption has some
independent positive motivation, as McCawley argued. Since then, further arguments in support of this view have been constructed by Bach
(1971) and Ross (1971). Since there are no known strong arguments
against it,[26] one might claim that McCawley's verb-initial proposal is a

---

[26] Underlying NP + VP structures involve several distinct claims, in particular, that
the subject NP precedes the Verb and that there is a fundamental binary break in
clause structure between subject and another constituent called VP. These two are

fundamental insight into the structure of English of the sort that linguists have only rarely been able to provide. This idea permits the actual formulation of a unitary rule of Raising in accord with Rosenbaum's basic view, which can then be regarded as valid. However, Rosenbaum's concomitant view—that Raising operates on the output of Extraposition—has been rejected.

We shall see later, in Chapter 7 and in Section 12.2, however, that the status of the verb-initial conception of English clause structure is not as unambiguous as these remarks suggest. This status is clouded, not by anything suggesting the validity of the more traditional NP + VP structure, but rather by two quite distinct factors. One is the possibility of a verb-final account of English clauses, recently argued for by Ross (to appear g). As various investigators have observed (see Chapter 7), a verb-final account permits A-verb and B-verb subject raising to be collapsed into a single rule just as readily as a verb-initial assumption. Second, the argument for the verb-initial view from the facts of subject raising depends crucially on the assumption that a rule like Raising is to be stated in terms of constituent configurations. If, however, such rules are, in fact, properly definable in terms of *grammatical relations,* as argued in Perlmutter and Postal (to appear a, to appear b), it turns out that a uniform rule is statable regardless of the position of the main verb in a clause. See Section 8.4. Despite these caveats, I shall continue to assume an underlying verb-initial character for English clauses in all sections of this work where the question is not explicitly under discussion, beginning with the following paragraph.

The situation under consideration thus seems to be a genuine case where a difficult problem in grammatical description, the formulation of a unitary rule of Raising, has been solved in the most desirable way.

---

obviously independent. Thus one could maintain underlying SVO structures without claiming that there is anything analogous to a VP constituent.

Although there has been some discussion of the validity of the Verb Phrase constituent, the near-uniform acceptance of underlying NP + VP structures for English clauses has not been supported, to my knowledge, by arguments favoring the subject-verb precedence feature. From the time that Chomsky first assumed it in work underlying *Syntactic Structures* (1957), it seems hardly to have been questioned seriously until McCawley's proposal (but see footnote 28). This is in marked contrast, for example, to the situation in German, where there was much discussion of whether German clause structure was underlying verb-second, verb-final, or verb-initial. See Bach (1962, 1971); Bierwisch (1963); Maling (1972); Ross (1970b).

One of the crucial features of the verb-initial proposal, as McCawley showed, was that, while permitting improvements in generalization in certain parts of the grammar, it has, as far as is known, no deleterious effects on any other. In particular, note that the rule needed to transform verb-initial order into NP-initial order, Subject Formation, is not an extra necessity,[27] since past NP + VP grammars had such a rule anyway, called Subject-Auxiliary Inversion, which was needed for questions and certain other constructions. In the new grammar, derivations formerly assumed to involve this rule are now taken to involve *non*application of Subject Formation, and conversely.

McCawley's analysis of these matters[28] has been widely if not uniformly accepted. However, Chomsky and some of his recent students have rejected McCawley's analysis, and Chomsky (to appear) has attempted to provide an alternative analysis of a new sort of certain constructions otherwise believed to involve Raising.

[27] Newmeyer (1971) argues that, despite McCawley (1970a), Subject Formation cannot be collapsed with the rule previously known as Subject-Auxiliary Inversion. However, his argument does not stand up, since it depends on ignoring the role of Raising in the relevant derivations. For analysis of this argument, see Postal (to appear b) and Section 12.3 of this book. Baker (1971: especially footnote 11) provides an argument with the same conclusion as Newmeyer's but based on entirely different facts. For discussion of this argument, see McCawley (to appear b).

[28] A verb-initial conception of English clause structure was also developed by Fillmore (especially 1968) and adopted by Stockwell, Schachter, and Partee (1968). This approach adopted the verb-initial idea in the context of so-called "case grammar" and did not, by and large, justify it independently of considerations internal to this approach. Moreover, it was embedded in a dubious account that divided clauses into a "Proposition," which had the verb-first structure, plus an independent "Modality," including tenses, auxiliaries, etc. This analysis, similar to that in Katz and Postal (1964) in certain respects, misses the verbal character of auxiliaries.

McCawley's contribution was then not so much to suggest verb-initial structure but to give justification for it independent of quite moot "case grammar" assumptions and to relate it to interesting typological and universal constraints.

2

An Alternative Approach

2.1 Background

Chomsky (1972: 86) states, in criticizing an analysis of the word *remind* (Postal, 1970a), which made some appeal to Raising, the following: ". . . I might mention that the permutation rule that gives (25) as well as subject-raising [into object position—this phrase not present in the original circulated version] seem to me to be at best dubious rules." This formulation (without the added clarification) might well have been confusing to some, as it was to the present writer, who, in some circulated but unpublished arguments, took it to be a general rejection of the existence of a rule Raising. However, in an earlier personal communication as well as in the published version, the author has clarified his position, indicating that what he had in mind rather was only to call into question the existence of a raising operation in the case of what I am here calling B-verbs.[1] That is, Chomsky does not question the existence of Raising for at least some A-verb constructions. Rejection of Raising for B-verb constructions is also briefly alluded to in Chomsky (1971) and sketched in greater detail in Chomsky (to appear).

Briefly, Chomsky recognizes, with Rosenbaum and almost all subsequent studies, that a subject-raising operation is involved in A-verb sentences like (1):

(1) a. Harry seems to be a weirdo.

   b. Harry happens to be Portuguese.

   c. Headway has begun to be made on that problem.

   d. The cat is likely to be out of the bag by then.

   e. There appear to be flaws in your first thirty-four arguments.

However, in contrast to Rosenbaum and the line of research that is inadequately outlined in Chapter 1, Chomsky now denies the existence of any raising operation with respect to B-verb configurations like (2):

---

[1] More generally, Chomsky would now, as the published text indicates, deny the existence of any subject NP raising rule that lifts NPs into superordinate clause *object* position.

(2) a. I believe that to be incorrect.

    b. Joan showed Melvin to be a Martian.

    c. The police proved the kids to be addicts.

    d. Jack found Cynthia to be unfaithful.

What is interesting about Chomsky's current view is its contrast with any past doubts about a Raising analysis for sentences like (2). Previous doubts, as far as I know, considered only the possibility that such sentences were analyzed *as involving complement subject deletion,* so that they would have underlying structures of the form of (3)a, or the like.

(3) a. NP B-verb NP S.

    b. NP B-verb S.

An obvious argument against this is that a different underlying structure must be provided for the *that*-clause analogues of (2), namely, one like (3)b. Another apparent argument against structures like (3)a for sentences like (2) is that it preempts the structure that has been assumed necessary for sentences like (4)a in contrast to those like (4)b in the face of the many now well-known contrasts between verbs like *persuade, convince, force,* on the one hand, and *show, believe, expect,* on the other.

(4) a. I persuaded him to be stubborn.

    b. I showed him to be stubborn.

(For one of several discussions of such contrasts arguing for a difference like (3)a, b, see Chomsky, 1967: 430–433.) However, I regard this as not too much of an objection to (3)a structures for sentences like (2), since I think the structure in (3)a is also quite inappropriate for sentences like (4)a. For some brief discussions, see Section 4.13 and Chapter 11.

In any event, Chomsky's current position is not anything like the claim that structures like (3)a underlie sentences like (2). On the contrary, he assumes that sentences like (2) and their *that*-clause analogues have essentially the same underlying structures. But, he claims that in the derived structure of an example like (2)b, the string *Melvin to be a Martian* is an S constituent, as it is in the underlying structure. Thus, no raising operation, ripping *Melvin* out of the subordinate clause and making it a constituent of the superordinate clause, is postulated to have been applied. According to this current view of Chomsky's, then, even in derived structure, infinitival and *that*-clause complements of B-verbs differ only in the internal form of complement marking (*that* complementizer + finite verbal form versus infinitival, nonfinite verbs). This is a position with respect to examples like (2) that, as far as I am aware, had never previously been contemplated.

An obvious and crucial consequence of a rejection of raising operations in B-verb complements is, of course, that the problem of constructing a unitary account of Raising for both B-verbs and A-verbs, which Rosenbaum, Lakoff, Ross, and others tackled without much success, and which, it was claimed previously, McCawley's verb-initial hypothesis solves, simply does not arise. A corollary is that raising operations provide no argument for the verb-initial hypothesis and, not surprisingly, Chomsky (to appear: footnote 33) rejects this hypothesis, remarking: "It is pointed out by McCawley (1970) that if English is a VSO language, then raising to subject and to object positions can be formulated as a single rule. There is, however, no persuasive independent evidence for the assumption, so far as I can see. If there is no rule of raising to object position, then there remains no substantial argument for the VSO analysis." I find this somewhat odd in the absence of any attempt to deal with the arguments for VSO order given by McCawley or that given by Bach (1971).

Moreover, in context, Chomsky's remarks may easily be read in an unjustified way. He asserts that there is no argument for the VSO analysis and adopts without explicit justification a version of the NP + VP analysis of English clauses which he has maintained since his initial transformational studies in the early fifties. One might take this to suggest that, in the absence of any arguments for the VSO analysis, the NP + VP analysis must be accepted. This is, obviously, utterly baseless. Neither of these interpretations has any known empirical or logical priority. Moreover, there are other alternatives, SOV structures, for example, as already noted. If there were no arguments for the VSO position, one would simply be unable to choose between this and the other positions—in particular, between it and the NP + VP position—unless there were definite arguments for the latter analysis. I am aware of no such arguments. Chomsky offers none. But clearly one must be wary of mistaking the historical priority of the NP + VP analysis, which is linguistically irrelevant, with some other kind.

Note, further, that there is no direct argument for NP + VP underlying structures, or, more generally, for NP + Verb underlying structures, on the ground that this is the order of surface clauses. Even if one were, mistakenly in my view, to adopt the principle that underlying structure is like surface structure unless there is evidence to the contrary (a principle that ignores totally the semantic character of underlying structure), the conclusion does not follow. Some English clauses have surface NP-initial structure, as (5)a–d, others have verb-initial surface order (ignoring adverbs), as (5)e–k:

(5) a. Harry likes birds.

   b. The truth is seldom recognized.

   c. That they are unhappy will become obvious.

   d. Jack escaped.

   e. *Shall we drink bourbon?*

   f. *Are you willing to vote for that?*

   g. *Never have I heard such a sad story.*

   h. That, *said Joe to Mary*, is very unlikely.

   i. Am I, *wondered Harry to himself*, really going to win?

   j. *Had Bill been there*, things would have been different.

   k. *Were you to learn French*, I would be surprised.

No one has ever shown how any conclusions about underlying order follow from such facts alone, nor does it seem possible to do so.

With reference to the main theme of this discussion, raising operations, it is evidently of considerable relevance to a good deal of English grammatical structure to determine which of the opposing views about raising operations for B-verb complements is correct. I shall argue later that the evidence for Raising with B-verb complements is decisive, but first I shall deal very briefly with the kinds of evidence that support NP raising rules, as well as with a fundamental difference between A-verb raising and B-verb raising which reveals why it is not completely implausible, at a certain level of observation, to accept the former and doubt the latter.

2.2 Interlude: Raising Justification in A-Verb Constructions

Given potential A-verb Raising sentences such as (6), what considerations are relevant to show that main clause subject NPs are actually former complement clause subjects which achieved their final locus through Raising?

(6) a. Melvin seems to speak fluent Gwambamambese.

b. Nuclear weapons happen to be useful for campus police.

The first point that might be made is that, semantically, such sentences are understood in such a way that the main clause subject NP and the infinitival complement represent jointly a single semantic "clause." Thus the logical structure of (6)a must reflect the fact that it consists of a part [SEEM] and another part [MELVIN SPEAK FLUENT GWAMBAMAMBESE], which are related in a certain way.[2] The Raising analysis naturally reflects this fact within terms of the general principle that, unless something special is said in the grammar, syntactic clauses correlate with semantic "clauses."

However, there are, within the rather fertile bed of theoretical suggestions now available, other possible analyses that would also, in at least many cases, embody this generalization. One would take sentences

---

2 Many *seem* sentences have, of course, an additional *to*-marked NP designating the "experiencer":

(i) It seems to me that corruption is increasing.

The principle seems to be that, with one exception discussed presently, this NP must be a coreferent of a higher verb, the performative in (i), the superficial verb in (ii):

(ii) Jane$_i$ said Melvin seemed to $\left\{ \begin{array}{l} \text{her}_i \\ \text{*her}_j \\ \text{*Max} \end{array} \right\}$ to be upset.

I suspect that "experiencer" NPs underlie all *seem* sentences, with those like (6)a in the text derived by a rule that deletes "experiencer" NPs of the generic *one* type, these being the exception noted previously. Sentences, such as (iii), containing explicit *to one* are generally unacceptable:

(iii) a. *It must have seemed to one that things were improving.

b. *John often seems crazy to one.

Therefore, this rule would appear to be obligatory (although there are some, especially British, idiolects that apparently accept things like (iii), so that for them the rule is optional).

like (6)a to involve a complement structure containing an NP subject that is a coreferent of the main clause subject, thus an underlying form for (6)a of the following form (using for discursive purposes NP-initial order):

(7) Melvin$_x$ seems [$_S$ NP$_x$ speaks fluent Gwambamambese$_S$].

Such an analysis would then derive the surface structure (6)a by claiming that the independently motivated rule Equi (NP Deletion) (see Postal, 1970b) operates to remove the complement subject. Thus, at first glance, an Equi analysis may seem just as plausible as a Raising analysis here.

There are, however, several arguments that disconfirm an Equi analysis like (7) of A-verb constructions. First, it does not seem that (7) gives a semantically relevant analysis, since there is no reason to assume that the logical structure of (6)a involves *two* occurrences of elements designating an individual named Melvin. That is, while it is probable that *seem* is logically transitive, as indicated in footnote 2, it does not, in a sentence like (6)a, relate a pair of terms designating Melvin and a proposition that Melvin speaks fluent Gwambamambese.

A second obvious argument against (7) is that it provides a representation for (6)a quite at variance with that possible for the generally parallel *that*-clause analogue in (8), for which an analysis like (7) is out of the question.

(8) It seems that Melvin speaks fluent Gwambamambese.

Hence, this analysis would complicate the insertion conditions for verbs like *seem*.

The incorrectness of structures like (7) for sentences like (6)a shows up, I believe, in the fact that there are many sentences for which the Equi analysis is simply impossible on various grounds. A sample includes the following:

(9) a. *There* seems to be trouble in the Congo.

    b. *The shit* seems to be about to hit the fan. (on idiomatic reading)

    c. *The jig* seems to be up. (on idiomatic reading)

    d. *Little heed* seems to have been paid to my suggestion.

    e. *The cat* seems to have his tongue. (on idiomatic reading)

The point here is that, as McCawley (1967, 1970b, 1970c, 1970d, to appear a), for example, has stressed in various places, Equi is a rule operating on NPs that correspond to coreferential indices in logical structure. But the italicized NPs in (9) are such that there is every reason to doubt that they correspond to any indices in logical structure at all. Consequently, for example, the coreference condition on Equi cannot possibly be met for an underlying structure like the following for (9)a:

(10) there seems [$_S$ there is trouble in the Congo$_S$]

Hence, at best, a new rule deleting complement subjects would be required to make an analysis along the lines of (8) even superficially adequate, a rule requiring deletion under a type of identity that has not been proved to exist in any other known cases, that is, constituent identity independent of coreference.[3] This point is worth stressing because of early attempts within transformational studies to formulate the coreference conditions of rules like Equi in terms of *constituent structure* identity rather than coreference. Such attempts can quickly be seen to be hopeless by noting examples involving quantifiers, generics, etc.:[4]

[3] This identity would also be distinct from the kind of identity of meaning required for deletions like VP Deletion (see Grinder and Postal, 1971). This follows since the latter really requires identity of portions of semantic structure, but such a requirement is senseless for elements like existential *there* and subparts of idioms, since these do not correspond to such portions.

The claim in the text that rules of deletion involving purely superficial identity are otherwise unknown is supported to some extent by examples of the sort pointed out to me by Kayne, such as (i) and (ii), in contrast to examples like (iii), for which coreference makes sense.

(i) a. There can't be peace without there being war first.
  b. *There can't be peace without being war first.

(ii) a. There can't be a fire in the closet without there being smoke there.
  b. *There can't be a fire in the closet without being smoke there.

(iii) John$_i$ can't be in the closet without (him$_i$) being visible.

However, other observations of Kayne's yield some problems (see footnote 56 of Chapter 4 and footnote 27 of Chapter 12).

[4] If sentences like those on the left in (11) were derived from structures like those on the right, the deletion rule would, at least, have to be supplemented with special "interpretive" principles of some sort to patch up the semantic incongruities implied by the syntactic structure. These problems involve chiefly quantifier scope and coreference. Other more obviously "syntactic" problems would arise as well. For in-

(11) a. Each senator wanted to be reelected ≠ each senator wanted each senator to be reelected.

    b. Americans hope to become famous ≠ Americans hope Americans become famous.

Correlated with the fact that analyses like (7) cannot make use of Equi for sentences like (9), and thus in general not at all, is the fact that such analyses require the direct generation as main clause subjects of NPs which are otherwise extremely restricted. Thus, for example, existential *there*, as in (9)a, occurs, outside of potential Raising A-verb constructions, only as the subject of clauses containing forms of *be* and a handful of other items like *exist, arise,* and *develop,* which tend to have the predicate EXIST as part of their meanings. If *there* is to be generated directly as a main clause subject of A-verbs, then this restriction must be redundantly repeated in some far from clear way to account for facts like (12):

(12) a. *There seems to know French.

    b. *There is likely to eat too much.

    c. *There appears to disperse.

    d. *There happened to work for the FBI.

Moreover, if there is a general "base rule" expansion of NP to *there,* then special ad hoc devices must be introduced to block its occurrence in all other cases, especially, nonsubject cases:

(13) a. *We discussed there at length.

    b. *Bob just loves there.

    c. *I don't understand there.

    d. *Joe gave there to the police.

---

stance, if sentences like (i) are derived from structures like (ii), with a quantifier in the complement as well, what would block this quantifier from floating off, as quantifiers can (see Section 4.5), yielding (iii) and (iv)?

(i) All of the girls tried to win.

(ii) [all of the girls tried for all of the girls to win]

(iii) *All of the girls tried to all win.

(iv) *The girls all tried to all win.

Parallels to such arguments can obviously be based on any other restricted NP like *little heed,* which can occur as A-verb subjects.

More generally, a structure of the form shown in (14) is a well-formed
sentence only when NP_a + infinitival complement$_j$ is a well-formed
infinitival clause structure.

(14) NP_a + A-verb + infinitival complement$_j$

That is, the intervening A-verb[5] is irrelevant to the selectional restrictions between NP_a and infinitival complement$_j$. As further examples,
note the following:

(15) a.   Swedes are friendly, nice, cheerful, gloomy.

    b. *A Swede is friendly, nice, cheerful, gloomy.

    c.   Swedes seem to be friendly, nice, cheerful, gloomy.

    d. *A Swede seems to be friendly, nice, cheerful, gloomy.

Also consider these examples:

(16) a. A Swede is outside, on top of your icebox, changing my tire.

    b. A Swede seems to be outside, on top of your icebox, changing my
       tire.

Along these lines, it is clear that a variety of arguments can be constructed to disconfirm an analysis of A-verb complementation along the
lines of (7). A sketch of such arguments is given in Section 12.1.

---

5 Actually, any sequence of intervening A-verbs is irrelevant:

(i) The important thing to me $\left\{ \begin{array}{l} \text{is sex} \\ \text{*bothers her} \end{array} \right\}$.

(ii) The important thing to me seems to $\left\{ \begin{array}{l} \text{be sex} \\ \text{*bother her} \end{array} \right\}$.

(iii) The important thing to me seems (?to be) likely to $\left\{ \begin{array}{l} \text{be sex} \\ \text{*bother her} \end{array} \right\}$.

(iv) The important thing to me seems to have ended up appearing to $\left\{ \begin{array}{l} \text{be sex} \\ \text{*bother her} \end{array} \right\}$.

I shall consider briefly later, in Section 5.2, why sentences like (iii) are not completely
acceptable with the post-*seems* occurrence of *to be.*

Another alternative, which has never been proposed as far as I know, would take the underlying syntactic structure of A-verb complementation to involve structures of the form shown in (17), that is, subject-*less* underlying infinitives.

(17) NP A-verb to VP

It would then be claimed that some kind of "interpretive" semantic rule connects the logical correspondent of the main clause subject with the logical correspondent of the complement. This "interpretive" rule would do the work in this proposal of the extra deletion rule required by the previous one to deal with the impossibility of utilizing Equi.[6] Independently of any general theoretical objections to "interpretive" rules, this proposal must obviously fail for the same reasons as the former. It also is burdened with the need to repeat redundantly the mass of idiosyncratic restrictions between the surface main clause NP and its noncontiguous related elements in the verbal phrase. Thus this most superficial analysis is disconfirmed by roughly the same arguments that dispose of the pseudo-Equi proposal. Since its possible competitors run into severe difficulties, it is hardly surprising that the Raising analysis of A-verb complementation, first proposed explicitly by Rosenbaum, has today no serious objectors.[7]

Notice, though, that the kinds of arguments disconfirming the Raising analysis competitors and hence supporting the Raising analysis depend, in the case of A-verbs, crucially on the fact that, with these main verbs, Raising, in combination with the action of Subject Formation, separates the raised NP from its original clause coelements and, in fact, can separate them to an unbounded degree, given successive embedding

---

[6] Such an "interpretive" rule will run into difficulties in the case of multiple A-verb embeddings like those in footnote 5, since it will be necessary for the rule to determine how far "down" the tree the connections are to be projected. A trivial formulation of the rule with a configuration like (17) must fail for complex cases.

[7] Although an explicit A-verb Raising analysis was first proposed by Rosenbaum, such a treatment is, in a sense, implicit in some instances of more traditional work, for example, in Jespersen's "split subject" treatment of A-verbs like *happen, fail,* and *seem.* See Jespersen (1969: 45–47).

The statement by Stockwell, Schachter, and Partee (1968: 56) thus seems to be as true today as when written: "It is quite analogous to the RAIS-SUBJ principle . . . which has been accepted in some form by virtually everyone who has examined sentences of this type."

of A-verb below A-verb as in (18), where multiple applications of Raising occur on successive cycles.[8]

(18) Jones only appears to be beginning to seem bored with Gladys.

It is a fact, however, that the putative Raising analysis of B-verb complementation does not have this property.

Thus, regardless of whether some version of Raising is or is not involved in the derivation of sentences like (19), the NP *Bill* is not linearly separated from its original clause coconstituents.

(19) Joan believes Bill to be a Finnish spy.

Because of this, arguments to show that Raising is relevant in such derivations must take a different form from those appealed to in A-verb cases. Thus, take the example of sentences with B-verbs analogous to A-verb cases like (9):

(20) a. Joan believes there to be trouble in the Congo.

     b. Joan believes the shit to be about to hit the fan.

     c. Joan believes the jig to be up.

     d. Joan believes little heed to have been paid to my suggestion.

These examples show little or nothing directly about the validity of the Raising hypothesis, since there is always the alternative, finally adopted by Chomsky, of taking the post-*believe* sequences in such cases to have simply their underlying organization as clauses. This proposal can be maintained, initially, against the Raising view, without any appeal to an analogue of an analysis like (7) or its "interpretive" alternative, just because of the lack of intervening material in these B-verb examples corresponding to the intrusive A-verb (sequence) in the A-verb constructions.

It is noteworthy, then, that the chief traditional arguments for Raising in B-verb sentences like (20) have a structure quite distinct from the traditional or nontraditional (see Section 12.1) arguments for Raising in A-verb cases.

---

8 For a discussion of the cyclical character of Raising, see Section 8.2. For an extremely interesting argument for the analogue of A-verb Raising in French based on this separation property, see Ruwet (1972: Chapter 2).

2.3 The Traditional Arguments for B-Verb Raising

There exist, I believe, three distinct arguments[9] that can reasonably be said to be the chief previous basis for the belief that a raising rule has applied in the derivations of sentences such as (20). Each of these arguments takes the form of showing that, while there is a clausal boundary between the B-verb and the following elements in the derived structure of sentences like (21), there is no such boundary between *believe* and the directly following NP in the type of sentence like (20).

(21) Joan believes (that) there is trouble in the Congo.

Each of the arguments tries to show this by exhibiting some process that, by assumption, is sensitive to clause boundaries. It is then claimed that in all three cases, the infinitival and *that*-clause complements of B-verbs differ with respect to the position of inferrable clause boundaries at the level of derived structure.

The three processes involved are passivization, reflexivization, and reciprocal marking. Gross contrasts between infinitival and *that*-clause complements are, of course, easily exhibited. Consider first passivization:

(22) a. Jack believed (that) Joan was famous.

  b. That Joan was famous was believed by Jack.

  c. *Joan was believed (that) was famous by Jack.

(23) a. Jack believed Joan to be famous.

  b. *(For) Joan to be (have been) famous was believed by Jack.

  c. Joan was believed to have been famous by Jack.

---

9 Stockwell, Schachter, and Partee (1968: 55) appear to give only one of these: "Consider now the motivations for claiming that the subject of the embedded clause in (85.c) [a *that* clause with *believe*] is raised to object of *believe* in (85.d) [an infinitival clause]. If the analysis did not raise the clausal subject *she* to object of *believe*, there would be no natural explanation of the fact that reflexivization is possible in this position: (85)g *she believes herself to be intelligent*."

There is, moreover, what can well be considered a fourth traditional argument for a raising operation in these cases, an argument that applies also to A-verb cases. This involves contrasts and noncontrasts in meaning correlated with passivization. See Rosenbaum (1967: 59–61, 73–74, 78). It is briefly discussed later, in Chapter 7 and again in Chapters 9, 10, and 11.

Hence, with *that* complements, passivization operates on the entire complement and is impossible with just the complement subject, while the opposite situation holds for infinitival complements. Traditionally, this was taken to be an argument for a Raising analysis of B-verb infinitival complements, because it was assumed that passivization was inherently restricted to clause-internal operation. Thus, if the complement subject stays in a subordinate clause, as in (22), it is not subject to passivization—hence the star on (22)c. After the application of Raising, however, main clause passivization becomes possible, since Raising lifts the NP into the main clause. In these terms, (23)b is blocked on both of its a priori possible branches of derivation. That is, either it would involve conversion to infinitival form with a B-verb without previous application of Raising (application of the de-finitization rule to a structure like (22)b), which is impossible (see footnote 8 of Chapter 1), or it would involve passivization of the whole underlying complement, that is, direct application of Passive to the string *Joan to be famous* in (23)a. But a Raising analysis automatically blocks this because at the point of potential application of Passive, a string like that is not even a constituent, as the tree in (24) indicates. But Passive, in anybody's formulation, can only form the derived subject of a passive sentence from an NP. Contrasts like those between (22) and (23) thus seemed to provide natural grounds for the Raising analysis of B-verb infinitival complements.

(24)

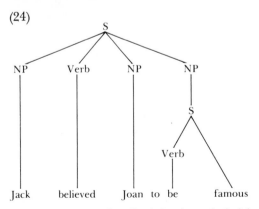

In the case of reflexivization, infinitival-*that*-clause contrasts are equally apparent:

(25) a.   Jack$_i$ believed (that) he$_i$ was immortal.

   b. *Jack$_i$ believed (that) himself$_i$ was immortal.

   c.   Jack$_i$ believed himself$_i$ to be immortal.

   d. *Jack$_i$ believed him$_i$ (he$_i$) to be immortal.

Coreference in such cases yields well-formed reflexivization only in the infinitival cases. Again, under the assumption that ordinary reflexive marking[10] is exclusively clause-internal, this leads to a result exactly parallel to, and hence consistent with, that in the passive cases. There is no clause boundary between *believe* and the directly following NP in (25)c, d, but there is in (25) a, b, a conclusion that follows directly from the Raising analysis and is inconsistent with a non-Raising analysis.

   The reciprocal marking argument is essentially identical to that involving reflexivization:

(26) a.   *They believed (that) each other were honest.

   b.   They believed each other to be honest.

Again, the facts would support the Raising analysis of B-verb infinitival complements, under the assumption that the operation of reciprocal marking is purely clause-internal. The consistency between these three arguments is apparent.

   We thus see how each of the past arguments for a Raising analysis of B-verb infinitival complementation depended on showing a contrast in

---

[10] I shall use the term "ordinary reflexivization" or "ordinary reflexive marking" to refer to the reflexive marking of verbal object NPs and prepositional phrase object NPs not embedded within larger NPs (unless their antecedents are also so embedded, as in (i), which I also regard as ordinary reflexivization).

(i) John's description of himself was ludicrous.

It is this range of reflexive marking in English which tends to have analogues in the reflexivization of other languages (see Postal, 1970, for one example), as opposed to the use of reflexives in contexts like the following:

(ii) a. That picture of himself$_i$ annoyed Mike$_i$.
   b. Melvin$_i$ said that physicists like himself$_i$ were misunderstood.
   c. Tom$_i$ said that as for himself$_i$ he$_i$ would rather eat beans.
   d. Tom$_i$ drew the snake toward $\begin{Bmatrix} him_i \\ himself_i \end{Bmatrix}$.

Ordinary reflexivization is always obligatory, while these other, more idiosyncratic to English uses of reflexives are often optional, as in (ii)d, for my idiolect at least.

clause boundary distribution between infinitival and *that*-clause complements, a demonstration based on assumptions about the role of clause boundaries in the statement of the rules involved in the processes of passivization, reflexivization, and reciprocal marking. There is an obvious contrast between these arguments and those traditionally given for Raising in A-verb cases, which did not involve clause boundaries.

2.4 Chomsky's Recent Counterproposals

In spite of these three traditional arguments, Chomsky (1971, to appear) rejects the claim that a raising operation for infinitival B-verb complements is supported by the nature of the three processes involved. While naturally granting contrasts such as those in (22)–(26), Chomsky denies that they are the function of the interaction of processes sensitive to clause boundaries with or without the raising of complement subjects. Rather, he claims that these contrasts are a function of general principles of grammar, relevant also to many other cases of varied sorts, which distinguish essentially tensed, or finite, clauses from nonfinite clauses. Since his discussion is quite wide ranging and only a portion of it is directly relevant here, the present discussion constitutes only a partial critique of his proposals.

Chomsky's approach (to appear: 8–9) to the questions here can be naturally introduced by the following remarks:

Consider once again the passive transformation which, reduced to essentials, applies to a phrase-marker of the form NP-V-NP-X, rearranging the NPs. Consider the sentence:

(17) I believe the dog is hungry

This can be analyzed into the successive substrings *I, believe, the dog, is hungry,* which are NP, V, NP, X, respectively, so that the transformation should yield "the dog is believed is hungry (by me)". In exactly the same way, the sentence "the dog is believed to be hungry (by me)" derives from (18), with the analysis indicated:

(18) [$_S$ [$_{NP}$ I] [$_{VP}$ [$_V$ believe] [$_S$ [$_{NP}$ the dog] [$_{VP}$ to be hungry]]]]

Notice that there is no problem in explaining why the passive transformation, with its domain defined in terms of a structural condition on phrase-markers in the conventional way, applies to (18); the problem, rather, is to explain why it does not apply to (17).

The most obvious distinction between (17) and (18) is that the embedded sentence in (17) is tensed (finite), while the corresponding sentence of (18) is nontensed. Suppose, then, that we propose the following tentative principle:

(19) items cannot be extracted from tensed sentences

This passage reveals clearly Chomsky's rejection of certain crucial assumptions necessary if the factual contrasts in (22)–(26) are to provide grounds for recognizing a raising operation. In particular, he rejects the view that passivization (and similarly reflexivization and reciprocal marking) are constrained to clause-internal operation. He claims, in fact, essentially the opposite—that, unless something special is said, Passive, for instance, as defined by the structural description he specifies, will automatically apply to his (18),[11] so that the problem according to him is only why it fails to apply likewise "down into" *that* complements, that is, why it does not apply to his (17), ripping out the complement subject. Chomsky proposes to answer this question, in large part, with his principle (19), or rather, ultimately, with a successively refined version of this principle plus others. These refinements will then draw a distinction between tensed and untensed clauses with respect to the application of extraction and insertion operations (not in completely parallel ways).

Under the analysis newly proposed, rules like Passive, Ordinary Reflexivization, and Reciprocal Marking are free to extract elements from subordinate clauses and to insert material into subordinate clauses. Their general failure to do so in the case of tensed clauses is then explained, Chomsky suggests, by restricting the application of grammatical operations across the boundaries of tensed clauses.

Unfortunately, although there are undoubtedly correct points em-

[11] Thus, Chomsky (to appear: footnote 15) claims:

Under any formulation of the theory of transformations so far proposed, it would require an extra condition on the transformation to exclude (18) from the domain of the passive with the structural condition (X, NP, V, NP, Y). One might imagine a different theory in which the domain of a transformation is defined not by a structural condition of the familiar sort but rather by a condition on grammatical relations: thus "passive" in this theory might be defined not in terms of the structural condition (X, NP, V, NP, Y), but in terms of the total configuration which expresses subject and object as relational terms. Under this revised theory, passive would not apply to (18) unless the configuration were modified by a transformation raising the subject of the embedded sentence to the object position of the matrix sentence. There is, however, no empirical motivation for such a revision of the theory of transformations. It would, furthermore, be ill-advised in the case of passive because of pseudo-passives . . . , double passives . . . or indirect object constructions, etc.

Chomsky thus considers a "relational" alternative to the standard conception of transformational application, which would block Passive from working into lower clauses, and wrongly, I think (see Section 8.4), rejects it. He does not consider, however, another alternative with the same consequences in these cases, which will be discussed in the text later.

bedded in these proposals, Chomsky does not, in my opinion, question sufficiently the logic of his rejection of the arguments given in the previous section, arguments that have in the past been taken to support Raising in the case of B-verb infinitival complements. In particular, this failure covers up the fact that, direct empirical issues aside, Chomsky's proposals about the way a rule like Passive operates require a definite *weakening* of linguistic theory, concomitant with the apparent strengthening added by principles like (19), or their refinements.

It is perfectly true, as Chomsky notes, that the traditional account of how transformational rules impose an analysis on potential input structures would not prevent a (Passive) rule with a structural description of the form shown in (27) from applying "across S boundaries," that is, from applying to (28) in terms of the imposed bracketing to yield, in this case, the ill-formed result given in (29).

(27) NP, Verb, NP, X
     1   2   3 4

(28) Jane - believes - Bill - is insane.
     1   2   3   4

(29) *Bill is believed is insane by Jane. (Or: *Bill is believed by Jane is insane.)

Consequently, if such considerations are taken into account, it is true that a rule like Passive as in (27) would apply to (30) to yield (31), with no need for an intermediate step of raising the complement subject:

(30) Jane - believes - Bill - to be insane.
     1   2   3   4

(31) Bill is believed to be insane by Jane.

It may appear then that Chomsky is correct in saying that, as opposed to the argument that assumed that contrasts like (28)–(31) support a raising operation in (31), it is really the ill-formedness of (29) which requires explanation, not possible apparently in terms of a raising operation.

This is, however, a superficial view. It assumes gratuitously, I think, that the only relevant thing that can be (and even has been) said about rules like (27) is how they impose a bracketing on potential input structures. Similarly, it assumes implicitly that the arguments from (22) to (26) for a raising operation make false assumptions.

The situation is, in fact, rather different. In several works at least, for instance, Ross (1967) and Postal (1971), a typology of constituent movement rules (in particular, NP movement rules) is proposed, under which, crucially, the attested examples of such rules are claimed to fall into a restricted set of types, roughly these:

(32) a. *Unbounded Rules,* that is, the *Wh* reorderings, Topicalization, and other rules that transport constituents over an unbounded number of higher clause boundaries.[12]

    b. *Bounded Rules,* restricted to crossing constituents over a finite number *n* of higher clause boundaries. These are of two subtypes:

       (i) *Raising Rules,* that is, Raising, Neg Raising, Predicate Raising, where the number *n* is exactly 1—such rules move a constituent from a subordinate clause into the immediately superordinate one.

      (ii) *Clause-Internal Rules,* that is, Dative Movement, Complex NP Shift, etc., where the number *n* is zero—such rules rearrange constituents without crossing them over any higher clause boundaries at all.

Within such a typology, which amounts to an extremely restricted

---

[12] If one thinks of clause boundaries as symbols dominated by S nodes, as shown in (i), then a *higher clause boundary* with respect to some constituent C is an occurrence that *commands* C.

(i)

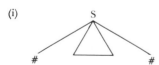

This usage is required to eliminate as irrelevant the clause boundaries in cases like (ii), which are "crossed" in the application of Passive, for example.

(ii) Melvin kissed the girl # who loved Bob # .

In (ii), the occurrences of # are higher clause boundaries only with respect to items inside the relative clause and not, for instance, with respect to *Melvin.*

hypothesis about extraction or movement rules in natural languages,[13] Passive was considered, obviously, to fall into type b (ii), of which there are a large number of clear examples.

Chomsky's proposal that Passive can, however, sometimes operate in such a way as to cross a constituent over a higher clause boundary, that is, when applying to (30) to yield (31), means that the typology of movement rules must on these grounds be extended, in other words, *weakened,* to allow a whole new type, namely, rules of this form:

(33) b. (iii) *Sometimes Clause-Internal Rules,* which in some derivations have the properties of (32) b (i) rules, in others of (32) b (ii) rules.

This is necessary, since obviously in the vast majority of cases, even in Chomsky's terms, operation of Passive will be purely clause-internal.

It is only by largely ignoring conditions like those implicit in (32) that Chomsky can claim that Passive will *automatically* apply to structures like (30) to yield (31) unless some special restriction is added, and it is only by ignoring (32) that he can claim that the "problem" is why Passive fails to apply to structures like (28).

If (32), or something essentially like it, is correct, there are strong theoretical grounds that not only prevent Passive from applying to structures like (28), under the unchallenged assumption that there is a clause boundary after *believes,* but also prevent application of Passive to (30) if there were, as Chomsky claims, a clause boundary at the relevant point after the occurrence of *believes.* Namely, the Passive rule that could apply both in such cases and in those like (34) to yield (35) is not, according to (32), a possible rule in a human language.

(34) Bob - attacked - the government - yesterday.
    1   2   3   4

(35) The government was attacked yesterday by Bob.

Thus, independently of other empirical facts,[14] an analysis like

---

13 There is, of course, no reason to think typologies like (32) are *complete.* In fact, they are not. For instance, in contrast to Chomsky and many of his recent students, who generally deny the existence of rules lowering quantifiers and elements like comparative *more* into lower clauses, I believe that a variety of such rules exist.

14 If Passive can, as Chomsky assumes, operate down into untensed clauses, it is not at all obvious what blocks incorrect passive sentences such as the *b* examples in (i) and (ii):

Chomsky's can be proposed only in a context where the set of constraints on constituent movement rules in (32) is weakened, where, to use his terms, the class of possible grammars is broadened—always, as he has often rightly stressed, an undesirable move. It is possible, of course, that (32) is incorrect in ways relevant to this discussion (distinct from those mentioned in footnote 13). I know, however, of no evidence or arguments directly indicating this. It is clear that in language after

---

(i) a. The authorities arranged for the building to be cleared.
   b. *The building was arranged by the authorities (for) to be cleared.

(ii) a. Harry planned for Sylvia to live there.
   b. *Sylvia was planned (for) to live there by Harry.

This is especially difficult in view of the fact that the main verbs here are, in other contexts, happy determinants of passivization, even across an intervening element with the construction *for*:

(iii) a. The authorities arranged for that.
   b. That was arranged for by the authorities.

(iv) a. Melvin planned for this expense.
   b. This expense was planned for by Melvin.

Analogous problems arise in the case of gerundive complements:

(v) a. They will resent him (his) coming late.
   b. *He will be resented coming late by them.

(vi) a. Arthur doesn't favor that sort of bomb('s) being used.
   b. *That sort of bomb('s) isn't favored being used by Arthur.

Chomsky apparently wishes to block cases like (v)b and (vi)b by reviving the A-over-A Principle, which prevents moving a constituent of type A out of a larger constituent of type A. This could work in cases like (v) and (vi), since Chomsky regards gerundive complements as NPs. It fails, of course, for (i) and (ii), since he denies NP status to infinitival complements. Moreover, this is the necessary device to allow passivization of the underlying subjects of B-verb infinitival complements, such as (vii), without any application of Raising.

(vii) a. Harry believes Joan to be pregnant.
   b. Joan is believed by Harry to be pregnant.

This is possible in Chomsky's terms, given the A-over-A Principle, because *Joan to be pregnant* is at no stage an NP in his system.

In his use of a weakened version of the A-over-A Principle, Chomsky makes no attempt to deal with the arguments in Ross (1967), which led to the conclusion that no such principle could be maintained. I shall not pursue this matter, since most of the motivation for the current appeal to this principle dissolves once it is seen that the passivized NP in cases like (vii) has undergone Raising, and once it is seen that infinitival clauses are in general NPs. These matters are treated in some detail in what follows.

language, there are a variety of rules restricted to purely clause-internal operation, for instance, as Ross (1967) has insightfully observed, every attested rule moving constituents *to the right*.[15] Chomsky (to appear: 38–38a) says: "Furthermore, it would be highly undesirable to extend the general theory of transformations so as to permit transformations to be restricted to a single clause, and so far as I can see, there are no strong empirical reasons motivating such an elaboration of the theory, given the general framework that we are exploring." It is difficult to know what to make of this, especially in view of the fact that there are a variety of languages, probably including most verb-final languages, in which no attested rule can move anything out of a clause,[16] and a variety

---

It should be said only that Chomsky's use of the A-over-A Principle to account for such passivization facts as those just discussed is paralleled by a similar application to other types of phenomena, in which the subjects of gerundive complements are systematically impervious to rules that, according to Chomsky, are free to operate into untensed clauses. Independently of questions of descriptive adequacy, note how this maneuver greatly decreases the empirical consequences of the claim that rules operate into untensed clauses, that is, weakens it. This follows since it is probably accurate to say that half of all untensed clauses are gerundive. In these terms, it becomes clearer, I think, how an approach to English grammar that attempts to dispense with a raising operation into superordinate object position is forced into strained and otherwise unmotivated paths.

15 This statement ignores those rules mentioned in footnote 13, which, if they exist, must, in a language like English, be unbounded movements to the right (under the assumption that English is verb-initial). It would not be hard, incidentally, to characterize formally the differences between this class of rules and those considered by Ross, so his constraint can be maintained for a restricted domain of rightward movement rules. Roughly, the difference seems to be that unbounded rightward movements necessarily destroy all of the structure to the left of the clause in which they end up. That is, they have the effect of turning a formerly subordinate clause into a new main clause. Thus they never leave behind, as do unbounded leftward movement rules, any "truncated" constituents. Ross's constraint would then hold for all rightward movement rules that leave behind "truncated" constituents.

Chomsky (to appear), following Dougherty (1969, 1970, 1971), considers a rightward movement rule that is not purely clause-internal, namely, one to derive structures like (ii) from those like (i):

(i) Each of them kissed the others; each of them wanted to kiss the others.

(ii) They kissed each other; they wanted to kiss each other.

This rule is, I think, very dubious for reasons beyond the fact that it violates the condition that rightward-moving rules are clause-internal. See Section 3.3.

16 Again, this probably requires considerable refinement. For example, I expect that all languages would contain an analogue of McCawley's rule of Predicate Raising, as

of individual rules in other languages which are restricted to clause-internal operation.[17]

Perhaps what Chomsky means is that in every case these clause-internal restrictions are to be regarded as a function of either (i) the particular formulation of the rule (either its structure index or the operation it performs) or (ii) the kind of general conditions (no extraction from tensed clauses, for example) that he is proposing. This would eliminate the possibility of saying for a particular rule, independent of its structure index, that it can apply only within clauses. However, given (32), this power is not in all likelihood required. It is probable that an inspection of the form of a rule indicates whether it is a type b (i) or b (ii) rule. If so, (32) is not to this extent inconsistent with Chomsky's claim. The latter just becomes irrelevant, since his formulation of Passive with no Raising in B-verb complements still requires replacement of (32) by the weaker (33). Thus implicit in Chomsky's proposals for dispensing with B-verb infinitival Raising is an otherwise unnecessary weakening of linguistic theory.

---

well as as analogues of quantifier and comparative lowering. Rather analogous to the situation referred to in footnotes 13 and 15, it may be possible to characterize the class of rules that permit escape from clauses in these languages as those that inherently destroy the clause from which elements are extracted. Consequently, the only rules that can extract in these languages are those that make the result appear as if nothing had been extracted—with no "truncated" clauses being left dangling in the output. But see Section 12.2.

[17] English cases of such rules include those operations involved in generating the b versions of the following pairs:

(i) a. That Bill lost is sad.
   b. It is sad that Bill lost.

(ii) a. A review of that book appeared.
    b. A review appeared of that book.

(iii) a. A boat which was loaded with heroin docked.
     b. A boat docked which was loaded with heroin.

(iv) a. Nobody $\left\{ \begin{array}{c} \text{but} \\ \text{except} \end{array} \right\}$ Melvin cheated.

    b. Nobody cheated $\left\{ \begin{array}{c} \text{but} \\ \text{except} \end{array} \right\}$ Melvin.

(v) a. The possibility that Bob is dead exists.
   b. The possibility exists that Bob is dead.

Unless (32) can be undermined, then, the fundamental assumptions of Chomsky's approach to the problems of passivization in connection with B-verb complements are just not correct. Within the terms of (32), the logic of the argument that assumed that contrasts like (22)–(23) support the postulation of a raising operation is correct. And the brute fact underlying the relevant portion of (32) remains. There are many clear cases of movement rules restricted to purely clause-internal operation, but Chomsky's version of Passive, in which sometimes operation is clause-internal, but sometimes operation goes "down" (equivalently "up") one clause, is a unique kind of reordering rule.[18-20] What would be necessary to justify such an analysis would be evidence showing that there are various other rules with the properties now uniquely attributed to Passive. But this task Chomsky does not undertake.

Incidentally, I do not think this argument is particularly important, since we shall see that there are a large variety of independent considerations showing that those cases assumed by Chomsky to involve passivization into a lower clause do not involve this, since the relevant

[18] Kayne (personal communication) suggests that the rule he calls L-Tous (see Kayne, 1969) sometimes operates clause-internally, sometimes across clause boundaries. Even if this is the case, however, it really does not bear much on the argument in the text. For L-Tous reorders quantifiers like *tous, chacun*. The properties of L-Tous thus cannot undermine a *restricted* version of (32) *governing only rules that reorder NPs*. Chomsky's version of Passive would still require an otherwise unnecessary weakening of this restricted principle. That is, even if (32) has to be weakened for some rules, this is no reason not to maintain it for other subclasses of rules, insofar as this is possible.

[19] This form of argument cannot be turned against a proposal involving Raising. That is, it cannot be claimed that the alternative to Chomsky's approach here is a unique type of rule, namely, a raising rule. For even Chomsky accepts the existence of type (32) b(i) raising rules, namely, at least the one operative with A-verbs.

[20] Ultimately, I believe that the principle that a cyclical rule like Passive is restricted to clause-internal operation is not a brute fact or even just a theorem of a relatively unenlightening typology like (32) but rather a theorem from much more interesting principles characterizing the nature of cyclical rules. Suppose it is the case that such rules in general must be defined in terms of grammatical relations like "subject of," "object of" and, in particular, that Passive is essentially defined as a rule which takes the direct object of a Verb V_u and makes it the subject of V_u. In such a theory, the clause-internal character of Passive is a direct consequence of the way the grammatical relations are defined, and there are quite deep reasons why Passive can never apply to underlying complement subjects unless these have been raised and hence turned into derived objects. For an introduction to the view that cyclical rules inherently involve grammatical relations see Section 8.4 and Perlmutter and Postal (to appear a, to appear b).

NP can be shown to have been raised. If the arguments given later are valid, then the extra power permitted in principle by Chomsky's account is even less justified, since, instead of *one* rule with unique properties, there are *no* attested cases of such a rule (see Section 12.6 for discussion of another relevant case), even though nothing in Chomsky's current version of syntactic theory—containing at best (33) instead of (32)—rules out such principles. On the contrary, they are ruled in.

It is by no means clear that one can give a parallel account to that just given for Passive with respect to the reflexive and reciprocal cases, since it is not clear what the analogue of (32) would be in these cases or even that such an analogue exists. This is evident because there is no agreement on what kind of rules these are, and I believe there is no reason to assume, as Chomsky does, that they are rules that insert morphological material (sometimes into lower clauses). Thus the question of whether these rules operate across clauses boundaries or not probably cannot be discussed usefully at this point on general theoretical grounds, as Passive in part can be. I shall therefore restrict myself almost entirely to purely empirical matters that bear on this question, in the context of a wider criticism of Chomsky's tensed-clause proposal for distinguishing infinitival from *that*-clause complements as an alternative to a raising operation into superordinate object positions.

Before turning to this question, I think it is worth noting that *if* Chomsky's proposals were extended to the analogous cases of potential B-verb Raising in languages like French, or languages with case marking like Ancient Greek, it would probably also be necessary to allow rules like cliticization of pronouns and case marking to work down into subordinate clauses. For example, in a case-marking language with analogues of both cases, one expects that in (36)a, NP_a will be in the case appropriate to its subordinate clause—nominative, or whatever.

(36) a. NP B-verb$_u$ that NP_a

  b. NP B-verb$_u$ NP_a to . . .

On the other hand, in (36)b, one expects NP_a to have whatever case is appropriate for the object of a verb—typically accusative. Ancient Greek might be such a case. For example, Andrews (1971: 138–140) presents an example that seems relevant, in which NP_a in the analogue to (36)b is dative, with a verb that determines dative case marking on its objects. If such cases can be substantiated, the facts will follow from a Raising analysis in conjunction with the principle given in (37):

(37) Case marking triggered by a verb is always internal to the minimal clause containing that verb.

This principle is otherwise valid (and also probably a function of a deeper principle analogous to that mentioned in footnote 20 that case marking is determined by grammatical relations). But an analogue to Chomsky's approach would reject Raising for the relevant examples and force case marking to operate down into the subordinate clause to mark the subject of the complement (which in such terms would bear no grammatical relation to the verb determining the case marking). See Section 12.2, dealing with Japanese, for further relevant facts.

In languages like French, where object pronouns cliticize onto their verbs, the situation is essentially parallel. Unfortunately, the analogue of Raising with B-verbs is at best severely restricted in French. But with *considérer* one can find the following:

(38) a. Je le considère (*être) intelligent.

b. Je considère Pierre intelligent.

c. L'homme que je considère (être) intelligent

The facts suggest that putative Raising with French *considérer* is limited to *être* complements and even then possible in most contexts only when *être* is deleted. Nonetheless, in essence the problems of English B-verbs arise here. If we say that there is Raising, then (38)a can be described as subject to the following principle:

(39) Cliticization of pronouns triggered by a verb is always internal to the minimal clause containing that verb.

But, again, an analogue of Chomsky's approach would reject Raising for cases like (38)a and require cliticization to operate on the subject of the complement within a lower clause, parallel to the situation with Passive (I ignore here the dubious possibility that it might be claimed that *le* in (38)a was *never* in any lower clause).

Furthermore, in languages that have verbs agreeing with both subjects and objects, facts parallel to those in the previous two paragraphs would, under a non-Raising analysis, force object agreement to work down into lower clauses, where otherwise the following regularity is valid:

(40) Agreement of a verb with NP is always limited to those NPs internal to the minimal clause containing that verb (in fact, probably to those NPs which are sisters of the verb and which, moreover, bear grammatical relations to it).

Mohawk and other Iroquoian languages have such agreement, but I have no relevant data in my notes. However, apparently relevant material has been discovered by Pam (see Pam, 1971; Hall, Hall, and Pam, 1971) for the Ethiopian language Tigrinya, which has verbal agreement with both subjects and (definite) objects. In particular, at least for the verb equivalent to 'want,' *dly*, sentences equivalent to "I wanted John to go to the city" have *dly* agreeing not only with "I" but also with "John." See, in particular, Hall, Hall and Pam (1971: 5–7). There are, in this case, reasons why "John" cannot have been the underlying object of main clause *dly* (an a priori implausible analysis on semantic grounds, obviously). Thus the alternatives would appear to be a Raising analysis, adopted by these authors, or a proposal analogous to Chomsky's, the latter requiring abandonment of principle (40).

It is very likely, then, that the situation vis-à-vis (32) and Passive in English will find analogues involving principles (37), (39), and (40) for parallel cases in other languages. Quite likely, then, principles (37), (39), (40) and a principle stating that rules like Passive are purely clause-internal will be obviously valid for most cases and questionable only for a class of examples where the doubt is resolvable by a Raising type of analysis. Or, to put it differently, if a Raising rule can be characterized as part of universal grammar, an idea considered in greater detail in Section 8.4 and Section 12.2, one class of justifications for such a rule will be that it permits the maintenance of a variety of restrictive constraints on grammars such as (37) and (39).

To conclude, in this discussion I have essentially been considering logical possibilities, because the available information about other languages is not adequate for serious empirical claims on my part. In particular, I have certainly not intended to suggest that Chomsky has committed himself to any particular analyses of facts of languages other than English.

3

Evidence for Raising with B-Verb Infinitival Complements I: Previously Discussed Classes of Facts

3.1 Passivization

In the preceding chapter, I gave essentially one argument for B-verb Raising, namely, a restatement of the older claim that the passivization contrasts between *that*-clause and infinitival complements support such an operation. The essence of the discussion was a justification of the past view that the operation of Passive is purely clause-internal. I argued that any attempt to claim that Passive can operate across higher clause boundaries requires an otherwise unmotivated broadening of the class of possible grammatical rules—an unnecessary weakening of linguistic theory. There is a little more to be said about passivization, however, particularly about how Chomsky's proposals are to generate sentences like (1) and simultaneously block those like (2):

(1) a. It was believed (by everyone) that Melvin was an addict.

    b. That Melvin was an addict was believed by everyone.

(2) a. *It was believed (by everyone) (for) Melvin to be an addict.

    b. *(For) Melvin to be an addict was believed by everyone.

It is particularly important to explain the latter cases of ill-formedness in contrast to cases like (3), which show that the relevant positions are not in general taboo for infinitival complements.

(3) a. It was inevitable for Melvin to become an addict.

    b. For Melvin to become an addict was inevitable.

In the more traditional analysis adopted here, (1)b is simply the normal passive with (1)a derived from the latter by optional application of Extraposition. Both (2)a and (2)b are blocked because there has been a deformation of a clause to infinitival form without the application of Raising, which triggers this. That is, Raising application is the only source of infinitival complements with B-verbs.

If Raising had applied, then automatically (4) would be generated instead of (2)b, since it is the raised NP that becomes the object of the main verb, directly post-(main) verbal, and hence subject to main clause passivization.

(4) Melvin was believed to be an addict (by everyone).

On the other hand, forms like (3) are not blocked, because, with predicates like *inevitable, nice,* and *bad,* the infinitival form is independent of Raising and is probably induced by a variety of semantic factors.

One problem in Chomsky's system is the fact that he reiterates by giving labeled bracketings in several places[1] that structures like (5) are analyzed in such a way that the *that* + S is *not* an NP.[2]

(5) NP B-verb (that) S

Thus for Chomsky, verbs like *expected* and *believed* have object NPs in (6)a, but not in (6)b:

(6) a. I $\left\{ \begin{array}{l} \text{believed} \\ \text{expected} \end{array} \right\}$ that.

　　b. I $\left\{ \begin{array}{l} \text{believed} \\ \text{expected} \end{array} \right\}$ that Melvin would escape.

This being the case, one asks how passives such as (1) can be derived at all. The only answer given, as far as I can tell, is in a terse, dense footnote, which I quote (Chomsky, to appear: footnote 57):

We might go on, following Emonds, to hold that instead of extraposition there is a rule of *it*-replacement that gives "for John to leave would surprise me", "that John left surprised me", etc.; we might also hold that the passive transformation does not apply to such forms as (20a, b), preposing the embedded S. Such forms as "that John left is (widely) believed" then derive by *it*-replacement from (A) "it is (widely) believed that John left", under these assumptions. If this is a root transformation, in Emonds' sense, it follows that we cannot have "I wonder whether that S′ is widely believed", though "I wonder whether the fact that S′ is widely believed" is all right. Speculating as to (A), we might

[1] See Chomsky (to appear: 8, 10, 11, 25, 29a, 31, 33, especially 65a).

[2] This represents a break not justified in Chomsky's paper with the position of Chomsky (1965: 200): ". . . as Peter Rosenbaum has pointed out, the sentential complement of (11) should be regarded as embedded in the Noun-Phrase Object of 'expect' " and also Chomsky (1967: 431). It is presumably motivated by the claims made in Emonds (1970). An immediate deleterious consequence, of course, is that the insertion conditions for B-verbs must be complicated to allow either [NP_____S] or [NP_____NP], because of noncomplement cases. (See footnote 11 of Chapter 1.)

take it to be in effect a base form, if VP $\longrightarrow$ Aspect $\overline{V}$, where Aspect $\longrightarrow$ (Perfect) (Progressive) (Passive). This analysis would require that both components of passive are obligatory if Aspect contains Passive (and, of course, NP-preposing is inapplicable if there is no NP following the verb, as in (A)); that a rule of interpretation relates *it* and sentential complements (thus there is no interpretation for "it is died by John," but there is for (A)); that *believe*, etc., must have a subject at the deep structure level, either a lexical subject or Δ; which will delete (by the rule of agent deletion) if it moves to the agent position (excluding *"it believes that S"); that *it* appears in the position of an otherwise unfilled subject.

It is, however, difficult to interpret this account in a way consistent with the generation of sentences like (1)a. Even granting Emonds's (1970) proposal that such structures are nearer to base forms than those like (1)b,[3] and granting the division of the passive rule into two operations, an agent-postposing rule and an object-preposing rule (as in Chomsky, 1970; see also Postal, 1971)[4] and even granting the dubious broadening (actually, weakening) of the topology of linguistic structures to include "empty" nodes in representations, that is, nonterminal nodes dominating no other nodes,[5] it is still unclear how to interpret the

3 Emonds's (1970) analysis rejects an Extraposition rule in favor of a rule that does roughly the opposite, with concomitant differences in assumptions about underlying structure. Strong counterarguments exist to this approach. See Section 12.4 and Higgins (1971).

4 Such a breakup of the older Passive rule is essentially automatic under a verb-initial analysis, in which the derived subject formation part of the rule is subsumed under the general Subject Formation rule, which positions all preverbal subjects.

5 Emonds (1970) allows both "empty" nodes what he calls "doubly filled" nodes. Although neither term has ever been defined precisely, the latter apparently refers to a situation in which a nonterminal node dominates two other nodes, *A* and *B*, where there is no "precede" relation between *A* and *B*. Logically, it would seem, the system allows for "doubly unfilled nodes," but no one has yet made use of these. Both of these utterly unmotivated alterations of the topology of linguistic structures represent weakenings of linguistic theory. Thus the former requires at least the elimination of the axiom given in (i), while the latter requires elimination of at least the principle given in (ii):

(i) All nonterminal nodes in all trees dominate some elements.

(ii) In all trees, if some node *N* directly dominates two nodes *A*, *B*, then either *A* precedes *B* or conversely.

It is perhaps worth noting that "empty" nodes are incompatible with Chomsky's previous formalization of the way transformations apply to phrase markers, since this depended entirely on a so-called proper analysis of the terminal string—a theory in which no nonterminal node could possibly be recognized by a transformation unless it dominated some element of the terminal string.

quotation in a way consistent with the generation of (1)a. Chomsky clearly says that *believe* must take an underlying subject, and we know that the *that* clause is for him not an underlying object NP. Hence, the underlying structure of (1)a would necessarily be for Chomsky something like (7). It is easy to see how the underlying subject NP can be moved by the postposing part of the division of Passive. The question is how the *it* is generated. All Chomsky says of relevance is that (i) "of course, NP-preposing is inapplicable if there is no NP following the verb, as in (A)" and (ii) "*it* appears in the position of an otherwise unfilled subject."

(7)

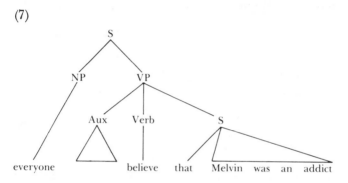

One initially assumes that the notion of "unfilled subject" here refers to a subject NP node that is "empty," in the sense discussed earlier, since this concept, though so far undefined, is one to which Chomsky makes frequent appeal. But even so, there is no way to turn (5) into (1)a. Since NP preposing must be inapplicable, there is no natural way to generate any derived subject NP *node* at all, empty or not, to become *it*. It might be claimed then that (7) is a wrong reconstruction of the author's intent, which might be to have an "empty" NP node generated after the B-verb in such cases. But this analysis, which would be essentially like that of Emonds (1970), is incompatible with Chomsky's statement of the VP rule for these cases as (8), which mentions no NP node.

(8) VP ⟶ Aspect + V.

There is, then, as far as I can see, only one remaining possibility. Namely, some newly invented rule must not only introduce the *it* again but also mark it as an NP, since this structure is required for later rules (such as, in Chomsky's system, Subject-Auxiliary Inversion) and, in any-body's system, Raising, because of examples like (9):

(9) It seems to have been believed that Melvin was an addict.

This necessary rule will cause some system-internal problems for Chom-sky, since it would not be "structure preserving," as he requires (con-trast Emonds's (1969) treatment of the insertion of existential *there* as involving a base-generated "empty" NP). However, it is not now pos-sible, I believe, to turn the need for this rule itself into a serious argu-ment against Chomsky's proposal, since the question of how to generate such expletive *its* has no well-founded answer in any other system. Kayne has pointed out such French examples as (10), where *il* is gram-matically masculine singular, but *trois femmes* feminine plural.

(10) Il est arrivé trois femmes.

Probably there is one general unsolved problem here involving exple-tive pronouns.[6]

However, an argument against Chomsky's proposals arises, I think, from the problems under discussion. Assume his system succeeds in somehow generating pairs of sentences like (11) from underlying struc-tures like (7).

(11) a. It was believed by everyone that Melvin was an addict.

   b. That Melvin was an addict was believed by everyone.

There is then nothing to prevent the perfectly parallel derivation of those like (12), since Chomsky's system must generate underlying struc-tures like (7) except that the complement S is infinitival.

---

6 That is, there seems to be some kind of principle guaranteeing in a certain class of cases that when an NP or at least its essential components are moved out of a cer-tain position, this position will be filled by an NP constituent that has the form of the maximally unmarked definite pronouns (neuter, singular, if there is such a cat-egory; otherwise, masculine, singular, etc.). The existence of such a principle would be one important reason for rejecting Rosenbaum's assumption (number (iv) of foot-note 6 in Chapter 1) that base rules in English generate underlying NPs of the form $[_{NP}$ *it* $S_{NP}]$, an idea otherwise ignored in this study. Because, given such a general rule, an ad hoc base generation for English misses the generalization involved. Rosen-baum's treatment gives no basis for the element before S having the form of a definite pronoun. It could as well have any other arbitrary form. For some interesting dis-cussion of typological contrasts across languages involving these expletive pronouns see Perlmutter (1971). See also Morgan (1968).

(12) a. *It was believed by everyone (for) Melvin to be an addict.

    b. *(For) Melvin to be an addict was believed by everyone.

Hence, an ad hoc statement must be added to block cases like (12). The need for this ad hoc statement counts against his approach.

It might be claimed that his statement is no more ad hoc than that required in a Raising system to explain (12). Recall that the latter must say that Raising application with B-verbs triggers infinitival marking. However, this claim of equivalence is incorrect. The reason is that even Chomsky's system must correlate infinitival form with Raising application, because of A-verbs:

(13) a. It seems that Melvin is an addict.

    b. *It seems (for) Melvin to be an addict.

    c. Melvin seems to be an addict.

Thus, in a grammar recognizing Raising for B-verb infinitival complements, the facts in (12) can be made a special case of the general principle needed for (13), specifically for (13)b and (13)c, namely, the following principle:

(14) A complement whose subject is raised is marked infinitival.

Of course, as we have seen, (14) is not, strictly speaking, correct, because of gerundive Raising cases like (15).

(15) Melvin ended up supporting the communists.

Ultimately then, (14) must be replaced by a statement that only de-finitizes such complements, with the infinitival-gerundive contrast predicted either by ad hoc statements or by so far unknown principles. In this version, incidentally, the principle may cease to be a part of English grammar at all. It is conceivable that any language (meeting certain conditions, perhaps) with an analogue of Raising has the affected complements de-finitized.[7, 8]

Concluding this discussion of passivization, I must say that there is

---

[7] A parallel statement must also be made about the operation of Equi (Postal, 1970b). Complement subject deletion also seems systematically linked with de-finitization.

However, while this is apparently uniformly the case for European languages, at least one counterexample seems to exist, namely, Japanese, where raising into object position is apparently possible without de-finitization. See Section 12.2.

nothing in Chomsky's discussion to suggest any error in the essentially traditional argument for B-verb Raising based on the facts of passivization, and there is nothing to suggest that his alternative account is really viable. The latter depends on the implicit assumption that (32) of Chapter 2 (at least for NP reorderings) is to be weakened, and the resulting system can block B-verb passives with infinitival complements like (12) of this chapter only at the cost of ad hoc statements, where the Raising analysis can make use of a principle at least necessary also for A-verbs, and possibly a feature of universal grammar.

3.2 Reflexivization

An approach to reflexivization in Chomsky's terms must be parallel to that for passivization.[9] It must be claimed that reflexivization of a pronoun by an antecedent is not inherently restricted to pairs of NPs that

---

Further, it is probably no accident that Tough Movement, operative in (iii), also is invariably connected with a nonfinite complement.

(i) It was tough that Mary kicked you.

(ii) It was tough for Mary to kick you.

(iii) You were tough for Mary to kick.

(iv) *You were tough (that) Mary kicked.

This suggests that the principle involved is even more general and is concerned with any raising rule that creates new derived subjects or objects (thus not relevant for rules like Topicalization, or the *wh* movements, which do not create new subjects or objects).

If the principle in question can, despite the situation in Japanese, somehow be assigned to universal grammar, the argument in the text for a Raising analysis of B-verbs, and against the requirement of a system like Chomsky's that there be an ad hoc statement ruling out text examples like (12), becomes even stronger. This would mean that the required de-finitization is, under a Raising analysis, a function of a principle of universal grammar, while in Chomsky's system it is just a peculiar accident. Thus the Raising analysis offers hope of actually explaining such facts, not merely of describing them.

8 In this sense, Chomsky is certainly pointing to a real feature of language with his tensed clause–nontensed clause distinction. But there are many problems (see footnote 12). In particular, no generally applicable definition of the notions has been given.

9 He does not give an explicit description of reflexivization within the system he develops, but the outlines of what would be required are directly derivable from the form of his statements. Thus he consistently makes use of the schema [No rule can involve . . .], then specifies the tensed clause as well as subject conditions, for ex-

are Clause Mates, but rather that the rule can operate between an antecedent and a commanded pronoun that is in a lower clause. The contrast between *that*-clause and infinitival reflexivization with respect to underlying complement subjects, as in (16), is then drawn in terms of the tensed-nontensed clause distinction.

(16) a. Harriet$_i$ believes that she$_i$ (*herself$_i$) is telepathic.

    b. Harriet$_i$ believes herself$_i$ (*her$_i$, *she$_i$) to be telepathic.

That is, it is to be claimed that Ordinary Reflexivization cannot work down into *tensed* clauses.

However, this will obviously not suffice since, even with infinitival forms, reflexivization is not possible with nonsubjects:

(17) a. Harvey$_i$ believes Joan to hate him$_i$ (*himself$_i$).[10]

    b. Lucy$_i$ proved Bill to have talked to her$_i$ (*herself$_i$) about ornithology.

To account for this and other parallel facts involving similar processes, Chomsky proposes a "specified subject" condition that says, very roughly, that rules cannot operate across a subject that is not deleted.[11] Hence, the erroneous reflexivization in (17) is to be blocked by the intervening (between antecedent and pronoun) putative subjects *Joan* and *Bill*. Note the lack of an intervening subject in (16)b. This, then, is supposed to explain why only subjects of infinitival complements reflexivize in terms of a higher clause antecedent.

There are two objections that might be considered with respect to this sort of analysis, which seems to offer hope of avoiding the conclusion that the contrasts here are simply a function of the traditional Clause Mate condition on Ordinary Reflexivization in combination

---

ample, as under the scope of the negative and existential quantifier. Hence, the first that the reflexivization rules fall under their scope follows trivially.

[10] Many speakers, including myself (for discussion, see Postal, 1970: 50–52; also Section 6.9), do not actually accept sentences like (17), even without the reflexives. This is, however, not really relevant here since, even for such speakers, there is no doubt that reflexivization makes the sentences far worse, indicating that there is a true constraint on reflexive marking manifested in such constructions. For these speakers, then, the markings in (17) are correctly indicative of relative grammaticality.

[11] Refinements turn even some deleted subjects into "specified subjects," depending on what NP controlled their deletion.

with the application or not of Raising. First, one might argue that the notions of tensed versus untensed clause and of specified subject are, particularly in the latter case, theoretically inadequate.[12] I shall not attempt to argue this here, however. For, even granting that these notions are formulated so that they categorize clauses in the way intended, they just give the wrong answers.

The purported interest of Chomsky's innovative account is that it reduces idiosyncratic facts, namely, whether or not Ordinary Reflexivization applies, to general principles—general at least for English—and

---

[12] The specified subject condition seems inherently redundant, since its definition includes, in effect, much of the conditions of application for Equi.

The chief problem with the tensed clause condition is that no definition is given of what a tensed clause is. It seems to be assumed that the notion is essentially self-evident for English and can be taken to include any clause whose main verb is inflected for "tense." Even were this the case, the notions are not characterized in such a way as to permit cross-linguistic application. Their general intuitive clarity, for a wide range of languages, suggests that there is indeed a valid notion here, as do facts like those in footnote 7.

Chomsky (to appear: footnote 13) assumes that certain clauses that are not superficially inflected for tense, namely, the "subjunctive" *that* clauses in examples like (i) are nonetheless to be accorded the status of tensed clauses by simply having an element "subjunctive" as one expansion in "deep structure" of the element Tense.

(i) a. I demand that he be arrested.
   b. It is mandatory that he visit the infirmary.

This is necessary because such clauses behave in every relevant way like inflected *that* clauses. However, this approach to such cases takes a long stride toward rendering any statement in terms of tensed clauses contentless.

Suppose, for instance, that some infinitival complement clauses behaved like tensed clauses with respect to the processes under investigation. What stops one from recognizing some further expansion of Tense, call it "Fix," which is present in just these cases? In short, if there are no independently valid principles for assigning the categorization "tensed clause," then clauses are assigned this status purely on the basis of their behavior with respect to the processes in question. Hence, to say that this principle explains such behavior is useless.

That the problem is more than hypothetical is indicated by observations of Ross, who observes that in pseudoclefts, verbs like *want*, which ordinarily take infinitival complements, allow "subjunctive" *that* clauses:

(ii) a. I want Bob to go.
    b. *I want that Bob go.

(iii) a. What I want is for Bob to go.
     b. What I want is that Bob go.

possibly even to principles of universal grammar, and, moreover, principles relevant to various other types of phenomena. For this purpose, however, the principles must at least constrain not only the reflexivization rule at work in (16)–(17) but other similar rules, and most certainly other reflexivization rules in English. But they do not.

First, reflexivization into so-called picture noun phrases is not constrained by tensed clause boundaries. While the phenomenon in such cases is quite restricted, such reflexivization with existential sentences, for example, is quite unimpeachable:

(18) a. Jack$_i$ thinks that there are pictures of himself$_i$ hanging in the post office.

b. Mary$_i$ feels that there is an unflattering story about herself$_i$ in the *Tribune.*

This judgment is, incidentally, not a new one. Such sentences are given, possibly for the first time, in Jackendoff (1969) with no hint of doubts. A related set of sentences involving picture noun reflexivization equally in violation of Chomsky's tensed clause principle was given by Ross (1970a: 232), who attributes their discovery to Gruber (1967):

(19) a. Tad$_i$ knew that it would be a story about himself$_i$.

b. Mike$_i$ will not believe that this is a photograph of himself$_i$.

c. I promised Omar$_i$ that it would be a poem about himself$_i$.

Thus it is clear that picture noun reflexivization does not obey the tensed clause principle. Examples like (19)a–c also show that it does not obey the specified subject principle either, since the respective subjects *it, this,* and *it* intervene between antecedent and reflexive in these.[13]

This suggests that infinitival clauses in general might be derived from "subjunctive" *that* clauses, a plausible enough idea on semantic grounds. Note in addition such complementarities as the following:

(iv) a. I desire that he win.
b. *I desire him to win.

This would mean, however, that the presence or absence of underlying "subjunctive" marking is not a possible basis for controlling rule behavior with respect to these clauses, for the "subjunctive" *that* clauses that keep the *that* marker behave like tensed clauses, while infinitival clauses in general do not.

[13] It is true, of course, as Langacker (personal communication) reminds me, that, in spite of (19), most cases of picture noun reflexivization across subjects are ill-formed.

Second, these principles also fail to constrain several other reflexivization operations discussed by Ross (1970a). Both principles are violated without ill-formedness by the unique type of reflexivization found in conjoined agent phrases, as in (20), where all of these examples were given by Ross:

(20) a. Tom_i believed that the paper had been written by Ann and himself$_i$.

b. I told Tom_i that the entries should be designed by Ann and himself$_i$.

c. That the paper would have to be written by Ann and himself$_i$ was obvious to Tom_i.

d. Tom_i thinks that I tried to get Mary to make you say that the paper had been written by Ann and himself$_i$.

Chomsky's principles also fail in the case of the reflexivization operation which applies in *like* phrases, again discussed at some length by Ross (1970a). Relevant examples include the following:

(21) a. I told $Albert_i$ that physicists like himself$_i$ were a godsend.

b. $Albert_i$ accused me of having tried to get his secretary to tell you that physicists like himself$_i$ were hard to get along with.

c. That physicists like himself$_i$ never got invited to horse shows didn't seem to faze $Albert_i$.

Finally, the tensed clause principle is violable without deviance with respect to the reflexivization operation found in *as* phrases, also discussed by Ross (1970a), who gave such examples as (22):

(22) a. $Harry_i$ told Glinda that as for himself$_i$ he wouldn't be invited.

b. Harry believes that the students know that $Glinda_i$ has been saying that as for herself$_i$ she won't be invited.

To take his example:

(i) *Tad_i hoped (that) Mary would tell a story about himself$_i$.

I think, however, that such blockages are due to something along the lines of the Intervention Constraint suggested by Grinder (1970) and applied by him (1970: 309–310) to picture noun reflexivization among a variety of other anaphoric processes.

Third, further evidence that the specified subject condition is not a correct constraint on reflexivization operations is provided by some observations of John Lawler.[14] He points out that there is a special reflexivization process associated with complement occurrences of such symmetrical or asymmetrical predicates as *similar, superior, more +* adjective:

(23) a. Joe$_i$ considers Mary (to be) superior to himself$_i$.

    b. I regard them as more liberal than myself.

    c. Mary$_i$ found Joan (to be) similar to herself$_i$.

But, in these cases, the reflexivization operates "across" a specified subject.[15] Note the contrast between these sentences and those involving predicates not of the special class for the same main verbs:[16]

(24) a. Joe$_i$ considers Mary (to be) in love with him$_i$ (*himself$_i$).

    b. I regard them as having been mean to me (*myself).

    c. Mary$_i$ found Joan to be faithful to her$_i$ (*herself$_i$).

It follows that principles involving tensed clauses and specified subjects do not give the right answers for (i) picture noun reflexivization, (ii) conjoined agent reflexivization, (iii) *like*-phrase reflexivization, (iv) *as*-phrase reflexivization, and (v) symmetrical predicate reflexivization, wrongly predicting that none of these processes can work into tensed clauses or across specified subjects.

In particular, principles like Chomsky's totally fail to account for such contrasts as those in (25):

(25) a. *I believe Bob to love myself.

    b. I believe Bob to be more liberal than myself.

The full set of reflexivization cases shows that there is no basis for assuming such principles to be relevant to the description of Ordinary

---

[14] I am indebted to G. Lakoff for bringing this to my attention.

[15] That is, it does so in Chomsky's terms. Under a Raising analysis, the former subjects have been raised before the reflexivization rule can be tested for application. It is for reasons parallel to this in other cases that Chomsky rejects postulation of a raising rule. That is, among other things, the specified subject condition and B-verb type Raising are incompatible. What is being argued here, then, is that one must choose the latter.

[16] See footnote 10.

Reflexivization, since the only apparently supporting cases of Ordinary Reflexivization into lower (untensed) clauses are susceptible to a Raising explanation. Consequently, the failure of Ordinary Reflexivization to operate into subordinate clauses in general must be a function of the constraint, almost uniformly recognized since the initial generative article on the subject by Lees and Klima (1963), that this rule is restricted to Clause Mates. Note especially that, once it is seen that tensed clause boundaries and specified subjects do not interfere with reflexivization operations in general, only the Clause Mate condition on Ordinary Reflexivization can block its operation into *relative clauses,* either restrictive or nonrestrictive:

(26) a. Bob$_i$ kissed the girl (who) he$_i$ (*himself$_i$) loved.

    b. Joan$_i$ called the man (that) she$_i$ (*herself$_i$) wanted to question.

    c. Joan$_i$ called Bob, who she$_i$(*herself$_i$)wanted to question.

    d. Bob$_i$ didn't like the book (which) it was incumbent on him$_i$ (*himself$_i$) to review.

It is doubtful, incidentally, that such facts can follow from anything other than an ad hoc restriction of Ordinary Reflexivization to Clause Mates. For example, in Japanese, reflexivization can work into both types of relative clause. See Kuno (1972a).

It follows that the other reflexivization operations discussed earlier are not subject to Clause Mate conditions. But, given the fact that Ordinary Reflexivization is subject to this condition, contrasts between pairs like (16) must be due to Clause Mate contrasts, which can only be a function of the operation of a raising operation in the infinitival cases, as traditionally recognized.

The discussion so far shows that Chomsky's tensed clause and specified subject conditions are too strong to correctly account for the reflexivization contrasts between pairs like (16), since, if adopted, they would block a wide variety of perfectly appropriate reflexive connections produced by at least five other reflexivization rules. But, *fourth,* in addition to the relative clause facts, there are other cases, showing that these principles are too *weak.* The underlying assumption, in contrast to the traditional view first adopted by Lees and Klima (1963), under which Ordinary Reflexivization is constrained by a Clause Mate condition, is that reflexivization operates freely into subordinate clauses unless blocked by independent conditions. But there are various cases, for which the tensed clause and specified subject principles are not relevant, in which this is not so:

(27) a. Joan$_i$ recognized the necessity for her$_i$ (*herself$_i$) to leave.

    b. Mike$_i$ hasn't decided on the best way for him$_i$ (*himself$_i$) to do it.

These cases[17] should be separated from those like (28):

(28) a. Nixon$_i$ is aware of the widespread wish for him$_i$ (*himself$_i$) to resign.

    b. I heard about a plan to fire me (*myself).

The point is that in (28) it is more than plausible to recognize that nominals like *wish* and *plan* have underlying pronominal subjects, and there is thus at least hope that it is these which block the erroneous reflexivization, according to the specified subject constraint. This will require ad hoc orderings, of course, but still there is some hope for such an analysis. However, most crucially, such an analysis fails for cases like (27), where there is no basis for recognizing such underlying subjects for the nominals but, on the contrary, many grounds for rejecting such a postulation. In particular, the meaning is inconsistent with such NPs in all cases, and such nominals can never show up with nondeleted subjects. Moreover, internal to Chomsky's system, such a postulation of subjects would be inconsistent with the fact that elements are extractable from the complements of elements like *necessity*, which would be blocked by the specified subject condition if *necessity* had a subject:

(29) The only thing which I recognize the necessity to change is the punctuation.

I know of no independent principles that will block the wrong re-

---

[17] I have found some speakers for whom the reflexive variants of (27) are well-formed. This has, however, no real bearing on the argument here, I think, because these speakers also accept the nonreflexive forms with coreferent readings. Hence, the reflexive rule at work for them is *optional*. However, as observed in Chapter 2, footnote 10, Ordinary Reflexivization is generally obligatory. This suggests that these speakers have some optional reflexivization not present in my type of idiolect, an optional rule *not* governed by a Clause Mate condition.

flexivization in cases like (28), under the assumption that Ordinary Reflexivization is free to operate down into untensed clauses. Nothing else that Chomsky suggests is relevant, as far as I can see. Hence, in the absence of the usual Clause Mate constraint on Ordinary Reflexivization, at best an ad hoc restriction must be invented to block cases like (28). But to do this is to destroy any lingering plausibility for the claim that this rule works down into subordinate clauses. What we have seen is that (i) there are absolutely no attested cases of Ordinary Reflexivization operating into putatively subordinate clauses except for those constructions where the Raising analysis permits the claim that application is subsequent to the movement of the relevant NP out of the subordinate clause; and (ii) there are cases where operation of this rule into untensed subordinate clauses must be blocked, but no independent principle suffices.

The conclusion seems to be that the traditional view that Ordinary Reflexivization in English is restricted to Clause Mates is correct. Chomsky's attempt to replace this condition by a combination of principles referring to tensed clauses and specified subjects fails, since these conditions are at once too weak and too strong to govern properly the ranges of the variety of English reflexivization operations. It follows that contrasts like those given in (30) provide the argument for Raising in B-verb infinitival complements that they have been traditionally thought to provide.

(30) a. I believe that I (*myself) am immortal.

b. I believe myself (*me) to be immortal.

3.3 Reciprocal Marking

A position such as that developed by Chomsky is more plausible initially in the case of the facts of reciprocal marking (distribution of the phrases *each other, one another*) than in the case of those involving reflexive marking. This is so because, by and large, there is no analogue to the variety of additional reflexivization operations, that is, no analogue of *as*-phrase reflexivization, coordinate *by*-phrase reflexivization, etc. Roughly, the scope of reciprocal marking is the same as the scope of Ordinary Reflexivization, with at least one important exception, namely, reciprocals also parallel the distribution of picture noun reflexives:

(31) a.   They hate each other (themselves).

   b. *They know that I hate each other (*themselves).

   c.   They bought pictures of each other (themselves).

   d. *They bought John's pictures of each other (*themselves).

I do not understand reciprocal marking very well, but I think certain prior generative ideas about it were substantially correct, as far as they went. These notions were that there are at least two, partially independent, processes, one operating essentially in contexts where Ordinary Reflexivization operates, called "Ordinary Reciprocal Marking," the other operating in contexts where picture noun reflexivization is possible (and possibly others), called "picture noun reciprocal marking." The former, it would have been argued, is restricted to those contexts where the antecedent and the reciprocal phrase are Clause Mates, analogous to the situation with Ordinary Reflexivization. This would have accounted for such contrasts as that shown in (32), on the assumption that Raising operates in the former, producing the required Clause Mate structures for the cycle of the main clause.

(32) a.   They believe each other to be intelligent.

   b. *They believe (that) each other are intelligent.

Chomsky discusses reciprocals extensively and in some detail throughout his paper; indeed, the facts involved form one of the cornerstones of his entire discussion. He rejects the Clause Mate explanation for cases like (32) and appeals instead to the distinction between tensed and untensed clauses. This argument is immediately suspect because, partially parallel to picture noun reflexivization, as illustrated in (18) and (19), picture noun reciprocal marking is not governed by tensed clause boundaries:

(33) a. Jack and Tom think that there are pictures of each other hanging in the hall.

   b. We feel that there are unflattering stories about each other in the *Tribune*.

(34) a. ?*They knew that there would be stories about each other.

   b. ?*Mike and Tom will not believe that these are photographs of each other.

c. ?*I promised Sally and Sue that there would be poems about each other.

Further cases include the following:

(35) a. We agreed that obscene photographs of each other should not be displayed.

b. They conceded to each other that unfair stories about each other had been circulated by immature aides.

If, however, the tensed clause principle does not block reciprocal marking in cases like (33) and (35), there is no basis for believing it is the operative filter in cases like (32)b. If, then, Ordinary Reciprocal Marking is not governed by a Clause Mate condition, a special ad hoc constraint is required to block (32)b.

However, it is probably the specified subject condition that bears the greatest burden in Chomsky's account of reciprocal distribution because of cases like (36):

(36) a.   They want to buy pictures of each other.

b. *They want Bob to buy pictures of each other.

However, (33)a and (33)b already show that reciprocal marking in general is not governed by such a condition.

Chomsky's approach to reciprocal marking takes the form of adopting essentially the analysis of Dougherty (1969, 1970, 1971), which assumes that reciprocals are formed by a reordering rule that actually moves the constituent *each* to its ultimate locus from the antecedent structure. Thus underlying (36)a would be something like (37)[18] with (36)a derived by application of the movement rule in question.

---

18 Chomsky (to appear: especially footnote 27) builds basic aspects of his system on the assumption that sequences like *they each* in (37) are constituents—in fact, NP constituents. There are at least three arguments that this assumption is, in general, incorrect. *First*, the quantifier can never accompany a *wh* form when these are moved:

(i) a.   the men, who each died
   b.   the men, who I think each died
   c. *the men, who each I think died

Second, the distribution of parenthetical elements is inconsistent with the assumption of constituent status:

(37) They each want to buy pictures of the other.

Given the similarities in meaning between structures like (36)a and (37), as well as the partial morphological similarity, such an analysis is attractive initially in spite of cases where the input and output are partially distinct in subtle aspects of meaning, several interesting examples of which are given by Chomsky. However, when looked at more closely, such an analysis seems to lose much of its appeal.

Cases like (38) show that the rule in question cannot be a simple movement rule.

(38) a. They talked to each other about each other.

b. They bought pictures of each other from each other.

Cases like (39) show that the naturalness of the source in some cases is paralleled by an impossibility in others, like (40):

(39) a. All of them were hitting and biting each other.

b. Some of them hate each other.

c. Tom and Bill hate each other.

(40) a. *Each (one) of all of them were hitting and biting the others.

b. *All of them each were hitting and biting the others.

c. *Each (one) of some of them hate the others.

d. *Some of them each hate the others.

e. *Each (one) of Tom and Bill hates the other.

Perhaps most serious[19] of all, in language after language, the morpho-

---

(ii) a. The officers, $\left\{ \begin{array}{l} \text{you know} \\ \text{I think} \end{array} \right\}$, each left separately.

b. *The officers each, $\left\{ \begin{array}{l} \text{you know} \\ \text{I think} \end{array} \right\}$, left separately.

Third, as pointed out to me by Stephen Anderson, the positioning of the genitive in gerundive clauses is inconsistent with such a view:

(iii) a.   ?The men's each leaving individually worries me.

b. **The men each's leaving individually worries me.

However, later, in Section 4.5, I shall argue briefly that there is an independent rule that does make such quantifiers part of the preceding NPs in just those cases where these NPs are definite pronouns like *we* and *they*.

19 Chomsky does not consider the implications for his account of reciprocal formation of sentences like the following:

logical structure used for the analogue of reciprocal marking is similar to or identical to that used for reflexive marking. Thus it seems very likely that the parallelism in distribution in English is not an accident but a consequence of the fact that these processes are closely related,[20] although neither Chomsky's analysis of reciprocals nor any other so far captures this similarity.

Thus Chomsky's underlying approach to reciprocal marking seems vulnerable.[21] I shall not pursue this point, however. For even if reciprocals were described correctly by the kind of rule Chomsky assumes, the tensed clause and specified subject conditions are not the appropriate metaprinciples for controlling the operation of this rule, under the as-

---

(i) Help each other.

(ii) People who help each other are happy.

(iii) $\left\{ \begin{array}{l} \text{People} \\ \text{Saints} \\ \text{Priests} \end{array} \right\}$ should love each other.

Example (i) indicates that he would have to allow *each,* but probably *each* alone among quantifiers, on the NP that is deleted in imperatives. Example (ii) shows that he would have to allow *each,* but *each* alone among quantifiers, on the relative pronouns of *restrictive* relative clauses, since these normally permit no quantifiers. Moreover, these *each* would be well-formed only if they underwent Chomsky's movement rule. Example (iii) shows that he would have to allow *each* to cooccur with generic NPs, which normally exclude all quantifiers.

[20] Notice that they both involve *coreference.* Thus, very roughly, the logical structures of (i) and (ii) can be approximated by (iii) and (iv), where the occurrences of *of* here represent partitive relations.

(i) They criticized themselves.

(ii) They criticized each other.

(iii) NP_x criticized NP_x.

(iv) Quantifier NP_i of NP_x criticised Quantifier NP_j of NP_x.

Thus while Chomsky tends to consider paraphrases for sentences like (ii) of the form given in (v), I suggest as more appropriate something like (vi):

(v) Each of them criticized the others.

(vi) Each one$_j$ of them$_x$ criticized (the) other one(s)$_k$ of them$_x$.

[21] A further problem for an attempt to use the specified subject condition in the description of contrasts like (i) and (ii) is that what I (Postal (1969b)) called *pseudoadjectives* behave in the same way as genitive NPs in (ii).

(i) They liked pictures of each other.

sumption required to handle cases like (32) without any appeal to Raising, that reciprocal marking can work down into subordinate clauses. Examples (33) and (35) already show that these principles are both too strong.

Consider also the following analogues of (27):

(41) a. *Joan and Betty recognized the necessity for each other to retire.

    b. *They haven't decided on the best way for each other to do it.

These are my judgments. It is clear that, for such an idiolect, the principles are also too weak, since they do not block these erroneous cases, while a Clause Mate condition would prevent Ordinary Reciprocal Marking from applying to them.

However, the situation is more complicated, as noted for the reflexive analogues in footnote 17, in that there are idiolects that place reflexives in the relevant positions of (27). For these same idiolects, examples like (41) are also well-formed. Unlike my idiolect, those idiolects which accept (41) are consistent with Chomsky's system, at least with respect to reciprocal marking. They are, however, inconsistent with a Clause Mate condition on Ordinary Reciprocal Marking, under the assumption that in these dialect types it is that rule which applies in (41). However, the latter assumption is by no means necessary. We have noted (i) the general parallelism between Ordinary Reflexivization and Ordinary Re-

---

(ii) *They liked Bob's pictures of each other.

Examples are as follows:

(iii) *They resented presidential attempts to visit each other.

(iv) They made attempts to visit each other.

(v) *They encouraged royal attacks on each other.

(vi) They encouraged attacks on each other.

Thus, to nail down the generalization, *presidential* and *royal* must also be regarded as subjects in a still further extension of the sense of this term. Chomsky (1972: 95) says that "perhaps" the subject relation must be extended to such forms. But to make the specified subject analysis handle cases like (iii) and (v), this becomes a necessity. Needless to say, a general definition of subject under which it follows that *presidential, royal,* etc., are subjects in cases like these (or any others) has not been offered. This is especially noteworthy since Chomsky (1972) strongly denies that pseudoadjectives are derived from underlying NPs, as I claimed, and continue to claim. Therefore, unless this position is abandoned, the definition of subject must be extended to cover *non-NPs*, although how it can be done is totally obscure.

ciprocal Marking and (ii) the fact that the relevant idiolects are only *optionally* reflexive in contexts parallel to (41), while Ordinary Reflexivization is invariably obligatory,[22] and (iii) the possibility of acceptable reciprocal marking in (41) correlates with acceptable reflexivization in (27). Therefore, we have some basis for assuming that the rules relevant for (27) and (41) in those idiolects for which these are well-formed are distinct from Ordinary Reflexivization and Ordinary Reciprocal Marking. Hence, the well-formedness of (41) in certain idiolects would not bear on the validity of a Clause Mate constraint on Ordinary Reciprocal Marking.

Other problematical cases remain, however. Thus consider the following:

(42) a. They believe that each other's theories are incorrect.

b. We must recognize that each other's positions have some merit.

For me, such examples seem at worst subtly deviant. Others, in particular those who accept (41), find them perfect. It is not clear how these cases are to be handled in either system. For the Clause Mate account, they provide an exception to the Clause Mate condition, if they are to be described by Ordinary Reciprocal Marking. They also provide an apparent counterexample to the parallelism between reflexive and reciprocal distribution.[23]

---

22 This comment is meant to exclude a potential free variant like (i):

(i) Jerry_i discussed $\left\{ \begin{array}{c} *\text{him}_i \\ \text{himself}_i \end{array} \right\}$.

As Langacker (personal communication) observes, however, under contrastive stress it is possible to have things like this:

(ii) George_i voted for Geórge_i.

In first person cases, this is possible even with pronouns:

(iii) I voted for mé.

But it is not so in third person clauses:

(iv) *George_i voted for hím_i.

23 However, the latter can be restored for these cases if one assumes, as is plausible, that reflexives in such contexts simply adopt the shape *own*:

(43) a. *They believe that themselves' theories are incorrect.

   b. *We must recognize that ourselves' positions have some merit.

But this might be due to a superficial constraint blocking genitives on reflexives.

For Chomsky's system, however, examples like (42) are simple violations of the tensed clause condition and go further toward showing that this is not a correct general metaprinciple governing reciprocal marking.

In summary, the situation seems to be this: There is ample evidence that reciprocal marking is not governed by the tensed clause and specified subject conditions, namely, (33), (35), (41) in one idiolect type, and (42). On the other hand, the Clause Mate condition on Ordinary Reciprocal Marking seems adequate for a range of cases, but it runs into problems with cases like (41) in one idiolect type and (42), where it must be supplemented by an additional rule, as is also necessary for many picture noun cases.

In general, then, reciprocals seem to be poorly understood, their overall distribution following from no principles and rules so far stated. In this sense, they provide strong evidence for no position at the moment. I think, though, that the best hypothesis at present is that there is a rule of Ordinary Reciprocal Marking parallel to Ordinary Reflexivization, thus governed by a Clause Mate condition. If so, then cases like (44) provide an argument for B-verb Raising.

(44) a. *We believe (that) each other are discontent.

   b. We believe each other to be discontent.

It is clear, however, that until the problems touched on can be resolved, this argument is by no means as clear-cut as was traditionally assumed. At the same time, Chomsky's alternative in terms of the tensed clause and specified subject conditions is evidently not sustainable.[24]

(i) They believe that their own theories are incorrect.

(ii) We must recognize that our own positions have some drawbacks.

This, of course, would raise important questions, since *own* is obviously not related to its antecedent by a strict Clause Mate condition. McCawley suggests that it is quite possible that in such cases reflexive pronouns simply merge in shape with non-reflexive genitive pronouns.

[24] After nearly completing the manuscript, I discovered such examples as (i), which, though slightly strained for some speakers, are perfect for others.

3.4 The Inclusion Constraint

In Postal (1966c), I noted and designated restrictions like the following as the "Inclusion Constraint":

(45) a. *I like us.

    b. *We like me.

    c. *He$_i$ praised them$_{i,\,j}$.

    d. *They$_{i,\,j}$ criticized him$_i$.

That is, certain pairs of NPs are not permitted to overlap in stipulated coreference. In Postal (1969a), I claimed that the characterization of which pairs depends on the notion of Clause Mate. Thus, consider the following:

(46) a. I believe that we can win.

    b. They$_{i,\,j}$ both claimed he$_i$ was innocent.

    c. We must call the girl who saw me.

If it is true that the proper account of pairs of NPs subject to the Inclusion Constraint depends on these pairs being Clause Mates,[25] then the phenomenon provides another piece of evidence for a raising analysis of B-verb infinitival complements and against a proposal to replace this with a nonraising approach that is backed by the tensed clause and specified subject conditions. This follows because, in general, infinitival and *that*-clause complements of B-verbs behave contrastively with respect to the Inclusion Constraint:

(47) a.   I believed (that) we were right.

    b. *I believed us to be right.

(i) a. They arranged for each other to live in comfort.
    b. They prayed for each other to prosper.

These seem to eliminate any possibility of sustaining a Clause Mate theory of Ordinary Reciprocal Marking and thus leave reciprocal facts showing nothing at all for or against B-verb Raising, as far as I can see.

[25] This leaves open at what point in derivations this condition holds. I suggest that it is true of cycle-final structures. That is, in general, coreference overlap is banned for pairs if they are Clause Mates at the end of some cycle, a condition analogous to that needed for reflexivization, I think. See Section 8.2.

(48) a.   Did you (singular) find that you (plural) were in agreement?

b. *Did you (singular) find you (plural) to be in agreement?

Thus, in the infinitival cases, which the Raising analysis claims involve derived Clause Mates, the constraint holds, but in the *that*-clause cases, where the Raising analysis does not assign derived Clause Mate status, the constraint predictably does not hold, apparently disconfirming again a system like Chomsky's, which does not differentiate infinitival and *that*-clause complements with respect to Clause Mate properties.

Chomsky deals with such facts at some length, arguing in effect that it is not the Clause Mate condition that is relevant but rather the tensed clause and specified subject conditions. This argument is made possible by claiming that the Inclusion Constraint is actually a function of "a rule that assigns the feature *(ungrammatical) to a sentence S dominating Pro_i-V-Pro_j-X, where Pro_i and Pro_j are both first person or second person," according to Chomsky (to appear: 16). This account, which seems to me wholly gratuitous,[26] is then generalized to eliminate

---

[26] My claim is that the restriction is a filter that marks derivations as ill-formed if at the end of any appropriate cycle (see Section 8.2) there are Clause Mates that overlap in coreference (subject to certain further conditions). No otherwise unmotivated apparatus of stars, etc., is required. The condition can be defined over natural, independently needed types of structures. Chomsky (to appear: 16) says: "Notice that it is difficult to see how RI can be construed naturally as anything other than a rule of semantic interpretation, operating at a fairly 'superficial' level (at or close to surface structure), at least if we wish to incorporate (44) and (45) under the generalization." His (44) is as follows:

(i) The soldiers shot the officers (among them).

This, as he notes, cannot be understood in such a way that the references of *soldiers* and *officers* overlap. However, the constraint in (i) is evidently distinct from the Inclusion Constraint discussed earlier. Note the contrast:

(ii) The soldiers said that the officers (among them) were infected.

(iii) He_i said that $they_{i,j}$ were infected.

Example (ii) does not differ in a relevant way from (i), while (iii) contrasts sharply with (iv).

(iv) *He_i shot $them_{i,j}$.

Thus the constraint in (i) is a general one that is not limited to Clause Mates.

Furthermore, the claim that the Inclusion Constraint must be stated at or near surface structure is unfathomable. Violations are unaffected by a variety of rules that radically alter the defining configurations:

the incorrect person references.[27] Chomsky refers to this rule as RI.

If we disregard objections to formulating the Inclusion Constraint as RI, the point is that, analogous to the facts for reflexives and reciprocals, RI controlled by the tensed clause and specified subject conditions instead of a Clause Mate condition gives the wrong answers. Thus, since neither of Chomsky's two principles can block application in the analogues to (27) and (41), such a system predicts that the parallel cases involving coreference overlap should all be ill-formed. As (49) shows, however, this prediction is uniformly incorrect.

(49) a. Do you (singular) recognize the necessity for you (plural) to resign?

b. Harry$_i$ understands the necessity for them$_{i, j}$ to vote liberal.

c. I was unaware of the possibility for us to hire her.

These examples are well-formed, as follows from an account of the In-

---

(v) a. *John said I hated us.
   b. *Us, John said I hated.
   c. I said John hated us.
   d. Us, I said John hated.

(vi) a. *It is difficult for me to shoot us.
    b. *We are difficult for me to shoot.

(vii) a. *It seems to me that he$_i$ loves them$_{i, j}$.
     b. *He$_i$ seems to me to love them$_{i, j}$.

Thus the definition of the constraint must refer to structures prior to the application of these rules, a condition met by the statement suggested in footnotes 25 and 26.

Finally, Chomsky says (to appear: 16): "The point seems to be that a rule of interpretation RI applying to the structure NP-V-NP (among others) seeks to interpret the two NP's as non-intersecting in reference, and where this is impossible (as in the case of first and second pronouns) assigns 'strangeness' marking the sentence with *." This strange formulation has, among other things, the drawback, vis-à-vis a filter like that suggested here, of turning a generalization into a disjunction. Thus Chomsky's rule says "Do X if you can, otherwise Y." The "interpretive" account thus necessarily misses the regularity. Overall, then, Chomsky's attempt to formulate the Inclusion Constraint as an "interpretive" rule RI seems to me both theoretically unmotivated and empirically impossible.

[27] To avoid confusion, I note that the original formulation restricted to first and second person and also the term "unlike person constraint" that Chomsky uses are due to Helke (1971), who independently rediscovered that aspect of the Inclusion Constraint which pertains to non-third-person elements.

clusion Constraint in which it is limited to pairs of Clause Mates. Incidentally, unlike (27) and (41), sentences like (49) do not seem to vary idiolectally. Those speakers I have checked who accept (27) and (41) treat (49) as my idiolect does, that is, the sentences of (49) are fine for these speakers as well. This is of some importance, because it suggests that there is an idiolectally variable rule not subject to Clause Mate restrictions for reflexivization and reciprocal marking, but that the Inclusion Constraint uniformaly operates on Clause Mates.[28]

Further evidence that the tensed clause condition plays no proper role in restricting the scope of the Inclusion Constraint is provided by the verbs *pray, arrange,* etc., which take infinitival complements but do not, even in a Raising system, trigger application of Raising, according to varied criteria (as will be seen later in section after section).

(50) a. I arranged for Bob to dine with us.

b. *Bob was arranged to dine with us.

c. *I arranged for myself to win.

Given that the Inclusion Constraint is governed by a Clause Mate condition, we predict the well-formedness of examples like (51):

(51) a. I arranged for us to dine with Sally.

b. I prayed for us to be allowed to marry.

c. He$_i$ planned for them$_{i,j}$ to live in Persia.

d. They$_{i,j}$ prayed for him$_i$ to get better.

This is correct. Chomsky's system, however, in which RI can work down into untensed clauses, predicts wrongly that these would be ill-formed. That is, a non-Raising account of B-verb infinitival complements has no known way of explaining contrasts like (52):

---

[28] I maintain that this is true as well for cases like (i) and (ii), since I would argue these are derived from underlying structures containing clauses of the form given in (iii) and (iv), etc.:

(i)   *our love for me

(ii)   *his$_i$ attack on them$_{i,j}$

(iii) *[we love me]

(iv)   *[he$_i$ attacked them$_{i,j}$]

(52) a.   I arranged for us to study French.

   b. *I expect us to study French.

   c.   I expect that we will study French.

It must thus appeal to an ad hoc constraint, say, one referring to the presence of *for*, in spite of the fact that prepositions in general do not block Inclusion Constraint violations:

(53) a. *I work for us.

   b. *I will speak for us.[29]

Significantly, though, the facts of Inclusion restrictions are, as pointed out to me by Ross, more complicated in at least one respect than allowed for either in my earlier discussion or in Chomsky's account. For many speakers, at least, including Ross and myself, there exist such contrasts as the following:

(54) a.   I expect Bob to call Sally.

   b.   I expect Bob to win.

   c. *I expect us to call Sally.

   d.   I expect us to win.

(55) a.   I believe Bob to hate Sally.

   b.   I believe Bob to be hated by Sally.

   c. *I believe us to hate Sally.

   d.   I believe us to be hated by Sally.

Possibly all speakers can discern relative differences here, even if they would not make discrete categorizations. What is at issue is the difference between (54)c and (54)d and between (55)c and (55)d. The general-

---

[29] Among the "further conditions" referred to in footnote 26 must be those that distinguish (i)–(iii) and (iv)–(vi):

(i)   *I understand us.

(ii)   I understand both of us.

(iii)   I understand us both.

(iv) *They$_{i,j}$ praised him$_i$.

(v)   ?Both of them$_{i,j}$ praised him$_i$.

(vi) ?They$_{i,j}$ both praised him$_i$.

ization appears to be that a violation ensues only when the underlying complement subject is either an *agent NP* (of a self-controllable predicate, in the sense of Kuno (1970), as in (54)c, hence the difference between *win* and *call*) or an *experiencer NP* in the sense of Fillmore (1968) or Postal (1970a). It seems then that in a Raising system one must say that the Inclusion Constraint is relatively absolute for underlying Clause Mates but holds for derivative Clause Mates produced by Raising subject to the conditions about agent and experiencer. These are strange conditions but not intolerable as part of a peculiar constraint.

But for a system like Chomsky's, facts like (54) and (55) cause further difficulties. For it will not do merely to add the analogue of the condition just discussed to his rule RI. It must further be explained why the same pattern is *not* found with *pray, arrange,* etc.:

(56) a. I arranged for Bob to call Sally.

　　b. I arranged for Bob to win.

　　c. I arranged for us to call Sally.

　　d. I arranged for us to win.

(57) a. ?I arranged for Bob to hate Sally.

　　b. ?I arranged for Bob to be hated by Sally.

　　c. ?I arranged for us to hate Sally.

　　d. ?I arranged for us to be hated by Sally.

The contrast between (54) and (55), on the one hand, and between (56) and (57), on the other, adds another piece of evidence to that provided by pairs like (52) that there is an important difference between the *for* . . . type of infinitival complement and the type possessed by B-verbs. A Raising system naturally characterizes this difference in terms of whether the underlying complement subject NP remains in its clause or not. But in a non-Raising grammar the difference is not naturally characterized in any known way. We shall see later, however, that the difference shows up for a variety of other grammatical properties as well.

Overall, then, the Inclusion Constraint facts provide counterevidence to a view that attempts to replace the Clause Mate condition on this filter with the tensed clause and specified subject conditions. If, however, the Inclusion Constraint is governed by a Clause Mate condition, then contrasts like (47) and (48) provide an argument for Raising.

4

Evidence for Raising with B-Verb Infinitival Complements II: New Classes of Facts

4.1 Complex NP Shift

Ross (1967) discovered and discussed a rule he called Complex NP Shift. This operation has the function of moving a "heavy" (that is, roughly, long and/or clause-containing)[1] NP from its normal position to the right of the end of its immediately containing clause:

(1) a. Jack bought a book from Melvin.

b. *Jack bought from Melvin a book.

c. Jack bought from Melvin—a book which taught him organic knitting.

d. I showed the cookies to Jack.

e. *I showed to Jack—the cookies.

f. I showed to Jack—all of the coffee ground + lettuce cookies.

g. They selected Joan as revolutionary of the month.

h. *They selected as revolutionary of the month—Joan.

i. They selected as revolutionary of the month—the most obnoxious member of Dominance Now.

While many problems about this rule remain unsolved, one principle, noted in Postal (1971: 133), constraining its operation is clear:

(2) Complex NP Shift does *not* operate on NPs that are subjects at the point of application.

Thus the result is cases like (3):

(3) a. *Are happy—all of the men who recovered from mononucleosis.

---

[1] This is very rough indeed. For instance, the presence of quantifiers is also sufficient, as (1)f shows. And, as Ross notes, this is true even when the quantifiers are in adjectival forms like *whole* and *entire*:

(i) a. I gave to Harry—all the sheep.
 b. *I gave to Harry the big sheep.
 c. I gave to Harry—the whole sheep.
 d. I gave to Harry—the entire sheep.

b. *That retired too soon—the man who founded this company is obvious.

c. *I regret the fact that were destroyed—so many of our priceless relics.

If, however, principle (2) is true,[2] it predicts a sharp difference in the acceptability of applying Complex NP Shift to the directly post-B-verb NP in pairs like (4):

(4) a. *Jim proved (that) were innocent—all of the gang members who had been caught.

b. Jim proved (?to be)[3] innocent—all of the gang members who had been caught.

c. *I believe (that) were tortured by Brazilians—the priests who are going to speak today.

d. I believe to have been tortured by Brazilians—the priests who are going to speak today.

---

[2] So far, the evidence offered for principle (2) is of uncertain force, since it might be claimed, for example, following Perlmutter (1971), that what is wrong with examples like (3) involves a surface constraint about tensed clauses having subjects, or the like. However, this claim seems to me to be incorrect, since I reject the view that subject deletion or movement triggers pruning of embedded S nodes (see Sections 6.5, 6.6). Consequently, all of the following italicized phrases seem to me to be subjectless tensed clauses:

(i) a. Jack entered the room and then *was seized by fourteen FBI agents in drag.*
b. Jack is taller than *is widely recognized.*
c. Who do you think *is the best man for this job?*

Moreover, it is difficult to see how any constraint referring to the need for subjects could allow (i)a, but not (ii)b:

(ii) a. Jack entered the room and then Bob was seized by fourteen FBI agents in drag.
b. *Jack entered the room and then was seized by fourteen FBI agents in drag—the outstanding bankrobber and rapist produced by the class of 1956.

Later, I shall provide considerable evidence that the subjects of untensed clauses are also not subject to Complex NP Shift, so that reference to tensed clauses is further shown to be inappropriate for cases like (3).

[3] It seems to me that examples like (4)b are not acceptable if *to be* is present. The reason for this is, I think, an interesting *transderivational* constraint that blocks Complex NP Shift derivations when the structure of the truncated clause minus the shifted NP is identical with that produced by another class of rules. Thus in the case of (4)b the sequence in (i) is independently derivable in the grammar, in fact, by

e. *Allen showed (that) were Martians—those teachers who continually gave him poor grades.

f. Allen showed to be Martians—those teachers who continually gave him poor grades.

The predicted differences thus exist.

Under an analysis of B-verb infinitival complements involving a raising operation, the contrasts in (4) follow directly from principle (2), since it can be claimed that Complex NP Shift can apply after the relevant Raising application,[4] and hence at a point when the former com-

---

Raising, since *prove* is an intransitive A-verb obligatorily triggering Raising application (see Section 9.2).

(i) Jim proved to be innocent.

However, (ii) is not independently derivable:

(ii) *Jim proved innocent.

Contrast also (4)d, where the sequence (iii) is not independently derivable, just as (ii) is not.

(iii) *I believe to have been tortured by Brazilians.

It is the same constraint that, I claim, also blocks things like (iv) because of (v), which is independently derivable by Equi.

(iv) *I can't conceive of going there—the man who said he hated Gladys.

(v) I can't conceive of going there.

And it is the same constraint that blocks examples first noted by Howard Lasnik, like (vi) because of (vii), also independently generated by Equi.

(vi) *I want to die—all those people who refuse to accept my authority.

(vii) I want to die.

Compare:

(viii) a. I want dead—everyone who refuses to accept my authority.
      b. *I want dead.

The existence of this constraint reduces the possibility of using principle (2) as a test for Raising application. Thus, if one did not know about this constraint, one might, as Lasnik has suggested, take (vi) to show that *want* does not trigger Raising. Example (viii) already suggests the incorrectness of this. For further discussion, see Section 12.5.

4 This possibility would exist under any of the assumptions that Complex NP Shift is (i) cyclical, (ii) postcyclical, (iii) last cyclical. That is, it is a weak and uncontroversial assumption.

plement subject has become an object, that is, a nonsubject, in the infinitival cases. But under Chomsky's analysis,[5] which assigns B-verb *that* and infinitival complements the same structure throughout derivations, except for the tensed clause distinction, the contrasts require an ad hoc statement to the effect that Complex NP Shift can apply to subjects only when these are in B-verb infinitival complements. In short, while a non-Raising system assigns subject status to post-B-verb NPs in infinitival complements throughout derivations, these supposed subjects do not behave like derived subjects with respect to Complex NP Shift, in accord with the Raising theory of these constructions.

There seems no hope of claiming that something like the distinction between tensed and untensed clauses generally controls Complex NP Shift. Note the quite regular failure of this rule to apply to true (derived) subjects even in nontensed infinitival clauses like these:

(5) a. For all of the girls who got pregnant to have abortions would be tragic.

b. *For to have abortions—all of the girls who got pregnant would be tragic.

c. *To have abortions—all of the girls who got pregnant would be tragic.

d. *To have abortions—for all of the girls who got pregnant would be tragic.

e. The necessity for them to invoke precedent is obvious.

f. *The necessity for to invoke precedent—the senators who are about to lose the tax fight is obvious.

g. *The necessity to invoke precedent—the senators who are about to lose the tax fight is obvious.

h. *The necessity to invoke precedent—for the senators who are about to lose the tax fight is obvious.

Similarly, observe the impossibility of applying Complex NP Shift to the subjects of such untensed clauses as the following:

[5] The argument is unaffected if principle (2) is revised to refer to the initial NP in clauses, or even to NPs in the context: [#——(to) Verb X]. Such characterizations will, in non-Raising terms, apply homogeneously to both infinitival and *that*-clause complements of B-verbs but will fail to account for the contrast in Complex NP Shift behavior between them.

(6) a. The nurse who he loved's refusing to marry him drove Don to despair.

    b. *Refusing to marry him—the nurse who he loved's drove Don to despair.

    c. Mary, Joan, Sylvia, and Sally's criticizing him bothered Ben.

    d. *Criticizing him—Mary, Joan, Sylvia, and Sally's bothered Ben.

Observe also such contrasts as these:

(7) a. I discouraged Bob's visiting Sylvia.

    b. I discouraged Bob from visiting Sylvia.

    c. *I discouraged visiting Sylvia—the young soldier who had a short leave's.

    d. I discouraged from visiting Sylvia—the young soldier who had a short leave.

While *discourage* is not, of course, a B-verb, I shall suggest later, in Section 4.14, that pairs like (7)a,b are also distinguished by the application or not of Raising. Under this assumption, such contrasts follow from principle (2).

It is hardly surprising, then, that Complex NP Shift fails also to apply to the subjects of various superficially untensed *that* clauses:

(8) a. I demanded that all of the filthy hippies be shot.

    b. *I demanded that be shot—all of the filthy hippies.

    c. Joan insisted that all of her attackers be punished.

    d. *Joan insisted that be punished—all of her attackers.[6]

    e. What is mandatory is that those students with C grades read structuralist manuals.

[6] For most of the subjunctive clauses, it might be claimed that the ill-formedness of examples like (17)b is a function of the impossibility of having a clause with an initial *that* and no subject NP, as discussed, say, in Perlmutter (1971: Chapter 4); see also Hudson (1972). However, in my idiolect, at least, *insist* does not require an initial *that*, as most subjunctive complement verbs do. Thus (i) is acceptable.

(i) I insist (that) Bob be fired.

Hence, no constraint about subjects and *that* independent of Complex NP Shift can explain (ii).

(ii) *I insist be fired—all of those workers who refuse to attend your coronation.

f. *What is mandatory is that read structuralist manuals—those students with C grades.

However, examples like (5)–(7) do not provide the strong argument for principle (2) that they first appear to. In the case of infinitival examples, it might be argued that the ill-formedness of (5)b,c,d,f,g,h is a function, not of a special constraint on Complex NP Shift referring to subjects, but rather of the constraint, noted by Ross (1967: 446–447), that the subject NP of a *for*-marked infinitival clause is simply frozen with respect to the operation of any movement rules, regardless of whether these reorder to the left or right. Such a constraint is evidently needed independently for *leftward* reorderings:

(9) a. *Melvin, I never arranged (for) to meet Greta.

    b. *For Melvin, I never arranged to meet Greta.

    c. *The only person who I never planned for to be investigated was Max.

    d. *The only person for whom I never planned to be investigated was Max.

And the errant Complex NP Shift cases with *for* infinitivals could then be covered by rejecting any right-left asymmetry for the principle that blocks (9) and (10).

Similarly, as pointed out to me by Emily Pope, one might argue that the violations in (6) and (7) are also a function of a principle independent of subjects, namely, the principle that blocks the reordering either to the left or to the right of such genitive-marked NPs as those in (10):

(10) a. I gave Bill's tent to Arthur.

    b. *Bill's I gave tent to Arthur.

    c. *Whose did you give tent to Arthur?

    d. *I gave tent to Arthur—the oldest son of my neighbor's brother's

Observe that the genitive subjects of gerundive clauses are also not reorderable to the left:

(11) a. I didn't like his slapping Sonia.

b. *Melvin's I didn't like slapping Sonia.

c. *The boy whose I didn't like slapping Sonia was retarded.

It might be argued, then, that there is no evidence for principle (2), at least in the case of untensed clauses, since those cases where Complex NP Shift cannot apply can quite plausibly be attributed to independent constraints having nothing to do with subjects. If this tack could be maintained, then the application of Complex NP Shift to the infinitival complements of (4) would not be an argument for a Raising analysis, but simply irrelevant to this question.

However, there is, I think, sufficient evidence to show that principle (2) is needed, even for untensed clauses, because of a variety of instances of untensed clauses whose subjects are not subject to Complex NP Shift, although no known independent principle predicts this. *First,* there is a need for principle (2) with respect to the subjects of infinitival clauses without *for* like those in (12):

(12) a. It will get cloudy in the evening, with rain to follow.

    b. *It will get cloudy in the evening with to follow—more rain than anyone has ever seen before.

    c. The horses will cross the river first, the elephants to follow.

    d. *The horses will cross the river first, to follow—all of those elephants wearing yellow beanies and pink jumpsuits.

Second, the principle relevant for (10) and (11) can be invoked only for those gerundive complements whose subjects are genitive-marked. In many cases, however, gerundive subjects need not be so marked, and, most crucially, in these cases the subjects are extractable by *leftward* movement rules:

(13) a. I don't favor that sort of person being allowed to join.

    b. That sort of person, I don't favor being allowed to join.

    c. The only kind of person that I don't favor being allowed to join . . .

(14) a. He is against drunks now becoming surgeons.

    b. ?Drunks, he is against now becoming surgeons.

    c. The only people who he is against now becoming surgeons are drunks.

(15) a. I didn't anticipate that happening.

    b. That, I didn't anticipate happening.

    c. The only thing that I didn't anticipate happening happened immediately.

However, in none of these cases can nongenitive subjects undergo Complex NP Shift:

(16) a. *I don't favor being allowed to join—that sort of rude, uncouth, ill-behaved person.

    b. *He is against now becoming surgeons—all of those drunks who are hanging around this medical school.

    c. *I didn't anticipate happening—any of those terrible unexpected things which we talked about.

Such cases must then be attributed to principle (2). Similarly, since the genitive is crucial for explaining cases like (6)b,d without appeal to principle (2) (by way of the principle relevant for (10)b,c,d and (11)b,c), only principle (2) can, as far as is known, account for the resistance to Complex NP Shift operation of the subjects of so-called nominative absolute constructions:

(17) a. Bob having been arrested, his wife had to get a job.

    b. *Having been arrested—the former choirboy and champion wrestler who hated to work, his wife had to get a job.

    c. All of the beer being gone, we had to drink 7-UP.

    d. *Being gone—all of the beer which we had smuggled into the country from Bavaria, we had to drink 7-UP.

    Finally, consider the failure of Complex NP Shift to apply to the subjects of the various untensed subordinate clauses in (18):

(18) a. Jim, his new red pants falling off, ran into the room.

    b. *Jim, falling off—his new red pants with the yellow stripes, ran into the room.

    c. The police dashed in, with Melvin following behind.

d. *The police dashed in, with following behind—the nervous reporter who was deathly afraid of firearms.

e. Nixon saying he is for law and order is a real scream.

f. *Saying he is for law and order—the chief of the notorious band of smugglers and thieves is a real scream.

Therefore, in spite of the fact that *some* cases of Complex NP Shift's failure with respect to subjects in untensed clauses can probably be treated in terms of independently needed principles other than (2), a range of cases for which this is not the case exists. Since (2) is, furthermore, evidently needed for tensed clauses and "subjunctive" clauses,[7] principle (2) remains well supported. The fact remains that there is no known case where Complex NP Shift applies to an NP that can be shown, independently of the controversy about Raising, to be a subject at the point of application.

The evidence then indicates that contrasts like those given in (4) must be attributed to principle (2), which is possible only if such pairs differ in the subject status of the relevant NP. But they can differ in this way only under an analysis that involves Raising for the infinitival cases. One concludes that the fact that Complex NP Shift is governed

---

[7] Further support for principle (2) comes from the fact that it also properly blocks application of Complex NP Shift to the subjects of *imperatives*, where no other known principle suffices:

(i) a. $Zeke_i$, you_i, Bob, Mike, Ted, Harvey, and George, go beat up the sheriff.
   b.*$Zeke_i$, go beat up the sheriff—you_i, Bob, Mike, Ted, Harvey, and George.

(ii) a. Tom_i, you $people_{i, j} \ldots$ with bad cases of bubonic plague or athlete's foot, sit over there.
   b.*Tom_i, sit over there—you $people_{i, j} \ldots$ with bad cases of bubonic plague or athlete's foot.

These also are presumably nontensed clauses, and hence contrast with the post-B-verb NP of infinitival complements, as predicted by principle (2) in conjunction with a Raising analysis.

Moreover, on the assumption that the NPs following *may* in examples like (iii) are subjects of *may*, principle (2) derives further support, since *may* here is untensed, and Complex NP Shift completely inapplicable, as shown in (iv):

(iii) a. May everyone who voted for him suffer from warts.
   b. May they survive unharmed.

(iv) a. *May suffer from warts—everyone who voted for him.
   b.*May survive unharmed—all of those thoughtful youths who have come to our aid.

by principle (2) provides a disconfirmation of any analysis failing to recognize a raising operation for B-verb infinitival complements, that is, for any analysis claiming that post-B-verb NPs in infinitival cases remain complement subjects throughout derivations.[8]

Not at all incidentally, it should be observed that Complex NP Shift causes a serious difficulty for Chomsky's attempt to justify the claim that the specified subject condition is responsible for contrasts like (19):

(19) a. They want to help each other.

b. *They want Bob to help each other.

[8] Perlmutter has suggested to me the possibility of an argument for Raising based on Complex NP Shift which is quite independent of principle (2). The argument would be founded on Ross's (1967) discovery that rightward-moving rules are upward bounded. Since Complex NP Shift is a rightward reordering, it naturally falls under this constraint. The argument would run as follows. In a Raising grammar, the italicized NP in a context like (i) is in the main clause in derived structure, while in a non-Raising grammar it remains at every point within the complement clause.

(i) I B-verb *NP* to . . .

Therefore, the upward-boundedness of Complex NP Shift would make distinct predictions with respect to the possibility of shifting the italicized NP across elements in the main clause. This should be possible if a Raising grammar is correct, but impossible otherwise. Consider, then, cases like (ii):

(ii) a. Arthur proved Mu-grammars to be recursive on the basis of Beanworthy's Lemma.

b. Arthur proved to be recursive on the basis of Beanworthy's Lemma—that subclass of Mu-grammars in which all rules precede themselves.

It appears that a Raising grammar is supported, since the post-B-verb NP is, in fact, transported to the right of an adverbial phrase that is clearly a constituent of the main clause, not the complement. Given the upward-bounded character of Complex NP Shift, this would be impossible if the underlying complement subject had not been raised into the main clause prior to the application of Complex NP Shift. Many other examples like (ii)b can be constructed.

It thus seems that the argument suggested by Perlmutter is correct and provides independent support for Raising from the interaction of complements with Complex NP Shift. While I believe that this argument can ultimately be validated, there are serious problems, which show that the claim of upward-boundedness for Complex NP Shift needs considerable refinement.

In particular, Witten (1972: IV-93) has discovered examples showing that Complex NP Shift is not, strictly speaking, upward bounded:

(iii) a. I have wanted to know exactly what happened to Rosa Luxemburg for many years.

b. I have wanted to know for many years—exactly what happened to Rosa Luxemburg.

The application of Complex NP Shift does not improve sentences such as (19)b, as can be seen in (20):

(20) *They want to help each other—the girl who they met on top of Mount Everest.

Nor is it correct to attribute what is wrong with (20) entirely to the principle discussed in footnote 3 and in Section 12.5. As evidence for this, note the following:

(21) a.   They want Bob near Sally.

   b. *They want Bob near each other.

   c. *They want near each other—the girl who they met on top of Mount Everest.

Here, as Witten notes, *for many years* is clearly a main clause constituent, and yet Complex NP Shift moves a complement constituent to the right of it.

Unless such examples can be dealt with by some refinements of the claim that Complex NP Shift is upward bounded, the argument for Raising based on examples like (ii) clearly collapses, as does the general claim made by Ross that all rightward-moving rules are upward bounded.

My approach to examples like (iii) is based on the notion of "quasi-clause", introduced in Sections 6.5 and 6.6. There, it is suggested that, instead of previous ideas about pruning, an embedded clause becomes a member of the quasi-clause category if it loses its subject NP through the action of cyclic rules. It is then suggested that clause boundaries that are quasi-clause boundaries are not as strong a barrier to grammatical processes as full clause boundaries. These notions can be applied to cases like (iii), since the complement from which an NP has unexpectedly been extracted in violation of the upward-boundedness constraint is a quasi-clause, formed when the subject is deleted by the rule Equi. If something like this were correct, we would expect contrasts in cases like the following:

(iv) a. I have expected that I would find the treasure since 1939.
   b. I have expected to find the treasure since 1939.

 (v) a. *I have expected that I would find since 1939—the treasure said to have been buried on that island.
   b. I have expected to find since 1939—the treasure said to have been buried on that island.

Thus there is some hope for ultimately constructing the argument suggested by Perlmutter with the help of a notion like quasi-clause and a slight weakening of the upward-boundedness condition to take account of it.

At least one further problem exists, however. It is that, if the word *Bob* is placed after *wanted* in the examples of (iii), then (iii)a remains well-formed but not (iii)b. Later it is shown that such sentences are the result of Raising, and it thus appears that quasi-clauses generated by Raising are more impervious to Complex NP Shift than those generated by Equi, a fact for which I have at present no explanation.

Example (21)c would not be blocked by the principle in footnote 3 because of (22), but it is still just as bad as (21)b:

(22) *They want near each other.

It might be thought that the problem of blocking (20), (21)c, etc., can be dealt with in a system like Chomsky's by rule ordering, by having Complex NP Shift simply follow the rule that moves *each* to form reciprocals. However, this is not possible in his terms because, for him, Complex NP Shift must be a cyclical rule, since it can apply at different levels of embedding. And, according to his current assumptions, such a rule is necessarily cyclical (I reject this consequence and regard the implication about Complex NP Shift as a good reason for doing so. For some general principles according to which Complex NP Shift cannot be cyclical, see Perlmutter and Postal, to appear b). Thus, in Chomsky's terms, Complex NP Shift would be able to apply on the lower cycle in cases like (20) and (21), while the *each*-movement rule would not become applicable in such cases until the next, or main clause, cycle. Rule ordering is thus irrelevant in such terms.

The only solution is an ad hoc, otherwise unmotivated claim that Complex NP Shift leaves behind a "trace," which would function somehow as a specified subject past the point when the rules that must be blocked by the specified subject condition have all been tested for application. Then some rule must be invented to delete the "trace."

The same problems will arise with respect to other sentential features like reflexivization and the Inclusion Constraint, where the facts also are unaffected by Complex NP Shift operation:

(23) a. I want Bob friendly to me (*myself).

   b. I want friendly to me (*myself)—all those men who own large businesses.

(24) a. I want Bob friendly to us.

   b. I want friendly to us—all those men who own large businesses.

4.2 *Not*-Initial NPs

Certain NPs in English can occur with an initial morpheme *not*. These are to be distinguished from NPs beginning with *no* (*nobody, nothing, no peaches,* etc.):

(25) a. Not many gorillas have learned to tap-dance.

b. Not much sense can be made out of that proposal.

c. Not many Turks speak Yiddish.

d. Not many Albanians have been interviewed by Sevareid.

e. Not many farmers are easy to convince.

The *not*-initial NPs in (25) all occur as superficial subjects. It turns out that other functional positions in which NPs occur do not permit *not*-initial NPs:

(26) a. *Joe kissed not many models.

b. *Jane earns not much money.

c. *Sally talked to Bob about not many problems.

d. *I bought kangaroos from not many Australians.

The generalization seems to be as follows:

(27) *Not*-initial NPs occur only in (derived) subject positions.

Principle (27) surely requires refinements.[9] It is, for instance, only a

---

9 It should be stressed that (27) does not hold for NPs of the form *not* $\left\{ \begin{array}{l} one \\ a\ single \end{array} \right\}$:

(i) a. I met not $\left\{ \begin{array}{l} one \\ a\ single \end{array} \right\}$ doctor.

b. He found not $\left\{ \begin{array}{l} one \\ a\ single \end{array} \right\}$ jar of chocolate butter.

Nor does it hold for those of the type cited in the text when these are *parts of adverbs*:

(ii) a. Not three hours ago, I saw Melvin over there.
b. I met him not many years before that.

Next, *not*-initial NPs can occur as parts of conjunct NPs forming a coordinate subject:

(iii) a. Not many colonels and not many majors were demoted yesterday.
b. Not much wheat and not much barley was sold to the Turks.

The whole must, however, be a subject:

(iv) a. *They demoted not many colonels and not many majors yesterday.
b. *They sold not much wheat and not much barley to the Turks.

Furthermore, the *many* or *much* preceded by *not* need not be an immediate constituent of a subject NP but can be an immediate constituent of a preposed genitive NP that is part of a subject NP:

(v) a. Not many people's mothers are movie stars.
 b. Not many citizens' passports were seized by the police.

However, the genitive NP must be part of a subject and must be preposed:

(vi) a. *I called not many people's mothers.
 b. *Friends of not many people('s) are outside.

Thus the constraint would appear to be, if adverbs and conjoined cases are ignored, that *not* be the leftmost constituent of a subject NP. It should be emphasized that none of the further statements about *not*-initial NP distribution just made have any real bearing on the argument in the text. For these refinements do not alter the fact that *not*-initial NPs distinguish subject from nonsubject positions.

The notion of derived subject relevant for principle (27) is not entirely clear. In general, I should like to maintain a universal notion of subject something like the following:

(vii) For any clause C (at any level of derivation), the subject NP of C is that NP, N which is the leftmost immediate constituent NP of C.

This would be supplemented by the notion "subject of verb," to say that N is the subject of that verb V which is the immediate constituent of C. These accounts need considerable refinement, though. For instance, one must guarantee that rules deleting subject NPs do not have the effect of turning objects into subjects under (vii), which we can do in terms of a global theory by restricting (vii) to just those NPs which are corresponding constituents of subject NPs—by (vii)—in cycle-final structures. In other words, an NP is a subject if it both meets (vii) and corresponds to a cyclic subject.

In these terms, then, it is probably possible to say that condition (27) refers to surface subjects, a claim that is consistent with Gapping cases like (viii) and (ix), since the *not*-initial NPs in the gapped cases meet both (vii) and the condition requiring correspondence to cyclic subjects.

(viii) a. Not many Greeks speak Turkish, and not many Turks speak Greek.
 b. Not many Greeks speak Turkish, and not many Turks Greek.

(ix) a. Many Greeks speak Spanish, but not many Spaniards speak Greek.
 b. Many Greeks speak Spanish, but not many Spaniards Greek.

It might be thought that a surface account of (27) fails because any definition that makes *not many Indians* a subject in (x)a will make *not many Indians* a subject in (x)b:

(x) a. Many Pakistanis were captured, but not many Indians (were captured).
 b. They captured many Pakistanis but not many Indians.

This is wrong, however. First, *not many Indians* in (x)a corresponds to a cyclic subject, while that in (x)b does not. But even more fundamentally, there is no reason to think that *not many Indians* is a constituent in (x)b, in contrast to (x)a. That is, we find also such cases as (xi), where the sequences *not* + X can never occur as constituents elsewhere.

necessary condition.[10] Note the ill-formedness of all of the following examples, in which subject NPs remain postverbal, owing to the regular failure of Subject Formation to apply in certain classes of environments:

(28) a. *Are not many policemen corrupt? (Note the necessity in a–d of reading *not* as part of the NP.)

    b. *Are there not many bars in Paris?

    c. *Did not many kangaroos eat the poisoned grain?

    d. *Will not much rice be imported by Greenland?

    e. *Were not many girls to come, I would be sad.

This will have no real bearing on the present discussion, however. The key point is that *not*-initial NPs are banned from derived nonsubject positions. It might be thought that such examples as (29) are counterexamples:

(29) There are not many blacks on the White House staff.

However, as Ross observes, the *not* here is not part of the NP, as proved by modal analogues like (30), contrasted with (31):

(30) There may not be many blacks on the White House staff (but . . .)

(31) *There may be not many blacks on the White House staff.

Hence, the generalization holds.

    Together with the Raising analysis, (27) predicts a contrast between B-verb complements of the *that* and infinitival varieties. And just such a contrast exists:

(xi) a. They captured Tom but not Bob.

    b. They investigated Melvin's return but not mine.

I think, then, that so far, nothing precludes an account of (27) in terms of surface subject.

10 Kayne has supplied the following examples, which illustrate further the lack of sufficiency of principle (27):

(i) *You'll soon know whether not many people like her.

(ii) *I'm in favor of not everyone leaving immediately.

(iii) *We were talking about not everybody's having registered.

Curiously, (iii), but not (ii), becomes well-formed when *many people* replaces *everybody*.

(32) a. Harry believes (that) not many pilots are familiar with Racine.

b. *Harry believes not many pilots to be familiar with Racine.

(33) a. Harry proved (that) not many of those formulas were theorems.

b. *Harry proved not many of those formulas to be theorems.

(34) a. Harry found (that) not much grain was stored in telephone booths.

b. *Harry found not much grain to be stored in telephone booths.

With respect to the distribution of *not*-initial NPs, the postverbal NPs in the infinitival complement cases behave like nonsubjects, just as the Raising analysis predicts. An account like Chomsky's offers, on the contrary, no basis for the contrasts between pairs like those in (32)–(34).

No appeal to the tensed versus untensed clause distinction can rescue a non-Raising analysis here, since *not*-initial NPs can occur as derived subjects in several types of untensed clauses:

(35) a. Not many guests having arrived, Melvin poured a stiff drink.

b. For not many of you to pass would be tragic.

c. It would be normal for not much to be done about that.

d. I would prefer $\left\{ \begin{array}{l} \text{for not much} \\ \text{*not much} \end{array} \right\}$[11] to be said about this.

e. ?Joan prayed for not many of them to be convicted.

f. ?I am in favor of not many of them being released.

Thus a non-Raising treatment of B-verb complements is disconfirmed by the behavior of *not*-initial NPs.[12]

---

[11] I shall return to contrasts between *prefer* NP/*prefer for* NP several times later on. In general, it turns out that, in the former, the NP behaves like a member of the main clause and, in the latter, like part of the complement. I take this to indicate that Raising operates optionally for *prefer*, similar to the way it works for *wish* and *desire*, as described in Section 4.16. If so, the grammar predicts that, by and large, the *for* cases will work like *that* clauses in contrast to the others without *for*. Comparison of (35)d with (i) is an initial indication that this is correct.

(i) I would prefer that not much be said about this.

[12] Baker observes that in his idiolect examples like the following are well-formed:

(i) Not many girls would Jack dance with.

(ii) Not many people can I think of who would put up with Oscar's manners.

4.3 *Alone*-Final NPs

Certain NPs can end with the form *alone* expressing essentially the meaning 'only':

(36) a. Gronzmeyer alone can help you.

    b. Jones alone knows the secret formula.

    c. My uncle alone was able to survive.

    d. Matilda alone is easy to seduce.

    e. Harrison alone can be forced to resign.

(37) a. *Call Bob alone.

    b. *I talked to Smith alone about the wombat question.

    c. *Melvin hires those plumbers alone.

    d. *We were freed by the soldier alone.

    e. I believe $\left\{ \begin{array}{l} \text{*that alone} \\ \text{only that} \end{array} \right\}$.

He thus suggests that the proper condition on *not*-initial NPs is not that they be subjects, but rather that they be clause-initial. This would automatically account for facts like (v) and (vi) in footnote 9. However, I find examples like (i) and (ii) somewhat ill-formed. But, in support of Baker's contention, the following is well-formed, probably for everyone:

(iii) those girls, not many of whom the judge is willing to parole,

If, then, a clause-initial proposal is to be adopted, it must be stated in such a way as to be consistent with examples like (35)b, c, d. It must also be compatible with examples like (iv) presumably only by a view of Adverb Preposing as involving Chomsky adjunction.

(iv) a. Ten years ago, not many people were eating soyburgers.

     b. Under those conditions, not many doctors will volunteer.

I shall make no decision here as to whether a clause-initial account is ultimately preferable to a subject one. Observe that this choice has no bearing at all on the validity of the argument for B-verb Raising. This follows since, in a non-Raising grammar, not only is the italicized NP in (v) not a derived subject, but there is also a clause boundary after *believes*, just as in (vi).

(v) *Jack believes *not many people* to be happy.

(vi) Jack believes not many people are happy.

Thus a non-Raising system is equally incompatible with a clause-initial account of *not*-initial NPs.

f. Jim $\left\{\begin{array}{l}\text{proved}\\ \text{expected}\end{array}\right\}$ $\left\{\begin{array}{l}\text{*that result alone}\\ \text{only that result}\end{array}\right\}$.

g. *I refuse to work with her alone.

The generalization seems to be similar to that for *not*-initial NPs:

(38) *Alone*-final NPs can occur only in (derived) subject positions.[13]

Thus, parallel to the situation with *not*-initial NPs, principle (38) predicts, given the Raising analysis of B-verb infinitival complements, contrasts between pairs like (39):

(39) a. Larry found (that) Bob alone had drunk the bourbon + vinegar mixture.

[13] I would propose of course, that the notion of subject defined in footnote 9 is also appropriate here.

Like principle (27), governing *not*-initial NPs, principle (38) is not strictly true. It seems that *alone* meaning 'only' can also occur in certain kinds of adverbial NPs:

(i) a. In that way alone can we be sure of winning.

b. ?Under those conditions alone will I agree to do it.

Moreover, Plath points out that there is a usage of *alone* in emphatic coordinate contexts:

(ii) a. I will tell this to you and to you alone.

b. The car was stolen by Jim and by Jim alone.

Even more peculiarly, it seems to me that *alone* can occur on the predictate NPs of cleft sentences:

(iii) It was the Germans alone who started doing that.

Amazingly, as pointed out by McCawley, this is apparently possible only when the predicate NP corresponds to the subject of the embedded sentence:

(iv) a. *It was the Germans alone who we defeated.

b. *It was the Germans alone who they sent money to.

c. *It was the Germans alone who they were contacted by.

These points have no real bearing on the argument in the text, however, since it remains true that such NPs cannot occur in normal object positions.

In some respects, *alone*-final NPs are freer than *not*-initial NPs. For example, they can occur in *unfronted* subjects:

(v) a. Did Bob alone call Sally on time?

b. Under no circumstances would she alone be chosen.

c. Were Tom alone to come, I would call Jack.

In others, however, as pointed out by Kayne, they are more restricted:

(vi) a. Bob alone studied organic knitting, and Tom alone studied conceptual art.

b. *Bob alone studied organic knitting, and Tom alone conceptual art.

b. *Larry found Bob alone to have drunk the bourbon + vinegar mixture.

c. They proved (that) Martha alone had been at the scene.

d. *They proved Martha alone to have been at the scene.

The fact that predicted contrasts exist would again be evidence that the post-main-verb NP in infinitival B-verb complements is not a derived subject. Principle (38) predicts directly the parallelism between such pairs as (40):

(40) a. *Larry believes that alone to be possible.

b. *Larry believes that alone.

Once more, this is a conclusion that cannot be undermined by appeal to the properties of untensed clauses generally. For *alone*-final NPs can occur as the derived subjects of untensed clauses:

(41) a. Harry alone having been arrested, I called his wife.

b. For Harry alone to be sent there would be unfair.

c. I would prefer $\left\{ \begin{array}{l} \text{for Harry alone} \\ \text{*Harry alone} \end{array} \right\}$ to be arrested.

d. It would be strange for you alone to be nominated on the first ballot.

e. I arranged for Tony alone to receive a secret message.

Thus the properties of *alone*-final NPs also at once support a Raising analysis and disconfirm an analysis like Chomsky's, which assigns subject status to the relevant NPs not only in underlying structures but throughout derivations.

It is worth remarking briefly on the logic of the three arguments given so far in this section. In the case of Complex NP Shift, we discovered a restriction that blocks a certain operation from applying to subjects. Since the two grammatical proposals in competition make contrasting claims about the subject status of certain NPs in derived structures, such a restriction permits differentiation of the two positions. Similarly, in the case of both *not*-initial and *alone*-final NPs, we discovered that these can occur only in derived subject positions. This kind of generalization also interacts with the difference between the competing positions to permit their empirical separation. We have seen in all three cases that the Raising analysis correctly predicts the non-subject status of those NPs which behave as nonsubjects, while a non-Raising system like Chomsky's gives the wrong answer in all three, predicting in each case that the NPs in question should behave like derived subjects, when they do not.

It follows that in searching for further empirical bases for distinguishing the consequences of Raising and non-Raising grammars of B-verb constructions, one should attempt, among other things, to find restrictions that are sensitive to derived subjects. It would be equally relevant to discover properties that were restricted to nonsubjects, or to derived objects. Such cases will be considered later.

4.4 Contraction

As has been stressed throughout, Chomsky's system assigns essentially identical derived structures to such pairs as (42), while a Raising analysis assigns sharply different structures, with a clause boundary before the *it* in (42)a but after the *it* in (42)b:

(42) a. Max believes it $\begin{Bmatrix} \text{is true} \\ \text{has vanished} \end{Bmatrix}$.

  b. Max believes it to $\begin{Bmatrix} \text{be true} \\ \text{have vanished} \end{Bmatrix}$.

If, however, one pays close attention to the pronunciation of the un-stressed vowel of *it*, one finds, in my speech and that of many others I have asked, a rather subtle contrast.

In (42)b the vowel can be greatly reduced to a very weak, centralized vowel, just as much as it can in (43):

(43) Max believes it.

In fact, the most reduced pronunciation of (43) can serve as a perfectly appropriate initial segment of the pronunciation of (42)b. However, the vowel in (42)a cannot be reduced to this degree, and (43) does not provide a proper beginning for (42)a.

A natural statement would thus be that the degree of reduction found in (42)b and (43) is typical of object pronouns cliticized onto preceding verbs, but not at all typical of subject pronouns separated from preceding verbs by clause boundaries. The claim would be that cliticization is possible only for objects of verbs. It is, however, only a Raising analysis that can assign the required object status in (42)a and the required nonobject status in (42)b. An analysis like Chomsky's does not differentiate the derived configurations of the two sentences.

The argument is, however, not airtight. Cliticization is restricted to pronouns. In general, there is a contrast between the shapes of pronouns that are the subjects of tensed clauses and the corresponding pronouns in all other positions. That is, there are the contrasts illustrated in (44):

(44) a. *I* versus *me*

    b. *he* versus *him*

    c. *she* versus *her*

    d. *we* versus *us*

    e. *they* versus *them*

Suppose, then, that a defender of a non-Raising system attempts to deal with the difference between (42)a and (42)b as follows. Let it be claimed that the pronouns on the left in (44) have some "syntactic feature," called [+Nominative], while those on the right have the feature [−Nominative]. It will naturally follow, then, that although the shapes of *you, it, one,* etc., do not differ in the positions where the contrasts in (44) manifest themselves, these words will nonetheless occur with contrastive values of [Nominative]. Instead of saying, then, that object pronouns cliticize, as is necessary if the argument I gave above for Raising is to stand up, let us say that [−Nominative] pronouns cliticize. The contrast between (42)a and (42)b is now explained in terms of a contrast between the [+Nominative] marking of *it* in (42)a and the [−Nominative] marking of *it* in (42)b.

There are several objections to this proposal, which, it seems to me, indicate it cannot save a non-Raising system from the contraction contrasts. *First,* as with other cases of independently unmotivated (nonsemantic) "syntactic features," the marker [Nominative] is otherwise unneeded. The contrast in (44) is completely predicted by independent structures, namely, just that needed to specify where one finds [+Nominative] or [−Nominative]. The feature is a mere notational device for coding this information. There is thus no reason to think that it exists.[14] But, if it does not, no general statement of the conditions of cliticization (hence contraction) is possible in a non-Raising system.

[14] Along these lines, I would argue that, in this sense, there are *no* syntactic features. For introductory discussion of this claim, see Postal (1972a, 1972c); Lakoff (1972).

Second, the feature proposal has the following empirical consequence. If there are verbs that take *directly* following complement subjects that are not raised but are not the subjects of tensed verbs either,
these will also cliticize and contract to the same degree as in (42)b, and
(43). And there are such cases. Thus for some speakers, including the
present writer, the verbs *resent* and *favor,* and the adjectives *for* and
against can have the typical genitive of gerundive complement subjects
absent, subject to peculiar restrictions:

(45) a. I $\left\{ \begin{array}{l} \text{resent} \\ \text{favor} \\ \text{am} \left\{ \begin{array}{l} \text{against} \\ \text{for} \end{array} \right\} \end{array} \right\}$ Bob's falling on me.

    Bob('s) falling on me.

b. *I $\left\{ \begin{array}{l} \text{resent} \\ \text{favor} \end{array} \right\}$ Bob falling on me.

c. *I $\left\{ \begin{array}{l} \text{resent} \\ \text{favor} \\ \text{am} \left\{ \begin{array}{l} \text{against} \\ \text{for} \end{array} \right\} \end{array} \right\}$ that's[15] happening to me.

d. I $\left\{ \begin{array}{l} \text{resent} \\ \text{favor} \\ \text{am} \left\{ \begin{array}{l} \text{against} \\ \text{for} \end{array} \right\} \end{array} \right\}$ that happening to me.

Consider now the following:

(46) I $\left\{ \begin{array}{l} \text{resent} \\ \text{favor} \\ \text{am} \left\{ \begin{array}{l} \text{against} \\ \text{for} \end{array} \right\} \end{array} \right\}$ it happening to me.

According to the feature proposal, the *it* in (46) should be as cliticizable

---

[15] For some discussion of a basis for the ill-formedness of examples like (46)a, see
Ross (1972).

as that in (42)b or (43).[16] This follows since the *it* in (46) is clearly in nonnominative position, as shown by (47):

(47) a. I resent him (*he) going there.

b. I favor her (*she) being allowed to resign.

c. I am against him (*he) running again.

One should thus expect the same degree of vowel reduction to be possible for the *it* of (46) as for those of (42)b or (43). While the judgment is subtle, this does not seem to be the case.[17]

---

[16] This assumes, of course, that there is no possibility of claiming that elements like *resent* and *favor* trigger Raising. It will be seen later in section after section that the various tests for Raising operation support this view. Here I shall note only that such elements do not permit passivization of the underlying complement subject:

(i) a. *It was resented happening to Bob.
    b. *That was favored being done immediately.

In addition, the underlying complement subjects cannot undergo Complex NP Shift:

(ii) a. I resent all sorts of bad accidents and other unpleasant occurrences happening to me.
    b. *I resent happening to me—all sorts of bad accidents and other unpleasant occurrences.

(iii) a. I favor everyone who disagrees with that policy being fired.
    b. *I favor being fired—everyone who disagrees with that policy.

Finally, as far as *for* and *against* are concerned, it must be noted that no other adjectives trigger Raising application into superordinate object position, so that regularity would be lost if Raising were advocated for such elements.

[17] Since *believe* and *resent* have rather different phonetic endings, one might claim that any difference in vowel reduction for the following *it* is due to these phonetic differences rather than to structural factors. It is worth considering, then, pairs like (i) and (ii), where the *it* after *want* behaves like that after *believe*.

(i) I don't want it to happen to me.

(ii) I don't resent it happening to me.

As will be argued, especially in Section 4.16, *want* also triggers Raising, as do *believe* and other B-verbs. But since the phonetic endings of *want* and *resent* are the same, differences in vowel reduction must be due to other factors.

Moreover, as Ross observes, there is further argument along these lines. Namely, when the following word is a cliticized object of the verb, the *t* of the *nt* cluster is elidable. But we find the contrasts in (iii), indicating further that the *it* in (iii)b and (iii)d are in contrasting structural positions.

(iii) a. I don't wan' it.
    b. I don't wan' it to happen to me. } = [wánɨt]

    c. I don't resen' it.
    d. *I don't resen' it happening to me. } = [rizénɨt]

Third, and most seriously of all, I believe, the feature approach to contrasts like (42)a and (42)b appears to miss a rather deep generalization. This proposal claims, in effect, that the cliticization facts are accidental peculiarities. In feature terms, they could just as well have been formulated in the opposite way. A Raising system offers, however, a basis for showing the facts to be a function of an independent principle. The principle would be that cliticization is, in general, blocked across major constituent boundaries, particularly across *clause* boundaries.[18] Processes like cliticization would be permitted only for those constituents which are, at late levels of derivation, *sisters*—and possibly only sisters of certain limited kinds of constituents. In other words, there is reason to doubt that the rule needed in the feature proposal to cliticize *it* to *believe* in (42)b is a possible rule in a human language.[19] This

[18] I should like to believe that rules like *Wh*-Q Movement work by Chomsky adjunction. Consequently, a sentence like (i)a has a derived structure like (i)b:

(i) a. Who will $\left\{ \begin{array}{l} \text{Jerry} \\ \text{he} \end{array} \right\}$ select?

   b. [$_S$ who [$_S$ will NP select $_S$] $_S$]

If so, then examples like (ii) indicate that S boundaries produced by Chomsky-adjunction operations do not have the power to impede cliticization with respect to the principle in question.

(ii) Who'll he select?

Langacker points out that genitive cases like (iii) are also apparent counterexamples to the principle, since the genitive in such cases is clearly part of the word *saw's* and hence inside the relative clause.

(iii) The boy who I saw's mother is sick.

Perhaps the way to protect the principle against such cases is to observe that the morpheme in question, the genitive, never occurs unattached. That is, for example, there is no uncliticized version of (iii). The principle in the text may then hold only for elements that are optionally cliticizable, elements that have the possibility of occurring as independent words. The distinction drawn here would in large part follow the traditional division between inflectional elements (genitive, etc.) and particles or clitics.

[19] There seem to exist parallel contrasts for the operation that turns $t + y$ to [č]. Thus, for me, this appears possible in (i) but not in (ii):

(i) He would preven*t* *y*ou from going there.

(ii) He would resen*t* *y*ou(r) going there.

But, as argued later, especially in Section 4.13, the NP after *prevent* is a derived object, and hence a sister of *prevent*, while *you*(r) with *resent* remains a complement subject. Hence, there is a clause boundary between *t* and *y* in (ii), but not in (i), which would explain the contrast if this contraction is also restricted from applying across clause boundaries. Such a principle is weakly supported by the lack of contraction in such cases as the following:

follows because in a non-Raising grammar there is a clause boundary between these two constituents.

This is not an original claim of mine or, in general, at all peculiar to a line of work foreign to Chomsky's general approach. Thus, in work as closely related to his as that of his recent student Bresnan, one finds an analysis that makes quite similar assumptions.

Bresnan (1971) is concerned, among other things, with the reduction of infinitival *to* from [tuw] to [tə], and ultimately even to [ə], as in *wanna, gotta*. She suggests the following (1971: 5–6):

> It is notable that this process of vowel reduction applies only to items which are syntactically dependent, in an obvious sense. (We may define a *syntactic dependent* to be a terminal node A, and by extension the item dominated by A, which is immediately dominated by a node dominating a node other than A.) For example, a preposition is a syntactic dependent, since it occurs under P in the following configuration:

(21)   PP

                          P   NP

Similarly, the infinitive marker *to* is a syntactic dependent, because it occurs in some such configuration as:

(22)   VP

                          Prt   V

                            |
                           to

In this terminology, what *To* Contraction does is make *to* a syntactic dependent of the preceding eligible verb:

(23)   V

                          V   Prt

                                        |
                                       to

(iii) I gave the man who found the ha*t* your phone number.

(iv) I met Mary, who is sitting on the ma*t*, yesterday.

(v) Shaking the po*t* yields few benefits.

Furthermore, she proposes (1971: 6):

(27) (Syncategorematic) vowel reduction can apply only to surface structure syntactic dependents.

While one might quarrel with details, this proposal seems rather plausible. But observe that the function of her *To* Contraction is essentially nothing else than to produce a derived structure that can permit contraction and reduction without these processes having to cross major constituent boundaries, in particular, the underlying boundary between a main verb like *want* and a following infinitive. If something like Bresnan's approach to contraction is correct in general terms, then the cliticization in (42)b can be only a function of a raising rule which makes the post-*believe* NP its sister.

I conclude that the feature proposal in all likelihood would necessarily involve an otherwise unnecessary expansion of the class of possible grammatical rules, that is, a weakening of the theory of grammar, to include independently unneeded cliticizations or reductions of structurally separated items. Therefore, it is not a serious alternative to a Raising analysis.

It might be noted that there is, to my mind at least, a perfectly clear correlative surface bracketing contrast between B-verb *that*-clause and infinitival complements. Thus for me, the bracketing of (48)a is (49), while that of (48)b is (50), an intuition essentially shared by Huddleston (1971: 159–160), so that *Bill* and the remaining words form a *derived* constituent only in (48)a:

(48) a. Tom believes Bill is clever.

    b. Tom believes Bill to be clever.

(49)

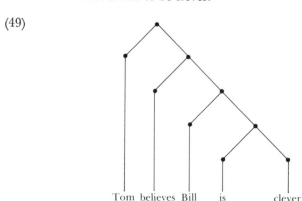

Tom believes Bill   is   clever

(50)

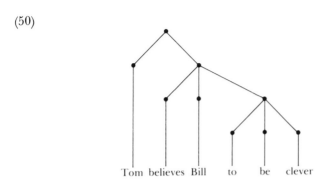

Tom believes Bill to be clever

One commentator suggests that contrasts like those in (49)–(50) are by no means clear, but that, even if real, they can be made compatible with a non-Raising analysis by recognizing a special "readjustment" rule to give the proper derived structure for the phonology. This "readjustment" rule could also solve the cliticization problem discussed earlier. But this is surely granting too much. The advocate of the traditional analysis of B-verb infinitival complements is necessarily sympathetic to the existence of a "readjustment" rule in such cases but must simply insist that the rule is not some extra addition to the grammar, as this commentator suggests, but is simply the Raising rule needed for A-verbs, as McCawley argued. There seems to be no way to avoid the conclusion that if the bracketing contrast in examples like (48) is real, as I claim, then it counts as a further piece of counterevidence to a non-Raising grammar.

4.5 Quantifier Postposing: A Seductive Nonargument

In this section I shall present a body of facts that on first analysis easily can be taken to yield an argument for Raising, but which, as observations of Kayne and Baker show, end up being neutral between Raising and non-Raising grammars.

In derived subject positions, the quantifiers *each, all,* and *both* can occur with relative freedom after the NP they bind:

(51) a. The men all left.

b. The guides each took a separate path.

c. We all were arrested.

d. The children both got dirty.

But in derived nonsubject positions, quantifier postposing is in general restricted to pronouns and restricted to *all* and *both*:

(52) a. I called them $\left\{ \begin{array}{c} \text{all} \\ \text{both} \\ *\text{each} \end{array} \right\}$.

   b. *Joe was arrested by the cops all.

   c. *I talked about that with them all.[20]

   d. *Mary hates the marines both.

This, then, seems to offer the basis for an argument for Raising with B-verb infinitival complements like one previewed earlier involving derived object constraints, since in one analysis of these there are derived objects, and in another there are not, and quantifier postposing seems sensitive to the status of NPs as derived objects. A first attempt to test the situation seems, surprisingly at this point, to support a non-Raising view, since one finds the case of (53), where (53)a, b are expected under both analyses, but where, under a Raising analysis, (53)d is apparently not expected, because of (52)d, etc.

(53) a. I believe they both left.

   b. I believe them both to have left.[21]

   c. I believe the soldiers both left.

   d. I believe the soldiers both to have left.

---

[20] For many speakers, even with pronouns and *all* or *both*, posterior position of quantifiers is not possible when the pronoun is the object of a preposition.

[21] Note the great degree of reduction of the vowel of *them* possible here, which is of some interest vis-à-vis the discussion of contraction in Section 4.4. Quantifier examples like (ii) seem to show the same contrast in degree of reduction noted for cases without quantifiers.

(i) a. Harry believes all of it is spoiled.
     b. Harry believes all of it to be spoiled.

(ii) a. Harry believes it all is spoiled.
     b. Harry believes it all to be spoiled.

Compare also (iii), where the vowel of *it* in (iii)b cannot be reduced to the extent of that in (iii)a, correlated with the fact that only the former becomes a derived object in a Raising grammar.

(iii) a. I believe it all to be spoiled.
      b. I resent it all being spoiled.

Thus (iii)b contrasts in reduction with (iv)b, while (iii)a does not contrast with (iv)a.

(iv) a. I believe it all.
     b. I resent it all.

Hence, it might seem that *the soldiers* in (53)d is not behaving like a derived object, in accord with a non-Raising analysis like that now advocated by Chomsky.

However, this conclusion is superficial. Although (53)d is well-formed, it is not really relevant. For, despite first impressions, (53)d is compatible with the Raising analysis. It will be naturally derived by the rule that reorders quantifiers into verbal phrases, that is, the rule responsible for sentences like (54):

(54) a. The men have all tried to escape.

b. The girls will all refuse.

c. The bombs probably were each placed by different individuals.

This rule will, in (53)d, move *both* into the verbal phrase from the NP *the soldiers*[22] on the cycle of the lower, or complement clause, when

[22] It is likely that the rule that inserts quantifiers into verbal phrases operates on the output of a rule that postposes quantifiers. Hence, schematically, we have (i) and (ii):

(i) $[_{NP}$all of the men$_{NP}]$ love Sylvia $\Rightarrow$ $[_{NP}$the men$_{NP}]$ all [love Sylvia] $\Rightarrow$

(ii) The men [all love Sylvia].

Thus postposing gets the quantifier out of the NP to a position following it. A different rule would make it part of the verbal phrase. The latter is possible only if the original NP was in subject position. Later, I suggest that in certain cases, namely, where the NP is a pronoun, the operation in (i) is, in effect, partly undone by a cliticizing rule that can attach a quantifier to the end of the NP. The second rule in (i) is necessary because in cases like (ii) *all love Sylvia* is a constituent. This assumes, though, that the same rule is operative in subject position as in object position, in other words, that the right-hand side of (i) is generated by the same postposing rule operative in (iii), which clearly does not adjoin the quantifier onto any following constituent.

(iii) I hate them all.

Hence, if this rule is involved in (ii), the derivation must be compound, with first a postposing and detachment from NP rule and second an adjunction. The latter is also consistent with the bracketing of cases like (iv), which probably has the right-branching structure shown in (v):

(iv) The girls recently reluctantly all resigned their positions.

(v)

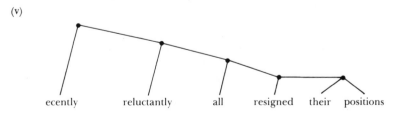

ecently   reluctantly   all   resigned   their   positions

the soldiers is still a subject, and hence not governed by the constraints illustrated in (52). There can be little doubt of the cyclical properties of the rules that reposition quantifiers here.[23] It follows, then, that even under the Raising analysis, (53)d is not an instance of quantifier postposing in object position from a nonpronoun, which is generally impossible, as (52) shows. So far, then, quantifier postposing seems irrelevant to the choice between Raising and non-Raising grammars of B-verb infinitival complements.

Persisting, though, in trying to show that this is not the case, one can note that there is a contrast between (53)b and (53)d, which differ only in *them/the soldiers*. Namely, in (53)d, the sequence *both to have left* is a derived constituent. However, while this is a possible analysis in (53)b, the latter also has a surface structure in which *both to have left* is not a constituent (while *them both* is), a bracketing unavailable for (53)d. This contrast follows from the assumption of the Raising approach. Both (53)b and (53)d would have derivations in which the quantifier is positioned by the rules relevant for subjects on the lower cycle. But only (53)b, with a pronoun head, would be subject to postposing of quantifiers on the higher cycle (or postcyclically), when the NP has become an object and is subject to the restrictions of (52).

However, although initially appealing, this argument cannot survive. It collapses in the face of observations by Kayne (personal communication), who notes insightfully that there are contrasts parallel to those between examples like (53)b and (53)d, for which all questions of Raising application are necessarily irrelevant. He provides such examples as:

(55) a.   They all, it seems to me, have the same outlook on politics.

  b. ?*Your brothers all, it seems to me, have the same outlook on politics.

One reason, stressed by Ross, for assuming that the rule that places quantifiers in the verbal phrase operates on the output of the postposing rule relevant for objects is that otherwise this postposing rule would work for objects but not subjects. But, as he points out, there are "primacy" conditions suggesting that this is, in general, impossible—that rules can work for subjects only, but not for nonsubjects only. See Ross (to appear c).

23 By saying these rules have cyclical properties, I mean to leave open the question whether they are simple cyclical rules of the ordinary sort or postcyclical rules with global environments sensitive to structure within the cycle. For arguments that the parallel processes in French are cyclical see Kayne (1969); Fauconnier (1971). This question is discussed in Postal (to appear c).

Here, when a parenthetical element separates the quantifier from the beginning of the verbal phrase, well-formedness results only with a pronoun. A natural suggestion would be, I think, that the output structure (56) is ill-formed, which accounts for (55)b. Example (55)a can survive then only because there must be some rule *which attaches the quantifier to the NP*,[24] yielding (57), which is not covered by a blockage on (56)-type structures. Let us call this rule Q-Pro Attachment. This rule might also account for such differences as (58), contrasted with (59), and more interestingly with (60), if there is also some constraint that rejects cases where a quantifier is the first element of a verbal phrase whose main verb is a form of *be*.

(56)

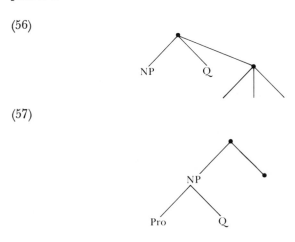

(57)

(58) a.   They all are happy.

b. ?*The soldiers all are happy.

(59) a. They are all happy.

b. The soldiers are all happy.

24 Kayne (1969: 25) observes French examples like (i):

(i) Eux tous partiront.

These probably manifest the same type of structure involved in our English examples, that is, one with the quantifier cliticized to the pronoun. Note that with ordinary intonation nothing can intervene between subject NP and Verb in French. Hence, we have (ii):

(ii) *Les chauffeurs tous partiront.

$$(60) \left\{ \begin{array}{l} \text{They} \\ \text{The soldiers} \end{array} \right\} \left\{ \begin{array}{l} \text{all} \\ \text{both} \\ \text{each} \end{array} \right\} \left\{ \begin{array}{l} \text{left} \\ \text{will leave} \\ \text{have left} \end{array} \right\}.$$

However, if there is a rule Q-Pro Attachment, and a constraint something like (56), then the contrast between (53)b and (53)d is explained without any appeal to Raising and the restrictions in (52).[25] That is, since Q-Pro Attachment is optional because one can find both (61)a and (61)b, the two structures for (53)b follow, while (53)d can have only one, since with its nonpronominal head, Q-Pro Attachment is not applicable.

(61) a. They [all left].

    b. They all [left].

Thus the facts of quantifier positioning still seem to offer no evidence for or against the Raising theory.

[25] Moreover, the combination of a rule like Q-Pro Attachment and a constraint such as (56) goes a long way toward explaining the constraints in (52). Only the contrast between *each/all + both* does not follow (but see the discussion of Baker's observations later). If this is right, it would predict that sequences of pronoun + quantifier in nonsubject position would have the surface structure in (i), not that in (ii):

(i) [pro Q]

(ii) [pro] Q

Consideration of examples like (iii) indicate that this is correct, since the superficial bracketing of (iii) appears to be (iv), not (v).

(iii) I saw them all yesterday.

(iv)

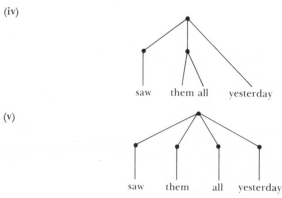

(v)

It would also seem that the likely existence of Q-Pro Attachment and a condition like (56) explain contrasts like (62):

(62) a. Malcolm proved *them* all, $\left\{ \begin{array}{l} \text{don't forget} \\ \text{he claimed} \end{array} \right\}$, to be vicious criminals.

b. *Malcolm proved *the soldiers* all, $\left\{ \begin{array}{l} \text{don't forget} \\ \text{he claimed} \end{array} \right\}$, to be vicious criminals.

Without these aspects of the grammar, examples like (62) would evidently provide a strong argument for Raising, since an analysis involving application of this rule would make the italicized elements derived objects in (62), and hence subject to the quantifier postposing constraints of (52), which they appear to be subject to. However, the combination of Q-Pro Attachment and (56) also explains (62) without any appeal to a derived object status for the italicized NP. So again the apparent argument collapses.

As a last gasp, then, one can try to form an argument for Raising based on restrictions like (52) by noting the fact that examples parallel to both (62)a and (62)b are ill-formed if the word *all* is replaced by the word *each*:

(63) a. *Malcolm proved them each, $\left\{ \begin{array}{l} \text{don't forget} \\ \text{he claimed} \end{array} \right\}$, to be vicious criminals.

b. *Malcolm proved the soldiers each, $\left\{ \begin{array}{l} \text{don't forget} \\ \text{he claimed} \end{array} \right\}$, to be vicious criminals.

Under a Raising conception, this would follow directly from the derived object status of the relevant NP plus the restrictions illustrated in examples like (64):

(64) a. *Malcolm proved them each.

b. *Malcolm proved the theorems each.

Compare (63), with its parentheticals, to (65):

(65) a. Malcolm proved them each to be vicious criminals.

b. Malcolm proved the soldiers each to be vicious criminals.

The difference between (63) and (65) is, of course, that the presence of the parenthetical expression prevents an analysis of the sentences in which the quantifier has been positioned by the rules that attach quantifiers to verbal phrases. These rules can, in (65), operate on the lower cycle, unaffected by constraints like those illustrated in (52) and (64), because, at that stage, the relevant NPs are still subjects. The presence of the parenthetical expression prevents this analysis for reasons that are unclear.[26] But the fact that it prevents it, in general, independently

[26] It might be thought that condition (56) suffices to explain the blockage. But this is not so. Example (56) would account for the absence of an analysis of a sequence such as (i) of the form shown in (ii):

(i) *The men all, I think, died.

(ii)

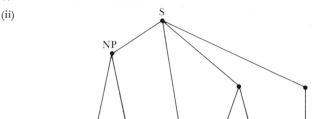

But it does not block equally impossible analyses of the form shown in (iii):

(iii) a.

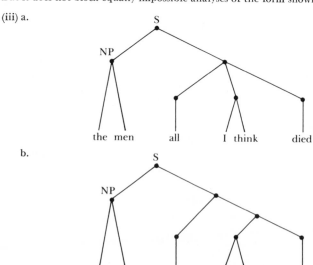

b.

of constructions relevant to present questions about Raising, is shown
by such examples as (66):

(66) a. The men, $\begin{Bmatrix} \text{don't forget} \\ \text{I think} \end{Bmatrix}$, $\begin{Bmatrix} \text{each} \\ \text{all} \\ \text{both} \end{Bmatrix}$[27] left at dawn.

b. *The men $\begin{Bmatrix} \text{each} \\ \text{all} \\ \text{both} \end{Bmatrix}$, $\begin{Bmatrix} \text{don't forget} \\ \text{I think} \end{Bmatrix}$, left at dawn.

c. The nearer caves, $\begin{Bmatrix} \text{Ed realized} \\ \text{you know} \\ \text{Bob says} \end{Bmatrix}$, $\begin{Bmatrix} \text{each} \\ \text{all} \\ \text{both} \end{Bmatrix}$ should be searched.

d. *The nearer caves $\begin{Bmatrix} \text{each} \\ \text{all} \\ \text{both} \end{Bmatrix}$, $\begin{Bmatrix} \text{Ed realized} \\ \text{you know} \\ \text{Bob says} \end{Bmatrix}$, should be searched.

The constraint illustrated in (66) then shows that in examples like (63)
the only analysis is one involving the kind of quantifier postposing
which can function in object positions. But this is allowed only for *all*
and *both,* with *each* banned. That is, the constraint in (64) explains the
constraint in (63), while the facts in (66) show that the well-formedness
of (65) is also to be expected. But the former explanation depends on
the assignment of derived object status, sanctioned only in Raising
grammars.

However, as Baker has pointed out to me, this last attempt to extract
a pro-Raising argument also fails. The facts in (63) are explained independently of Raising by simply specifying that Q-Pro Attachment is
blocked, in the idiolects in question, with the quantifier *each.* More-

---

This is, I think, highly suspicious and suggests that there should be some more
general principle that blocks both (iii) and the cases for which (56) correctly filters
unwanted structures. I am, however, not able to formulate such a condition.
27 To get truly well-formed cases here with the *each* option, one should in many
cases add an adverb like *separately* or a phrase like *by different people.*

over, this specification is independently necessary because of the following case:

(67) a. *They each, I think, left separately.

   b. *You each, he claimed, made contradictory claims.

Finally, Baker's claim that the constraint illustrated in (63) is the same as that in (67) is supported by the fact that there exist speakers, particularly my colleague F. Damerau, for whom Q-Pro Attachment evidently generalizes to *each,* so that examples like (67) are well-formed. But for him, examples like (63) are also well-formed. Thus Baker's claim that the properties of Q-Pro Attachment account for facts like (63) independently of Raising seems validated, and the last attempt to extract an argument for Raising from the constraints in (52) also fails. Note that nothing said here offers any evidence *against* a Raising analysis, however.

   Although all attempts to extract support for Raising from the restrictions in (52) have apparently failed, I have let this section remain because of the inherent interest of the facts involved and, more importantly, because I think this discussion illustrates the great difficulty involved in validating empirical arguments for grammatical proposals, the great care that must be taken in reaching conclusions, and the always existing possibility that independent, unconsidered factors can always render an apparently clear argument untenable.

4.6 A Fundamental Pronominalization Constraint
It has been known since late 1966 that a basic constraint on stipulated coreferential pronominalization in English (and, no doubt, other langauges) is the following:

(68) A pronoun cannot both precede and command its antecedent NP.[28]

Recall that one constituent, which it neither dominates nor is dominated by, A, commands another, B, if the first S node above A also dominates B. Hence, in the configurations of (69) there are the command relations among non-S nodes given in (70).

---

28 This formulation is due to Langacker (1969). See Ross (1969b) and Postal (1970b, 1971) for further discussion.

(69) a.

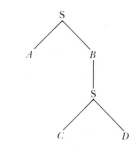

   b.

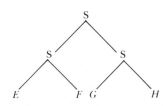

(70) a. *A* commands *B*.

    b. *A* commands *C*.

    c. *A* commands *D*.

    d. *B* commands *A*.

    e. *C* commands *D*.

    f. *D* commands *C*.

    g. *E* commands *F*.

    h. *F* commands *E*.

    i. *G* commands *H*.

    j. *H* commands *G*.

The principle in (68) accounts for an enormous range of facts, briefly and inadequately indicated by the following narrow selection:

(71) a. *He$_i$ wants Jane to kiss Bob$_i$.

    b. *They$_{i,j}$ didn't believe I would help the employees$_{i,j}$.

    c. *She$_i$ called the man who annoyed Joan$_i$.

    d. *He$_i$ visited Jane, who used to know Bob$_i$.

While the exact point or points in derivations where (68) is applicable have never been specified precisely,[29] it seems clear that these must include a stage after the application of cyclic NP reordering rules (like Passive), for reasons such as (72):

(72) a. *He$_i$ called all of the girls who Bob$_i$ knew.

    b. ?All of the girls who Bob$_i$ knew were called by him$_i$.

While sentences like (72)b are less than perfect for many speakers, they do not manifest the complete block on coreferential linkages found in those like (72)a. Hence, the constraint in (68), which is responsible for the character of (72)a, must be sensitive to the structures produced by a rule like Passive in order to prevent the assignment of the status of examples like (72)a to passive sentences like (72)b.

One of the most obvious properties of raising operations is that *they alter command relations*. In particular, if there is a raising operation associated with B-verb infinitival complements, this operation permits the raised NP to command certain elements after it is raised which it did not before, since it is moved into a higher clause. Consequently, the way is open in principle for the Raising analysis, in conjunction with principle (68), to generate certain pronominalization contrasts that a system without Raising in these cases would not predict. In short, (68) offers another empirical possibility for differentiating Raising versus non-Raising grammars for B-verb complements.

Moreover, some sentences discovered by Bach (1970) turn the theoretical possibility into an actuality. Bach notes that in his speech and that of many others (myself included) the following sorts of contrasts exist:

(73) a. Joan believes (that) he$_i$ is a genius even more fervently than Bob$_i$ does.

    b. *Joan believes him$_i$ to be a genius even more fervently than Bob$_i$ does.

    c. Tom proved (that) she$_i$ was telepathic just as easily as Joan$_i$ did.

    d. *Tom proved her$_i$ to be telepathic just as easily as Joan$_i$ did.

That is, if we choose the first pair for discussion, *he* and *Bob* can be stipulated coreferents in (73)a, but *him* and *Bob* cannot be in (73)b. Under the Raising analysis of B-verb infinitival complements, this is an

---

[29] This question is considered in Postal (to appear d), where it is argued that the constraint must be defined at more than one stage of derivation and is, consequently, global.

automatic consequence of principle (68),[30] since after application of Raising *him* will command *Bob,* although before application it would not have. These characteristics would follow from tree structures something like those shown in (74). Here (74)a represents the *that*-clause case and (74)b the infinitival structure *after* Raising has applied. It can be seen that, while in (74)a the first S node (S_1) above *he* does not dominate *Bob* and hence *he* does not command *Bob,* in (74)b the first S node (S_0) above *him* does dominate *Bob,* and hence *him* does command *Bob.* Therefore, it would follow from principle (68) that *him* and *Bob* cannot be coreferential in (73)b, while (68) is inapplicable in the case of

(74) a.

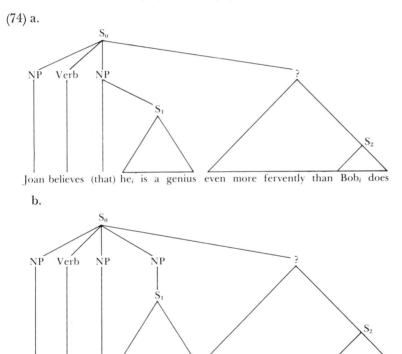

b.

---

30 That is, automatic under the assumption that the constraint is sensitive to the output of Raising. However, since it has already been seen that the constraint is sensitive to the output of Passive, and since Passive operates, in a system with B-verb Raising, on the output of Raising, it follows that the constraint must consider the output of Raising. Parallel to (72) is the case of (i) and (ii):

(i) *He_i believed all of the girls who knew Bob_i were happy.

(ii) All of the girls who knew Bob_i were believed by him_i to be happy.

he and *Bob* in (73)a, accounting for their possible coreferentiality. However, this contrast depends on the difference in command relations generated by Raising application in the infinitival cases and its nonapplication in the *that*-clause case.

I can think of one possible objection to this argument, which would take advantage of the fact that our knowledge of the constituent structures of comparative clauses is far from definitive. A critic might then claim that there is no basis for attaching the unlabeled nodes in (74) to the node S_0. He might claim that these are actually attached at some higher point, so that the structure would be the one shown in (75) rather

(75)

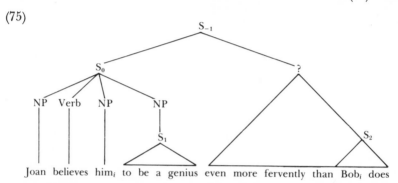

Joan believes him$_i$ to be a genius even more fervently than Bob$_i$ does

than (74)b. If this were the case, then, even in (73)b, *him* would not command *Bob,* and principle (68) would not be relevant to the example. The critic might then claim, weakly to be sure, that some as-yet-unknown principle blocks the coreference linkage in sentences like (73)b,d. Because of the loss of generality in the description of pronominalization constraints, and because (75) is not motivated, this objection seems to me to have at worst little force. However, even this problem can, I think, be eliminated by embedding sentences like (73) *as gerundive nominals:*

(76) a. Joan's believing (that) he$_i$ is a genius even more fervently than Bob$_i$ does worries me.

   b. *Joan's believing him$_i$ to be a genius even more fervently than Bob$_i$ does worries me.

For here it is known independently that a verb like *worries* determines gerundive form for the main verb of its complement subject. But if the appropriate structure for the revelant cases were like (75) instead of (74),

(77)

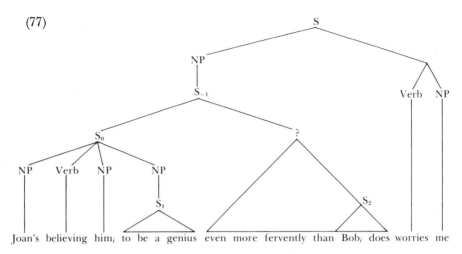

Joan's believing him$_i$ to be a genius even more fervently than Bob$_i$ does worries me

the structure of a sentence like (76)b would be like (77). But in such a structure, *believing* is not the main verb of the complement clause but rather of a clause embedded within that. The complement clause itself, S_{-1}, does not even have a main verb in any accepted sense. Hence, given structures like (77), the rules determining the relation between main verbs like *worry* and the gerundive form of their complement subjects would be unnecessarily complicated. Thus (75) is not an appropriate structure, and the objection to the argument collapses.

In conclusion, the sentences observed by Bach reveal a contrast in terms of principle (68) which is a direct consequence of the Raising analysis. Chomsky's system, on the other hand, assigns both B-verb infinitival and *that*-clauses structures that differ at no point in command relations, and thus it predicts that contrasts like those in (73) and (76) do not exist. Any such non-Raising system is thus falsified by Bach's observations.

It is, of course, possible that an opponent of Raising might suggest ad hoc constraints as the basis for contrasts like those in (73) and (76), constraints having nothing to do with the general principle (68). One further thing should be said about this. Clearly, examples like (73) and (76) are extremely marginal—in the sense that a speaker could naturally live his entire life without ever encountering this particular example of backward pronominalization. Far from weakening the argument for Raising derivable from such examples, this type of marginality greatly strengthens it. Because of the marginality, it follows that the linguistic experience of speakers will not dependably provide them with the opportunity to come in contact with the relevant examples. Thus they would, in general, have no basis for adding to their grammars any special constraints designed to handle contrasts like those in (73) and (76) independently of principle (68). Consequently, the definite judgments available to English speakers about such cases must follow from general principles that are internalizable independently of such marginal sentences, principles like (68), which are either universal and innate or at least capable of being induced on the basis of a wide variety of not-at-all-marginal examples. Thus, while it is conceivable that ad hoc constraints for examples like those underlying the present pro-Raising argument could achieve descriptive adequacy, they could never provide any basis for justifying their own incorporation into the grammar; that is, explanatory adequacy would be impossible. This general form of argument, in which the marginality of a phenomenon actually strengthens the force of evidence for Raising, can be applied to many of the other phenomena found relevant in this study to justifying the choice of a Raising system.

4.7 Backward Equi

The Equi rule works *backward,* or with the antecedent on the right, to delete coreferential pronouns in a variety of contexts like that of (78):

(78) a. Shooting himself amused Tony.

b. Losing his wallet annoyed Max.

This deletion provides an argument for the Raising analysis of B-verb infinitival complements rather like that in the preceding section. This follows since, in general, backward application of Equi is restricted to cases where the potentially deleted pronoun is commanded by its antecedent, as in (78). Compare the following:

(79) a. *Shooting himself$_i$ amused Barbara because Tony$_i$ was unpleasant.

b. *Criticizing himself$_i$ annoyed the girl who loved Tony$_i$.

c. *Studying himself$_i$ interested Joan, who loved Tony$_i$.

d. *Ingratiating himself$_i$ with the Queen made me realize that Bob$_i$ was a spy.

Thus there is the principle given in (80):

(80) A pronoun P to be deleted under Equi controlled by a following antecedent A must be commanded by A.

Consider, then, these cases:

(81) a. *Criticizing himself$_i$ proved (that) Bob$_i$ was humble.[31]

   b. ?Criticizing himself$_i$ proved Bob$_i$ to be humble.

Everyone agrees that sentences like (81)a are impossible. Some people find those like (81)b acceptable; others find them deviant. But even the latter speakers recognize, I think,, a contrast of relative acceptability between (81)a and (81)b. Given principle (80), the Raising analysis accounts for the contrast in the same way as it explained those in the previous section. A non-Raising grammar offers, however, no non-ad-hoc basis for such differences.[32]

4.8 Right Node Raising

There is a rule in English and many other languages that I shall refer to as Right Node Raising (henceforth: RNR).[33] Its operation is illustrated by such examples as these:

[31] The structure underlying (81)a must be realized with a surface structure pronoun, that is, as follows:

(i) His$_i$ criticizing himself$_i$ proved that Bob$_i$ was humble.

[32] Because of constraints on the class of possible underlying subjects with complement-taking verbs, this argument is not applicable to all B-verbs, thus not to *believe* and *find*, since they cannot take sentential subjects. However, it applies to *show*, as well as to *prove*:

(i) a. *Criticizing himself$_i$ showed (that) Bob$_i$ was humble.

   b. ?Criticizing himself$_i$ showed Bob$_i$ to be humble.

[33] For discussion, see Hankamer (1971), and Maling (1972), who independently show that RNR is actually the rule involved in what had previously been called Backward Gapping (Ross, 1970b).

   RNR has also often been called Conjunction Reduction, which, I think, amounts to a confusion between the rule operative in (82) and that involved in the derivation of such examples as the following:

(i) a. Joe and Tom weigh, respectively, 150 and 200 pounds.

   b. Harry danced and sang.

Notice these involve no sharp intonational marking and no requirement that the identical sequences be on right branches, both typical features of RNR derivations.

(82) a. Jack may be—and Tony certainly is—a werewolf.

   b. Tom said he would—and Bill actually did—eat a raw eggplant.

   c. Tony should have—and Pete probably would have—called Grace.

   d. Terry used to be—and George still is—very suspicious.

Roughly, given certain paired sequences of identical constituents in disjoint clauses, RNR places a double of the sequence on the right, by Chomsky adjunction, and deletes all original occurrences.[34] Note the characteristically extremely sharp intonation breaks at the points of deletion indicated by dashes in (82). Hence, schematically (82)a would be derived as shown in (83). While there are myriad problems in achieving a precise formulation of RNR, its crucial feature for the present discussion is, fortunately, simply the property that the identical sequences, a copy of which is added on the right, *are always constituents*—in fact, I think, even in examples like (82)b–d, NP constituents, but this does

(83) a.

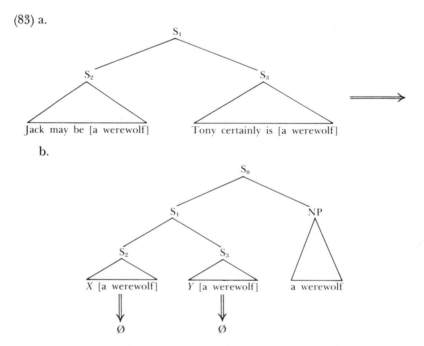

   b.

---
34 Alternatively, but less plausibly, one might argue that one of the original sequences is adjoined, with the other(s) deleted.

not matter here. Since *that* clauses are constituents, one is not surprised that these undergo the rule, as shown in (84).

(84) a. Harry has claimed—but I do not believe—that Melvin is a communist.

 b. The *News* may have reported—but I do not accept—that Nixon did that.

 c. Harry may have believed—but I certainly don't believe—that the war is justified.

 d. Henry claimed—but nobody has so far proved—that Mu-grammars are recursive.

Note further that the *that* clauses undergoing RNR include those forming the complements of B-verbs.

As we have seen, in Chomsky's system, the basic structure of infinitival and *that*-clause complements for B-verbs is the same. Both are simply S, with all further distinctions being clause internal. No raising operation affects either. There is, then, nothing to predict any contrast in behavior under RNR operation. In a descriptive system that involves a raising operation for B-verb infinitival complements, however, the situation is different. Here, (cyclic) Raising operation guarantees that, at the earliest point where RNR might apply, the original single constituent clause has been broken apart in the infinitival cases. That is, at the point where RNR might apply, a Raising system claims, in contrast to a system like Chomsky's, that examples such as (85) do not have a derived structure in which *Bill to be a spy* is a constituent.

(85) Harry believes Bill to be a spy.

If so, then a Raising analysis necessarily predicts that such sequences cannot undergo RNR, in contrast to *that*-clause complements which, not undergoing Raising, remain constituents. And this prediction is borne out:

(86) a. I find it easy to believe that Tom is dishonest, but Joan finds it hard to believe that Tom (he) is dishonest.

 b. I find it easy to believe Tom to be dishonest, but Joan finds it hard to believe Tom (him) to be dishonest.

(87) a. I find it easy to believe—but Joan finds it hard to believe—that Tom is dishonest

b. *I find it easy to believe—but Joan finds it hard to believe—Tom to be dishonest.

The sharp contrast in behavior is exactly that predicted by the Raising analysis of B-verb infinitival complements, but not predicted at all by a non-Raising system, which makes only clause-internal distinctions between the relevant infinitival and *that*-clause complements.

Moreover, adding some ad hoc condition on RNR referring to the internal structure of the relevant constituents, that is, distinguishing tensed from untensed clauses, not only would be lacking in generality in comparison with the automatic predictions of the Raising analysis but also would not be empirically viable. In fact, nontensed, infinitival clauses can undergo RNR when they clearly meet the condition of constituency:

(88) a. I think it would be unwise for John to marry Laura, but Tom feels it would be clever for him to marry her.

b. I think it would be unwise—but Tom feels it would be clever—for John to marry Laura.

(89) a. I like to visit new places, but Tom doesn't like to visit new places.

b. I like—but Tom doesn't like—to visit new places.

I conclude that the contrast in RNR behavior between B-verb infinitival and *that*-clause complements is at once a strong argument in favor of the Raising conception of English grammar and a critical counterexample to a non-Raising grammar like that advocated by Chomsky. The facts follow directly from an interaction of the constituent condition on RNR plus the Raising analysis but are in conflict with the predictions of Chomsky's system.[35]

[35] One possible line of defense for a non-Raising system has been suggested to me by Howard Lasnik. He notes that while RNR operates on *that* clauses, it does so only correlated with the actual surface occurrence of the *that*. Hence, compare (87)a in the text with (i), which seems no better than the infinitival case (87)b.

(i) *I find it easy to believe—but Joan finds it hard to believe—Tom is dishonest.

A non-Raising defender might argue then that what is wrong with (i), and also with (87)b, is not incorrect application of RNR but occurrence of a clause in a certain position without a complementizer required in that position. As support, note that

4.9 Gapping

An argument similar to that just given for RNR can be based on sentences involving the Gapping rule.[36] The key facts are such contrasts as those following:

(90) a. I believe that Tom is weird, and Joan believes that Sally is paranoiac.

b. I believe that Tom is weird, and Joan that Sally is paranoiac.

(91) a. I believe Tom to be weird, and Joan believes Sally to be paranoiac.

---

well-formed untensed clause examples like (88)b have the element *for* in clause-initial position.

So far, however, this approach has not developed to the point where it forces abandonment of the argument in the text. Crucially, it has not been shown that the suggested constraint is independently motivated. To account for the contrast between (87)a and (i), it would suffice to specify precisely the possible conditions for deletion of the *that* of a *that* complement, which, with a few exceptions like (ii), require as a necessary (but not sufficient) condition that the *that* clause directly follow the verb of which it is the complement.

(ii) It seems to me (that) Bill is unhappy.

Moreover, examples like (89)b and (iii) show that clauses, with or without subjects, can occur in the position in question without explicit clause-initial complementizer.

(iii) Harry wanted to discuss—but we didn't actually discuss—(Tom's) dating Greta.

Nor is this conclusion avoidable by an even further extension of nonhomogeneity in the notion of complementizer by trying to extend it to genitives. For observe (iv):

(iv) Harry may not resent—but I do resent—that sort of thing going on.

Finally, note such contrasts as the following:

(v) a. I didn't think I would prefer for Wallace to win, but Tom said I would prefer for Wallace to win.
   b. I didn't think I would prefer—but Tom said I would prefer—for Wallace to win.

(vi) a. I didn't think I would prefer Wallace to win, but Tom said I would prefer Wallace to win.
   b. *I didn't think I would prefer—but Tom said I would prefer—Wallace to win.

So, all in all, I see little hope of anyone succeeding in attributing the ill-formedness of examples like (87)b to the absence of a complementizer, which is what would be required to overthrow the argument for Raising along the lines suggested by Lasnik.
36 For discussion of this rule see Ross (1967, 1970b); Hankamer (1971, to appear); Maling (1972); and Jackendoff (1971).

b. *I believe Tom to be weird, and Joan Sally to be paranoiac.

As such, Chomsky's system, with its assignment of parallel structures to B-verb infinitival and *that*-clause complements, offers no explanation for such contrasts. What of the Raising analysis?

First, observe that, under a Raising approach, in which *that* clauses are NPs, the derived structure of a gapped clause like the second in (90)b is simply [$_s$NP NP$_s$]. However, under this analysis, the derived structure of gapped clauses like those in (91)b is [$_s$NP NP NP$_s$], with the subjectless infinitive maintaining its original NP over S structure. Does this contrast, automatic when Gapping combines with the Raising analysis, predict the contrast between pairs like (90)b and (91)b? There is evidence that it does. In general, gapped clauses ending up as [NP NP] are, of course, fine. However, as Jackendoff (1971: 25–26) noted, "With two unlike constituents [besides the subject], the acceptability of Gapping varies. With two NP's, the result is marginal at best. . . ." He then gave the following examples:[37]

(92) a. *Arizona elected Goldwater Senator, and Massachusetts(,) Mc-Cormack(,) Congressman.

b. *Millie will send the President an obscene telegram, and Paul(,) the Queen(,) a pregnant duck.

See Hankamer (to appear) for some discussion. It thus seems that independently of B-verb complements, clauses resulting from Gapping of the form [NP NP NP] are ill-formed. Further examples would be as in (93):

(93) a. I bought roses for Sally, and Jack bought lilies for Jane.

b. I bought roses for Sally, and Jack lilies for Jane.

c. I bought Sally roses, and Jack bought Jane lilies.

d. *I bought Sally roses, and Jack Jane lilies.

[37] If, as I would argue, prepositional phrases have the structure shown in (i), then one must note that the restriction in question does not hold for NPs that begin with prepositions, as (93)b will show.

(i)

Since, however, the Raising analysis, but not Chomsky's system, assigns just this structure to clauses like the final one in (91)b, it follows that Gapping provides further evidence for the Raising analysis.[38]

This argument, however, probably cannot be regarded as being as strong as the previous one involving RNR. That argument depended basically on the condition, surely unchallengeable, that this rule operates only on constituents. But the Gapping argument depends on the assumption that the ill-formedness of examples like (92) and (93)d is a function of a restriction blocking gapped clauses with the output form [NP NP NP].[39] Given the obscurities surrounding Gapping, however, this assumption is probably more challengeable than that made about RNR.

[38] Much to my embarrassment, after writing up this argument, I was reminded by Huddleston (1971: 160) that it was originally given by R. Lakoff (1968: 37).

[39] Again, parallel to the discussion about RNR in footnote 35, an alternative claim might be made involving complementizers. Thus it could be pointed out that sentences like (90)b become ill-formed if the *that* is removed:

(i) *I believe that Tom is weird, and Joan Sally is paranoiac.

I shall argue here that (i) follows simply from the condition blocking *that* deletion except directly following the verb. And to see that clauses need not have complementizers to occur in gapped clauses, observe these examples:

(ii) Bob resents this happening to him, and I that happening to me.

(iii) Joan discussed Bob's kissing the gorilla, and Marsha Tom's caressing the penguin.

(iv) Jack tried to cheat Bob, and Tom to fool Melvin.

If there is no such need, then contrasts like that between (91)b and examples like (v) provide further evidence for the existence of Raising for the former.

(v) I arranged for Bob to win, and Tom for Sally to lose.

Note also (vi):

(vi) a.   I would prefer for Bob to lose, and Tom for Sally to win.
     b. *I would prefer for Bob to lose, and Tom Sally to win.

Finally, consider sentences like (vii):

(vii) a. I believe Bob to be Italian and Marsha to be Polish.
      b. I expect Arthur to win and Jack to lose.

These might at first glance be taken to indicate that sequences like *Marsha to be Polish* and *Jack to lose* are constituents in these cases, apparently contrary to the claims of Raising analyses of the infinitival complements of *believe* and *expect* (see Section 4.16). However, although I am far from understanding sentences like (vii),

4.10 Pseudocleft Sentences

An argument parallel to the previous two, but closer to that involving RNR, can be formulated on the basis of the pseudocleft sentence construction, illustrated by sentences like (94):

(94) a. What I want is to become a millionaire.

   b. What he doesn't seem to understand is that money doesn't grow on trees.

   c. What Melvin proved is that there is a proof of every set of proofs.

Here what is crucial is the sequence after the main verb *be*. While the overall derivation of these sentences is unclear, complex, and controversial, one thing seems evident, as with the sequences operated on by RNR. Namely, the post-*be* sequence is a constituent in derived structure.

  Compare (95), on the one hand, with (96), on the other.

(95) a. What I believe is that Bill is intelligent.

   b. What Harry proved is that Tony was a Venusian.

   c. What Joan found was that Barbara was pregnant again.

(96) a. *What I believe is Bill to be intelligent.

   b. *What Harry proved is Tony to be a Venusian.

   c. *What Joan found was Barbara to be pregnant again.

---

this anti-Raising conclusion is unjustified. For the same pattern exists even with a verb like *promise*:

(viii) a. I promised Bob to leave and Sally to stay.

    b. Joan promised me to come early and you to come late.

But here it is out of the question to regard sequences like *Sally to stay* as representing the realization of underlying complement clauses, since the actual subject of *stay* is a coreferent of *I*, deleted by Equi, with *Sally* the indirect object of the deleted occurrence of *promise*. I conclude, therefore, that if such sequences as *Sally to stay* in (viii)a or *Marsha to be Polish* in (vii)a are actually derived constituents, the constituent they represent is that corresponding, not to the complement of the second clause, but to the whole second clause. Thus for (vii)a, *Marsha to be Polish* would be the remnant of the underlying constituent *I believe Marsha to be Polish*, while for (viii)a *Sally to stay* would be the remnant of the underlying *I promised Sally (I to stay)*. Undoubtedly, Gapping is involved in such derivations, but it apparently combines in mysterious ways with other processes capable of reducing coordinate structures.

That is, pseudocleft sentences can be based on B-verb complements only when these are *that* clauses, not when they are infinitival. Under the Raising analysis of B-verb infinitival complements, this can be taken to follow automatically from the fact that under such an analysis in examples like (97) the italicized string of elements does not form a derived constituent, a direct consequence of the deformation produced by Raising.

(97) I believe *Bill to be intelligent.*

Under a conception like Chomsky's, however, the external structures of the two types of complement in (95) and (96) do not differ, and the contrast between them is unexplained.

Similar to the previous two arguments, questions of complementizers arise again. As discussed in footnotes 35 and 39 for the relevant contexts of those arguments, the *that* is not deletable in examples like (95):

(98) a. *What I believe is Bill is intelligent.

b. *What Harry proved is Tony was a Venusian.

c. *What Joan found was Barbara was pregnant again.

Again, however, I attribute this to the same condition blocking *that* deletion when the *that* clause does not immediately follow the verb of which it is the complement.[40] Examples like the following show that a complementizer is not uniformly required for clauses in the position of the pseudoclefts in (98):

(99) a. What I resented most was there being no beer.

b. What I am in favor of is Nixon being shipped to Pakistan.

c. What I hate is to miss obscenity trials.

Therefore, the contrast between examples like (96) and sentences such as (100) favors Raising.

(100) a. What I arranged (for) was for Bob to come in last.

b. What I prayed for was for Sally to return.

---

[40] That is, I assume that underlying (98)a, for example, is something like this:

(i) [the thing which I believe is *I believe* that Bill is intelligent]

Deletion of the italicized material then blocks *that* deletion, as in the RNR and Gapping cases. Evidently, this restriction on deletion is sensitive to surface structure, at least in a system with no extrinsic rule-ordering statements.

Note also example (101):

(101) a.   I would prefer Bob to win.

     b.   I would prefer for Bob to win.

     c. *What I would prefer is Bob to win.

     d.   What I would prefer is for Bob to win.

Here the contrast can be naturally explained by recognizing Raising application in (101)a, its absence in (101)b, as in several earlier cases of *prefer NP, prefer for NP* contrasts. See Section 4.16.

4.11 Adverbs I

Throughout Chapter 4 of this book, I have been searching for properties of English sentences which distinguish B-verb infinitival and *that*-clause complements in such a way as to bear on the existence of B-verb Raising. The behavior of adverbs offers several possible lines of comparison in this regard, which will be treated in this section and the following one.

Consider first the contrasts given in (102):

(102) a.   I believe very strongly that Tony is honest.

     b. *I believe very strongly Tony to be honest.

These illustrate the point that a B-verb can be separated from a following *that* clause by an interpolated adverb, but not from a following NP + infinitive. This is a general principle:

(103) a.   Jack proved quite easily that Tony was on hash.

     b. *Jack proved quite easily Tony to be on hash.

(104) a.   They found recently that the money was missing.

     b. *They found recently the money to be missing.

The question then arises as to how the grammar of English imposes these different characteristics on the constructions in question. Within a Raising system, an answer seems to be naturally available. It is a quite general fact about English that elements cannot be interpolated between a verb and its directly following object NP (direct, or indirect):[41]

---

[41] It will appear, because of examples like (i) and (ii), that the constraint holds only for "short" NPs.

(105) a. *I proved easily $\left\{\begin{array}{l}\text{that}\\\text{your theorem}\\\text{the results}\end{array}\right\}$.

b. *I love very much $\left\{\begin{array}{l}\text{her}\\\text{Sally}\\\text{my mother}\\\text{everyone}\end{array}\right\}$.

(106) *I handed slowly $\left\{\begin{array}{l}\text{Jane}\\\text{her}\\\text{your dog}\\\text{someone}\end{array}\right\}$ the apple.

But in a Raising analysis the former complement clause subjects have become main clause objects. Thus, in such terms, examples like (102)b, (103)b, and (104)b have an object NP separated from its verb by an interpolated adverb, just as (105) and (106) do. Thus it appears that in a Raising system the constraint operative in (105) and (106) also suffices to block (102)b, etc. Nothing extra appears to be needed to deal with the B-verb infinitival interpolation examples.

It seems, then, that in a Raising system all is handled by the independently needed condition (107), however this is to be formulated precisely.

(107) *Verb X ($\neq \emptyset$) object NP.

This is not the case, though. For, given (107) and structures in which *that* clauses are NPs as well as Ss, all examples like (102), with interpolated adverbs before *that* clauses, would be marked as ill-formed by (107). Something is wrong. The problem here is, I claim, essentially that noted in footnote 41.

There seems to be a class of exceptions to (107) when the object NP in question is "long" or "heavy" in some sense that is difficult to specify.

(i) I just proved easily the theorem which I had formerly struggled with for hours.

(ii) I love very much the old woman who visited me in the orphanage.

This point is discussed in the text later, where this formulation is rejected.

(108) a. *I loved very much $\left\{ \begin{array}{l} \text{her} \\ \text{Joan} \\ \text{everyone} \end{array} \right\}$.

　　 b. I loved very much $\left\{ \begin{array}{l} \text{the woman who came to see me} \\ \text{all of the children who I offered to adopt} \\ \text{most of the people in my class} \end{array} \right\}$.

It might seem, then, that one must reformulate (107) at the least to take account of the difference between "short" and "heavy" NPs. There is, however, an alternative, which I claim is correct. Namely, let us reformulate (107), to be sure, but not in a way which refers to "heaviness." Rather, let us reformulate it to guarantee that the verb and object NP *are sister constituents*. Hence, we have (109). If this is done,[42] one can then explain the contrast between pairs like (108)a, b in terms of the

(109)

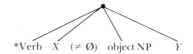

*Verb　X　(≠ Ø)　object NP　　Y

[42] Principle (109), suitably refined, may yield an interesting argument for the view that auxiliaries *do, will, can*, etc., are members of the same category of verb as *smell, punch, believe*, etc., and not members of some distinct category, as in the line of work initiated by Chomsky (1957). A modification of (109) so that it is not restricted to object NPs could also correctly predict the impossibility of interpolating an element between an initial verb, auxiliary or not, and its following *subject* NP in cases where independent conditions prevent subject fronting. Hence, we have the following:

(i) *Will, do you think, the man there win easily?

(ii) *Did slowly Bob hand over the gun?

(iii) *Under no conditions should now you retire.

In particular, note the parallelism between the preceding cases, where the verbal is an auxiliary, and such cases as the following, with parenthetical clauses:

(iv) a. John is, said Pete to Sally, going to lose.
　　 b. *John is, said slowly Pete to Sally, going to lose.

(v) a. Are you, asked Bob recently, going to retire?
　 b. *Are you, asked recently Bob, going to retire?

This argument is developed in Postal (to appear e).

operation of Complex NP Shift, discussed in Section 4.1. The immediate virtue of this method is that it explains why the notion of "shortness" or "heaviness" relevant to such pairs is exactly that relevant for Complex NP Shift.

What I am proposing, then, is that while sentences like (108)a have the derived structure shown in (110), those like (108)b have the derived structure shown in (111) under the assumption that Complex NP Shift

(110)

(111)

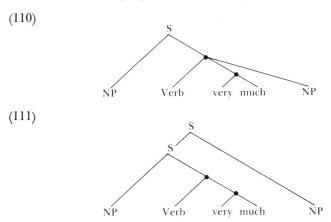

operates by Chomsky adjunction, creating a new S node above the original. The structure in (110) is subject to condition (109), but that in (111), which follows from the Complex NP Shift operation, is not. This requires, of course, the claim for sentences like (108)b that Complex NP Shift has operated "vacuously" from the point of view of the terminal string. A further virtue of this analysis, and a piece of evidence for it, is that the intonation of such sentences seems to be that expected under Complex NP Shift derivation, that is, with an intonation break before the final NP.[43]

---

[43] Perlmutter points out that there is a sharp contrast in the intonation contours of pairs like (i), with (i)a having sustained intonation at the point of the dash and (i)b having a falling contour corresponding to the comma.

(i) a. I believe to be very clever—the author who is being interviewed today.
   b. He is very clever, the author who is being interviewed today.

This is true even though both sentences would have a derived structure of the form shown in (ii), under the assumption that Complex NP Shift operates by Chomsky adjunction.

Other more striking evidence is available, however. It is a consequence of the Complex NP Shift plus condition (109) theory of sentences like (108) that even the necessary "heaviness" of an NP will not save the structure if there is following material aligned in such a way as to indicate that Complex NP Shift could not have applied. And such examples exist. We expect (112)b to be wrong because it has an adverb interpolated between a verb and its sister object NP, which is short:

(112) a.   I handed her the book.

b. *I handed slowly her the book.

Crucially though, and just as the Complex NP Shift account of the (108) type examples predicts, well-formedness is unattainable by replacing *her* by a "heavy" NP:

(113) a. *I handed slowly the woman who came to see me the book which she wanted.[44]

b. *I handed slowly the tall, dark, beautiful nurse who Tony had married the poison-dipped blade which she had so passionately requested.

Such facts would be directly inconsistent with a formulation of the no-interpolation constraint that made direct reference to the "heaviness"

(ii)

An explanation for the contrast would lie, I believe, in the fact that in cases like (i)b, the initial clause is complete in an intuitively obvious sense, the final element serving only to identify further the subject NP. In (i)a, however, the structure before the dash is incomplete. One correlate of this contrast is that the precomma sequence in (i)b can be an independent sentence, but the predash sequence in (i)a cannot be. The latter turns out to be quite a crucial fact about Complex NP Shift derivations, as noted in footnote 3, and discussed further in Section 12.5.

44 It is necessary for the direct object NP here to be complex, as it is, to eliminate any possibility of attributing the ill-formedness to the constraint independent of adverb interpolation, which operates in (i):

(i) I handed the woman who came to see me $\begin{Bmatrix} \text{*it} \\ \text{*everything} \\ \text{?*the book} \end{Bmatrix}$.

of the object NP. Such examples show that the constraint on interpolation is absolute, not relative to "heaviness." What is relative to the latter property is the legality of applying Complex NP Shift.[45]

Let us return now to examples like (102)a and (103)a, which were,
as we saw, incorrectly predicted to be ill-formed by a constraint like
(107). We have now, in effect, solved that problem. Such sentences are
well-formed in this analysis because *that* clauses, being NPs, are subject

[45] The need for a Complex NP Shift analysis of apparent exceptions to a principle
like (109) is argued in detail in Ross (to appear d) on the basis of a general theory
of "niching," referring to points where elements can be interpolated in tree structures.

There is an apparent difficulty in claiming that *that* clauses undergo Complex NP
Shift, derivable as follows. Sentences like (i) are ill-formed:

(i) *I believe that Bob knows French to be likely.

But this is expected because they have in some sense an "internal" *that* clause, which
(as noted first in Ross, 1967, and also in Kuno, to appear a) is not permitted. So (i) is
ill-formed for the same reason as (ii) is:

(ii) *Did that Martha lost worry you?

However, since *that Bob knows French* is an NP in our terms and is subject to Complex NP Shift, we expect (iv) to be grammatical, just as (iii) is:

(iii) I believe (to be) likely to occur—all of the events which you talked about.

(iv) *I believe (to be) likely—that Bob knows French.

But this expectation is frustrated; in fact, there are, as far as I have been able to
determine, no cases where a *that* clause may successfully be postposed from the
object position of a B-verb by Complex NP Shift. At first glance, this fact seems to
offer some support to those, like Emonds (1970) and Chomsky, who would deny the
NP status of *that* clauses in "Deep Structure," granting it at best only to those which
have replaced it in the course of derivations. (But see Section 12.4.) However, this
conclusion is unwarranted. For, although these authors dispute the NP status of
that clauses, and infinitive clauses, they stress the NP status of gerundive clauses,
which is not, as far as I know, disputed by anyone.

However, the constraint illustrated in (iv) is paralleled by (v):

(v) a. I believe Joan's insulting the mayor to have been discussed by the committee.
    b. *I believe to have been discussed by the committee—Joan's insulting the mayor.

And it is equally general that no gerundive NP can be successfully postposed from
between a B-verb and an infinitive by Complex NP Shift. Therefore, under the
assumption that *that* clauses are NPs, the ill-formedness of (iv) would follow from
the independently needed (by everyone) constraint on clausal NPs illustrated by (v)b.
Violations like (iv) can thus lend no comfort to enemies of the NP status of *that*
clauses.

to Complex NP Shift. Hence, an example like (102)a has the derived structure shown in (114), which does not come under the scope of principle (109).[46]

(114)

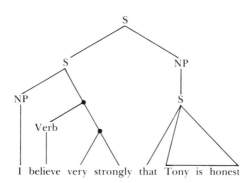

It follows that a Raising analysis, combined with the independently needed principle (109) and Complex NP Shift, automatically accounts for contrasts like (102) and (103). This provides, naturally, a very strong argument for B-verb Raising. The more so because a non-Raising analysis cannot make use of principle (109) to block examples like (102)b and (103)b. For in such a system, the postadverbial NP is not an object, that is, a sister, of the main verb at any point, this crucial structure being assigned only in Raising systems.

One reader (personal communication) has argued, however (on the basis, to be sure, of the essentially undeveloped version of the preceding argument found in an unpublished note of mine),[47] that the virtues of Raising in this regard are illusory. His key observation is that sentences like (102)a and (103)a become as ill-formed, probably, as (102)b and (103)b, if the *that* is removed:

(115) a. *I believe very strongly Tony is honest.

   b. *Jack proved quite easily Tony was on hash.

   c. *They found recently the money was missing.

---

[46] It hardly needs stressing that the argument here provides grounds for rejecting Chomsky's assumption, in accord with Emonds (1970), that *that* clauses are not NPs. See Section 12.4.

[47] Entitled "More on Raising," a sequel to an earlier, also unpublished, note entitled "Arguments for Raising in Random Order."

This was a point overlooked in my note. This reader tentatively suggests that what is wrong with examples like those of (115) as well as (102)b, (103)b, and (104)b is that the position indicated in (116) blocks interpolation, where the NP is "short," regardless of whether the NP is object of the verb or not.

(116) Verb _____ NP.

(It is not, of course, in Chomsky's non-Raising system for examples like (102)b.)

This proposal, which offers hope of saving the non-Raising position from otherwise unexplained contrasts like (102) and (103), cannot, however, be sustained. As should be clear from previous discussion in the sections dealing with RNR, Gapping, and pseudocleft sentences, I claim that what is wrong with examples like (115) is simply that the marker *that* has been elided when the *that* clause is not directly postverbal in surface structure. Nothing new need be said beyond the conditions on *that* deletion required anyway.

As to this reader's suggestion, which differs from (107) in that he explicitly rejects a condition that the NP be an object of the verb (to cover the cases handled by Raising), evidence has already been provided that it cannot stand. Namely, examples like (113) show that a pure output condition like this reader's, which refers to "shortness" and is independent of Complex NP Shift, is inadequate.

More interesting counterevidence is available. The offered suggestion claims that an example like (102)b, repeated here as (117), is ill-formed because it has an adverb interpolated between a verb and a "short" NP.

(117) *I believe very strongly Tony to be honest.

This claims that a well-formed sentence results if one replaces *Tony* by an appropriately "heavy" NP. But this is not the case:

(118) a. *I believe very strongly the man who I met yesterday in the submarine to be honest.
      b. *I believe very strongly all of the nurses who Tony says he has made love to twice to be pregnant.

If anything, "heavy" NPs make these sentences worse. The properties of (118), which are the rule for B-verb infinitivals, follow from principle

(109) plus a Raising grammar for B-verb infinitival clauses. For no matter how long or complex the relevant NPs become in such a grammar, they remain derived objects of *believe* and hence under the domain of (109). Complex NP Shift is irrelevant to (118), because it has demonstrably not applied. If it does apply, the NPs in question are, of course, moved past the infinitive, yielding, as expected, well-formed sentences of no particular relevance:

(119) I believe very strongly to be honest—the man who I met yesterday in the submarine.

These facts provide, I think, sufficient refutation of this proposal.

However, further counterevidence is available. In particular, a constraint like (116), which indiscriminately lumps subjects and objects together, is in conflict with the general well-formedness of examples like the following:

(120) a. I resent very much your kicking my dog.

b. I liked very much his refusing to be cowed.

c. I have watched very closely his lying and cheating.

If, moreover, it is proposed that an ad hoc limitation on (116) be made to specify that the NPs be nongenitive, this can be shown to fail in both directions. That is, some cases with genitives must be marked as ill-formed, and some gerundive cases without genitives must escape. As to the former, we have (121)a, b; as to the latter, observe (121)c, d, e:

(121) a.   I like his.

b. *I like very much his.

c.   I resent very much there being no more beer.

d.   They resented very strongly it being too late to buy more.

e.   We all resented very strongly Sally behaving like an autocrat.

Compare in particular (121)c with (122):

(122) *I believe very strongly there to be no more beer.

The point about *resent,* of course (see footnote 16), is that it does not trigger Raising but simply permits loss of the genitive from the subject of its gerundive complement in certain cases. Hence (121)c could never come under the scope of (109), in contrast to (122). But an account like the anonymous reader's fails to distinguish them.

In particular, what has been refuted is the suggestion that examples like (115) are ill-formed for the same reason as those like (102)b, namely, that both violate a simple constraint on interpolation between verb and short NP. I claim it is simply a misleading accident that both (115) and (102)b are ill-formed. As further evidence of the independence of the ill-formedness of the former from any considerations having to do with a constraint like (116), note the following. Just as (116) predicts falsely that examples like (118), containing complex NPs where (102)b has a short one, should be well-formed, it also predicts falsely that the same substitution on (115) yields well-formed results:

(123) a. *I believe very strongly the man who I met yesterday in the submarine is honest.

b. *I believe very strongly all of the nurses who Tony says he has made love to twice are pregnant.

Again, though, ungrammaticality like (123) follows from the analysis advocated here, which attributes the ill-formedness of examples like (115) to deletion of *that* from a *that* clause that is not directly post-verbal, an explanation that holds for sentences like (123) as well as for (115).

I conclude that contrasts like those between (102)a and (102)b, (103)a and (103)b, (121)c and (122) are so far completely unexplained in any system that has no rule of Raising operating in B-verb infinitival complements. Examples like (115), originally overlooked, turn out to be irrelevant. A Raising analysis correctly explains the basic facts discussed here in conjunction with independently motivated features of the grammar, like principle (109). The conclusion follows that the interaction of adverb interpolation with B-verb constructions provides at once strong confirmation of a Raising system and strong refutation of non-Raising grammars.

It is worth noting that the behavior of adverbs documented here is essentially paralleled by emphatic reflexives:

(124) a. John believes himself that the world is ending.

b. *John believes himself the world to be ending.

c. *John believes himself the world is ending.

The same comments hold, of course. Recall that principle (109) does not mention adverbs per se, and hence is as applicable to (124)b, given B-verb Raising, as to (102)b. Example (124)c is ill-formed for the same reason that (115) is. And parallels like (125)a, b are accounted for.

(125) a. *Harry proved himself the formula.

   b. *Harry proved himself the formula to be a theorem.

Similarly, nonparallels like (125)c, d are automatic, since, for instance, (125)c is well-formed because its NP has undergone Complex NP Shift, while if this is applied to the parallel NP in (125)d the result is not (125)d but (126).

(125) c. Harry proved himself—the formula which you were interested in yesterday.

   d. *Harry proved himself the formula which you were interested in yesterday to be a theorem.

(126) *Harry proved himself to be a theorem—the formula which you were interested in yesterday.

This is ill-formed. But the reason seems intuitively obvious and is related, I think, to the constraint discussed in footnote 3 and in Section 12.5. That is, in (126) the operation of Complex NP Shift has left an initial clause that looks as though it had been independently derived in the grammar. However, unlike those cases briefly touched on in footnote 3, which involved mostly overlaps that were a function of Equi, the overlap in (126) involves Complex NP Shift and Raising.[48]

Basically, though, the facts of emphatic reflexive distribution follow equally well from the Raising analysis suggested here, and thus add further support for this analysis. This is not surprising because, given (109) and a Raising grammar, it is predicted that any process that shifts elements after a verb will come to grief in B-verb infinitivals because of (109) and the derived object structure produced by Raising. Thus we have the following:

[48] Baker observes that examples like (i) are also ill-formed, possibly providing an additional basis for the ungrammaticality of those like (126).

(i) *Harry proved the formula which you were interested in yesterday himself to be a theorem.

(127) a. Tom believes, he said, that Melvin is a Martian.

b. *Tom believes, he said, Melvin to be a Martian.

(128) a. Tom believes, or at least I think he believes, that Melvin is a Martian.

b. *Tom believes, or at least I think he believes, Melvin to be a Martian.

(129) a. Tom believes, if I am not mistaken, that Melvin is a Martian.

b. *Tom believes, if I am not mistaken, Melvin to be a Martian.

I have assumed in this discussion the adequacy of (109) as a formulation of the ban on interpolating elements between verbs and objects. Later, in Section 8.2, I consider some evidence suggesting that (109) may be only one component of what is, in fact, a global constraint. This matter has, however, no bearing on the argument of the present section, as far as I can see.[49]

[49] One difficulty with (109) which does require comment has been pointed out by Perlmutter. He observes that, as is, this principle would apparently block double object sentences like (i), since these have the structure shown in (ii), with *Arthur* and *the girls* erroneously in the X position.

(i) a. I gave Arthur an apple.
   b. Jim bought the girls necklaces.

(ii)

     Verb   X ($= $ NP and hence $\neq \emptyset$)   object NP

There are various ad hoc moves one could make to handle this situation, by specifying, for instance, that interpolation is not blocked for NPs, but only for adverbs, parentheticals, etc. This is pretty clearly unsatisfactory, however. My approach to this problem is to stress that the notion of object NP in principle (109) must be taken literally. And I deny that *an apple* and *necklaces* are objects of verbs in sentences like (i). The basis of this claim would be the assumption that such sentences are derived from underlying representations of the form (iii), in which the italicized NPs are the direct objects of the verbs.

(iii) a. I gave *an apple* to Arthur.
   b. Jim bought *necklaces* for the girls.

Sentences like (ii) are then derived by a rule called Dative Movement. This rule has the function of taking the objects of *to* and making them the direct objects of the

4.12 Adverbs II

The argument of this section is due to Kuno (1972b). In the previous section, I considered contrasts between B-verb infinitival and *that*-clause complements having to do with placing adverbs and parenthetical elements after the main verb. Here I shall be considering the properties of sentences in which such elements are inserted after the underlying complement subject NP. Thus of interest will be such pairs as the following:

(130) a. *Jane believes that Bob, if I am not mistaken, is Hungarian.

   b. Jane believes Bob, if I am not mistaken, to be Hungarian.

(131) a. Jane proved that Bob, unfortunately, was a werewolf.

   b. Jane proved Bob, unfortunately, to be a werewolf.

In (130) there is a contrast in grammaticality, in (131) a contrast in meaning. The word *unfortunately* in (131)b "modifies" the main clause. Hence (131)b means that it is unfortunate that Jane proved what she did prove. In (131)a, however, *unfortunately* "modifies" *was a werewolf*. Such contrasts seem general:

(132) a. I believed that Nixon, incorrectly, was interested in ending the war.

   b. I believed Nixon, incorrectly, to be interested in ending the war.

Example (132)b refers to an incorrect belief on the part of the speaker, (132)a to an incorrect interest on Nixon's part. Similarly:

(133) a. I have found that Bob recently has been morose.

   b. I have found Bob recently to be morose.

Example (133)a refers to recent moroseness, (133)b either to that or to a recent finding. Thus the following is conceivable:

---

relevant verbs. I assume that when this happens, there is a general principle guaranteeing that the former direct objects cease to bear any relations at all. Hence, I suggest that the proper formulation of (109) will involve direct reference to grammatical relations, including the substantive assumptions just outlined. For an introduction to a theory of grammar in which grammatical relations play the kind of role assumed here, see Section 8.4 and Perlmutter and Postal (to appear a, to appear b).

(134) ?Somebody found Germany recently to have been relatively justi-
     fied in the *Lusitania* sinking.

But never:

(135) *Somebody found that Germany was recently justified in the
     Lusitania sinking.

Other examples follow:

(136) a. I can prove that Bob easily outweighed Martha's goat.

     b. I can prove Bob easily to have outweighed Martha's goat.

Here again, in the infinitival case, the adverb can be ambiguously construed as "modifying" either the main clause or just the complement.
But in the *that*-clause case, it can be construed only as modifying the
complement.

   How shall the grammar of English account for these differences? In
a Raising system, a natural answer would be available along the following lines. "Sentential" adverbs can be placed at various points in a sentence subject to constraints that include this principle:

(137) A "sentential" adverb can*not* be inserted in a complement clause.

Thus (137) would permit insertion of main clause "sentential" adverbs
between the immediate constituents of the main clause but not in positions inside complement sentences. Since Raising guarantees that the
former complement subject NP becomes a constituent of the main
clause, "sentential" adverbs could be placed after the raised NP without
violating (137). But placement of such an adverb after the subject of a
that clause, which is not raised, necessarily violates (137).

   It is not clear at all what an advocate of a non-Raising system would
suggest instead of (137). Suppose, given what we know of Chomsky's
particular account of non-B-verb Raising grammar, that (138) is suggested instead:

(138) A "sentential" adverb cannot be inserted in a *tensed* complement
     clause.

This would also correctly distinguish the contrasting pairs considered
so far.

   However, unlike (137), (138) fails to account for the fact that "sentential" adverbs are never insertable within those nontensed clauses which are not analyzable as cases of Raising application in a Raising grammar:

(139) a. I recently arranged for Bob to meet my niece.

b. I arranged for Bob recently to meet my niece.

c. I arranged for Bob to recently meet my niece.

(140) a. John, unfortunately, is hard for me to deal with.

b. *John is hard for me, unfortunately, to deal with.

In particular, note the contrast with the verb *prefer*:

(141) a. *Harry would prefer for Bob, unfortunately, to marry Sheila.

b. Harry would prefer Bob, unfortunately, to marry Sheila.

And also consider (142), where *recently* can go only with the complement.

(142) I resented it recently happening to me.

There are, in fact, no independently specifiable cases where an adverb inside a complement clause is construable as "modifying" the main clause. Hence the fact that a non-Raising system requires just this possibility to handle examples with B-verbs shows that non-Raising systems miss the generalization embodied in (137), which cannot correctly be *weakened* to (138).

There is at least one class of cases that might be taken as counterexamples to the claim just made, those in which one might argue that a "sentential" adverb is inside a complement clause but construed with the main clause. I refer to such examples as (143):

(143) a. It is important for us, unfortunately, to visit Tony.

b. It would be impossible for them, regrettably, to have survived.

c. It was possible for me, thank God, to reach the ladder.

Here one might claim that there are complements of this form:

(144) [$_S$ for NP, "sentential" adverb, to + Verb Phrase$_S$]

This structure would directly falsify (137), since in each example the "sentential" adverb is construed with the main clause.

However, I claim that the structure (144) for sentences like (143) is incorrect. The issue is complicated a bit because sentences like the following, *without adverbs,* do have structures parallel to (144):

(145) a. It is important for us to visit Tony.

b. It would be impossible for them to have survived.

c. It was possible for me to reach the ladder.

But I believe that these also have a distinct structure, in which the bracketing is, instead, as shown in (146):

(146) It is important for us [to [   ]].

Thus my claim is that, while examples like (145) are structurally ambiguous, with the *for* phrase either an immediate constituent of the complement clause or not, sentences like (143) are not ambiguous in this way and have only the structure in which the *for* phrase is not part of the complement.

As an indication of the ambiguity of examples like (145), they have at least two possible intonational divisions, that is, either like (147) or like (148), with a sharp break after the adjective or after the *for* phrase.

(147) It is A—for . . .

(148) It is A for NP—to . . .

The key issue is what evidence is available to argue that cases like (143) have *only* the structure of (148).

First, if, contrary to my claim, structure (144) were an accurate analysis of (143), then the sequences *for* . . . would be (S) constituents. Observe, then, that parenthetical sequences can be placed between adjectives like *important* or *impossible* and following S constituents:

(149) a. It is important, I assume, for us to arrive on time.

b. It is impossible, you realize, for most men to run four-minute miles.

On the other hand, such parentheticals are *not* permitted between such adjectives and *for* prepositional phrases:

(150) a. *That is important, I assume, for us.

b. *Doing that would be impossible, you realize, for him.

At least this is so where the NP head of the prepositional phrase is "short" (in the sense relevant for Complex NP Shift).

Therefore, if (144) provides a valid analysis of (143), we should expect to be able to find the analogues to (143) with parentheticals after the adjectives. However, this is impossible:

(151) a. *It is important, I assume, for us, unfortunately, to visit Tony.

　　b. *It would be impossible, you realize, for them, regrettably, to have survived.

Under the suggested analysis of such examples, in which sentence adverbs like *unfortunately* and *regrettably* cannot occur in complements, the *for* phrases in (151) are part of the main clause; hence, the structures in (151) are in relevant respects like those in (150) and are ill-formed for the same reason. The contrast between (149) and (150) then confirms the view that the sentence adverbs in examples like (143) are not complement-internal.

A second argument for the nonsubject status of the *for* phrases in examples like (143) can be based on the following fact. When sentences like (143), but with the sentence adverbs missing, have the reading in which *for* + NP is not part of the complement, the sentences have meanings in which the property defined by the adjective is attributed to the entity dominated by the NP following *for*. In certain cases, particularly for *important,* it is a consequence of the meaning that this NP designate a mind-possessing entity, that the NP be, in other words, what has traditionally but rather misleadingly been designated "animate." For the other reading, the property is not attributed to the entity designated by the NP following *for*.

However, while one can find both (152)a and (152)b, there is a sharp contrast when the post-*for* NP does not designate a mind-possessing entity, as shown in (153):

(152) a. It is important for John to be investigated.

　　b. It is important for John, unfortunately, to be investigated.

(153) It is important for $\left\{\begin{array}{l}\text{your suggestion}\\\text{this analysis}\\\text{that mercury}\end{array}\right\}$ *(, unfortunately,) to be investigated.

This is inexplicable if one fails to recognize an ambiguous structure for sentences like (152)a. But it follows naturally from this assumption plus the claim that interpolated adverbs are possibly only on one term of the ambiguity, namely, the one in which the *for* phrase is associated with the main clause, and not the complement. Because the latter analysis requires a meaning in which what is important is important to the entity designated by the post-*for* NP. And this must yield an anomaly if this NP designates something without (by assumption)[50] a mind. Contrasts like those in (153) thus show further that the *for* phrases in examples like (143) are not parts of complements. Baker notes the existence of examples like (154)a, which should be contrasted with (154)b:

(154) a.   To be investigated is important for John.

     b.   *To be investigated is important for that analysis.

These show further that the adjective *important* occurs with its own *for*-phrase NP, which must designate an entity with a mind.

    Other arguments are also available for the analysis required to preserve principle (137). Thus, in Sections 4.2 and 4.3 it was observed that *not*-initial and *alone*-final NPs can occur only in subject positions. So if the claim about examples like (143) made here is correct, interpolated adverbs will be impossible where the post-*for* NP is a *not*-initial or an *alone*-final NP. And this is true.

(155) a.   It is important for not many of us to be arrested on the first day.

     b.   *It is important for not many of us, unfortunately, to be arrested on the first day.

     c.   It is important for Bob alone to be arrested on the first day.

     d.   *It is important for Bob alone, unfortunately, to be arrested on the first day.

---

[50] That is, as usual with "selectional restrictions," these are dependent on speaker assumption. Hence, in cases like fairy tales, where one is willing to impute minds to odd things, the relevant sentences will be all right:

(i) It was important for the little engine, unfortunately, to get the toys over the hill.

This is acceptable, I claim, only when *the little engine* designates a mind in a railroad suit.

Furthermore, the fact that RNR, discussed in Section 4.8, can deal only with constituents indicates that sentences like (143) do not have complements beginning with *for*:

(156) a. It is possible for Bob to meet Sally, but it would be unwise for Bob (him) to meet Sally.

b. It is possible—but it would be unwise—for Bob to meet Sally.

c. It is possible for Bob, fortunately, to meet Sally, but it would be unwise for Bob (him), fortunately, to meet Sally.

d. *It is possible—but it would be unwise—for Bob, fortunately, to meet Sally.

Example (156)c is a bit strained, but it has nothing of the completely impossible character of (156)d. The latter thus requires a special explanation, which is provided (given our knowledge that RNR obeys at least a constituent condition) by the fact that, with interpolated adverbs, sequences of the form *for NP, adverb* . . . are not complement clauses and not even constituents.

Finally, if, contrary to what I have been arguing here, the bracketed sequence in (157)a had the same possibility of being a clause constituent as that in (157)b, then what could account for the contrast in (157)c and (157)d?

(157) a. It is important [for Bob, unfortunately, to defeat Lou].

b. It is important [for Bob to defeat Lou].

c. *For Bob, unfortunately, to defeat Lou is important.

d. For Bob to defeat Lou is important.

That is, in a context like (157)c, d, where the sequence *for* . . . must be a full clause, the adverb is impossible, just as the analysis that denies the clausehood of the bracketed sequence in (157)a predicts.[51]

---

[51] It is worth noting that some of the adjectives under discussion can occur with *that* clauses, and, more significantly, these cooccur with *for* phrases:

(i) It is important for our country that electricity consumption be reduced.

It would thus follow that such elements must be allowed to occur with *for* phrases that are not part of complements. McCawley adds that there are also sentences like (ii), which make the point even more effectively.

(ii) It is important for me for you to visit my mother.

Sentences like (i) raise some problems for the claim that such noncomplement *for*

I take it as established, then, that interpolated adverbs are possible before infinitives of elements like *possible* and *important* only when any *for* phrase present is not part of the complement. Thus sentences like (143) provide no evidence at all contrary to principle (137).

Let us return now to the contrasts with which we began this section, namely, those like (131), repeated here as (158):

(158) a. Jane proved that Bob, unfortunately, was a werewolf.

   b. Jane proved Bob, unfortunately, to be a werewolf.

We can see here that Kuno's obervation that only the latter permits construal of the adverb with the main clause must—given principle (137), which has no known exceptions—serve as a strong argument in favor of a Raising grammar and against a non-Raising system like that suggested by Chomsky. For in the latter system, it is necessarily an unexplained exception that only the "subjects" of B-verb infinitival complements permit following adverbs to be interpreted as main clause modifiers. Such an analysis thus requires special statements to say this, while the facts are a direct consequence of the basic effect of Raising application, which is the reattachment of a complement clause constituent as part of the main clause.

Huddleston (1971: 160), however, raises the following difficulty:

There is thus strong syntactic evidence supporting the subject-raising rule, One thing it does not account for is the deviance of (xvii)a (in contrast to the well-formedness of b):

(xvii) a. *I expected John quite confidently to give the lecture
       b. I persuaded John quite easily to give the lecture

where the adverbs modify the matrix verbs, not *give*.

---

phrases must designate mind-possessing entities. Here I refer, not to cases like (i), where words like *country* reveal only a rather common feature of "institutional" nouns being treated as if they designated minds, as in (iii), but rather to sentences such as (iv):

(iii) The United States feels that bombing those countries is justifiable.

(iv) It is important for that theory that all carbon atoms be purple.

Such sentences in no way attribute any mind to the theory designated. I don't understand this, but it is possibly related to usages like those in (v), where *theory, article,* etc., occur in contexts typical of mind-designating NPs.

(v) a. This theory says that all carbon atoms are purple.

   b. This article $\left\{ \begin{matrix} \text{argues} \\ \text{tries to argue} \end{matrix} \right\}$ that Nixon is intelligent.

Although I agree with Huddleston's judgments, I do not consider this a serious problem. For it evidently involves some special feature of the adverbial expression chosen rather than of the B-verb plus NP context. This can be seen from the fact that the analogues of his (xvii)a are well-formed under the matrix verb "modification" reading when other adverbial expressions are substituted for *quite confidently*—in particular, *quite without reason, in spite of protests, with my usual false optimism,* etc. On the other hand, insertion of these words after *John* in the *that*-clause analogues of his (xvii)a fails completely, so that despite (xvii)a, *expect* behaves in accord with the Raising hypothesis.

I think there is some likelihood that principle (137) is an element of universal grammar, rather than a peculiarity of English. It is observed by Kuno (1972b) that a formally identical constraint operates in Japanese (see Section 12.2). If such a principle is a universal, then the argument for English Raising based on (137) is, of course, even stronger than our discussion has assumed.

4.13 Gerundive Complements

Chomsky's proposal to dispense with any operation of Raising into superordinate clause object position attempts to take advantage of the fact that infinitival complements of B-verbs, in surface word order at least, superficially have the structure of clauses. More than a dozen arguments that this is not really the case, however, have already been provided. These arguments show that the underlying clause structure of B-verb infinitival complements has been deformed by the raising of the subject NP, as the older analysis involving application of a Raising rule predicts.

Consider now such examples as (159), on the one hand, and those like (160), on the other:

(159) a. I prevented Jack from kissing the gorilla.

    b. They stopped him from embarking.

    c. She kept us from winning.

    d. They prohibited Jack from carrying weapons.

(160) a. I dissuaded Jack from kissing the gorilla.

    b. I deterred him from embarking.

c. We restrained her from jumping.

d. They discouraged me from taking that flight.

One finds with these verbs of "negative causation" (henceforth: N-verbs) superficial structures of this form:

(161) N-verb + NP + *from* + subjectless gerundive complement

However, there is rather immediately evident an important difference between the N-verbs in (159) and those in (160). Namely, the postverbal NP in (159) is quite free,[52] but that in (160) must designate a mind-possessing entity:

(162) a.   I prevented the bomb from going off.

b. *I $\begin{Bmatrix} \text{deterred} \\ \text{dissuaded} \\ \text{discouraged} \end{Bmatrix}$ the bomb from going off.

---

[52] Against this statement, Perlmutter points out to me that there are constraints on the verb *prohibit*, distinguishing it from *prevent*, *stop*, and *keep*. In particular, he observes the impossibility of such examples as the following:

(i) a. *They prohibited the bomb from going off.
   b. *They prohibited snow from falling.

It might appear, then, that *prohibit* acts like the verbs in (160) and that (i) is simply a special case of (162). This is not the case, however. The verbs in (160) require the immediately following NP to designate a mind-possessing entity. But *prohibit* does not.

(ii) a. *They dissuaded weapons from being carried.
    b. They prohibited weapons from being carried.

It seems that *prohibit* involves the weaker constraint that a mind-possessing entity somehow be involved in the (non)event referred to in its complement. Perlmutter suggests further that contrasts involving *prohibit* like (iii) are of the same order as those with *need* in (iv):

(iii) a. *They prohibited bombs from going off.
     b. They prohibited investigations from taking place.

(iv) a. *There needs to be an explosion.
    b. There needs to be an investigation.

This seems correct and gains substance from such contrasts as those in (v):

(v) a. *They prohibited explosions from taking place.
   b. They prohibited investigations from taking place.

Let us ignore this difference for the moment and concentrate on N-verbs of the (159) type. How should constructions like (159) be analyzed? My answer is that they are simply cases of the operation of Raising, parallel to application in the infinitival complements of B-verbs.[53] They are given schematically in (163). I shall turn to some arguments for this presently. But, first, a few points about the relation between sentences like (159) and Chomsky's proposals should be stressed.

Chomsky was able to suggest, in contrast to the facts for A-verbs, that B-verb sentences like (164) involve no raising operation because there is

(163) a.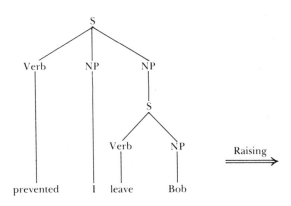

b.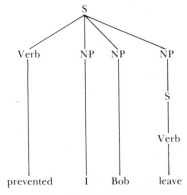

[53] This is oversimplified in crucial respects. In particular, I argue that at a deeper level *prevent* and N-verbs in general must at least have a structure containing separate elements CAUSE and NOT, ultimately combined by McCawley's (1970) rule of Predicate Raising. Hence there would be at least one further echelon of structure in the underlying representation of (163). See Chapter 11.

at least an outside possibility of claiming that *Bob to be unfaithful* is a surface clause.

(164) I believe Bob to be unfaithful.

This is possible since, as stressed earlier, in Section 2.2, the raising operation, if any, in such cases does not result in any morphemic material intervening between those constituents which were earlier immediate constituents of the underlying complement clause. In the case of N-verb complements, however, the situation in this regard is more nearly parallel to that with A-verbs. That is, with examples like (165) there seems to be no possibility of claiming that *Bob from leaving* is a surface clause.

(165) Jim prevented Bob from leaving.

The considerations that prevent such a conclusion are as follows. *First,* the word *from* is a preposition, and English verbal phrases do not, to say the least, customarily begin with prepositions. Nor, obviously, can one seriously claim that only in N-verb complements can English subject NPs end with prepositions. That is, it makes no sense to claim that *Bob from* is a subject NP in the derived structure of (165). Thus the claim that the post-N-verb NP is part of the complement clause in derived structure would require ad hoc patching statements of a transparent sort. *Second,* and more serious, the sequences in question, if surface clauses, would be constituents. But they do not meet the test of constituency with respect to a rule like RNR:

(166) a.   I wanted to prevent Bob from leaving, but I couldn't prevent Bob (him) from leaving.

   b. *I wanted to prevent—but I couldn't prevent—Bob from leaving.

   c.   Tony hopes to stop the bomb from going off, but only I can stop the bomb (it) from going off.

   d. *Tony hopes to stop—but only I can stop—the bomb from going off.

Third, post-N-verb NPs can undergo Complex NP Shift freely:

(167) a. I prevented from leaving—all of those men whose shirts were splattered with blood.

   b. We must keep from escaping—anyone who might convince the
   newspapers.

But, as shown in Section 4.1, subject NPs cannot undergo Complex NP
Shift. It follows that the post-N-verb NP is not a subject, hence not, in
derived structure, part of the complement clause.[54] It is evident, then,
that one cannot apply an analogue of Chomsky's analysis of B-verb infinitival complements to N-verb complements.

   This seems to leave two possible contenders for the correct analysis of
N-verb constructions like (159): a Raising analysis and an Equi analysis.
The latter would, in contrast to (163)a, take the structure of a sentence
like (168) to be of roughly the form shown in (169).

(168) I prevented Bob from leaving.

(169)

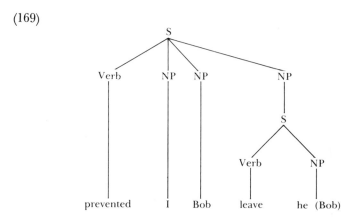

   That is, an Equi analysis would recognize such N-verbs as taking both
an underlying object NP and a complement, with the requirement that
the complement subject be a coreferent of the object NP. Such an analysis would treat these verbs in the same way as traditional analysis of
"positive causative" verbs like *force* and *persuade,* which have frequently been regarded as entering into underlying [Verb + NP + S]

---

[54] With regard to the unsuccessful argument of Section 4.5 concerning quantifier postposing, it is worth noting the ill-formedness of examples like (i) and (ii), which
might plausibly be taken to support the nonderived subject status of the post-N-verb
NP, again, no doubt, incorrectly.

(i) *I prevented the men each from leaving separately.

(ii) *They stopped the girls each from disrobing.

structures (see Rosenbaum, 1967; Chomsky, 1965: 22–23; 167: 148–153; Stockwell, Schachter, and Partee, 1968).

However, certain of the same sort of considerations that argue against an Equi analysis of A-verb constructions, as discussed in Section 2.2, likewise preclude such a treatment of N-verb constructions like those in (159) and (168). In particular, the directly post-N-verb position can be filled by many of those peculiar, limited-distribution NPs, like existential *there* and idiom chunks, which have traditionally been taken to support Raising analyses of A-verb constructions:

(170) a. He prevented there from being a riot.

   b. Harry kept tabs from being kept on Joan's movements.

   c. We must prevent any heed from being taken of his suggestions.

   d. Nobody can stop it from snowing in the Himalayas.

Earlier, it was argued that such NPs[55] preclude an Equi analysis in the case of A-verb sentences, and they do so here to the same degree. Thus

[55] Although such NPs can occur as the derived object NPs of N-verbs like *prevent*, and although *prevent* in general permits its object NPs to passivize, these NPs are unpassivizable:

(i) a. I prevented there from being a riot.
   b. I prevented tabs from being kept on Lucy.
   c. I prevented the wall from falling down.
   d. I prevented Harry from escaping.

(ii) a. *There was prevented from being a riot.
   b. *Tabs were prevented from being kept on Lucy.
   c. ?The wall was prevented from falling down.
   d. Harry was prevented from escaping.

These are a few facts out of dozens that make incomprehensible to me a statement like that of Chomsky (to appear: 2–3):

Thus the structural condition defining the [Passive] transformation can be given in the form (X, NP, V_x, NP, Y). The transformation rearranges the noun phrases in a fixed way. It will, therefore, apply to the phrase markers underlying the sentences of (1), converting them to the corresponding passive forms:

(1) (a) Perhaps—John—read—the book—intelligently
   (b) John—received—the book
   (c) John—regards—Bill—as a friend
   (d) John—painted—the wall—gray
   (e) John—expects—the food—to be good to eat

Evidently the semantic and grammatical relation of the main verb to the following noun phrase varies in these cases (there is no relation at all in (e)), but these relations are of no concern to the transformation, which *applies blindly in all cases* [emphasis mine], producing "perhaps the book was read intelligently by John", "the book was received by John", "Bill is regarded as a friend by John", "the wall was painted

an Equi analysis of sentences like (170)a of the form illustrated in (171) can be maintained in only two ways.

(171) He prevented there [$_s$there be a riot$_s$].

The first is by generating existential *there* as an object of N-verbs, when otherwise it is uniquely inserted by transformational rule as a derived subject of existential clauses. The second is by adding a unique deletion

---

gray by John", "the food is expected to be good to eat by John". By requiring that all transformations must be structure-dependent in this specific sense, we limit the class of possible grammars, excluding many imaginable systems.

But evidently the notion of "structure dependence," referred to by Chomsky here and in several other recent works in the same context of passivization (Chomsky, 1971, 1972), is obscure. Chomsky has picked a few examples that work properly under a "blind" application of a rule with the stated structure index. But there are many cases, of which (ii)a, b are only a tiny example, where it breaks down. Evidently, then, either Passive is not the "blind," purely "structure-dependent" rule that Chomsky indicates or, more likely, an attempt to make the latter precise would reduce its content to little more than the faith, surely shared by most of us, that ultimately it will be possible to state Passive and all other grammatical rules precisely.

A few further cases where "blindness" leads to error follow:

(iii) a. I prevented anyone from leaving.
   b. *Anyone was prevented from leaving by me.
   c. Jack drives a truck for a living.
   d. *A truck is driven by Jack for a living. } (contrast noted by John Lawler)
   e. You remind me of Bob in the way you talk.
   f. *I am reminded of Bob in the way you talk by you.
   g. Joan wants Bob to leave.
   h. *Bob is wanted to leave by Joan.
   i. I love you next to me.
   j. *You are loved next to me by me.

In fact, for me at least, one of Chomsky's own examples of a "blindly" produced passive is ill-formed, namely, "the food is expected to be good to eat by John," since I get at best only "the food is expected by John to be good to eat." An hour's work would, no doubt, provide several hundred other such cases, which prove simply that we do not know how to correctly constrain the derivations involving Passive. Any talk of its being a "blind" operation on phrase markers defined exclusively in terms of superficial categories like verb and NP must, if interpreted literally, be grotesquely inaccurate and, if interpreted in some other way, a mere smokescreen to cover up the lack of justification for any division of phenomena into those governed by "blind" transformations and others not so governed. Among other issues involved in this question of "blind" transformations is, of course, the question of whether there is an "autonomous" syntax free of semantic reference. The very area of passivization chosen by Chomsky as a model of this situation appears to argue against such a thing, since many of the violations in (iii), such as (iii)d, seem to involve semantic restrictions on passivization.

rule of a type (noncoreference) otherwise unknown.[56] That is, as stressed in Section 2.2, the rule that can turn (171) into (170)a could not be Equi, requiring stipulated coreference, which is meaningless in cases like (170)a, but some new creation. The term "Equi analysis" is thus a misnomer. Analogues of the first type arise for the different forms in (170)b, c, etc. Moreover, underlying [Verb + NP + S] structures like (171) are quite redundant, the apparent object NP adding no information. This means, in effect, that the "extra" NP in such a structure is semantically unmotivated. Such underlying structures would, therefore, be impossible in a natural grammar ("generative semantic") framework.[57]

[56] Actually, such a claim is somewhat too strong, as observed by Kayne. He points out the existence of such examples as (i), in which the subject of the *before* clause has been deleted.

(i) Around here, it always snows before raining.

This clearly requires identity with the subject of the preceding clause:

(ii) a. *Around here, the wind always rises before raining.
 b. *Around here, the sky darkens before raining.
 c. Around here, it always sleets before raining.

However, there is no sense in which this identity is coreference. I should like to say, then, that in addition to coreferential deletion, there is a perhaps universal rule that can delete the maximally unmarked definite pronoun, in English *it*, under superficial identity with an antecedent occurrence of the same pronoun. Such a rule could also account for examples of the sort discovered by Morgan (1968), such as (iii), where again the *it* of the second clause is removed, but there is no possibility of invoking coreference.

(iii) It is a mistake to trust him but obvious that some people do.

However, even if there is such a rule of unmarked pronoun deletion, it does not suffice to explain all of the facts. For instance, it fails to account for various selections in these cases:

(iv) a. *Around here, it is a mistake to trust anybody before raining.
 b. *It is a mistake to trust him but raining.

[57] For the N-verbs *prevent* and *stop* it might be argued that underlying Verb + NP structures are independently necessary so that the "extra" NP analysis complicates the insertion conditions for these verbs:

(i) a. I prevented Bob's concluding that Mary was pregnant.
 b. ?They stopped Harry's working on Sundays.

But these seem unacceptable in many cases and strained in others. Moreover, parallel sentences are out of the question with *keep*:

(ii) *They kept Bob's concluding that Mary was pregnant.

Hence this argument has limited force at best.

Another argument against structures like (169) has to do with truth value equivalence under passivization, a type of argument first utilized in the discussion of complements by Rosenbaum (1967). This is touched on in the following discussion of his (1967: 89–91), which is essentially that of the present analysis, minus the assumptions discussed earlier in Chapter 1, footnote 6, and minus the view adopted by Rosenbaum that *from* is a complementizer:

... As an illustration, consider these sentences:

(152) a. I prevented the doctor from examining John

b. I prevented John from being examined by the doctor

It will be observed immediately that sentences (152a) and (152b) have the same truth value synonymy, a fact which could not be explained on the assumption that the sentences in (152) are instances of transitive oblique noun phrase complementation as are the sentences (145a) and (149a). On this assumption, the underlying structures, and hence the semantic interpretation, of the sentences in (152) are different. In (152a), the underlying object of "prevent" is "the doctor," while in (152b), the underlying object is "John."

The second problem which arises with respect to (152) is that a transitive oblique noun phrase complement analysis predicts incorrectly the grammaticality of the pseudocleft sentences in (153).

(153) a. *what I prevented the doctor from was examining John

b. *what I prevented John from was being examined by the doctor

Both of these problems can be resolved if it is assumed that the morpheme "from" in (152) is not an instance of PREP but a complementizer of the basic form "from-ing." ...

This analysis has several virtues that offset, perhaps, the cost of the required restriction on the obligatory complementizer deletion transformation. First, the synonymy of the sentences in (152) is explained by the fact that the two sentences do not differ in their underlying structures except for the constituent marking the obligatory passive transformation which does not affect the semantic interpretation. Second, the nonoccurrence of the pseudocleft sentences in (153) is explained in precisely the same way as the nonoccurrence of such sentences in constructions containing main verbs of the "believe" class, that is, the application of pronoun replacement transformation destroys the environment on which the pseudocleft sentence transformations must be defined. Similarly, this analysis explains the introductory "there" phenomenon in sentences like (155).

(155) a. Wyatt Earp prevented there from being trouble on the range

b. shelters will not prevent there from being great destruction

Finally, this analysis allows us to explain the synonymy of the sentences in (156) with those in (152).

(156) a. I prevented the doctor's examining John

   b. I prevented John's being examined by the doctor

In the sentences in (156) the complementizer is "POSS-ing" rather than "from-ing" but the underlying structures of the two pairs of sentences are identical in every respect. Their semantic interpretations, therefore, must be the same.

I shall return to the argument for Raising involving truth-functional equivalance under passivization in diverse types of constructions in Chapters 7, 9 (Section 9.4), 10, and 11.

Summing up, we can say that a Raising analysis of constructions like (159) is the only one that does not run into obvious difficulties. Therefore, a rule raising NPs into superordinate object position is required in English independently of the treatment of B-verb infinitival constructions, and this fact provides further support for the positing of Raising for the latter. The rule is needed anyway, independently of considerations showing that the rule of Raising for A-verb constructions need not be modified to carry out B-verb raising as well in a verb-initial system, as McCawley showed.

What about constructions like (160), however? In traditional terms, it would seem that a Raising analysis of these is difficult to justify, since the class of empty NPs like *there* and *tabs* cannot occur in the post-N-verb position with verbs like *dissuade* and *deter*. Equally seriously, there are the "selectional restrictions," which require the NP in this position to designate something with a mind. In particular, the latter fact would, as in the case of the positive verbs *persuade, force,* etc., be taken to justify a [Verb + NP + S] underlying structure, as in Rosenbaum's (1967) widely accepted analysis. I think, however, that such conclusions are far from justified. The matter is briefly discussed in Chapter 11.

4.14 A Bracketing Contrast

In Section 1.4, I discussed an argument about derived constituent structure, given originally by Lakoff and Ross, that Raising does not operate on the output of Extraposition. The argument involved sentences like (172):

(172) a. It is widely believed that Melvin is an ex-priest.

   b. Melvin is widely believed to be an ex-priest.

The point was that in (172)b *widely believed to be an ex-priest* is a constituent, although this is not the case for the sequence *widely . . . priest* in (172)a.

Consider now the following:

(173) I believe it to be obvious that Melvin is an ex-priest.

In fact, the derived constituent structure of (173) is certainly parallel to that of (172)a. Both sentences appear to have binary surface bracketings, with the *that* clause being the rightmost immediate constituent. This kind of fact was one among several that led Ross (1967) to argue that rules like Extraposition must be last-cyclical, since operation of Extraposition on any cycle before that of *believe* in (172)a or (173) would not yield the appropriate structure. However, at least in the case of (173), this argument presupposes a Raising analysis, for it is only that method which allows the *that* clause ever to become a main constituent, and hence subject to Extraposition on the main clause cycle.

A more telling argument for Raising based on this phenomenon is derivable from contrasts like the following:

(174) a. I believe it to be possible for them to have visitors.

b. I want it to be possible for them to have visitors.

c. I resent it being possible for them to have visitors.

Example (174)a involves a B-verb, and hence Raising in our terms.[58] While *want* is not a B-verb, I also take it to involve Raising (see Section 4.16). However, *resent* takes gerundive complements and has the peculiarity, utilized already several times earlier, of permitting its complement subjects to dispense with the genitive marker in certain cases. No Raising application is possible with *resent* (note that it is factive).[59]

Observe, however, that there is a bracketing contrast between (174)a,

[58] From this point on, I shall consider all members of the class *expect, hate, intend, like, mean, need, prefer, want,* and *wish* as elements that trigger Raising in a fashion parallel to B-verbs such as *believe* and *prove*. I shall refer to these jointly as W-verbs. Evidence showing that these do function like B-verbs with respect to Raising is systematically considered later, in Section 4.16.

[59] As observed by Kiparsky and Kiparsky (1970), Raising in general operates only with nonfactive main verbs. There are, however, some apparent counterexamples in the A-verb class, for instance, *stop* and *continue*. This matter is very briefly discussed later, in Section 9.2.

b, on the one hand, and (174)c, on the other. The *for* clause is a main clause constituent in the former two, but it is a constituent of the complement clause in the latter. One need not rely simply on bracketing intuitions for this contrast. First, there is a difference in acceptability of parenthetical insertions:

(175) a. I believe it to be possible, said Melvin, for them to have visitors.

   b. I want it to be possible, said Melvin, for them to have visitors.

   c. ?I resent it being possible, said Melvin, for them to have visitors.

(176) a. I believe it not to be feasible, despite what you say, for us to balance the budget.

   b. I want it not to be feasible, despite what you say, for us to balance the budget.

   c. ?I resent it not being feasible, despite what you say, for us to balance the budget.

Second, and more interesting, there is a contrast in extractability of elements from the extraposed clauses.

Here, however, there is some background required. In recent, so far unpublished, work,[60] Ross has observed that the past practices of lumping all unbounded movement rules together with respect to their possibilities of extracting items and of dividing contexts in a binary fashion into islands and nonislands are both unrealistic. He has shown that there are two hierarchies, one of rule strengths, and the other of environment resistance to extraction. Thus while some contexts are islands for all extraction rules, others block only rules of weak strength. The immediate relevance of this observation is that gerundive complements with *resent* are rather weak islands—they do not block all extraction but block only that carried out by rather weak rules. Thus observe that if one chooses strong movement rules like those involved in cleft sentence constructions, it is possible to rip relative pronouns out of these complements:

(177) a. The only person who I resent your dating is Sylvia.

   b. What I resent your hiding is the fact that Bob is a Venusian.

   c. It is the fact that Bob is a Venusian that I resent your hiding.

60 But see Ross (to appear e).

But the rule of Adverb Preposing, for example, is a rather weak rule and, in particular, too weak to pull elements out of the gerundive complements of *resent*:

(178) a. On Thursday, I resented your calling Sally.

     b. Under those conditions, I would resent him being elected.

     c. For that reason, I would resent you choosing them.

Thus, in no sentence of (178) is the fronted adverbial expression interpretable as part of the complement. Rather, in each case, the adverb "modifies" the occurrence of *resent*, and was thus never inside the complement. Notice, however, that neither *believe* nor *want* complements block Adverb Preposing:

(179) a. On Thursday, I want you to call Sally.

     b. Under those conditions, I believe it would be impossible for him to win.

     c. For that reason, I believe he would refuse to run.

Thus in (179)a the adverb can "modify" *call*, and in (179)b it can "modify" *impossible*, and in (179)c *refuse*.

With these extractability differences established, consider the following examples:

(180) a. On Thursday, I believe it to be impossible for him to come.

     b. On Thursday, I want it to be impossible for him to come.

     c. ?On Thursday, I resent it being impossible for him to come.

Examples (180)a, b are perfectly normal sentences, in which the adverb can "modify" *come*. Strikingly, however, this is impossible in (180)c, and the adverb must "modify" *resent*, giving the sentence a peculiar, strained character at best. Given the extractability facts about Adverb Preposing established earlier, however, this contrast follows directly from the Raising contrast posited between the *believe* and *want* type of verbs, on the one hand, and *resent*, on the other. In the former cases, the *for* clause is raised out of the complement when it is still subject of *impossible*, and extraposed only on the higher cycle, and this application of Extraposition makes it a main clause constituent. However, when the *for* clause in (180)c is the subject of *impossible*, it cannot be raised, since *resent* does not trigger application of Raising. For this reason the clause must extrapose on the cycle of the complement and must stay a complement constituent. Therefore, the impossibility of extracting the adverb from the extraposed *for* clauses with *resent* follows simply from the fact, illustrated in (178), that the complement of *resent* blocks extraction by a rule as weak as Adverb Preposing.

Consequently, there is a correlation of contrasts between main verbs like *believe* and *want,* on the one hand, and *resent,* on the other—a correlation between bracketing, parenthetical possibilities, and extraction possibilities. These contrasts are naturally explained by a Raising grammar of the former type of verbs, which permits the extraposable clauses of relevance to be first raised and then subjected to Extraposition on the cycle of the main verb in the former case, while the impossibility of Raising with *resent* forces Extraposition to be a complement-internal process in this case.

Favor, a verb that acts much like *resent,* manifests parallel behavior with respect to the relevant parameters, as do the adjectives *for* and *against*:

(181) a. ?I favor it being possible, said Melvin, for them to have visitors.

b. ?I am $\left\{ \begin{array}{l} \text{for} \\ \text{against} \end{array} \right\}$ it being possible, said Melvin, for them to have visitors.

(182) a. On Thursday, I favor it being possible for them to have visitors.

b. On Thursday, I am $\left\{ \begin{array}{l} \text{for} \\ \text{against} \end{array} \right\}$ it being possible for them to have visitors.

It is worth stressing that the facts in this section are consistent with the results to be expected from the RNR rule. We saw earlier that the NP + infinitive sequence after a B-verb is not a constituent from the point of view of this rule. But the sequences after *resent, favor,* etc., which contrast with B-verbs and W-verbs with respect to the properties discussed in this section *do* meet the constituency requirement of RNR:

(183) a. I didn't use to favor prisoners' being released, but I now do favor prisoners' being released.

b. I didn't use to favor—but I now do favor—prisoners' being released.

(184) a. I didn't want to resent it happening to me, but I did resent it happening to me.

b. I didn't want to resent—but I did resent—it happening to me.

Compare (183)b and (184)b with W-verb examples:

(185) a. I didn't expect to want Nixon to win, but I ended up wanting Nixon to win.

b. *I didn't expect to want—but I ended up wanting—Nixon to win.

(186) a. I didn't think I would need it to slide, but I did need it to slide.

b. *I didn't think I would need—but I did need—it to slide.

These facts thus provide independent support for the claim that *favor, resent*, etc., do not trigger Raising, while W-verbs, as well as B-verbs, do. This difference accounts for the fact that the postverbal material is a constituent for the former elements, but not for the latter. Raising is thus supported as a basis for the contrasts of this section.

The failure of *favor, resent*, etc., to trigger Raising is also supported by the fact that their complements can undergo Topicalization with passable acceptability:

(187) a. I would no longer resent that happening to me.

b. That happening to me, I would no longer resent.

(188) a. I really don't favor bombs being set off in public places.

b. Bombs being set off in public places, I really don't favor.

The nontopicalizability of the sequences after *believe, want*, etc., on the other hand, does not show much, since, as Ross has stressed, infinitival phrases, with or without subjects, never seem to topicalize even when their constituency is not in question.

(189) a. I want Bob to win.

b. *Bob to win, I want.

(190) a. I believe Fred to know Greek.

     b. *Fred to know Greek, I believe.

(191) a. I arranged for Bob to win.

     b. *For Bob to win, I arranged.

(192) a. I am not anxious for you to win.

     b. *For you to win, I am not anxious.

(193) a. I wish to succeed.

     b. *To succeed, I wish.

Nonetheless, we have succeeded in illustrating several contrasts of a sort that follow from a Raising analysis of B-verbs and W-verbs and a lack of such an analysis for elements like *favor* and *resent*. We have also provided independent support for the respective claims of Raising application and nonapplication.

In particular, Raising explains directly why the bracketing in pairs like (194) is identical, since a Raising analysis alone guarantees that the *that* clause is a constituent of the main clause in both cases at the point of applying Extraposition.

(194) a. Harry believes it to be obvious *that Nora is a revolutionary.*

     b. It is believed to be obvious *that Nora is a revolutionary.*

In Chomsky's analysis, on the other hand, at best the *that* clause would be a main clause constituent only in (194)b,[61] when it is in the position ultimately occupied by *it,* but the *that* clause would be a complement constituent in (194)a. The bracketing similarity thus would remain inexplicable in such terms.

Finally, it should be pointed out that contrasts in bracketing like that discussed here for Extraposition also are found for several other rules that project constituents to the end of clauses:

(195) a. I believe the claim to have been made *that Nixon is a zombie.*

     b. I resent the claim being made *that Nixon is a zombie.*

[61] It would have become such through the application of Chomsky's formulation of Passive, which (recall from Sections 2.4 and 3.1) can reach down into a subordinate clause to turn the complement subject directly into the new main clause subject in B-verb infinitival cases.

(196) a. I believe a man to have arrived *who was from Philadelphia*.

   b. I resent a man('s) having arrived *who was from Philadelphia*.

(197) a. I believe a review to have appeared *of a book by Melvin*.

   b. I resent a review('s) having appeared *of a book by Melvin*.

(198) a. I believe no one to have survived *except Melvin*.

   b. I resent no one('s) having survived *except Melvin*.

Here also in each case the italicized sequence is bracketed as a main clause constituent in the *a* example, as a complement clause constituent in the *b* example. This would also follow in a Raising system, if the appropriate rules are characterized in the same way as Extraposition, that is, if some principle, last cyclicity or not, guarantees that they cannot be applied before the last cycle is reached.

4.15 Comparative Reduction

There is a process of reducing comparative clauses which involves, among other things, the loss of the main verb of that clause and (sometimes) the appearance of an auxiliary form like *do*:

(199) a. Bill works harder than Tom (does).

   b. Bill attends church as regularly as Joan (does).

If we assume a deletion analysis, at least the verb *works* has been removed in the case of (199)a, and at least the verb *attends* plus the following NP *church* in (199)b. Let us extend a term introduced by Jackendoff (1971) and refer to the removed sequence in such cases as the "gap."

   Gaps are also found in more complex cases involving complements:

(200) a. Joe promises his mother to give up drinking more often than Tom does his sister.

   b. Joe asked the police to help him less often than Jim did the FBI.

In (200)a, the gap is discontinuous and has the form *promise . . . to give up drinking*.[62] In (200)b, the discontinuous gap is *asked . . . to help him*.

---

[62] For some discussion of discontinuous gaps produced by the Gapping rule, see Jackendoff (1971), Hankamer (to appear). The latter should be consulted as background for this section.

Such cases suggest that the reduction rule in question—Comparative Deletion (Comp Del)—eliminates the main verb plus other identical elements, leaving behind the subject of the compared clause, an auxiliary form, and possibly an additional NP contrasting with one in the antecedent clause. These are, however, by no means the only possibilities.

Consider now the following:

(201) a.   Jim believes Betty to be incompetent even more fervently than Bob does Joan.

    b. *Jim believes (that) Betty is incompetent even more fervently than Bob does (that) Joan.

(202) a.   Alan proved the red mixture to be explosive more easily than Bob did the blue one.

    b. *Alan proved (that) the red mixture was explosive more easily than Bob did (that) the blue one.

It appears that Comp Del can produce a discontinuous gap of the type B-verb . . . NP when the complement in the antecedent clause is infinitival, but not when it is a *that* clause.

A ready explanation for such contrasts might be that Comp Del gaps cannot include proper subparts of *tensed* clauses. That this is, at best, insufficient is indicated by examples like (203):

(203) a. *I arranged for Bob to get a job more easily than Ted did (for) Sylvia.

    b. *Jim prayed for them to release his wife more emotionally than Tom did (for) his sister.

    c. *Joan planned for Jack to visit Ohio more carefully than Lou did (for) Melvin.

Here the gaps cannot include proper parts of these untensed infinitival clauses. It is similar with the following gerundive clauses:

(204) a. *I discussed Bob's studying French more intensively than Ted did Harry's.

    b. *I considered Sylvia's working more seriously than Jack did Greta's.

    c. *Joan would resent you(r) confessing more intensely than Jack
    would Sally('s).

Thus it is not true in general that Comp Del can cut into untensed
clauses. Hankamer (personal communication) has, however, suggested a
principle that predicts the ill-formedness of cases like (203) and (204)
and that also distinguishes the pairs in (201) and (202), while the tensed
clause statement can at best do the latter. Namely, he suggests[63] that the
gap generated by Comp Del cannot consist of a proper part of a clause,
although it can contain a whole clause (other than the rightmost compared clause itself). Thus, in cases like (200)a, the gap contains the
whole clause *to give up drinking* (whose subject was previously removed
by Equi); in (200)b, the gap contains the whole clause *to help him,* with
the subject missing for the same reason. In (201)b, though, the gap includes a proper part of the clause *Joan is incompetent,* namely, *is incompetent.* Similarly, in (202)b, the gap includes a proper part of the
clause *the blue one was explosive,* namely, *was explosive.* And clearly,
in (203) and (204), the gaps all include proper parts of clauses distinct
from the entire post-*than* clause.

    Why, then, are (201)a and (202)a, which are apparently parallel to
(201)b and (202)b, respectively, well-formed? A Raising analysis naturally explains this, given the assumption about gaps not containing
proper parts of clauses. For in each relevant case, Raising of course
moves the subject of the complement out of that clause. Therefore,
when Comp Del applies, it produces as a gap a removed sequence that
contains the entirety of the remaining complement clause. In short,
given the gap restriction, one can see that post-B-verb NPs with infinitival complements do not behave like parts of complement clauses
in derived structures, just as a Raising analysis predicts. On the contrary, though, and in accord with the Raising conception, the post-B-
verb NPs with *that*-clause complements do behave like part of the
complements in derived structure, regardless of whether or not the *that*
is deleted.

[63] Hankamer's proposal is actually more general and is suggested as a constraint on
a whole class of deletion rules. Namely, the gaps produced by rules that delete the
material represented in a rule by a variable cannot contain proper parts of clauses.
If this proposal can be sustained (see later discussion for some necessary revision),
then the property of Comp Del which is relevant for the argument of this section is
not an ad hoc feature or accident but rather a theorem of a deep property of
radical reduction rules in general.

N-verb and W-verb structures reveal the same pattern of behavior. Since, under a Raising analysis, the NP directly following the main verb in such cases has ceased to be part of the complement, this system predicts that the remaining part of the complement can be part of a Comp Del gap in such cases. And this is correct:

(205) a. I stopped Joan from sinking more easily than Jack did Louise.

b. I want Bob to win more strongly than Ted does Francis.

c. I wish Jane to survive as fervently as Max does Minerva.

Compare in particular the following:[64]

(206) a. I prevented the first plane from leaving as easily as Tom did the second plane.

b. *I prevented the first plane's leaving as easily as Tom did the second plane's.

c. I wish Nixon to lose as strongly as Tom does Agnew.

d. *I wish (that) Nixon would lose as strongly as Tom does Agnew.

e. Jack meant Shirley to die as surely as Tom did Gladys.

f. *Jack meant for Shirley to die as surely as Tom did (for) Gladys.

It follows that the clause-integrity restriction on Comp Del gaps suggested by Hankamer provides an argument for Raising in the disputed class of derivations which is as strong as the evidence for the appropriateness of the restriction itself.

However, in spite of what has been said, so far, there seem to be obvious objections to the principle that the gaps for Comp Reduce cannot cut into clauses. Observe these cases:

(207) a. Jim wants to kiss Betsy more than he does Sally.

b. Bill is as anxious to begin looking for an apartment as Sally is to begin looking for a new car.

c. Bill wishes to be able to drive the car more desperately than (he does) the tractor.

---

[64] The point in (206)c, d is that *wish*, like *want*, is a W-verb triggering Raising in the infinitival case. But, unlike *want*, it can also occur with *that* clauses, and hence without any application of Raising. In (206)e, f, *mean* is also a W-verb, but one that can occur with infinitival clauses independently of Raising. See Section 4.16.

Here one finds gaps of the respective forms, given in (208), each one of which cleaves a clause (distinct from the entire post-comparative element clause) at an internal point.

(208) a. wants to kiss

 b. anxious

 c. (he) wishes to be able to drive

Hence all of these gaps contain proper parts of clauses. On the face of it, such examples seem to falsify the principle suggested by Hankamer, limiting Comp Del gaps to those not containing proper parts of clauses. It seems to me possible, however, to preserve the principle despite such examples by refining it somewhat.

It turns out that, in comparison to the cases where the principle as first stated works properly, the examples in (209) have a unique, otherwise not found property. Let us take (207)a for discussion. In this sentence, Comp Del cuts apart the clause *want to kiss # Sally,* similarly, the included clause *to kiss # Sally,* at the point of the number sign. These clauses thus do not serve as barriers to Comp Del. However, in derived structures these clauses do not contain subject NPs, these having been either deleted by Equi (this is the case for the clause headed by *kiss*) or raised by Raising (this is the case for the clause headed by *want,* under an analysis where the auxiliary *do* is a verb triggering Raising, like *happen* and *seem*). In much earlier work, it is denied that such phrases are derived clauses; often they are called verb phrases, or some other special category is invented distinct from the S defining clausehood. However, in Sections 6.5 and 6.6, it is proposed in essence that the clausehood of such phrases can be maintained, even in derived structure, by adopting the following proposal. Clauses that *cyclically* lose their subject NPs through the operation of rules like Equi or Raising are assigned to a derivative category of clauses called "quasi-clauses." In general, such clauses impose much less of a barrier to various syntactic processes than full clauses do.

Therefore, I suggest that the principle that a Comp Del gap cannot contain a proper part of a clause be reformulated to take account of the distinction between full clauses and quasi-clauses. The principle would now say that a Comp Reduce gap cannot contain a subpart of a non-quasi-clause, that is, a subpart of a full clause, one still containing its subject. Given this somewhat weakened revision, cases like (207) cease to be counterexamples.[65, 66]

I know of no real exceptions to the refined version of the principle, which, however, provides exactly the same basis for the argument in favor of Raising as the original. I think, therefore, that the principle so refined is essentially correct and that it does provide a good argument for the existence of Raising operation in the disputed class of derivations involving movement into superordinate clause object position.

One proviso is necessary, however. Because of cases like (207)b, our reformulation holds only if an element like *be* is treated as a main verb triggering either Equi or Raising (in fact, Raising). In this case the second clause of (207)b has a remote structure of the form shown in (209), in which the quasi-clause becomes such because its subject has been lifted out by Raising on the cycle of the main verb, *is*.

(209) Sally is [$_{quasi-S}$ anxious to begin looking for a new car $_{quasi-S}$].

Note, on the contrary, that under an auxiliary analysis anything like

---

[65] On the basis of the facts with Gapping, maintenance of the general constraint on gaps mentioned in footnote 63 will require reference to the distinction between quasi-clause and full clause. For example, Hankamer (to appear: 14) gives an example like (i), in which the gap contains a subpart of the clause *to persuade Ira to get lost,* namely, *to persuade . . . to get lost.*

(i) a. Max wanted Ted to persuade Alex to get lost and Max wanted Walt to persuade Ira to get lost. Gapping $\implies$

　　b. Max wanted Ted to persuade Alex to get lost and Walt, Ira.

However, this clause is a quasi-clause, not a full clause, since its subject has undergone Raising, triggered by the W-verb *want.*

[66] Another type of example in which quasi-clausehood plays a key role is obtainable from Hankamer (to appear: 4). Thus in example (i) the gap contains a subpart of the clause *seem likely to get along with Martha,* namely, *seem likely to get along.*

(i) a. Joe seems more likely to get along with Sue than he seems likely to get along with Martha. Comp Del $\implies$

　　b. Joe seems more likely to get along with Sue than (he does) with Martha.

Again though, this is a quasi-clause, generated by Raising, triggered by *does.* Just so, *likely to get along* is a quasi-clause, produced by Raising triggered by *seem.* Finally, *to get along* is a quasi-clause, produced by Raising triggered by *likely.* Thus while there would be multiple violations of the original principle, there are none of the revised one.

that introduced by Chomsky (1957), in which *be* and other auxiliaries are not recognized as (main) verbs, there would be no basis for the quasi-clause status of the post-*is* phrase in (209). In that sort of analysis, *be* is a part of the Auxiliary constituent of simple clauses, rather than a main verb with a complement, as shown in (210), and no clause ever loses its

(210)

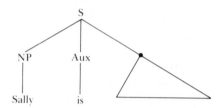

subject in such derivations. It thus appears that the behavior of Comp Del offers an interesting and unexpected argument in favor of attributing the properties of verb, main verb, and Raising-triggering element to so-called auxiliaries.

4.16 W-Verbs as under the Domain of Raising
Although the primary concern of the present study has been to support the relevance of Raising for B-verb infinitival complement derivations, I have also discussed the role of Raising in N-verb complements briefly in Section 4.13. Moreover, beginning in Section 4.9, I have sporadically utilized verbs like *want* and *wish* as elements that trigger Raising. Earlier, I introduced contrasts between *prefer* NP and *prefer for* NP, arguing that the former involved a case of Raising. In the present section, I shall briefly survey in a more unified way the evidence that these elements, and a number of others that I shall refer to jointly as *W-verbs,* do trigger the application of Raising. I shall therefore be concerned with the properties of infinitival complements after *expect, hate, intend, like, mean, need, prefer, want,* and *wish,* but apparently not *desire,* with sentences like the following:

(211) a. *I desire you to do that.

    b. I expect her to come.

    c. I (would) hate you to say things like that.

    d. I intended him to die.

e.   I (would) like you to visit me.

f.   I meant him to crash.

g.   I need you to help me.

h.   I (would) prefer you to call me Rocky.

i.   I want you to love me.

j.   I wish you to succeed.

It can be observed that W-verbs, in contrast to B-verbs, are similar in several ways. First, their complements designate states of affairs, rather than propositions. Second, the complements tend to have a future orientation. Third, such verbs trigger application of Equi when the main clause subject NP and complement subject NP are coreferential.

One point that should be made immediately about W-verbs, in contrast to B-verbs, is that some occur with contrasting types of infinitival complement, as already partly seen in the case of *prefer*:

(212) a. *I desire for you to do that.

b. *I expect for her to come.

c.   I (would) hate for you to say things like that.

d.   I intend for him to die.

e.   I (would) like for you to visit me.

f.   I meant for him to crash.

g. *I need for you to help me.

h.   I (would) prefer for you to call me Rocky.

i. *I want for you to love me.

j.   I wish for you to succeed.

Moreover, even when this is not possible in directly postverbal position, it is sometimes possible, as stressed by Howard Lasnik, with an intervening adverb:

(213) a.   I desire very much for you to do that.

b. *I expect very much for her to come.

c. *I need very much for you to help me.

d.   I want very much for you to love me.

Finally, many W-verbs can occur, at least in formal language, with (subjunctive) *that* clauses.

(214) a. ?I desire that you do that.

    b. I expect that she will do that.

    c. *I hate that he say things like that.

    d. I intend that he die.

    e. *I like that he visit me.

    f. ?I meant that he crash.

    g. *I need that you help me.

    h. I prefer that you call me Rocky.

    i. *I want that you love me.

    j. I wish that you knew Turkish.

Naturally, I shall assume that Raising has not applied in (212)–(214), although it has in (211). If so, then the variety of tests showing that an NP is, in fact, a (derived) main clause constituent should differentiate the corresponding NP in (211) and, for example, (212). It should also provide an even sharper test of Raising than the typical B-verb contrasts of infinitival and *that* clauses, since here all talk of the difference between tensed and untensed clauses is necessarily irrelevant. These contrasts will then be the systematic analogues of contrasts between *prefer* NP and *prefer for* NP somewhat randomly appealed to in earlier sections.

The best way to pursue this matter will be to examine in order the arguments of Chapters 3 and 4.

Let us turn to Chapter 3 first. Here, passivization yields the following factual array:

(215) a. *You are desired to do that.

    b. You are expected to come.

    c. *You are hated to say things like that.

    d. You were intended to die.

    e. *You are liked to visit us.

    f. You were meant to crash.

g. *You are needed to help us.[67]

h. *You are preferred to call me Rocky.

i. *You are wanted to love me.

j. *You are wished to succeed.

Clearly, passivization is limited with the preinfinitival NPs of W-verbs.[68] For all but *expect, intend,* and *mean,* this might be taken to indicate, on the assumption that Passive cannot "cross" higher clause boundaries, that the postverbal NPs in sentences like (211) are still parts of the complement during the cycle of the main clause. I think this conclusion is unwarranted, however. Even without surface complements, some of these verbs will not trigger application of Passive:

(216) a. Bob wants that.

b. *That is wanted by Bob.

c. Bob wishes for that.

d. *That is wished for by Bob.

One might try, then, to attribute the ill-formed examples in (215) to special constraints on passivization associated with the verbs in question, rather than to structural factors. However, this will not do in general, as Ross observes:

(217) That was generally $\left\{ \begin{array}{l} \text{hated} \\ \text{liked} \\ \text{needed} \\ \text{preferred} \\ \text{*wanted}^{69} \end{array} \right\}$.

---

[67] For those who accept examples like (215)g, it is likely that the sentences have a noncomplement structure, such as (i), in which the infinitival clause is part of a purpose adverbial.

(i) NP needs you for [$_S$ you help us $_S$]

[68] In the context of these idiosyncratic restrictions on Passive with W-verb complements, it is appropriate to stress again the criticisms of Chomsky's claim about "blindly" applying rules in footnote 55.

[69] To see further the complexity of the relevant passivization constraints, consider the following further array of facts from my idiolect:

It seems, therefore, that the ill-formedness typical of contexts like (215) requires a special statement in a Raising system. Such restrictions greatly limit the possibility of using passivization to support Raising. Note, though, that the facts in (215) are unexplained both in Chomsky's system and in one based on Raising, since nothing in his account predicts that Passive will distinguish the putative subjects of W-verb infinitival complements from those of B-verb infinitival complements.

The argument based on reflexivization is, by and large, inapplicable. Reflexivization depends on coreference, but with W-verbs a complement subject that is coreferential to the main clause subject is always subject to Equi, and hence obligatorily deleted. The one exception is *expect,* where sentences like (218) are at least marginally possible for many speakers, in accord with a Raising grammar.

(218) Melvin expected himself to do better than that.

I noted at the end of Section 3.3 that reciprocal facts do not show anything, and hence that phenomenon must be ignored here. This brings us to the Inclusion Constraint analysis, with respect to which one finds the following:

(219) a. *I desire us

    b. *I expect us

    c. *I (would) hate us

    d. *I intend us

    e. *I (would) like us

    f. *I meant us

    g. *I need us

    h. *I (would) prefer us

    i. *I want us

    j. *I wish us

$\left.\begin{array}{l} \\ \\ \\ \\ \\ \\ \\ \\ \\ \\ \end{array}\right\}$ to be slim.

(i) a. *The things which are $\left\{\begin{array}{l} \text{desired} \\ \text{liked} \\ \text{wanted} \end{array}\right\}$ by most people are worthless.

    b. The things $\left\{\begin{array}{l} \text{desired} \\ \text{liked} \\ \text{wanted} \end{array}\right\}$ by most people are worthless.

These facts are consistent with the view that the postverbal NPs are derived main clause constituents. Moreover, such examples must be interpreted in context with the analogous cases for those W-verbs which take *for*-marked infinitives:

(220) a. I (would) hate
   b. I intend
   c. I (would) like } for us to be slim.
   d. I meant
   e. I (would) prefer
   f. I wish

While some of these examples are possibly strained, the contrast with (219) seems clear.

Let us now turn to Chapter 4 and consider the interaction of W-verbs with Complex NP Shift. Here, because of the constraint discussed in footnote 3 and in Section 12.5, one cannot expect application in general when the full infinitival clause is present. However, in special cases this is at least marginally possible:

(221) a. I only want to become doctors—those students who have a real interest in a high income.

   b. I only wish to criticize themselves—those of you who are not afraid of public ridicule.

More significantly, in cases of reduced complements, application is relatively free, as expected under a Raising analysis:

(222) a. I want fired—anyone who refuses to accept our authority.

   b. I wish removed from the room—all of those students who have dirty socks.

Thus the argument from Complex NP Shift supports the Raising analysis of W-verbs.

This is also true of the *not*-initial argument. Observe the following:

(223) a. *I desire
　　 b. *I expect
　　 c. *I (would) hate
　　 d. *I intend
　　 e. *I (would) like
　　 f. *I meant   } not many people to be hired.
　　 g. *I need
　　 h. *I (would) prefer
　　 i. *I want
　　 j. *I wish

(224) a.　I (would) hate
　　 b.　I intend
　　 c. *I (would) like
　　 d.　I meant   } for not many people to be hired.
　　 e.　I (would) prefer
　　 f. *I wish

In each case, *not*-initial NPs are ill-formed in (223), as predicted by the subject constraint on such phrases in conjuction with a Raising analysis. On the other hand, the fact that over half of the sentences in (224) are well-formed is indicative of the subject status of the post-*for* NP. Examples (224) c, f must be attributed, then, to some special constraints on the particular main verbs.

　　The *alone*-final argument gives similar results:

(225) a. *I desire
　　 b. *I expect
　　 c. *I (would) hate
　　 d. *I intend
　　 e. *I (would) like
　　 f. *I meant   } Bob alone to win.
　　 g. *I need
　　 h. *I (would) prefer
　　 i. *I want
　　 j. *I wish

(226) a. I (would) hate
    b. I intend
    c. I (would) like
    d. I meant   } for Bob alone to win.
    e. I (would) prefer
    f. I wish

Again, the subject status of the post-*for* NPs and the lack of such a status for NPs directly following W-verbs is revealed.

A Raising analysis of W-verbs predicts that the degree of vowel reduction in the *it* of the examples in (227) should be greater than that in the examples in (228), according to the argument of Section 4.4.

(227) a. *I desire
    b. I expect
    c. I (would) hate
    d. I intend
    e. I (would) like
    f. I meant   } it to happen to you.
    g. I need
    h. I (would) prefer
    i. I want
    j. I wish

(228) a. I resent
    b. I favor
    c. I am for   } it happening to you.
    d. I am against

This is so because in (228) Raising cannot be invoked, and the *it* occurrences are necessarily (derived) parts of the complement clause. I believe this is correct, though this sort of judgment is, of course, quite subtle.

Next, let us turn to the quantifier-postposing argument of Section 4.5. But, as we saw, that argument did not stand up. Therefore, the following data indicate not that the postverbal NPs are main clause constituents in derived structure, as one would have hoped, but only the correctness of

Baker's observation that in most dialects *each* does not undergo Q-Pro Attachment:

(229) a. *John desired

    b. *John expected

    c. *John (would) have hated

    d. *John intended

    e. *John (would) have liked

    f. *John meant   } them each, he said, to be fired.

    g. *John needed

    h. *John (would) have preferred

    i. *John wanted

    j. *John wished

These facts have no bearing on the issues then.

    The pronominalization argument of Section 4.6 should next be dealt with. The following data indicate that the post-W-verb NPs have been raised:

(230) *I $\left\{ \begin{array}{l} \text{would hate} \\ \text{would like} \\ \text{would prefer} \\ \text{want} \\ \text{wish} \end{array} \right\}$ him$_i$ to become famous even more strongly

        than Bob$_i$ $\left\{ \begin{array}{l} \text{does} \\ \text{would} \end{array} \right\}$.

The contrast with (231) is, I think, surprisingly clear, supporting the view that only in the *for* cases does the underlying complement subject stay a complement subject throughout the derivation.

(231) I $\left\{ \begin{array}{l} \text{would hate} \\ \text{would like} \\ \text{would prefer} \\ \text{wish} \end{array} \right\}$ for him$_i$ to become famous even more strongly

        than Bob$_i$ $\left\{ \begin{array}{l} \text{does} \\ \text{would} \end{array} \right\}$.

The argument of Section 4.7 cannot be applied to W-verbs because of requirements on the class of subject NPs these can take. We come therefore to contrasts under the RNR rule:

(232) a. I didn't expect to $\left\{ \begin{matrix} \text{prefer} \\ \text{want} \\ \text{wish} \end{matrix} \right\}$ that to happen, but I did $\left\{ \begin{matrix} \text{prefer} \\ \text{want} \\ \text{wish} \end{matrix} \right\}$ that to happen.

b. *I didn't expect to $\left\{ \begin{matrix} \text{prefer} \\ \text{want} \\ \text{wish} \end{matrix} \right\}$ —but I did $\left\{ \begin{matrix} \text{prefer} \\ \text{want} \\ \text{wish} \end{matrix} \right\}$ —that to happen.

Contrast these cases:

(233) a. I didn't expect to $\left\{ \begin{matrix} \text{prefer} \\ \text{wish} \end{matrix} \right\}$ for that to happen, but I did $\left\{ \begin{matrix} \text{prefer} \\ \text{wish} \end{matrix} \right\}$ for that to happen.

b. I didn't expect to $\left\{ \begin{matrix} \text{prefer} \\ \text{wish} \end{matrix} \right\}$ —but I did $\left\{ \begin{matrix} \text{prefer} \\ \text{wish} \end{matrix} \right\}$ —for that to happen.

Thus the behavior of RNR indicates that the post-W-verb sequence [NP + infinitive] is not a derived constituent, as a Raising analysis predicts.

The argument based on Gapping also applies to W-verbs:

(234) a.   Bob $\left\{ \begin{matrix} \text{expects} \\ \text{hates} \\ \text{intends} \\ \text{likes} \\ \text{means} \\ \text{needs} \\ \text{prefers} \\ \text{wants} \\ \text{wishes} \end{matrix} \right\}$ Tom to win, and Ed $\left\{ \begin{matrix} \text{expects} \\ \text{etc.} \end{matrix} \right\}$ Bill to lose.

b. *Bob $\left\{ \begin{matrix} \text{expects} \\ \text{etc.} \end{matrix} \right\}$ Tom to win, and Ed Bill to lose.

Note these cases in contrast:

(235) a. Bob $\begin{Bmatrix} \text{hates} \\ \text{etc.} \end{Bmatrix}$ for Tom to win, and Ed $\begin{Bmatrix} \text{hates} \\ \text{etc.} \end{Bmatrix}$ for Bill to lose.

b. Bob $\begin{Bmatrix} \text{hates} \\ \text{etc.} \end{Bmatrix}$ for Tom to win, and Ed for Bill to lose.

Consequently, the discussion of Section 4.9 carries over to W-verbs.

Similarly, the behavior of pseudocleft sentences provides the same argument for Raising with W-verbs as it does for B-verbs:

(236) a. What he $\begin{Bmatrix} \text{wants} \\ \text{wishes} \end{Bmatrix}$ is $\begin{Bmatrix} \text{for us to lose} \\ \text{*us to lose} \end{Bmatrix}$.

b. What he would prefer is $\begin{Bmatrix} \text{for us to lose} \\ \text{that we lose} \\ \text{*us to lose} \end{Bmatrix}$.

One arrives, next, at the two arguments in Sections 4.11 and 4.12, based on adverbs. Applying the first, we find such contrasts as those in (237):

(237) a. *Tom $\begin{Bmatrix} \text{expects} \\ \text{wants} \\ \text{wishes} \end{Bmatrix}$ very $\begin{Bmatrix} \text{strongly} \\ \text{much} \end{Bmatrix}$ Bill to win.

b. Tom wishes very much for Bill to win.

Thus again the NPs preceding *to* in the sentences without *for* behave like sisters of the main verb, in accord with Raising application, while the NPs in the *for* cases clearly behave as nonsisters of the main verb.

The second adverbial argument also applies as well to W-verbs as to B-verbs:

(238) a.   Tom $\begin{Bmatrix} \text{expects} \\ \text{wants} \\ \text{wishes} \end{Bmatrix}$ Bob, obviously, to do well.

b. ?*Tom wishes for Bob, obviously, to do well.

Here the adverb can be construed as a main clause "modifier" only in (238)a, which is in accord with the principle that such "modifiers" cannot be inserted into complement clauses if sentences like (238)a are

Raising-derived, and consequently in contrast with those like (238)b with respect to derived clause membership of the underlying complement subject NP.

The bracketing contrast argument of Section 4.14 also applies to W-verbs, but this point was illustrated in that section already, at least for *want*. Note also the bracketing contrast between (239), where the main break in the verbal phrase is in front of *for*, and (240), where, on the contrary, *it being possible for . . . visitors* is a constituent.

$$(239)\ \mathrm{I} \left\{ \begin{array}{l} \text{expect} \\ \text{(would) hate} \\ \text{intend} \\ \text{(would) like} \\ \text{mean} \\ \text{(would) prefer} \\ \text{wish} \end{array} \right\} \text{it to be possible for them to have visitors.}$$

$$(240)\ \mathrm{I} \left\{ \begin{array}{l} \text{resent} \\ \text{favor} \\ \text{am} \left\{ \begin{array}{l} \text{against} \\ \text{for} \end{array} \right\} \end{array} \right\} \text{it being possible for them to have visitors.}$$

As shown before, this is a direct consequence of the clausal NP constituent underlying *it* having been raised in (239), but not having been raised in (240).

Finally, it remains only to recall the comparative reduction argument. But it should not be necessary to go over this further, because the argument as originally formulated utilized W-verbs.

In conclusion, it should be clear that despite problems with a few arguments and the nonapplicability of others, the overall weight of evidence strongly supports the hypothesis that *for*-less infinitival complements with W-verbs are Raising-derived.

5

Some Arguments against B-Verb Raising

5.1 Extraction from Complex Nominals

In Chapters 3 and 4 of this study I have attempted to formulate arguments showing that Raising functions for B-verb infinitival complements and related elements like N-verbs and W-verbs. (Several additional arguments are found in the final sections of Chapter 12.) Insofar as these arguments are valid, they falsify the claims of non-Raising systems, one version of which has been recently elaborated by Chomsky. Chomsky's challenge to Raising operation into main clause object position is largely implicit, in the sense that he does not attempt so much to give arguments against the B-verb type of Raising as to present and support an alternative point of view. Nonetheless, he does give several explicit arguments that, he claims, count against the view that B-verb Raising exists, and it is thus necessary to consider these arguments.

Chomsky's first negative argument, given on page 29a and in footnote 31 of the prepublication version of Chomsky (to appear), is based on the claim, which I shall not dispute here,[1] that NPs that are proper parts of subject NPs cannot in general be extracted from the subject NP containing them. Thus, NPs can be extracted from phrases like (1) when these occur as nonsubjects in (2):

---

[1] Chomsky (to appear: especially condition (99), reformulated as condition (110) (ii)) actually states a condition that would block all extraction of proper parts of subject NPs. This condition is clearly too strong. It ignores such operations as the one in (i)–(iii):

(i)   a. The important thing to me is money.
    b. To me the important thing is money.
    c. I think the important thing to me is money.
    d. To me, I think the important thing is money.

(ii) a. I think that only Martha of all the girls in my class is Irish.
    b. Of all the girls in my class, I think that only Martha is Irish.

(iii) a. I think that everybody in this office except (for) Bob is incompetent.
    b. Except for Bob, I think that everybody in this office is incompetent.

This does not bear on the argument in the text, however, since, for the class of phrases relevant there, extraction is banned.

(1) a. pictures of _____

   b. stories about _____

(2) a. Who did you buy pictures of?

   b. Melvin, I told several stories about.

   c. The only person who I have never heard any rumors about is Ted.

But this is not possible when the complex NPs are themselves subjects:

(3) a. Pictures of Bob lay on the table.

   b. *Bob, pictures of lay on the table.

   c. *Who did pictures of lay on the table?

   d. *The only one who pictures of lay on the table was Sylvia.

(4) a. Bill thought pictures of Sally were on the table.

   b. *Sally, Bill thought pictures of were on the table.

   c. *Who did Bill think pictures of were on the table?

   d. *The only person who Bill thought pictures of were on the table was Lulubelle.

Thus, if one ignores the phenomena discussed in footnote 1, there is the following regularity:

(5) NPs cannot be extracted from a complex NP, N, where N is a subject.

Given (5), Chomsky can argue that the ill-formedness of examples like (6) shows that the complex NP remains a subject.

(6) a. *Who did you believe pictures of to be on sale in Tunisia?

   b. *Who did the police prove stories about to be in Zelda's files?

This would follow under the assumption that it must be a subject at the point when extraction rules like *Wh*-Q Movement in (6) become applicable. In Chomsky's system, all such unbounded movement rules are supposed to operate in the fashion I have described (Postal, 1972c) as *successive cyclic*, which means that these rules apply on each cycle, moving elements successively forward in a series of jumps. But he has conditions that independently block application on the inner cycle in the relevant cases here, so that, for purposes of this argument, the situation is the same as if he assumed, as I do, that such rules work in one bound when their higher triggering element is reached. In either case, for examples like (6), if a rule of Raising is relevant, it will have applied before the extraction can be applied, and the complex NP will no longer be a subject. Thus Chomsky's argument seems to stand up, since apparently examples like (6) can be blocked generally by the same principle relevant for (3) and (4) only if there is no Raising application in (6).

Chomsky's actual examples for this argument are his (92)b and (94)b, repeated here as (7), utilizing the main verb *expect*.[2]

(7) a. *Who did stories about terrify John?

   b. *Who do you expect stories about to terrify John?

Here it is the parallelism between the unquestioned subject *stories about NP* in (7)a and the NP in (7)b which is crucial for the argument. Chomsky's formulation of the argument, given in footnote 31, runs as follows:

This analysis of course assumes, as throughout, that there is no raising rule assigning the subject *stories about who* of the embedded sentence of (94) to the object position of the matrix sentence. If there were such a rule, *wh* movement should apply, giving (94)b, analogous to "who did you see pictures of last night," "who did you tell stories about at the campfire"—which, though hardly elegant, seem to me much more acceptable than (94)b, as we would expect on the assumption that there is no rule of subject-raising to object position.

However, although interesting and plausible, this criticism of Raising does not stand up, for reasons not uncommon to argument failures in grammar. Namely, although the argument's *stated* premises can all be accepted, it depends crucially on an *unstated* premise, which does not withstand analysis.

---

[2] In Section 4.16, *expect* was treated as a member of the class of W-verbs. Since its complements designate states of affairs and are future oriented, and since *expect* triggers application of Equi, this categorization is quite natural. Because of examples like (i), it might also be regarded as simultaneously a marginal member of the class of B-verbs.

(i) Melvin expects himself to do 100 pushups every day.

In any event, it functions as an element that triggers application of Raising.

The essence of the argument is that triples like (8) must be handled by the same constraint (which refers to subjects).

(8) a. *Who is a picture of on the table?

  b. *Who do you believe a picture of is on the table?

  c. *Who do you believe a picture of to be on the table?

I concur with the essence of this view. The implicit premise made, however, with which I do not concur, and without which there is no argument against Raising for cases like (8)c, is that the phrase in question must be a subject at the point in derivations when the extraction rule is tested for application. In other words, it has been implicitly assumed that the constraint (5) is a *local* constraint, with "subject" interpreted to mean "subject at this point." There is, in terms of global grammar, an obvious alternative, however. Namely, specify (5) in terms of the notion "cyclic subject," where an NP at any point in derivations is a cyclic subject if it has a corresponding constituent NP that is the subject of a clause at the end of some cycle. This notion is needed for many other rules, for instance, as Andrews (1971) and Lakoff (1970a) have argued, for the statement of Classical Greek case agreement.

If, however, one reformulates (5) as (9), then the constraint applies to all examples like (6), (7)b, (8)c, regardless of whether the complex NP has been raised or not, since, even in a Raising system, the complex NP *was* a subject at the end of the complement cycle, and hence is subject to (9).

(9) NPs cannot be extracted from a complex NP, N, where N is (that is, corresponds to) a cyclical subject.[3]

Given (9) as the statement of the constraint found uniformly in (8),

---

[3] Notice that Extraposition (see Section 12.4) is consistent with this claim on the assumption that it extracts an S, not an NP. However, under the assumption that prepositional phrases are actually NPs, the operation in (i) requires either a special statement about such phrases or an appeal to a difference between leftward and rightward movements.

(i) a. A review of Harold's symphony was published today.

   b. A review was published today of Harold's symphony.

The latter method could also be relevant to Extraposition, under the assumption that the extracted constituent there is an NP as well as an S.

no known facts permit the formulation of any argument based on (8) against Raising. Moreover, (9) is a stronger constraint than (5), ruling out in principle more cases than (5), and is hence a priori to be preferred unless the extra power can be empirically falsified. I know of no cases that could show that and thus conclude that on current evidence (9) must be accepted.

It might be argued, though dubiously, given the existing literature already showing the need for global rules, that (9) as against (5) requires a weakening of linguistic theory, compared with the type of global rule-free grammar advocated by Chomsky, and hence that (9) should be rejected. This claim, however, cannot be taken seriously. As has already been pointed out (Postal 1972a; 1972c; Lakoff, 1972a), Chomsky's conception of grammar, in which one can make use of arbitrary syntactic features, permits the formulation of the bulk of possible global rules. In particular, it is quite trivial to formulate principle (9) in "nonglobal" terms making use of syntactic features.

It can simply be claimed that there is a rule, the last rule to apply on each cycle, which assigns to any subject NP the syntactic feature [+Cyclic Subject], this rule being the only source of the positive value of this feature. It is then only necessary to restate (9) as (10):

(10) NPs cannot be extracted from a complex NP, N, where N is marked [+Cyclic Subject].

Again all of the facts are covered, regardless of the disposition of claims about Raising.

Thus, in either a system with explicit global rules or one like Chomsky's which has feature devices capable of coding global statements, the argument against Raising does not hold.[4, 5]

---

[4] Kuno, McCawley, and Ross (see especially Kuno, to appear b) have all pointed out that the restrictions involved in constraints like (9) may very well be more general and have nothing to do in particular with subjects. Thus they point to the unacceptability of extraction of phrases in cases like the following:

(i)   a. I consider one picture of Betty terrible.
      b. *Betty, I consider one picture of terrible.

(ii) a. He finds photos of Agnew erotic.
      b. *The only one who he finds photos of erotic is Agnew.

It is doubtful if Chomsky could consider the containing NPs here subjects at any stage (although I do, of course). Subjecthood appears even more unlikely in examples like the following, provided by McCawley:

5.2 Interaction with Tough Movement

A second argument given by Chomsky to oppose the claim that Raising operates into object position is found in footnote 33 of Chomsky (to appear). Here Chomsky refers to observations of Kimball's, which have also been made independently by several other people, namely, that NPs putatively raised into superordinate object position are not subject to subsequent operation of Tough Movement. To quote:

> Another problem is suggested by some observations of John Kimball, who points out that from "it was easy for Jones to force Smith to recover" we can derive "Smith was easy for Jones to force to recover", but from "it was easy for Jones to expect Smith to recover", we cannot form "Smith was easy for Jones to expect to recover". Assuming subject-raising, the two sentences are identical at the point where *it*-replacement [my Tough Movement] takes place. If there is no subject-raising, the rule of *it* replacement can make the required distinction by permitting the NP moved to be followed by S (as in "Bill is easy to persuade that the moon is made of green cheese").

This is everything that Chomsky says on this score. His argument

---

(iii) a. I gave a disciple of the Swami a lot of money.

   b.*The scholar who I gave a disciple of a lot of money is in jail.

Although I do not regard it as being out of the question that *a disciple of NP* is the cyclic subject of some verb (a natural consequence of a Predicate Raising analysis of *give* involving CAUSE + HAVE), a grammar of the type advocated by Chomsky would certainly not assign it subject status at any stage at all. Such cases seem to show, therefore, that there is no basis, internal to Chomsky's system, for regarding the relevant restrictions as involving subjects. And this conclusion seems likely even for grammatical approaches not making any of Chomsky's particular assumptions. Thus it is even clearer, I think, that the facts in question do not serve as the basis for any argument against a Raising grammar of English.

5 For many speakers, including the present writer, there is either a stronger version of (9) or a similar constraint that also blocks extraction from elements that were formerly subjects at one stage, even if not formerly cyclical subjects. Thus, in this dialect, the *b* examples in the following are also ill-formed:

(i) a.   There is a picture of Bob (on the table).

   b. *Who is there a picture of (on the table)?

(ii) a.   Tom was annoyed by a picture of Bob.

   b. *Who was Tom annoyed by a picture of?

Here the complex NPs were never cyclical subjects, because in (i) *there* was inserted before the end of the first cycle, while in (ii) Passive applied before the end of the first cycle. Violations like (i)b and (ii)b do not seem as bad as violations of (9), however, which might argue for their being a function of a distinct constraint.

again utilizes *expect,* but this adds no special complication. The same thing hold for B-verbs:

(11) a. It is hard to believe Bill to be insane.

    b. *Bill is hard to believe to be insane.

(12) a. It was no problem to prove Melvin to be a Venusian.

    b. *Melvin was no problem to prove to be a Venusian.

Chomsky's formulation of the argument seems to be as follows: Tough Movement can operate on an NP in the context (13) as in (14), but not, evidently, in the context (15):

(13) X Verb _____ S.

(14) a. It was tough to - force - Bob - to leave.
             X   Verb   NP   S

    b. Bob was tough to force to leave.

(15) X Verb [$_S$ NP . . .

But under a Raising analysis, sentences like (11)a and (12)a will have the structure (13), just as (14) does, and the contrast will not be marked.

Chomsky has thus argued that an explanation is available for certain contrasts in a non-Raising grammar which is unavailable given Raising into superordinate object position. However, although the facts are again significant, the second argument also does not stand up to scrutiny. For the ill-formedness of examples like (11)b and (12)b is due, not to applying Tough Movement to the putative output of Raising, but rather to other causes. Observe such contrasts as these:

(16) a. It is hard to consider Jones (to be) competent.

    b. *Jones is hard to consider to be competent.

    c. Jones is hard to consider competent.

(17) a. It will be easy to prove Melvin (to be) guilty.

    b. *Melvin will be easy to prove to be guilty.

    c. Melvin will be easy to prove guilty.

Here (16)b and (17)b have the properties that Chomsky predicts, but

(16)c and (17)c behave contrastively. If it is really the fact that *Jones* and *Melvin* in the variants of (16)a, (17)a with the *to be* present remain in the lower clause that blocks (16)b and (17)b, then the well-formedness of the *c* examples shows that, in the variants of (16)a and (17)a without the *to be,* these NPs are in the higher clause. Thus, in the non-Raising account, one is immediately driven to the (to me) a priori unacceptable requirement[6] of different underlying structures for the variants of (16)a and (17)a, depending on whether *to be* shows up.

Moreover, not only is the conclusion dubious theoretically, but it can also be quickly eliminated on empirical grounds, which show that the clausal status of the NP is not distinguished in the cases with and without *to be.* Restricting ourselves to the cases without *to be,* we notice *first* that under a non-Raising account, the post-B-verb NPs are not and never were subjects. This follows since, if they were derived subjects, they would, according to Chomsky's account, block Tough Movement. On the other hand, if they had been underlying subjects, they could only have ceased to be subjects through the application of Raising, which is denied. But if the relevant NPs are not and never were subjects, one immediately loses, in either Chomsky's terms or mine, an account of the kind of extraction blockages discussed in Section 5.1:

(18) a. I considered a picture of Joan indecent.

　　 b. *Who did you consider a picture of indecent?

(19) a. They proved a memo about that inaccurate.

　　 b. *Who did they prove a memo about inaccurate?

Second, the relevant sentences can, with a bit of strain, contain existential *there*:

(20) ?I consider there unlikely to be further violence.

But we know independently that this is inserted only in subject posi-

---

[6] Such a conclusion is impossible in natural grammar, that is, a system in which the underlying structures of sentences are determined by their logical structures. In such terms, the semantic identity of the variants with and without *to be* forces identical underlying structures.

tion.[7] Thus both of these considerations show that the post-B-verb NPs in the cases without *to be* here are at the worst former subjects.

A *third* piece of evidence is derivable from facts involving floating emphatic reflexives, like *himself* and *in itself*. The generalization for these reflexives is that they can float away only from subject NPs:

(21) a. Bob is himself unwilling to do that.

b. *I gave Bob a book himself.

c. That is in itself sufficient reason.

d. *I talked about that to Bob in itself.

But there is also this case:

(22) a. I consider Nixon unlikely to himself commit acts of shoplifting.

b. They proved that insufficient in itself to yield the result.

The *fourth,* and final, point[8] is that there are adverbial expressions that can occur only in connection with subjects, for example, *by X-self*:

(23) a. John talked to Betty by himself.

b. *John talked to Betty by herself.

c. *I gave Joan a lift by herself.

d. *I discussed Joan with them by herself.

---

[7] Idiom chunks work the same way and provide an independent argument of the same sort. Hence *advantage* occurs only as the object of *take* and becomes a subject only through application of Passive. But one finds the following:

(i) I consider real advantage unlikely to be taken of that offer.

[8] Floating quantifiers, discussed briefly in Section 4.5, suggest an independent argument. Thus, if the italicized NPs in the following examples had never been subjects, it would be difficult to account for the distribution of the quantifiers, since quantifiers really float away only from subjects, and *unlikely* and *begin* are elements that trigger Raising, not Equi.

(i) I consider *them* unlikely to each leave separately.

(ii) I found *those managers* beginning to all question further promotions.

Thus (i) is well-formed, for example, because (iii) is:

(iii) It is unlikely that they will each leave separately.

And under Raising, (iii) leads to the generation of (iv), which, I claim, underlies the structure embedded under *consider* to form (i).

(iv) They are unlikely to each leave separately.

But note the following:

(24) a. I consider Nixon unlikely to go by himself.

b. They proved John incapable of doing that by himself.

Hence, on a variety of grounds, it is clear that the post-B-verb in a sequence like (25) must once have been the subject of a lower clause, just as it would have been for everyone, including Chomsky, in cases where *to be* intervenes between B-verb and adjective.

(25) X + B-verb + NP + Adjective + Y.

But now let us return to examples like (16). According to Chomsky's argument, (16)b is ill-formed because the NP moved by Tough Movement was a subject. Therefore, since (16)c is well-formed, the moved NP must *not* have been a subject at the point of Tough Movement application. But we have just shown that it must have been a subject earlier. And the only device known to account for the change of status is, of course, Raising. Hence when one expands the domain of fact to include cases like (16)c and (17)c, as well as (16)b and (17)b, not only do the data fail to argue against Raising, but they would, in fact, support Raising if the assumptions of Chomsky's argument were correct, that is, if the (16)b type of examples were ill-formed because Tough Movement cannot work in contexts like (15).

However, there is no reason to think that anything like (15) is relevant to such violations. There is good reason to conclude rather, as first suggested by Ross, that these blockages are due to the presence in the output of the marker *to*. It is a general fact, observed independently by many people, including Kayne, Lakoff, Perlmutter and myself, that even with unquestioned Raising into subject position, leaving more than one "successive" infinitive marker *to* decreases acceptability:

(26) a. ?Joe seems to be likely to win.

b. Joe seems likely to win.

c. ?Joe was believed to be likely to win.

d. Joe was believed likely to win.

We are dealing here with cases where a single NP is multiply raised, since *likely, seem,* and *believe* all trigger Raising. It has been claimed in passing that, in general, NPs can be raised an unlimited number of times if there is a proper underlying structure containing a "sequence" of successively embedded main verbs that trigger Raising. The iteration then follows, I claim, from the fact that Raising is cyclical (see Section 8.2). Lakoff (1967) was one of the first to illustrate such multiple applications of Raising within a single derivation, presenting such examples as the following:

(27) a. Max expected that Irving would believe that the bagel had been eaten by Seymour.

   b. Max expected Irving to believe the bagel to have been eaten by Seymour.

   c. Max expected the bagel to be believed by Irving to have been eaten by Seymour.

   d. The bagel was expected by Max to be believed by Irving to have been eaten by Seymour.

Here, under an analysis in which Raising is operative for B-verb complements, the NP *the bagel* has been multiply raised in (27)c and d. Lakoff apparently considered both of the last two examples to be unexceptionable. But, to me, they have rather the dubious status of (26)a, c. Deletion of *to be* cannot improve such examples because it is not generally permitted with participles. In the following example there is an equally unacceptable result:

(28) ?The bagel was expected by Max to seem to be rotten.

However, just as with Chomsky's examples involving Tough Movement, the violation is eliminated by deleting *to be*:

(29) The bagel was expected by Max to seem rotten.

I suggest, then, that it is the fact that the marker *to* is left behind in cases of multiple movements of a single NP as the result of either successive applications of Raising or combinations of Raising and Tough Movement that are responsible for the ill-formed examples of this section.

   Cantrall (1969:124) has observed that, whereas multiple raisings involving ordinary NPs yield somewhat unhappy results (with trailing *to*), they yield absolute ungrammaticality with existential *there*. Thus he gives the analogues to Lakoff's sentences (27):

(30) a. Max expected that Irving would believe there was a bagel in his lunch box.

   b. Max expected Irving would believe there to be a bagel in his lunch box.

   c. *Max expected there to be believed by Irving to be a bagel in his lunch box.

   d. *There was expected by Max to be believed by Irving to be a bagel in his lunch box.

Moreover, Perlmutter and I have observed that essentially the same thing is true of idiom chunks and weather *it*:

(31) a. I believe that Tom expects that tabs will be kept on her movements.

   b. I believe Tom expects tabs to be kept on her movements.

   c. ?I believe that tabs are expected to be kept on her movements.

   d. *I believe that tabs are expected by Tom to be kept on her movements.

   e. *Tabs are believed to be expected (by Tom) to be kept on her movements.

(32) a. Joe believes Ira found that little heed had been taken of her suggestion.

   b. Joe believes Ira found little heed to have been taken of her suggestion.

   c. ?Joe believes little heed was found by Ira to have been taken of her suggestion.

   d. *Little heed is believed to have been found (by Ira) to have been taken of her suggestion.

(33) a. Joe believes Melvin found that it was raining in Madrid.

   b. Joe believes Melvin found it to be raining in Madrid.

   c. Joe believes it was found (*by Melvin) to be raining in Madrid.

    d. *It is believed to have been found (by Melvin) to be raining in Madrid.

It thus seems that all of the "empty" NPs like *there,* weather *it,* and idiom chunks yield ill-formed sentences when they are multiply raised in such a way as to leave trailing *to.* However, when they are placed in contexts where the *to* can be elided, multiple applications of Raising are all right:

(34) a. *There seems to be likely to be a riot.

    b. There seems likely to be a riot.

(35) a. *Tabs appear to be likely to be kept on her movements.

    b. ?Tabs appear likely to be kept on her movements.

(36) a. *Little heed appears to be likely to be taken of my suggestion.

    b. Little heed appears likely to be taken of my suggestion.

These facts show, among other things, that Cantrall's (1969) view that facts like (30)c, d cast doubt on the very existence of Raising is unsupportable. In fact, it is not true that "empty" NPs cannot be multiply raised; it is only that this multiple raising must not leave behind "too many" trailing infinitive markers. The point seems to be that multiple raisings are better if they do not generate (by the rule that de-finitizes clauses when their subjects are raised) multiple occurrences of *to* between the original locus of the NP and its terminal point, and in the case of an empty NP, the constraint seems even stricter.

    Although I have no precise formulation to offer, it seems that a generalization that covers cases like (16)b, and (17)b as well as those like (26), (28), and (30)–(33) lies in the direction of talking about "raising" rules per se and of subsuming both Raising and Tough Movement under this category.[9] This is of further interest, because the parallel be-

[9] However, any such account must deal with the following contrast, pointed out to me by Baker:

(i) a. Bill is tough *to* persuade *to* smoke cigars.
    b. *Bill is tough *to* believe *to* smoke cigars.

Perhaps the difference lies in the fact that in (i)b the pair of immediately successive (in the obvious sense) *to*'s are generated through the operation of Raising. That is, the second *to* exists only because *believe* has triggered Raising. But in (i)a, neither *to* is a function of raising rules per se, since underlying (i)a would be (ii), which has both *to*'s in it.

havior of Tough Movement and Raising derivations here actually offers some evidence for Tough Movement, which has so far been very thin.

If it is really true that the violations of this section are a function of too many trailing *to*'s as suggested by Ross, then multiple raisings that do not have this consequence should in general be permitted. We have already seen that this is so in those cases where *to be* is deleted. It should also be so in cases where the de-finitized clauses produced by Raising are of gerundive form. The following examples show that this assumption is correct:

(37) a. It seems that John ended up supporting the communists.

  b. John seems to have ended up supporting the communists.

(38) a. I prevented it from seeming that John ended up supporting the communists.

  b. I prevented John from seeming to end up supporting the communists.

(39) a. It ended up seeming that John began supporting the communists in 1939.

  b. John ended up seeming to have begun supporting the communists in 1939.

Note that this is even true of "empty" NPs:

(40) a. It seems that there ended up being a riot.

  b. There seems to have ended up being a riot.

(41) a. It seems that tabs first began being kept on her in March.

  b. Tabs first seem to have begun $\begin{Bmatrix} \text{being} \\ \text{*to be} \end{Bmatrix}$ kept on her in March.

Thus Ross's view that the violations involve, not multiple raisings per se, but the generation of intervening infinitival markers is further supported.[10]

(ii) It is tough to persuade Bill to smoke cigars.

Clearly, we have only begun to scratch the surface of these *to* violations.

[10] This question bears on the claim that auxiliaries, including modals, are verbs that trigger Raising. For multiple raisings are possible with such elements, since in (i)a,

I conclude, then, that (i) Chomsky's argument against Raising does not hold up; (ii) its premise that (15) is the relevant structure for blocking examples like (16)b is almost certainly incorrect; and (iii) what is relevant is probably the constraint suggested by Ross generating unacceptability when de-finitization operations generate too many occurrences of the infinitival marker. What is required then is work directed toward providing a precise specification of the constraint in (iii).

Given something like (iii), it seems natural to assume, as have several people independently at various times, including Kayne, Ross, and myself, that the facts actually can provide a strong argument *for* Raising. That is, given (iii), violations like (42), as compared with (43), are due to the extra *to* generated when Raising is triggered by *certain*.

(42) a. *There is certain to be believed to be a spy in your class.

b. *There is certain to be about to be a riot.

(43) a. It is certain that there is believed to be a spy in your class.

b. It is certain that there is about to be a riot.

This is A-verb Raising, accepted even by Chomsky. But violations such

---

for example, *been, have,* and *may* would all have triggered applications of Raising on successive cycles.

(i) a. John may have been sick.
   b. The bomb should have gone off.
   c. There may have been a riot.

However, such sentences are consistent with the theory that auxiliaries are Raising-verb triggering elements since there are no dangling *to*'s in such cases. This theory should predict that the one modal that does require this *to*, namely, *ought*, would induce violations in the parallel cases:

(ii) a. George may seem to be healthy.
    b. ?George ought to seem to be healthy.
    c. George ought to seem healthy.

(iii) a. There may not seem to be too much pressure in the tube.
    b. *There ought not to be too much pressure in the tube.

As (ii)b and (iii)b show, this is correct. Thus Ross's insight about *to* shows that the possibility of examples like (i) is in no way incompatible with a Raising theory of auxiliaries.

as (44), as compared with (45), involve on the second cycle at best B-verb Raising.

(44) a. *I believe there to be certain to be a spy in your class.

    b. *I believe there to be certain to be a riot if . . .

(45) a. I believe that there is certain to be a spy in your class.

    b. I believe there is certain to be a riot if . . .

Hence, if the constraint actually does refer to occurrences of *to* generated by applications of Raising, or even by "raising" rules in general, the violations in (44) support the view that there is Raising operation with B-verb infinitival complements.

Whether this argument in favor of Raising can be sustained or not is, however, unclear to me. It depends in part on whether or not parallel violations are produced by processes other than Raising which induce infinitival form. For instance, at first glance the following examples seem to show that the *to* violations are not exclusively linked to Raising:

(46) a. *I prayed for there to be certain to be a riot.

    b. *I arranged for there to be sure to be witnesses present.

    c. *It would be impossible for there to be about to be a riot.

    d. *It is not nice for John to be believed to be insane.

If these are ill-formed for the same reason as earlier examples involving Raising, then the argument for Raising would dissolve. Ross suggests, however, that there is an independent basis for the ungrammaticality in (46), namely, verb-verb selectional restrictions blocking superordinate-subordinate linkages of (47):

(47) a. *pray-certain

    b. *arrange-sure

    c. *impossible-about

    d. *nice-believe

In certain cases, this claim is supported:

(48) a. *I prayed for it to be certain that there would be a riot.

b. *I arranged for it to be sure that there would be witnesses
present.

That is, on the basis of (48), examples like (46)a, b are explained with
no appeal to extra *to* violations, and the necessary linkage between *to*
violations and Raising is maintained. However, the *that*-clause analogue of (46)d is not all that bad, and it is certainly better than (46)d.

(49) ?It is not nice for it to be believed that John is insane.

These matters certainly require much further investigation, as do
the problems raised by Baker's observations in footnote 9. At the
moment, one must hesitate to take the *to* violations as a definite pro-
Raising argument. But they surely deserve the status of a potential
argument, like numerous other sets of facts to be considered in Chapter 6.

5.3 A Reciprocal and Inclusion Constraint Argument
Chomsky (to appear: footnote 33) offers one further argument against
Raising applications of the sort in question. This is given essentially
as follows:

As already noted, it is difficult to incorporate a rule of raising of the
familiar sort within the present framework. . . . There are other examples too which indicate that the allegedly raised subject continues
to behave as the subject of the embedded sentence rather than the
object of the matrix sentence. Thus consider the sentence "the men
each were told to expect John to kill the other(s)." If *John* is raised on
an internal cycle, it will no longer be a subject when the matrix cycle
is reached, so that *each* movement should apply, giving *"the men
were told to expect John to kill each other." Similarly, we have "we
were told to expect John to kill me" but not "we were told to expect
to kill me", the former inconsistent with subject-raising. . . .

However, the entire force of this pair of examples clearly depends on
Chomsky's assumptions, already argued to be untenable in Chapter 3,
that (i) there is a rule *Each* Movement underlying reciprocals; (ii) both
this rule and the Inclusion Constraint are controlled by the specified
subject condition. This argument against Raising operation into superordinate object position is thus internal to Chomsky's descriptive system and has no independent force. Given the array of evidence for
B-verb, W-verb, and N-verb Raising already presented, such cases are

properly interpretable, I suggest, only as showing further the incorrectness of the specified subject condition.

5.4 Summary

As far as I can determine, the three arguments just presented are the only ones that Chomsky explicitly offers against a system involving Raising operation into superordinate object positions. None of them holds up. I am, moreover, unaware of any other arguments that would suggest any problems with Raising into matrix object positions. Consequently, I conclude that the positive arguments in favor of matrix object Raising systems found in Chapters 3 and 4 (also Chapters 6 and 12) are not currently balanced by any known negative indications.

6
Potential Arguments

6.1 Comments

In Chapters 3 and 4 (see also Sections 12.6, 12.7, and 12.8), I have attempted to construct arguments showing that Raising is indeed operative with B-verb infinitival complements, W-verb infinitival complements, and N-verb complements. Generally, in order to formulate such arguments, it is necessary to have a certain degree of understanding of some independent aspect of English grammar. That is, it is necessary to depend on some generalization, rule, or constraint that makes reference to such notions as "derived subject," "derived object," "command," "Clause Mate," or, in general, some property that distinguishes the status of raised and unraised NPs. I am of the opinion that the at least eighteen arguments already given suffice to justify the claims advocated here. Nonetheless, given our extremely limited knowledge of English grammar as a whole, and the possibility that any argument can be overthrown by further empirical investigation (consider the fate of the argument in Section 4.5), I think it is not possible to have too many arguments for claims about English grammar as fundamental as those involving Raising. It is therefore of some interest to ask if it is possible to formulate further arguments with some force.

I believe there are further areas that will yield such arguments when they are studied further, although my own current understanding of them is not sufficient to claim that they really do so at present. I have thought it worthwhile to point out such areas here, along with some indication of the logic of their relation to Raising and with an account of some of the problems preventing final formulations at the moment.

Although the cases that follow are regarded only as potential arguments, it should be stressed that in most cases the formulations are developed sufficiently to suggest, I think, that the burden of proof is at least as strong for those who would reject these arguments as for those who would attempt to solidify them.

6.2 *Each* Shift

There is a process in English that has the effect of moving the quantifier *each* out of the NP corresponding to the variable bound by *each*[1] and attaching it to (or after) the end of a usually numerically quantified NP whose numerical quantifier is under the scope of the *each*. The process in question is illustrated by the *b, d* examples in the following:

(1) a. Each of the boys kissed her three times.

   b. The boys kissed her three times each.

   c. I gave each of them five dollars.

   d. I gave them five dollars each.

As far as I know, this aspect of English grammar has been studied directly only in Hudson (1970).[2]

I shall assume that constructions like (1)b and (1)d are derived by a rule of quantifier movement, called *Each* Shift, which transports the form *each* from one NP (henceforth in general the "*each*-source") to the end of another[3] (henceforth in general the "*each*-target"). One should distinguish this rule from that involved in moving all of the quantifiers *all, both,* and *each* into positions in the verbal phrase. The latter rule was the basis of the ill-fated argument of Section 4.5. *Each* Shift operates only on *each,* but with the proviso that in many contexts *each* can apparently be realized as the form *apiece*:

(2) I gave them ten dollars apiece.

One should also sharply distinguish *Each* Shift from the rule, mentioned earlier, which Dougherty (1969) and Chomsky (to appear) assume to underlie the process of reciprocal formation.

As noted by Hudson (1970), in some cases an *each*-target can be connected to two distinct *each*-sources, as in (3), where the *each*-source is ambiguously either the subject or the indirect object.

---

1 Actually, this is a simplification, since I claim that NPs like (i) have the structure (ii), and *each* binds only the NP whose head is *one*, not the whole large NP or that headed by *dancers*.

(i) each (one) of the dancers.

(ii) $[_{NP} [_{NP}$ each one $_{NP}]$ of $[_{NP}$ the dancers $_{NP}]$ $_{NP}]$

2 I have benefited a good deal from Hudson's discussion even though I have adopted here an analysis of the sort that he rejects.

3 I have no sharp evidence that the *each* is actually attached to the end of the *each*-target rather than being placed after it. This is immaterial for the present discussion, in which the former is assumed for convenience.

(3) They gave us two pounds each.

However, although one can find cases like (4), it is not possible for *Each Shift* to reorder both occurrences of *each,* as in (5):

(4) Each of them gave each of us two pounds.

(5) *They gave us two pounds $\left\{ \begin{array}{l} \text{each each} \\ \text{apiece apiece} \\ \text{apiece each} \\ \text{each apiece} \end{array} \right\}$.

However the third choice seems far better than any of the others in (5). This constraint on *Each* Shift might be a function of the fact that a shifted *each/apiece* must be the terminal element of the *each*-target NP. This is consistent with the following facts on the assumption that nonrestrictive relatives are parts of NPs:

(6) a. *He gave them six apples each, which were wormy.

    b. He gave them six apples, which were wormy.

    c. ??He gave them six apples, which were wormy, each.

There are several different sorts of constraints on *Each* Shift: *First,* there are constraints on the internal nature of the *each*-target:

(7) a. Each of the boys showed me (the) five pigs.

    b. The boys showed me (*the) five pigs each.[4]

(8) a. I gave each of them $\left\{ \begin{array}{l} \text{some} \\ \text{three gallons of} \end{array} \right\}$ water.

    b. I gave them $\left\{ \begin{array}{l} \text{*some} \\ \text{three gallons of} \end{array} \right\}$ water each.

(9) a. I gave each of them three of my horses.

    b. *I gave them three of my horses each.

Second, there are constraints on the position of the NP to which *each* is attached. For instance, in my speech, but probably not that of many

---

4 In reality, the ill-formedness of (7)b when the definite article is present is, no doubt, simply a function of the constraint that the numeral quantifier must be under the scope of *each*. This is impossible when the NP is definite.

others, *Each* Shift seems inapplicable whenever the *each*-target is the head of a prepositional phrase:

(10) a. Each of the heroes was given three medals by two ministers.

b. The heroes were given three medals each by two ministers.

c. *The heroes were given three medals by two ministers each.

(11) a. Each of us talked to two girls.

b. *We talked to two girls each.

(12) a. Each of us $\left\{ \begin{array}{l} \text{frightened} \\ \text{was frightening to} \end{array} \right\}$ two nuns.

b. $\left\{ \begin{array}{l} \text{We frightened} \\ \text{*We were frightening to} \end{array} \right\}$ two nuns each.

It should be noted, however, that violations of this constraint are not as severely ill-formed as many other wrong applications of *Each* Shift,[5] and, moreover, this constraint is idiolect variable. Another restriction of the same sort involving subjects will be discussed later. *Third,* there are constraints on the relative positions of the *each*-source and *each*-target. Here the most obvious restriction seems to be that the former must precede the latter (let us say at the point of application; this will be justified later).

(13) a. He sent three men to each of the stores.

b. *He sent three men each to the stores.

(14) a. Harry bought three diamonds for each of those girls.

b. *Harry bought three diamonds each for those girls.

c. For those girls, Harry bought three diamonds each.

d. The girls, for whom Harry bought three diamonds each, are happy.

---

[5] Observe that there is no parallel restriction on the *each*-source, which can freely be part of the head NP of a prepositional phrase:

(i) a. To each of us he sent at least two packages.
    b. To us, he sent at least two packages each.

(ii) a. For each of those girls, Max bought at least two orchids.
     b. For those girls, Max bought at least two orchids each.

(15) a.   Jack explained four problems to each of the students.

b. *Jack explained four problems each to the students.

c.   To the students, Jack explained four problems each.

d.   The students to whom Jack explained four problems each failed.

Sentences like (14)c, d and (15)c, d show, of course, that the positions produced by unbounded leftward movement rules (like Topicalization, Adverb Preposing, and *Wh* Rel Movement) can determine proper application of *Each* Shift, even when the original positions prior to the application of such rules would not have. This is of considerable importance in cases like (16), where the unbounded movement rule has moved the *each*-source to a point well out of its original containing clause.

(16) a.   For those girls, I am sure Harry bought three diamonds each.

b. For those girls, it was later learned that he had bought three diamonds each.

This means that, if we assume that *Each* Shift operates on the output of the unbounded NP movement rule in such cases,[6] the rule transports an *each* between an *each*-source and an *each*-target which are *not* Clause Mates into the input structure of *Each* Shift.[7]

[6] There is a (global) alternative, namely, to have *Each* Shift operate prior to such movements subject to a global condition that "looks ahead" to make sure that at later stages the *each*-source precedes the *each*-target, even if this is not the case at the point of application. However, such an alternative would at best be highly complex because, as noted in the text later, the left-to-right precedence condition between *each*-source and *each*-target is *not* a property of surface structures.

[7] The claim that a formulation of *Each* Shift as applying to the output of unbounded leftward movement rules means that in many cases *each*-source and *each*-target are not Clause Mates in the input structure to *Each* Shift depends on the assumption that unbounded movement rules transport traveling constituents in a single bound from their point of origin to their terminal location (under that rule). Thus, take an underlying structure like (i):

(i) [$_S$ I think [$_S$ Harry bought three orchids for each of those girls $_S$] $_S$]

If Topicalization directly generates (ii), with no intermediate structures, then *Each* Shift application to (ii) involves *each*-source and *each*-target, which are not Clause Mates in the input—that is, *each of those girls* and *three orchids* are not Clause Mates in (ii).

(ii) For each of those girls, I think Harry bought three orchids.

On the other hand, Jackendoff (1969) and Chomsky (to appear) have suggested a cyclical, multiple-jump conception (called "successive cyclic" in Postal, 1972c) of un-

It might then seem that a Clause Mate condition plays no role in the description of the relative positions of *each*-source and *Each* Shift. This is not the case, however. For consider (17):

(17) a. I (think I) told three girls that he would never give five dollars to each of those kids.

   b. *I (think I) told three girls that he would never give five dollars each to those kids.

   c. *I (think I) told three girls each that he would never give five dollars to those kids.

   d. To those kids, I (think I) told three girls that he would never give five dollars each.

---

bounded movement rules in which the traveling constituent reaches its ultimate locus in a series of hops, moving to the front of each successive clause. In this conception, the proper precedence relations between *each*-target and *each*-source would be derived for sentences like (ii) at a point when these NPs can still be taken as Clause Mates, that is, in the intermediate structure (iii):

(iii) I think [$_S$ for each of those girls Harry bought three orchids $_S$]

However, there are, I think, deep grounds for rejecting a successive cyclic account of such rules. For some initial discussion, see Postal (1972c), Perlmutter (to appear).

A key point in distinguishing unbounded movement rules from true cyclic rules is that the former do not interact with any other clearly cyclic rules. This is an automatic consequence of a postcyclic, one-move theory of such rules, but it requires special otherwise unmotivated conditions in a successive cyclic theory. That is, in the latter system the interactions with other cyclic rules predicted by a cyclic formulation must be blocked by additional statements. One such statement in Chomsky's account (to appear) is a principle that permits elements inside the constituent Comp (where unbounded rules place constituents) to move only to another Comp. This condition, whose ad hoc character is at best thinly disguised by the claim that it is a part of universal grammar, is needed by Chomsky to prevent, among other things, Passive from applying to structures like (iv), generating (v), since, it will be recalled, Chomsky claims that Passive can work down into untensed clauses.

(iv) Jack learned [$_S$ Comp to call $_S$].
                     |
                     NP
                     |
                    who

(v) **Who was learned to call by Jack; or **who was learned by Jack to call?

Such potential derivations never can arise, of course, in systems in which either Passive is strictly clause-internal, or unbounded movement rules are postcyclic, or where both conditions are met.

e. *To those kids, I (think I) told three girls each that he would never give five dollars.

The preposing of *to those kids* generates a good *Each* Shift sentence in (17)d, but not in (17)e. These contrast according to whether *each*-source and *each*-target were Clause Mates prior to application of the unbounded movement rule. Nonetheless, (17) provides only a weak argument for a Clause Mate condition on *Each* Shift.

It can be observed that in (17)a the quantifier *three* is not under the scope of *each*. Therefore, it can be argued that (17)e is blocked because *each* can be shifted only to an *each*-target containing a numerical quantifier under the scope of *each*. While the latter argument is not decisive, since in the type of case in question it is seemingly a Clause Mate condition that determines the relative scopes, it certainly clouds the issue sufficiently to preclude basing a case on contrasts like (17)d, e alone.

What is needed is a case where the underlying form meets the scope inclusion condition but where *Each* Shift is still blocked when the Clause Mate condition is not met (and in contexts where no other known constraints on *Each Shift* are operative). I think such a case is provided by examples like the following:

(18) a. I talked to each of the senators about (my) blocking three bills.

b. *I talked to the senators about (my) blocking three bills each.

c. I talked to each of the advisors about displaying three pictures of myself .

d. *I talked to the advisors about displaying three pictures of myself each.

The point here is that, in both (18)a and (18)c, *three* is under the scope of *each*,[8] yet *Each* Shift is still blocked. It is natural to explain this in terms of the failure of the *each*-source and *each*-target to be Clause Mates, since there is a clause boundary after the word *about*.

Within ordinary transformational terms, it would be natural to assume that the Clause Mate condition is imposed on the inputs to *Each* Shift, like the source-target precedence condition. However, examples like (14) and (15) have already shown that the condition that *each*-source pre-

---

[8] That is, it *can* be. The relative scopes of *each* and *three* are ambiguous in (18)a, (18)c.

cede *each-target* is definable only *on the output* of unbounded movement rules, even though a Clause Mate condition would be met only in cases like (14)c and (15)d at a point prior to the application of unbounded rules (given the remarks of footnote 7).

In short, under the assumption that the unbounded rules operate (postcyclically) in a single swoop, it appears that *Each* Shift must be regarded as a global rule, since the condition that *each*-source and *each*-target be Clause Mates refers to a different level of structure than the condition that *each*-source precede *each*-target. With present inadequate knowledge, it appears that there are two alternative global formulations. On the one hand, *Each* Shift could be defined as applying at a stage prior to the unbounded movements (say, cyclically), in which case the Clause Mate condition is a restriction met by the trees' input to the rule, but the left-to-right condition is a global condition "looking ahead from the point of application" to later stages. On the other hand, *Each* Shift could be characterized as a postcyclical rule (on the assumption that the unbounded movements are all postcyclical), in which case the left-to-right condition can be made a constraint on input trees, while the Clause Mate requirement is a global condition "looking back" from the point of application to earlier stages. Although it does not matter for present purposes which of these formulations is chosen, there is some evidence favoring the latter, postcyclical, "look back" account.

This evidence consists of the fact that it is difficult to formulate a "look ahead" condition because it does not seem to be the case that the *each*-source–*each*-target precedence condition holds at any distinguishable levels of grammatical structure. In particular, it need not hold in surface structure, as the following cases show:

(19) a. Able to afford two mistresses though each of them is, they only have one.

b. Able to afford two mistresses each though they are, they only have one.

(20) a. ?Sure to win three races, each of them isn't.

b. Sure to win three races each, they are not.

Thus, if *Each* Shift applies before unbounded movement rules, it is not clear how a general account of the precedence condition can be given.

This is evidence for the latter formulation if it can be shown that under a postcyclic definition of *Each* Shift, in which the precedence condition holds at the point of application, there is a natural way to characterize generally the Clause Mate restriction as a "look back" condition. A first attempt might be to say that this condition holds for the correspondents of *each*-source and *each*-target at the end of the whole cycle, in so-called "shallow structure." That this will not do, however, is easily seen on the basis of A-verb Raising cases like (21):

(21) a. They are certain to give me five dollars each.

   b. They seemed likely to send two men each.

   c. They ended up loaning her two hundred francs each.

At the end of the cycle, Raising has already applied, in (21)b twice, with each of the elements *certain, seemed, likely,* and *ended up* serving as the triggering factor (see Section 9.2). Consequently, in the structures resulting from the application of the last cyclic rule, *each-source* and *each-target* are not Clause Mates, since there are clause boundaries before the word *to* in (21)a, b and after the word *up* in (21)c.

However, I suggest that a somewhat different condition suffices, namely, that *each*-source and *each*-target (more precisely, their correspondents) must be Clause Mates at the end of some earlier cycle,[9] not necessarily the last. This condition is met in (21), because the relevant NPs will be Clause Mates at the end of the complement cycles in (21)a, c, and at the end of the lowest cycle in (21)b, before the *each*-containing NPs have been raised even once.

Thus there is a general "look back" formulation of the Clause Mate condition, but no general "look ahead" formulation of the precedence condition. This leads to a choice of a grammar in which *Each* Shift is regarded as a postcyclically-applying rule in which *each*-source must precede *each*-target in the input, subject to a global Clause Mate condition

[9] This formulation sounds as if the relevant point in derivations were to be picked out by quantification over the class of cycle-final trees, a highly undesirable approach, as stressed by Lakoff. This is, in fact, unnecessary since there is a function picking out the relevant cycle-final structures, namely, one that specifies the lowest cycle covering the sets of corresponding constituents of the pair *each*-source and *each*-target, where by "covering cycle" I refer to one defined by an S that dominates a member of each set of corresponding nodes. This function is, I suggest, also that needed for pronominalization constraints, particularly reflexivization. For some further discussion, see Section 8.2, especially footnote 2 of Chapter 8.

defined over the ends of certain cycles. As already noted in footnote 9, it will be seen later that an analogous cycle-final Clause Mate condition plays a role in reflexivization (see Section 8.2). This formulation is compatible with examples like (19)b and (20)b, since it can be assumed that *Each* Shift and the rules that produce the marked word orders in these sentences are *unordered* post-cyclical rules. Hence, *Each* Shift can apply before the word order shifts, at which point the precedence conditon still holds, the latter being a constraint only on the inputs to *Each* Shift.

Some additional support is available for the claims that there is a Clause Mate condition on *Each* Shift and that it is defined on the ends of cycles. First, this account correctly predicts the facts in (22):

(22) a.   Each of the lawyers showed that Joan called at least three doctors.

   b.   Each of the lawyers showed Joan to have called at least three doctors.

   c.   Joan was shown by each of the lawyers to have called at least three doctors.

   d. *Joan was shown by the lawyers to have called at least three doctors each.

In this case, Raising and Passive can apply only on the cycle of the main verb *showed* or *shown*. Even though the source-target precedence condition is met postcyclically in the case of a potential input like (22)c, and even though the scope condition is met, *Each* Shift is properly blocked in accord with (22)d, since there is no cycle-final structure in which the relevant NPs are Clause Mates. While (22)d supports a Clause Mate condition, it does not provide support for assigning this condition to the relevant cycle-final structures in particular, since there is *no* tree at all in the derivation of (22)d in which the NPs involved are Clause Mates. Evidence for a Clause Mate condition that does support assignment on this condition to the level of covering cycle-final trees is, however, derivable from processes that reduce or truncate clause structures.

Let us consider comparatives first. It is generally recognized that examples like (23)b have *than* phrases that are, in fact, reduced variants of the full clauses in examples like (23)a:

(23) a. Joan is taller than those boys are.

    b. Joan is taller than those boys.

Consider, then, variants of (23)b containing *each*:

(24) a. Each of the girls is taller than at least three boys.

    b. *The girls are taller than at least three boys each.

Here, although *three* is under the scope of *each,* and the precedence condition is met, *Each* Shift is inapplicable. Moreover, *each of the girls* and *at least three boys* would appear to be Clause Mates in derived structure. However, the ill-formedness of (24)b will follow automatically from a Clause Mate condition defined on the ends of cycles, for there is no *cycle-final* structure for (24)b in which the *each*-source and *each*-target correspondents are Clause Mates, under the natural assumption that the clause truncation process for comparatives is postcyclical.

    Similarly, there is a process of reduced answers to questions (discussed further from the point of view of reflexivization and adverb interpolation in Section 8.2) illustrated by (25):

(25) a. Q: Who should we hire?

    b. A: They think we should hire Melvin.

    c. A: They think Melvin.

Clearly, the process of reduction responsible[10] for examples like (25c) makes the subject of *think* and the post-*think* NP Clause Mates. However, under the natural assumption that this process is postcyclical, it will follow from our account of *Each* Shift as subject to a cycle-final Clause Mate condition that this rule is not applicable in cases of Clause Mates generated only by the reduction in question. But this is the case, for observe the following:

(26) a. Q: Should we hire three women or four men?

    b. A: Each of my colleagues thinks we should hire three women.

    c. A: Each of my colleagues thinks three women.

    d. A: My colleagues think three women each.

---

[10] Any doubts that sentences like (25)c are properly described as reductions of full sentences like (25)b (in contexts defined by particular questions like (25)a are, I think, fully eliminated by the arguments in Morgan (to appear).

Here, although *three* in (26)c is under the scope of *each*, *Each* Shift is inapplicable. This is shown by the total nonequivalence of (26)c and (26)d. The latter could only be derived along the lines of (27), that is, in a derivation in which *Each* Shift applies according to structures generated *without* the answer reduction process.

(27) a. Q: Should they hire three women each or only two women each?

    b. A: My colleagues think they should hire three women each.

    c. A: My colleagues think three women each.

Hence a cycle-final Clause Mate condition seems to properly control the interaction of *Each* Shift and the answer reduction process, where no independent principles are known to be relevant.

This long, apparent digression has provided us with some grounds for concluding that there is a rule of *Each* Shift that: (i) operates postcyclically on an input structure in which *each*-source precedes *each*-target; (ii) attaches the *each* to the end of an *each*-target containing an appropriate quantifier under the scope of the *each*; (iii) does not operate into prepositional phrases (subject to idiolect variation); (iv) is apparently subject to a global "look back" condition requiring the correspondents of *each*-source and *each*-target to be Clause Mates at the end of the lowest cycle covering both of them.

Assuming such a rule, let us turn to some typical environments where the question of Raising application arises, that is, cases involving B-verbs, N-verbs, etc.:

(28) a. Each of the students proved (that) three formulas were theorems.

    b. *The students proved (that) three formulas each were theorems.

(29) a. Each of the doctors showed (that) two classes of microbes were harmless.

    b. *The doctors showed (that) two classes of microbes each were harmless.

(30) a. Each of the ministers believed (that) three officers were spies.

    b. *The ministers believed (that) three officers each were spies.

It is evident, in the cases of B-verbs with *that*-clause complements, where there is no question of Raising application, and hence no question that the underlying complement subject remains a complement subject throughout the cyclic part of the grammar, that *Each* Shift cannot move a quantifier from the main verb subject, despite the fact that the quantifiers of the potential *each*-targets are under the scope of the relevant *each*. However, this follows automatically from our assumptions so far since, although the scope condition and the left-to-right condition are both met, the Clause Mate condition is not. That is, there is no cycle in (28), (29), or (30) at the end of which *each*-source and *each*-target are Clause Mates.

Moreover, there is, in some idiolects, an independent reason why examples like (28)b, (29)b, and (30)b are ill-formed. For many speakers, including myself, there is an additional condition on *Each* Shift, namely, that it cannot attach an *each* to an NP in subject position. Thus:

(31) a. At least three girls sent invitations to each of those officers.

b. *At least three girls each sent invitations to those officers.

c. *To those officers, at least three girls each sent invitations.

(32) a. At least two requests were made by each of the prisoners.

b. *At least two requests each were made by the prisoners.

c. *The prisoners, by whom at least two requests each were made,

Here the *b* examples are blocked by the left-to-right condition. But nothing said so far blocks the *c* examples, since the scope condition, the left-to-right condition, and the cycle-final Clause Mate condition are all met. Evidently, for those who reject (31)c, (32)c, etc., there is an additional nonsubject condition blocking attachment of *each* to a potential *each*-target in subject position.[11]

It follows that examples like (28)b, (29)b, and (30)b in the idiolects of those who do not accept (31)c, (32)c, etc., violate both the Clause Mate condition and the nonsubject condition, accounting for their truly ungrammatical character.

Now consider the infinitival analogues of (28)–(30):

(33) a. Each of the students proved three formulas to be theorems.

b. ?The students proved three formulas each to be theorems.

(34) a. Each of the doctors showed two classes of microbes to be harmless.

---

[11] This condition is crucially vague in not specifying on what level of structure the relevant notion of subjecthood is to be defined. I shall return to this presently.

b. ?The doctors showed two classes of microbes each to be harmless.

(35) a. Each of the ministers believed three officers to be spies.

   b. ?The ministers believed three officers each to be spies.

I find the infinitival examples generated by *Each* Shift[12] somewhat strain-ed. But there can be no doubt of the sharp contrast in acceptability be-tween these and the corresponding *that*-clause examples, which are far worse. This difference is naturally predicted by a Raising grammar of the infinitival cases in conjunction with the Clause Mate and nonsubject condition on *Each* Shift. The strained character of (33)b, etc., is, of course, not explained.

A potential account is, however, also conceivable in the terms worked out so far. Significantly, this strain is apparently not present in the idiolects of those who accept (31)c, (32)c, etc.[13] That is, the strained qual-ity of examples like (33)b seems to correlate with the nonsubject condi-tion. Suppose it is claimed, then, that this condition does not apply to the output trees generated by *Each* Shift, but rather that the condition is that the *each*-Target cannot be a *cyclical subject,* that is, the subject at the end of some cycle. It should be stressed that this is a property un-affected by subsequent Raising application. Hence, in (33)b, even though, in a Raising grammar, *three formulas* is not in subject position postcyclically, when *Each* Shift would thus apply, this NP is nonetheless the cyclical subject of *be.* Consequently, a global account of the non-subject condition in these terms offers some hope of simultaneously ex-plaining both the strained character of (33)b, etc., for those possessing this constraint and the perfectly natural character of such examples for those who do not possess it.[14]

---

12 In many cases, examples like (33)b have irrelevant readings in which the *each* is construed as part of the verbal phrase and hence as having been placed by the rule discussed in Section 4.5. This irrelevant reading can be eliminated by insertion of a parenthetical expression, as in (i):

(i) ?The students proved three formulas each, if I am not mistaken, to be theorems.

All relevant examples should then be read as having the structure in (i).

13 I am indebted to my colleagues F. Damerau and S. Petrick for information about this idiolect type.

14 Even this leaves unexplained the fact that examples like (33)b are not, in my idiolect, as bad as (31)c, and also the fact that (35)b seems worse than (33)b or (34)b.

Our account would also predict that, in idiolects with the nonsubject condition, for N-verb cases like (36) and (37) the *b* examples would be strained, while the same examples would be fine in the idiolect type without the nonsubject condition.

(36) a. Each of the men prevented two muggers from escaping.

b. ?The men prevented two muggers each from escaping.

(37) a. Each of the women deterred two salesmen from entering.

b. ?The women deterred two salesmen each from entering.

This also seems to be the case.

It appears, then, that those cases which receive derived Clause Mate status in a Raising grammar of B-verbs, N-verbs, etc., behave under *Each* Shift as if they had just such a derived Clause Mate status, in contrast to the *that*-clause cases, which behave as if they lacked such a status. The only account of these facts that can avoid postulation of Raising would appear to be one claiming that *Each* Shift does not work down into *that* clauses because of something like Chomsky's tensed clause condition. However, that this is insufficient at best is shown by the fact that for all idiolects those infinitival clauses which clearly exclude a Raising analysis block *Each* Shift from the main clause as firmly as do *that* clauses:

(38) a. Each of the men arranged for at least three girls to come.

b. *The men arranged for at least three girls each to come.

(39) a. Each of the novices prayed for at least two angels to appear.

b. *The novices prayed for at least two angels each to appear.

The former might well be attributed to a general principle that violations that are "visible" in surface structure are worse than those whose violation depends on computation of some level of underlying structure. The latter may well be a function of a constraint on *Each* Shift existing in my idiolect, but not, for instance, in Damerau's, according to which its operation is much less acceptable, if at all, when the main verb is stative:

(i) a. Each of us loves three girls.
   b. ??We love three girls each.

(ii) a. Each of them $\begin{Bmatrix} \text{speaks} \\ \text{understands} \end{Bmatrix}$ two languages.

   b. They $\begin{Bmatrix} \text{speak} \\ \text{??understand} \end{Bmatrix}$ two languages each.

(40) a. Each of the managers planned for at least six secretaries to be present.

b. *The managers planned for at least six secretaries each to be present.

(41) a. Each of the killers intended for at least three witnesses to be killed.

b. *The killers intended for at least three witnesses each to be killed.

It follows, I think, that a Clause Mate condition is necessary in distinguishing the impossible, (38)b–(41)b (in all idiolects as far as I know), from those which are at worst strained, (28)b–(30)b.

The behavior with respect to *Each* Shift on NPs in differing kinds of complements thus seems to me to offer the basis for an important argument in favor of Raising with B-verb infinitival complements, N-verb[15] complements, etc. I have, however, regarded the account here only as a potential argument because of the great complexity of facts relating to *Each* Shift, the intricacy of several of the points serving as foundations for the argument, and the fact that I have not been able to study the phenomena involved in anything like the required depth.[16]

[15] It will be observed that I have provided no interactions of *Each* Shift with W-verb complements. This is due to the fact that such sentences seem generally unacceptable, I believe, as a function of the constraint illustrated at the end of footnote 14.

(i) a. Each of us wants (to find) three apples.
b. ??We want (to find) three apples each.
c. Each of us wants three secretaries to be hired.
d. ??We want three secretaries each to be hired.

It is for this reason, I think, that in my idiolect there is so little contrast between such non-Raising/Raising pairs as the following:

(ii) a. *They would prefer for three secretaries each to be hired.
b. ??They would prefer three secretaries each to be hired.

(iii) a. *We intended for two bombs each to go off.
b. ??We intended two bombs each to go off.

[16] I have formulated the argument in this section in terms of a global description of *Each* Shift, a view based crucially on the assumption that the unbounded movement rules like *Wh* Rel Movement are postcyclical rules transporting constituents in a single jump. While I believe that this approach is correct, it should be stressed that the argument for Raising based on *Each* Shift depends, not on the global formulation, but only on the claim that *Each* Shift is, in fact, subject to a Clause Mate condition.

6.3 Quantifier Scope

For all the examples given in this section, it is important to assign normal, noncontrastive stress-intonation patterns. In particular, they must *not* be read with contrastive stress on the quantifiers.

Consider examples like (42):

(42) a. I believe that someone insulted Arthur.

    b. I believe someone to have insulted Arthur

For me, (42)a has ambiguous scope possibilities for the existential quantifier associated with the form *some*. This quantifier can have a purely complement-internal scope (henceforth: "narrow scope") or a scope that includes the main verb (henceforth: "wide scope". Thus the two readings of (42)a can be paraphrased as follows:

(43) a. I believe that there is someone who insulted Arthur.

    b. There is someone who I believe insulted Arthur.

However, I find that (42)b has only the wide scope reading like (13)b.

There also appears to be a parallel difference between similar pairs involving the vague amount quantifier *few*:

(44) a. The FBI proved that few students were spies.

    b. The FBI proved few students to be spies.

Perhaps the facts are even clearer here. Example (44)a has either wide or narrow scope for *few,* but (44)b only wide scope.

Finally, contrast (45)a and (46)b:

(45) a. Melvin showed that none of the formulas were theorems.

    b. Melvin showed none of the formulas to be theorems.

Again, (45)a is ambiguous, while (45)b is possessed of wide scope for the quantifier associated with *none*.

Within a Raising system, such contrasts are not overly surprising. For, in Raising terms, the ultimate positions of the quantifier differ as to their *command* relations with the main verbs. In the *a* examples, the quantifiers are both preceded and commanded by the main verbs, and they do not command the main verbs or precede them. Thus they are related to the main verbs asymmetrically along both of the major primacy parameters. In the *b* examples, however, the command relations have become symmetrical, since the quantifiers and main verbs are derived Clause Mates—hence they command each other. If, therefore, as Lakoff (1969) suggested, quantifier scope were in part controlled by precede and command relations in derived structures, there would be a natural formulation of the constraints which would distinguish the scope properties of pairs like (42), (44), and 45.

It is interesting, in this regard, to consider the passive versions of the *b* examples:

(46) a. Someone is believed to have insulted Arthur.

b. Few students were proved (by the FBI) to be spies.

c. None of the formulas were shown to be theorems.

Here the situation of the *a* examples in (42), (44) and (45) is reversed. The quantifiers now precede the main verbs and, in a system where *be* is a main verb triggering Raising, asymmetrically command them as well. And, as expected, only the wide scope is possible.

Baker has suggested a general principle underlying the restriction to wide scope in cases like (42)b, (44)b, (45)b and (46), namely:

(47) "A quantifier cannot have as its scope [only] a clause which does not contain it in Surface Structure."

That is, if *few students* in (44)b had narrow scope, which it does not, it would violate principle (47), under the assumption that it has undergone Raising and, in surface structure, is not part of the complement. If something like (47) can be maintained as a universal of grammar, then the requisite appeal to Raising for cases like (42)b provides an even stronger argument than appeared at first.

It thus appears that we have essentials of an argument for B-verb Raising from our analysis of quantifier scope. An alternative in terms of a system like Chomsky's would be to appeal to the difference between tensed and untensed clauses. One immediate disadvantage of this alternative would be that these concepts are not otherwise known to play a role in describing quantifier scope, while clause membership, command, etc., will be needed no matter what is finally said about Raising. Moreover, this appeal does not give the right answers. Thus narrow scope appears possible for the quantifier in all of the following cases with untensed complement clauses:

(48) a. I arranged for few of the girls to receive promotions.

    b. I resent none of you offering to help us.

    c. Tom discussed someone's insulting Arthur.

    d. It would be sad for none of them to get raises.

Thus it is not at all clear how a non-Raising grammatical system can avoid ad hoc patchwork statements about contrasts like those in (42), (44) and (45).

    Observe also such differences as the following with N-verbs and W-verbs:

(49) a. ?I prevented few men's leaving.

    b. I prevented few men from leaving.

    c. I $\left\{ \begin{array}{l} \text{intend} \\ \text{would prefer} \end{array} \right\}$ for none of them to arrive late.

    d. I $\left\{ \begin{array}{l} \text{intend} \\ \text{would prefer} \end{array} \right\}$ none of them to arrive late.

Despite the strained character of (49)a, it can have ambiguous scope for *few*. But in (49)b, *few* must have wide scope. Although both (49)c and (49)d have untensed clauses, I have ambiguous scope only in (49)c, while (49)d has only wide scope for *none*. Appeal to the difference between finite and nonfinite clauses thus seems without force.

    Finally, as an indication that, independently of questions of Raising per se, raising operations must induce "alterations" in possible scopes, consider such contrasts as (50):

(50) a. It will be easy for me to find some girls.

    b. Some girls will be easy for me to find.

    c. It would be difficult for Jim to talk to few girls.

    d. Few girls would be difficult for Jim to talk to.

Here Tough Movement operation (recognized by Chomsky, to appear) leaves only wide scope for the quantifiers in (50)b, d, while that in (50)a, c is ambiguous. This contrast is not, of course, as interesting as it might be, since Tough Movement in these cases changes precedence as well as command relations. This remark also holds for cases of Raising with A-verbs, where scope is also affected:

(51) a. It appears that few students passed.

     b. Few students appear to have passed.

I conclude that there are certain B-verb, W-verb, and N-verb scope contrasts naturally accountable in Raising terms, for which non-Raising grammars seem to offer no insight. I have regarded these facts as a potential rather than a real argument because of the inordinate complexity of quantifier scope phenomena and the lack of any firm generalizations covering reasonable portions of the known data. But the facts uncovered so far certainly offer promise of providing confirmation for the kind of Raising analyses advocated in this study.

6.4 Nonrestrictive Relatives on Pronouns

Nonrestrictive relatives can occur on definite pronouns:

(52) a. I, who am Turkish, refuse to accept that decision.

     b. He, who I had never met before, was repulsive.

     c. Joe said that they, who were about to move, were broke.

In these cases, though, the pronouns of relevance are unquestionably superficial subjects. [17] When one considers pronouns in object positions, however, nonrestrictive relatives seem impossible:

(53) a. *They shot him, who I had never met.

     b. *I sent him, who was tall, a pair of suspenders.

     c. *They spoke with her, who had complained about quitting.

     d. *You shouldn't talk like that to me, who you only just met.

This case might suggest the following generalization:

(54) A pronominal NP, N can take a nonrestrictive relative clause only if N is in superficial subject position.

---

[17] It might be thought that Gapping examples like (i) bear on the notion of "superficial subject" required.

(i) a.   Marvin likes apples, and she, who is from Texas, likes peaches.
    b. ?*Marvin likes apples, and she, who is from Texas, peaches.

But this is doubtful since (i)b seems to illustrate only a general fact about NPs, pronominal or not, stranded by Gapping:

(ii) ?*Marvin likes apples, and Gloria, who is from Texas, peaches.

Given (54), such contrasts as (55)–(57) would support the claim of
B-verb Raising, since only operation of this rule would generate the derived nonsubject status for the pronouns in the *b* examples needed to
predict their ill-formedness under principle (54).

(55) a.   They proved that he, who was Turkish, had lied forty-four
          times.

   b. *They proved him, who was Turkish, to have lied forty-four
          times.

(56) a.   Joan believes that I, who wine tends to nauseate, drink heavily.

   b. *Joan believes me, who wine tends to nauseate, to drink heavily.

(57) a.   George found that they, who I have never met, were radicals.

   b. *George found them, who I have never met, to be radicals.

The argument here is parallel in a way to that in Section 4.4 about
contraction. There, it will be recalled, we raised the possibility of replacing a generalization about objects with one involving syntactic features.
Here also it might be claimed that the rule is not (54) but rather a rule
stating that nonrestrictive relatives cannot go on [−Nominative] pronouns. Contrasts like (58) would then be due to the same contrast, here
invisibly manifested with respect to pronoun shape.

(58) a.   They believe that you, who Tom would like to meet, have a good
          chance to win.

   b. *They believe you, who Tom would like to meet, to have a good
          chance to win.

But the arguments that rejected such a feature in the earlier discussion
of course apply here automatically, since it is the same class of cases.

It might appear that the argument just given is as strong as several in
Chapter 4, which raises the question of why it has been discussed here.
One reason is that problems arise with respect to the character of exam-
ples like (59):

(59) a. They would prefer for him, who only Jane recommended, to
          come tomorrow.

   b. She arranged for them, who I have not yet met, to come today.

   c. Tony prayed for her, who the doctors couldn't help, to survive the
          accident.

If, as I later claim (see footnote 7 of Chapter 10), the definition of *sub-ject* relevant for (54) is unaffected by the presence of prepositions like *for,* then these examples should be as well-formed as cases involving nonrestrictives on nominative-shape pronouns. For me, however, this does not seem to be quite the case. Examples (59)a and (59)b seem all right, though possibly strained, but (59)c, for unknown reasons, is prob-ably worse. None seems to have, however, anything like the character of (53) or of (55)b, (56)b, (57)b. To this extent, then, something like (54) is further supported, while the feature approach, rejected already on theoretical grounds, is seen here to be empirically inadequate.

Non-third-person examples seem to have the same general properties:

(60) a. Jack would prefer for me, who Tony wouldn't hire, to go to school.

　　b. Jack arranged for you, who I still can't hire, to work in the market.

　　c. Jack prayed for us, who the police are after, to be vindicated.

Although the judgments are quite subtle, I find the examples with *me* and *us* passable but somewhat strained, but that with *you* is better. Since *you* is the only object pronoun form (with the exception of *it,* which cannot take nonrestrictives in any position)[18] that is shape-identical to a (finite) subject pronoun form, the strain in examples like (59) and (60) is somehow a function of the shape similarity of these subject pronouns with object pronouns, normally inhospitable to nonrestrictive relatives.

There is a further complication for sentences like (59) and (60) when the nonrestrictive relatives chosen have the relative pronoun as subject, and particularly subject of a form of *be*:

(61) a. *Tom arranged for us, who are happy, to live in the rear apart-ment.

　　b. *Tom arranged for me, who $\left\{ \begin{array}{l} \text{is} \\ \text{am} \end{array} \right\}$ happy, to live in the rear apartment.

　　c. Tom arranged for you, who are intelligent enough, to work in the office.

　　d. *Tom arranged for him, who is intelligent, to work in the office.

---

18 Presumably, this is due to the fact that *it* cannot bear strong stress, and an NP in construction with a nonrestrictive relative must have a high degree of stress.

   e. *Tom arranged for her, who is intelligent, to work in the office.

   f. *Tom arranged for them, who are intelligent, to work in the office.

Clearly, these examples are all unacceptable except for the single case with *you,* whose object and subject forms are the same. Presumably, what is going on here is a restriction on having a relative pronoun that is a coreferent of a pronoun which even looks like an object pronoun triggering verbal agreement. This is a transderivational restriction, in the sense that the underlying notion involves comparison of the forms in distinct derivations.

   In conclusion, although I suspect that for certain idiolects, at least, something like principle (54) can be maintained, along with a consequent argument for B-verb Raising derivable from contrasts like (55)–(57), there are too many obscurities in the facts—and I have not studied the matter in sufficient detail—to regard this as more than a potential argument.

6.5 Multiple-Question-Word "Binding"

The present discussion is due essentially to observations of Kuno and Robinson (to appear). Although Baker (1970a) observed that there are cases in English where more than one *wh* word is "bound" by a single interrogative marker (hence more than one must be replaced by "constants" in the answer), there are very strong restrictions on this phenomenon. In particular, in at least some idiolects, including my own, such multiple "binding" is possible for *who* and *what* (but not *which,* which figures crucially in Baker's examples and seems to be somewhat freer) only in certain contexts.

   Thus compare the sentences of (62), which are all acceptable, with those of (63), which seem hopeless.

(62) a. Tell me who kissed who.

   b. Tell me who you talked to about who.

   c. Tell me what bumped into what.

   d. Tell me who convinced who that it was time to leave.

(63) a. *Tell me who thought Joan kissed who.

   b. *Tell me who convinced Joan (that) Bob kissed who.

c. *Tell me what caused Bob to believe I had bumped into what.

d. *Tell me who forced Joan to say Arthur kissed who.

Kuno suggests initially that the relevant condition is that multiply "bound" *who* and *what* must simply be Clause Mates in the structures that are input to Wh-Q Movement. This condition is met in (62) but not in (63). Let us call this proposal the "Clause Mate Binding Constraint" (CMBC).

If CMBC is correct, it will combine with the Raising analysis of B-verb complements to predict contrasts between the infinitival and *that-*clause complements of such verbs with respect to multiple "binding." And such contrasts exist:

(64) a. *Who believes (that) who is guilty?

b. Who believes who to be guilty?

(65) a. *What proved (that) what was correct?

b. What proved what to be correct?

(66) a. *Who showed (that) who was a spy?

b. Who showed who to be a spy?

These facts seem not only to give further support to CMBC but also, more significantly for present concerns, to offer striking support for the Raising hypothesis about B-verb complements. For it is only the latter that can provide the derived Clause Mate status for the *wh* words in the *b* examples, which CMBC requires.

Kuno observes most strikingly, that CMBC receives further support from comparative contrasts like the following:

(67) a. John is taller than Bob is.

b. John is taller than Bob.

(68) a. *Who is taller than who is?

b. Who is taller than who?

As argued by Ross (1967, 1969), there is strong reason to believe that there is a clause boundary after *than* in examples like (67)a and (68)a, but none after *than* in (67)b and (68)b. This follows, he argues, in spite of the fact that the *b* examples are derived from structures like the *a* examples, because the deletion of the *than*-clause verb prunes the S node defining that clause.[19]

Further apparent support for CMBC comes from unquestioned cases of A-verb raising:

(69) a. *To whom did it seem (that) who was a spy? [20]

b. Who seemed to who(m) to be a spy?

So far, then, CMBC seems well justified. If so, contrasts like those in (64)–(66) add justification to the Raising analysis of B-verb infinitival complements. Moreover, sentences like (70) indicate that the data also are consistent with a Raising analysis of W-verbs and N-verbs, which we have also advocated earlier.

(70) a. Who wants who to go?

b. Who prevented who from leaving?

Again, though, there are important complications that at the least cloud these conclusions. First of all, CMBC does not, I believe, prepare us for such examples as (71):

(71) a. Who wants to marry who?

b. Who wants Bob to marry who?

c. Who expects to do what?

d. Who expects Jane to do what?

These also seem acceptable. Yet they can be made consistent with CMBC

---

[19] However, Kayne points out that in such terms the following examples are inexplicably bad:

(i) a. *Who do you talk to John as often as to?
   b. *The guy to whom I talk to John more often than.

(ii) a. *Who do you talk to John as often as to?
   b. *I know who you talk to more than to whom.

[20] Examples like (69)a do not, for many speakers at least, provide a strong test of the contrast with those like (69)b because they violate the independent constraint, discussed in Postal (1970a) and illustrated also in (i):

(i) ?To whom did it seem that Joan was a spy?

Nonetheless, examples like (69)a are not completely irrelevant, since violations like that in (i) are rather subtle, while that in (69)a is flagrant, indicating operation of some factor beyond that manifested in (i).

only under the assumption that *both* Raising and Equi have the effect of pruning the S nodes of clauses whose subjects they remove. With this pruning assumption, the original complement clause boundaries would be erased, and CMBC would fail to block (71) as desired. However, although past discussions of pruning (see Ross, 1967, 1969; Perlmutter, 1971; Postal, 1971: 113) have assumed that removal of the subject of a complement clause causes the pruning of its defining S node, there are objections to this assumption.

For example, as discussed in Postal (1972) there is a natural explanation of the failure of infinitives and gerundive constituents to "pied pipe" if no such pruning takes place, since intervening S nodes block Pied Piping, as Ross (1967) showed in his original discussion of this phenomenon. Hence, if Raising and Equi prune S nodes, the explanation for examples like (72) is lost.

(72) a. *The gorilla to kiss whom John wanted is outside.

   b. *The car to buy which Melvin wanted Sally was a Chevrolet.

   c. *The man from shooting whom I prevented the cop was arrested.

   d. *The drama which seeing over and over Bill likes really bores me.

   e. *The money to have stolen which I believed Bill has not been recovered.

Second, as previously known (see Perlmutter, 1971: 118–120), the pruning assumption causes difficulties with other phenomena believed to be characterized in part by Clause Mate conditions, such as reflexivization. In particular, given the discussion of reflexivization in Section 3.2, it is not clear, with this type of pruning, what would block examples like (73), since on the second cycle the pairs of antecedent + reflexive would be Clause Mates.

(73) a. *I want Bill to shoot myself.

   b. *Joan$_i$ believes us to have deceived herself$_i$

A completely analogous problem would arise for Inclusion Constraint cases. That is, we find cases like (74), where, if Raising pruned the complement S, we should expect violations.

(74) a. I want Bill to help us.

   b. I believe him to hate us.

Thus I cannot accept the view that the loss of a subject by a complement clause entails the pruning of the S node defining that clause.[21]

If not, then examples like (71) are direct counterexamples to CMBC. It might be asked, then, whether a correct reformation of CMBC should not involve some appeal to the difference between tensed and untensed clauses. Cases such as (75) indicate that this idea is untenable.

(75) a. *Who would prefer for who to win?

    b. *Who arranged for what to happen?

    c. *Who prayed for what to be saved?

    d. *To whom would it be important for what to happen?

    e. *Who discussed whose dying?

    f. *Who resented whose complaining?

    g. *Who favors whose running?

Although I have no elaborate analysis to offer, because the facts are dealt with in this domain of potential arguments, I think that the proper solution lies in the direction of a modification rather than a rejection of CMBC. This modification should, I suggest, take advantage of something correct in the idea that Raising and Equi trigger pruning. Namely, as contrasts like those between (71) and (75) suggest, clauses that have been subjected to either Raising or Equi do have a rather special status. One proposal to account for this involves pruning. But there are others. For example, as already touched on in Section 4.15 and footnote 8 of Chapter 4, one might attempt to define in universal grammar a notion called "quasi-clause" (a term suggested by Perlmutter) covering complement clauses that have lost their subjects through application of Raising or Equi. Quasi-clause boundaries would then not be as strong a barrier to at least some syntactic phenomena as full clause boundaries. In particular, one could then go on to define quasi-Clause Mates as elements separated at most by higher (in the sense of footnote 12 of Chapter 2) quasi-clause boundaries. Thus ordinary Clause Mates would also be

---

21 The pruning concept rejected here is distinct from that appealed to in the discussion of comparative examples like (67) and (68), in spite of the fact that Ross's original discussions ended up effectively merging them. The distinction is between saying that loss of the main verb of an embedded clause causes pruning and saying that loss of the subject of such a clause by Raising or Equi operation causes pruning. It is perfectly consistent to accept the former claim while rejecting the latter.

quasi-Clause Mates. But the italicized pairs in such examples as (76) would be quasi-Clause Mates as well, although they are not Clause Mates (at any stage).

(76) a. *I* want Bob to help *me*.

  b. *John* wants to kiss *Joan*.

  c. *I* prevented Tom from calling *Betty*.

However, the italicized pairs in examples like (77) are neither Clause Mates nor quasi-Clause Mates.

(77) a. *I* arranged for Bob to help *me*.

  b. *I* would prefer for you to call *me*.

  c. *I* would prefer that you called *me*.

Given such definitions, one could revise CMBC in a natural way to refer to quasi-Clause Mates instead of Clause Mates, covering all of the data dealt with correctly so far. Although I shall not pursue this line of discussion, it seems promising to me. The most crucial question to be answered is exactly what formal definition can be formulated for the notion of quasi-clause. However, while this question remains open, such contrasts as those between (71) and (75) already show a class of cases naturally distinguished in a Raising theory but unmarked in any natural way otherwise. Thus I think we have good reason to expect that the ultimate explication of multiple "binding" constraints will yield a serious argument for the operation of Raising into superordinate object positions.

It will be seen in the following sections that the notion of quasi-clause has further potential application in English grammar. I should like to stress, however, that a serious justification of this notion will depend on its suitability for dealing with cases in other languages of the same sort—those previously handled by appeal to pruning. One of the clearest and most elaborate cases of this sort is provided by Rivero (1970), who argues that there are constraints on Spanish clitic movement and negative distribution which require the view that the Spanish analogue of Equi causes the pruning of the S node defining the complement clause whose subject Equi deletes. She shows that, in general, clitics cannot move across S boundaries and that at most one negative particle *no* can occur per (simple) clause. However, when Equi applies, clitics can move out of the complement, and ill-formedness results if both main clause and complement contain *no*. As fas as I can see, however, these facts are equally describable in the quasi-clause framework, where what must be said is that clitics cannot cross clause boundaries that are not quasi-clause boundaries. (A term is evidently going to be needed for this notion. My suggestion is "strict clause boundaries.") Furthermore, quasi-clauses cannot contain more than one occurrence of *no*; that is, pairs of *no*'s cannot be quasi-Clause Mates. Decisive evidence between pruning and quasi-clause accounts would appear to require knowledge of what happens when Equi applies backward in Spanish. If earlier remarks about quasi-clauses are correct, this approach would predict that the double *no* constraint would not be violated, while the pruning theory would predict violations.

Similar cases involving the movement behavior of clitics in South Slavic languages have been studied by Perlmutter (personal communication), where apparently the analogue of Equi also permits movement across clause boundaries, which otherwise impose a barrier to such re-ordering (see Browne, 1968). Again, however, the basic facts are as compatible with a quasi-clause statement as with a pruning statement, although the latter was previously assumed for these cases.

Clearly, then, there is plenty of non-English material that should ultimately prove relevant for confirming or disconfirming proposals about quasi-clauses.

6.6 Double Negatives
We shall find in this section a group of facts that are formally parallel to those discussed in the previous section. That is, there is a regularity apparently statable in terms of Clause Mates which breaks down in roughly the same class of context as that in which CMBC broke down.

There is a traditional rule for English which prohibits more than one negative[22] word in the "same sentence." Although sometimes regarded as purely prescriptive, this rule actually functions in many dialects of English and appears to be one factor serving to define what is called standard English. Hence, we have these cases.

---

22 Of course, the term "negative word" is excessively vague and must exclude at a minimum those cases involving negative prefixes *un*, *dis*, *in/il/ir*, etc., as well as *non*. A further exclusion is discussed in the text.

(78) a. *I didn't do nothing.

    b. *Nobody didn't come.

    c. *Jane never doesn't behave badly.

Clearly, there exist constraints blocking structures in which multiple negatives exist (at some stage of derivation) within certain constructions. The traditional statement defines this construction class as the "same sentence." But this is obviously too loose a characterization:

(79) a. Nobody believes that you don't have enough money.

    b. That Bill didn't come doesn't worry us.

    c. I didn't urge that Bob not be chosen.

    d. No candidate who isn't a millionaire can win.

Evidently the notion "same sentence" must be restricted to cover only a circumscribed class of structures. Noting that in (78) the pairs of negative elements are Clause Mates, while this is not the case in (79), one might suggest plausibly as part of an initial statement of the double negative restrictions that violations ensue only when the pairs of negatives are Clause Mates. Moreover, in the absence of immediate evidence to the contrary and in accord with the general line of argument in McCawley (1968), one could assume that the relevant stage of derivations is surface structure.[23] Thus a preliminary statement might be as follows.[24]

[23] Considerable doubt is cast on this view by examples like (i), since one wishes to attribute the ill-formedness of (i)b to the same constraint found in (ii).

(i) a. What Nixon isn't is nice.
    b. *What Nixon isn't is proud of no one.

(ii) *Nixon isn't proud of no one.

But I have no better formulation to offer at this point.

[24] McCawley (1968) argues that there are two variants of standard English with respect to multiple negations. One variant, his in particular, accepts examples like (i), and another rejects them.

(i) Not many of the boys didn't talk to John.

McCawley suggests roughly that these variants differ in that the former rejects pairs of negatives within the same verb phrase, hence allowing (i), while the other, more restrictive version is specified in terms of Clause Mates. If, as I suggest later, core double negative violations must involve *no* NPs, then sentences like (i) are irrelevant here, and those who reject them have a quite separate constraint.

    Incidentally, McCawley's argument that double negative violations involve an

(80) A surface structure is ill-formed if it contains two negatives that
are Clause Mates.

The surface filter (80), in combination with the Raising analysis of
B-verb, W-verb, and N-verb complement structures then predicts that
there should exist contrasts like the following:[25]

(81) a. I couldn't believe that none of the sailors kissed Sally.

  b. *I couldn't believe none of the sailors to have kissed Sally.

(82) a. No one proved that no one was honest.

  b. *No one proved no one to be honest.

(83) a. Melvin didn't expect that none of the soup would be pure.

  b. *Melvin didn't expect none of the soup to be pure.

(84) a. *John didn't want no one to come.

  b. Joan didn't wish that no one would survive.

  c. *Joan didn't wish no one to survive.

  d. *I didn't prevent no one from surviving.

The correctness of the prediction seems to argue anew in favor of the
Raising analysis of the relevant cases, which is the only factor capable of

---

output or surface structure constraint was unfortunately formulated almost entirely
in terms of *not*-initial NPs like those in (i), considered in Section 4.2. However,
most of the examples that McCawley considered ill-formed because of double
negative violations are ill-formed for a quite different reason: namely, they violate
the constraint that *not*-initial NPs must be superficial subjects (or clause-initial,
however it turns out). Hence his examples, particularly (3), (4)b, (5)a, (7)b, (7)c, (8)b,
(8)c, and (9) all remain ill-formed even if the left occurrence of *not* is removed. Thus
his (7)b is given here as (ii):

(ii) *Handouts weren't given to not many of the beggars.

But, of course, (iii) is also ungrammatical.

(iii) *Handouts were given to not many of the beggars.

Nonetheless, McCawley's argument is partially sustainable, since examples like (ii)
are much worse than those like (iii).

25 These should be read with ordinary intonation, in particular, without contrastive
stress on the *no* forms.

  Contrasts involving *believe* like those in (81) were first noticed by McCawley
(1968:2).

accounting for the needed derived Clause Mate status in (81)b, (82)b, (83)b, and (84)a, c, d.

In addition to contrasts in grammaticality in (81)–(84), there are, at least with noncontrastive stress on words like *none,* interpretation contrasts as well. The *a* examples of (81)–(83) are understood to involve *two* logical negatives. Hence (81)a might be represented logically as (85):

(85) Not [I could believe (Not [Exists s such that s kissed Sally])].

However, the *b* examples are understood to involve only one logical negative (both for those whose idiolects reject such sentences and for those who accept them). Hence (81)b is logically like (86):

(86) Not [Exist s such that I could believe (s kissed Sally)].

This is, however, quite parallel to the meaning of examples like (87), which may be represented as (88):

(87) *I couldn't believe none of their claims.

(88) Not [Exist c such that I could believe c].

In short, it appears that in Clause Mate cases, multiple negatives are (i) ungrammatical in the standard language; and (ii) interpreted as correspondents of a single logical negative in both standard and other dialects. Another way of putting (ii) is that in this class of cases, the second of a double negative pair is understood in the standard language as a wrongly produced negative form of *any,* where a plain *any* is required.[26]

So far then, principle (80) and contrasts like those in (81)–(84) seem to offer further justification for the Raising analysis of B-verb constructions and similar complement cases. However, the situation is much more complicated than so far indicated, but not in totally unexpected ways. Observe these examples:

(89) a. *I don't want to kiss no gorillas.

[26] It is natural to assume that *no* forms are produced by a doubling rule (see Klima, 1964) placing the *no* in the position of an *any,* leaving an intermediate stage containing both the original negative and the new occurrence. This stage then survives into surface structure in much colloquial speech, so-called substandard dialects, etc. In the standard language, however, the original negative must be deleted.

b. *I don't want Bob to kiss no gorillas.

c. *I don't believe Bob to have kissed no gorillas.

These have exactly the acceptability and meaning characteristics of (78)a, (81)b, (82)b, (84)c, d, and (87). However, barring a theory in which subject loss causes pruning of S nodes, the negatives in (89) are not Clause Mates, and hence principle (80) would necessarily fail to mark the observed deviances. It should be apparent, though, that the problem here is analogous to that involving multiple "binding" of *wh* words discussed previously. The same notion of quasi-clause needed for "binding" would apparently apply correctly here to block cases like (89), if principle (80) is modified to refer to quasi-Clause Mates rather than to Clause Mates.

That something along these lines is appropriate rather than, for example, some appeal to the finite nonfinite clause distinction, is suggested by the contrast between putative Raising and Equi cases and those like the following:

(90) a. I didn't arrange for none of them to survive

   b. I didn't pray for none of the planes to land safely   that is, it just happened.

   c. I didn't plan for none of the cops to get bribes

   d. I don't resent no one's contributing to the fund.

In particular, compare these examples:

(91) a. ?I wouldn't prefer for none of them to survive.

   b. *I wouldn't prefer none of them to survive.

   c. I didn't intend for none of them to be arrested.

   d. *I didn't intend none of them to be arrested.

It is interesting that in the case of double negatives, one can actually find some evidence that argues against a pruning view and in favor of something more like the quasi-clause approach. In particular, *backward* application of Equi uniformly fails to induce any double negative violations:

(92) a. Eating nothing didn't faze Bob.

   b. Learning nothing that day didn't worry Joan.

   c. To discover no new arguments wouldn't bother me.

But if complement subject loss leads to S pruning, these would have the derived Clause Mate structure referred to in principle (80). On the other hand, in an account based on quasi-clauses, facts like (92) are not counterexamples. Either the definition of quasi-clause can be extended to take account of facts like (92), specifying that only postverbal subject loss leads to quasi-clause formation, or else the double negative principle itself can be restricted.

It seems then that if the quasi-clause approach can be developed precisely, the facts of double negatives will provide a further support for Raising in the disputed cases.

However, the facts of negativity are everywhere extremely complicated and poorly understood, and there are relevant difficulties involving double negatives. First, not all cases of *forward* operation of Equi and other deletions of subjects induce negative violations:

(93) a. I didn't discuss finding nothing.

b. Jack doesn't like doing nothing.

c. Most authorities don't approve of eating nothing for breakfast.

Under the assumption that the rule operative in (93)c is a postcyclical deletion, one might account for (93)c by claiming that only cyclical subject loss induces quasi-clauses. But this does not help to explain (93)a and (93)b, which are Equi-derived. One might attempt to appeal to the gerundive character of the complements here, in contrast to the typically infinitival cases considered earlier, but this fails for cases like (94), pointed out by Ross.

(94) a. Jack doesn't like to do nothing on weekends.

b. Jack won't agree to say nothing.

I simply have no idea what is going on here.

Second, principle (80), or its modified version restricted to quasi-clauses, refers only to negatives (subject to the remarks of footnote 22). That this is insufficient is shown by examples like (95):

(95) a. I don't want not to kiss the gorillas.

b. I don't want Bob not to kiss the gorillas.

c. I don't believe Bob not to have kissed the gorillas.

Although these may seem a bit strained, they have nothing of the quality of (89). Contrast also the following:

(96) a. *I wouldn't prefer none of them to stay.

    b. I wouldn't prefer them not to stay.

(97) a. *I didn't intend none of them to vote yes.

    b. I didn't intend them not to vote yes.

The differences between such pairs, (97)a, b in particular, are that in the ill-formed cases one of the negatives is part of a *no* NP. I think that core double negative violations of the sort under discussion here are, in fact, inherently linked to the occurrence of such NPs. Thus a proper reformulation of principle (80) must involve reference not only to quasi-Clause Mates rather than Clause Mates but also to the fact that at least one of the negatives involved must be of the *no* NP variety.

Despite the many problems and obscurities involving negatives, contrasts like those between (89), (90), and (91) remain, and they provide a basis for believing that the ultimate statement of core double negative violations will produce a serious argument for Raising analysis, probably on the basis of something like the quasi-clause notion.

6.7 *As* Constructions

I believe that constructions containing constituents beginning with *as* will ultimately provide some evidence for Raising. Such constructions were utilized early in the development of generative grammar, particularly by Chomsky, who pointed out such striking contrasts in "grammatical relations" as those in (98):

(98) a. I regard Max as (being) incompetent.

    b. Max strikes me as (being) incompetent.

Here, despite the differences in surface word order, *Max* is related to *incompetent* in the same way in both cases. It seems to be generally the case, as here, that *as* phrases are intuitively the realization of deformed complements based on the verb *be*. But with *strike* at least, *have* is also a possible basis:

(99) Melvin strikes me as having lost his judgment.

I shall suggest in Chapters 11 and 12 that *strike* is an A-verb, triggering Raising in the same fashion as *seem, appear,* etc., and differing chiefly in that its truncated complement must undergo the further mappings that insert *as* and determine that the complement is gerundive rather than infinitival.

More interesting for present concerns are those verbs like *regard, recognize,* which would, if involved with Raising, behave more like B-verbs. In fact, since it is doubtful that anyone would want to claim that the postverbal NP is a surface subject, it would follow that merely positing an underlying clause structure for *regard, recognize* complements requires appeal to Raising to account for the derived object status of the pre-*as* NPs. It is, moreover, not hard to find arguments for the derived object status of such NPs. In particular, the considerations of Section 4.6 about pronominalization constraints show this:

(100) a. *I regarded him$_i$ as (being) incompetent sooner than Bob$_i$ did.

    b. I recognized that he$_i$ was incompetent sooner than Bob$_i$ did.

    c. *I recognized him$_i$ as being incompetent sooner than Bob$_i$ did.

Similarly, the inability of *not*-initial or *alone*-final NPs to occur in that position shows that the NPs in question cannot be considered superficial subjects:

(101) a. *I $\begin{Bmatrix} \text{recognize} \\ \text{regard} \end{Bmatrix}$ not many men as great lovers.

    b. *She $\begin{Bmatrix} \text{recognizes} \\ \text{regards} \end{Bmatrix}$ Bob alone as intelligent.

Finally, the fact that such NPs can undergo Complex NP Shift reveals the same point:

(102) I $\begin{Bmatrix} \text{recognize} \\ \text{regard} \end{Bmatrix}$ as incompetent—all of those people who planned this incredible fiasco.

It follows that an analogue to Chomsky's treatment of B-verb infinitival complements is impossible for *as* constructions with verbs like *regard.* Other *as* verbs that appear to have the same properties include *consider, select, choose, elect,* and *pick.*[27] An anti-Raising analysis of

27 There is a large class of verbs taking *as,* including, *want, need, wish, desire, like,* etc., in sentences such as (i), in which there is a clear relation to sentences containing a complement verb *have,* as in (ii).

such cases would then apparently be forced to take the form of an Equi analysis:

$$(103)\ \text{NP} \begin{Bmatrix} \text{regard} \\ \text{choose} \\ \text{etc.} \end{Bmatrix} \text{NP}_i \text{ as } [_s \text{NP}_i \ldots {_s}]$$

By and large, "empty" NPs like existential *there,* idiom chunks, and weather *it* cannot occur in the pre-*as* position, so it is difficult to immediately reject such an analysis in a way parallel to that invoked for N-verbs in Section 4.13, or traditionally for B-verb constructions. However, as Ross insightfully observes, weather *it* is possible in some such cases when it is the underlying subject of an adjectival rather than a verbal predicate:

(104) a. I regard it as being foggy enough to cover our retreat.

   b. He recognizes it as being too windy to sail.

Such examples already cast considerable doubt on the merits of an Equi analysis and suggest that the absence of existential *there* cases is due to some special constraint.

   While I know of no further definitive arguments against Equi analysis of *as* cases[28] (nor of any arguments of the opposite sort), certain considerations are not without relevance. In particular, emphatic reflexives

---

(i) a. I want you as my friend.
   b. I need you as my assistant.
   c. Joan likes Bob as her neighbor.

(ii) a. I want to have you as my friend.
   b. I need to have you as my friend.
   c. Joan likes having Bob as her neighbor.

Sentences like (i) do not seem to me to bear on Raising in any visible way so far, although they may provide some evidence for McCawley's rule of Predicate Raising, the latter being the rule that, I suggest, combines the main verb with *have* to form examples like (ii).

[28] As Ross points out, if the claim of subject relevance involved in the extraction argument proposed by Chomsky and discussed earlier, in Section 5.1, were correct, examples like (i) would strongly counter any Equi analysis and force a Raising view in which the complex NP has been a subject.

(i) *Who would you regard a picture of as indecent?

However, such cases probably only support further the view of Kuno, McCawley, etc., that such violations are independent of subjecthood.

can float away from NPs that are raised (in anyone's terms) and appear within the complement, as shown by cases involving A-verb Raising:

(105) a. Jack seems to have himself called Sylvia.

   b. Jason appears unlikely to himself finish first.

This does not, however, seem possible with unquestioned Equi cases like (106)a, b in contrast to its evident possibility in *as* cases:

(106) a. *Jack wants to himself call Sylvia.

   b. *Harry expects to have himself moved by then.

   c. Jack strikes me as having himself overestimated the opposition.

   d. I regard Jack as being unlikely to himself visit that commune.

   e. I regard Jack as having himself violated the agreement.

If, in spite of the parallelism between (106)c, d, e and (105), and in spite of the contrast between (106)a, b, and (106)c, d, e, it is argued that the emphatic reflexives in the latter three sentences have floated away *from deleted NPs* and not from ultimately raised NPs before Raising has applied to remove them from the complement clause, even further special principles will evidently be needed to block (107):

(107) a. *Jack himself strikes me as having himself overestimated the opposition.

   b. *I regard Jack himself as being unlikely to himself visit that commune.

   c. *I regard Jack himself as having himself violated the agreement.

That is, an analysis that allows emphatic reflexives to float away from deleted NPs predicts multiple emphatic reflexives cooccurring, while a Raising analysis does not. The impossibility of a piling up of emphatic reflexives in these cases thus further argues against an Equi analysis of *as* constructions.

   I suspect, then, that the ultimate analysis of *as* constructions will yield further cases where Raising operates into superordinate object positions, cases distinct from B-verb, N-verb, and W-verb complements that form the major basis for the conclusions of this study.

6.8 A Deletion Rule

There is a coreferential deletion rule associated with such adverbial expressions as *too, enough,* and *sufficiently* (see Ross, 1967; Hankamer, 1971).

(108) a. Melvin$_i$ is too mean (for him$_i$) to help her.
$$\Downarrow$$
$$\emptyset$$

    b. Jean$_i$ worked hard enough (for her$_i$) to have won.
$$\Downarrow$$
$$\emptyset$$

    c. Bob$_i$ is sufficiently qualified for us to hire (him$_i$).
$$\Downarrow$$
$$\emptyset$$

    d. Jack$_i$ is too old for me to work with (him$_i$).
$$\Downarrow$$
$$\emptyset$$

Evidently, this rule, called Elide, can delete NPs of various functional types, subjects, objects, and objects of prepositions.

Interestingly, one can find contrasts like the following:

(109) a. Bob$_i$ is too honest for me to believe (him$_i$) (*to be)[29] capable of that.
$$\Downarrow$$
$$\emptyset$$

    b. *Bob$_i$ is too smart for me to believe (that) (he$_i$) is capable of that.
$$\Downarrow$$
$$\emptyset$$

(110) a. They$_i$ are too shifty for us to prove (them$_i$) (*to be) guilty.
$$\Downarrow$$
$$\emptyset$$

    b. *They$_i$ are too shifty for us to prove (that) (they$_i$) are guilty.
$$\Downarrow$$
$$\emptyset$$

Thus one must ask what constraints on Elide account for this. One might claim that the restriction is that it will not work into tensed clauses. This claim is evidently correct. I know of no cases where Elide does erase an element of a tensed clause. However, while this principle suffices to distinguish pairs like those in (109) and (110), it does not properly segregate cases like these:

[29] The impossibility of *to be* here is reminiscent of the restriction discussed at the end of Section 5.2, and may be a function of the same constraint.

(111) a. *Bob$_i$ is too popular for me to arrange (for him$_i$) to live alone.
$$\Downarrow$$
$$\emptyset$$

  b. Bob$_i$ is too popular for me to believe (him$_i$) to live alone.
$$\Downarrow$$
$$\emptyset$$

(112) a. *Bob$_i$ is too clever for us to pray (for him$_i$) to be content with
      that.
$$\Downarrow$$
$$\emptyset$$

  b. Bob$_i$ is too clever for us to prove (him$_i$) (*to be) content with
      that.
$$\Downarrow$$
$$\emptyset$$

Thus those cases previously taken to involve Raising seem to permit operation of Elide, while those for which Raising would not have been invoked do not. Examples like (113) make a similar point.

(113) a. Joan$_i$ is too dumb for us to expect (her$_i$) to pass.
$$\Downarrow$$
$$\emptyset$$

  b. Joan$_i$ is too skillful for us to prevent (her$_i$) from winning.
$$\Downarrow$$
$$\emptyset$$

  c. *Joan$_i$ is too nice for us to resent (her$_i$) praising herself.
$$\Downarrow$$
$$\emptyset$$

It is tempting, then, to suggest that Elide must simply operate on a constituent of S_i in a context like (114) but must not "cross" any internal S boundaries defining clauses embedded within S_i.

(114) $X, \begin{Bmatrix} \text{enough} \\ \text{sufficiently} \\ \text{too} \end{Bmatrix}, \text{(Adjective) } [_{S_i} \qquad \quad {_{S_i}}], \, Y$

Under a Raising analysis, this would explain the differences in sets like (111)–(113) and would also simultaneously handle those in (109) and (110) without a special statement about tensed clauses.

However, this claim that Elide can delete constituents of only the immediately lower clause is too strong:

(115) a. Mary$_i$ is too lazy for us to try to train (her$_i$).

$$\emptyset$$

b. Nancy$_i$ is sufficiently clever for them to begin teaching French
to (her$_i$).
⇓
∅

A generalization that blocks Elide from working "across" any S boundaries within the S$_i$ of (114) can be made consistent with examples like
(115) only through a theory in which application of the rules Equi and
Raising causes pruning of the S nodes defining the clauses whose subjects have been removed. But grounds have already been offered for rejecting such a theory.

I suspect, therefore, that the correct generalization about Elide is that
its domain is given by (114), as before, but that instead of a blockage on
"crossing" any clause boundaries within S$_i$, the correct restriction is the
weaker one that it cannot "cross" any clause boundaries in S$_i$ which are
not also quasi-clause boundaries in the sense of earlier discussions of this
notion, that is, that the rule cannot "cross" strict clause boundaries.
Thus in (115)a, the object of *train* can be elided, despite the clause
boundary after *try*, because this boundary is a quasi-clause boundary,
induced by the deletion under Equi of the subject NP of *train*. Similarly, in (115)b, Elide can delete the object of the preposition *to,* in
spite of the clause boundary after *begin,* because this also is a quasi-
clause boundary, induced by the operation of Equi, triggered by the
active, transitive verb *begin.* On the other hand, operation is blocked in
a case like (112)a because the clause boundary after *pray* is not a quasi-
clause boundary. Example (113)a works the same way, since the boundary after *arrange* is also not a quasi-clause boundary. [30, 31]

Clearly, though, *if* this analysis of the range of Elide in terms of
quasi-clauses is correct, cases like (109)a and (110)a must involve quasi-
clause boundaries, induced by the operation of Raising in B-verb infinitival complements. Thus the quasi-clause account of the range of Elide

---

[30] The quasi-clause account automatically covers the *that*-clause cases in (109) and
(110), since boundaries of *that* clauses are never quasi-clause boundaries. Thus the
quasi-clause specification of the range of Elide is stronger than the tensed clause
proposal and has the latter as one of its consequences.

[31] Among the things ignored here are the conditions under which Elide is optional
or obligatory. It is obligatory, for instance, in examples like (108)a, but optional in
(108)c, d. It is also optional in all of the remaining examples. This suggests that it is
optional except for the subject NP of S$_i$ in (114).

provides a significant argument for B-verb Raising. I consider this only a potential argument so far, though, because I have not studied derivations involving Elide in anything like sufficient depth to determine how effectively the quasi-clause statement accounts for the facts, and because the quasi-clause notion itself is not well worked out.[32]

6.9 A Coreference Constraint

In Postal (1970a: 50–52) I discussed a constraint on coreferential pronominalization which is part of the grammar of some speakers, includ-

---

[32] There is at least one further problem with the argument for Raising based on a quasi-clause account of the scope of Elide. The key facts in the argument so far are the contrastive behavior of B-verbs like *believe* and *prove* and non-B-verbs like *arrange* and *pray*. However, the latter type of element triggers Equi, while the former does not.

(i) a. I arranged (for me) to be in France. $\overset{\text{Equi}}{\Rightarrow}$ I arranged to be in France.

　 b. I prayed (for me) to be elected. $\overset{\text{Equi}}{\Rightarrow}$ I prayed to be elected.

It follows then that in ill-formed cases like (81)a, repeated here for convenience as (ii), Elide would have to delete an NP in a position where Equi operates.

(ii) *Bob$_i$ is too popular for me to arrange (for him$_i$) to live alone.

It is striking, therefore, that the sentence that should result from Elide, namely (iii), is, in fact, understood to have been derived by Equi, with the underlying subject of *live* being *me* and the derivation not making use of Elide at all.

(iii) Bob is too popular for me to arrange to live alone.

It is conceivable, therefore, that there is a kind of transderivational blockage on Elide derivations when the structures these derive overlap with Equi derivations. In view of the fact that constraints of this general type seem to be required (see Chapter 4, footnote 3 and Section 12.5), such an account can by no means be ruled out a priori. But if such a principle could be justifiably invoked, the argument for Raising based on contrasts between B-verbs and verbs like *arrange* and *pray* dissolves.

There is also some empirical evidence against such an account. Thus, *expect* triggers Equi, but examples like (13)a in the text, repeated here as (iv), seem to me all right on the Elide interpretation.

(iv) Joan$_i$ is too dumb for us to expect (her$_i$) to pass.

Similarly, *keep* triggers Equi, as in (v):

(v) I kept from laughing.

But sentences like (vi) seem fine under the Elide interpretation.

ing myself.[33] One class of cases manifesting this constraint involved clear cases of A-verb operation of Raising:

(116) a. It seemed to Bob$_i$ that Jane loved him$_i$.

   b. *Jane seemed to Bob$_i$ to love him$_i$.

(117) a. It must appear to you that I despise you.

   b. *I must appear to you to despise you.

Similarly, *strike* sentences show the same properties, consistent with the claim here that *strike* is also an A-verb:

(118) a. It struck Tom$_i$ that George had lied to him$_i$.

   b. *George struck Tom$_i$ as having lied to him$_i$.

For such cases, it seems that an NP that is an immediate constituent of a complement clause cannot be coreferential with an NP in a main clause, when the subject of the complement is raised into the main clause. This formulation refers directly to the operation of Raising. If such reference is appropriate, then cases like (119) and (120), which

---

(vi) Joan$_i$ is too persevering for us to keep from trying to do that.

The situation is clouded, however, by the fact that most W-verbs, which systematically trigger Equi, do not yield well-formed Elide structures:

$$(vii) \ \ *Jim_i \ is \ too \left\{ \begin{array}{c} foolish \\ smart \end{array} \right\} for \ us \ to \left\{ \begin{array}{c} hate \\ intend \\ like \\ mean \\ need \\ prefer \\ want \\ wish \end{array} \right\} \begin{array}{c} (him_i) \\ \Downarrow \\ \emptyset \end{array} \left\{ \begin{array}{c} to \ win \\ (to \ be) \ happy \end{array} \right\}.$$

Therefore, if these sentences are not blocked by an overlap with Equi, as (iv) and (vi) suggest they cannot be, then it is quite unclear what does exclude them.

[33] I shall ignore here the formulation given in Postal (1970a), since it involves irrelevant complications and at least one wrong assumption. Namely, there I overlooked the existence of violations in sentences like (119)b in the text, assuming wrongly that they were found only in examples like (116)b, and (120)b. I claimed and still claim that these involve application of rules on the cycle of the main clause which move the raised NP, namely, Psych Movement in (116)b and Passive in (120)b. Thus I wrongly assumed that such movement was a necessary concomitant of Raising application to induce the coreference violations, where sentences like (119)b now show this subsequent movement to be irrelevant.

seem to manifest parallel constraints, would argue in favor of the existence of Raising in the derivation of sentences like (119)b and (120)b.

(119) a.   Joan$_i$ believes (that) Bob hates her$_i$.

     b. *Joan$_i$ believes Bob to hate her$_i$.

(120) a.   It is believed by Joan$_i$ that Bob hates her$_i$.

     b. *Bob$_i$ is believed by Joan to hate her$_i$.

This would follow from a formulation of the constraint in question something along the lines of (121).

(121) Given a structure

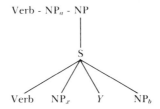

in which NP$_x$ undergoes Raising, NP$_a$ and NP$_b$ cannot be co-referents.[34]

However, there are problems that immediately prevent the outright acceptance of a constraint like (121), which offers the hope of bringing together properties of A-verbs and B-verbs in such a way as to yield an argument for Raising for the latter. In particular, consider the verb *prove,* which we have taken to be a B-verb. Despite (121), there does not appear to be a contrast in (122) or in (123):

(122) a.   Joan$_i$ proved (that) Bob had cheated her$_i$.

     b.   Joan$_i$ proved Bob to have cheated her$_i$.

[34] This formulation presupposes both the verb-initial structure and the Psych Movement analysis of verbs like *seem,* in which an example like (116)b would have an underlying structure as shown in (i) with the raised NP, *Jane,* becoming main clause subject through the application of Psych Movement, before final operation of Subject Formation.

(i) seemed Bob [$_S$ loved Jane him$_S$]

The underlying structure of *seem* sentences is thus taken to be essentially like that of *think* or *believe* sentences.

(123) a. It was proved by Joan$_i$ that Bob had cheated her$_i$.

     b. Bob was proved by Joan$_i$ to have cheated her$_i$.

Principle (121) fails to account for the difference between (122) and (123), on the one hand, and (119) and (120), on the other, wrongly predicting that *prove* should behave like *believe* with respect to the properties in question.

Similarly, I have argued that W-verbs trigger application of Raising. Yet there are no violations in sentences like (124):

(124) a. Jim$_i$ wants you to call him$_i$.

     b. Jim$_i$ needs you to help him$_i$.

     c. Jim$_i$ wishes you to write him$_i$.

Further, such violations are also absent in the case of N-verbs:

(125) a. Joe$_i$ prevented Joan from stabbing him$_i$.

     b. The king$_i$ prohibited anyone from approaching him$_i$.

Therefore, at the least, in order to extract any argument for Raising from these facts, it will be necessary to properly limit (121) so as to distinguish *seem, appear, strike,* and *believe,* on the one hand, from *prove, want, wish, prevent,* etc., on the other.

Such a differentiation does not seem hopeless, however. Those verbs which we have taken to trigger Raising, but which do not induce violations of coreference under (121), appear to fall into two classes distinct from verbs like *believe,* which do. Either these verbs are themselves active, like *prove* and the N-verbs, or they necessarily take semantically future infinitival complements like *want* and *wish.* A generalization to cover these two might take the form of specifying that structures involving these necessarily involve reference to *an event,*[35] which is not the case with *believe.* Principle (121) might then be restricted to non-event cases. This appears consistent with the A-verb cases, since *seem,*

---

[35] This formulation runs into difficulties with sentences like (i), where the event status of the complement is not obvious, to say the least.

(i) a. Larry wants to know Turkish.

   b. Joan wishes to understand Hinduism.

Perhaps the idea can be rescued here by noting the inchoative character of the complement. Thus these complements are semantically future and involve the desire to come to know or to come to understand. The change of state would then be the required event.

appear, and *strike* with infinitival complements do not necessarily involve reference to events.

This proposal makes some predictions about cases not yet considered. For example, the verb *find* is a B-verb like *believe,* with no event reference necessary, while *expect* is a W-verb like *want.* But it is true that the former yields violations under (91), while the latter does not:

(126) a. $Jane_i$ found that Jim loved her_i.

   b. *$Jane_i$ found Jim to love her_i.

(127) a. $Jane_i$ expects that Bob will help her_i.

   b. $Jane_i$ expects Bob to help her_i.

Although this account remains far from adequate, it suggests that some revision of (121) which would correctly divide up the cases may be possible. If so, the ultimate formulation of (121) will provide an argument for Raising.[36] This argument will depend not only on the facts gone over so far but also on the assumption that complement cases for which Raising cannot be invoked never induce coreference violations of the sort in question. This assumption seems to be true:

(128) a. $Joan_i$ arranged for Bob to help her_i.

   b. $Joan_i$ prayed for Tom to call her_i.

   c. $Joan_i$ planned for Bob to meet her_i.

   d. $Joan_i$ resented Bob's kissing her_i.

   e. $Joan_i$ was against Bob staying with her_i.

The infinitival cases here are not very significant, however, since they involve semantically future complements like *want.* What is relevant is the contrast between the following pair, where the semantic properties of the complements, independent of considerations of coreference, are identical:

(129) a. $Jim_i \begin{Bmatrix} \text{wishes} \\ \text{would prefer} \end{Bmatrix}$ for Jane to hate him_i.

   b. *$Jim_i \begin{Bmatrix} \text{wishes} \\ \text{would prefer} \end{Bmatrix}$ Jane to hate him_i.

---

36 Examples like (i), pointed out to me by Ross, suggest that the argument of this section dovetails with that in Section 6.7 based on *as* constructions.

(i) a. *$Jack_i$ regards Martha as inferior to him_i.

   b. *$Jack_i$ recognizes Martha as superior to him_i.

And there is, of course, also the fact, illustrated in (116)a, (117)a, (118)a, (119)a, and (120)a, that *that* clauses never yield the relevant violations.[37] Thus there seems to be a chance that the coreference constraint in question does involve Raising, either directly, as in my formulation of (121), or indirectly, by way of reference to the pre- and post-Raising configurations. If so, then this constraint offers an argument for Raising in the disputed cases like *believe* complements.

6.10 Another Nonargument

I have been considering bodies of data that offer hope of providing further arguments for the existence of Raising in the contested class of derivations. It should be clear that there is a fertile field of phenomena beyond that dealt with in Chapter 3 and 4 which bears on the justification of Raising.

It is worthwhile also to point to factors that do not seem relevant. One such case, involving quantifiers, has already been touched on (in Section 4.5). Given such obvious superficial contrasts as those between the pronoun shapes in (130) and (131), it is tempting to argue in favor of Raising on the basis of the parallelism between (130)b, (131)b, and (132).

(130) a. I believe (that) he (*him) is honest.

b. I believe him (*he) to be honest.

---

37 It should also be pointed out that there are no relevant violations in cases like the following, where it has been traditionally assumed that the italicized NPs have not been raised:

(i) a. John$_i$ persuaded *Joan* to help him$_i$.

b. Jerry$_i$ forced *Louise* to marry him$_i$.

c. Tom$_i$ pressed *the governor* to appoint him$_i$.

I believe that this analysis is wrong, however: I suggest that these constructions involve *both* Raising and Equi, as well as Predicate Raising, with (i)a having, for example, an underlying structure something like (ii):

(ii) CAUSE John$_a$ (AGREE Joan$_i$ [HELP she$_i$ him$_a$]).

Here Equi is relevant on the second cycle, Raising on the third, with Predicate Raising also applying on the third cycle to combine CAUSE and AGREE as the basis for *persuade*. See Lakoff (1970b) and Chapter 11.

It is not at all necessary to reject the involvement of Raising in derivations like (i) if the event limitation on (121) can be maintained, for all of the complements in (i) are eventlike and thus escape (121) on that ground, like W-verb and N-verb constructions.

(131) a. Jack proved (that) she (*her) was pregnant.

     b. Jack proved her (*she) to be pregnant.

(132) a. I believe him (*he).

     b. I like her (*she).

Huddleston (1971:159) actually offers contrasts like (130) as an argument for a Raising analysis.

    The argument would obviously depend on the following statement, which could account for the *believe, prove*, etc., cases only given the derived object status produced by Raising:

(133) The objective case of pronouns is used for (derived) objects.

However, further scrutiny indicates that this argument has little or no force. The trouble is that the objective case pronouns *me, him*, etc., are found not only in derived objects but more or less everywhere except as the subjects of finite clauses. Thus they are found as subjects in cases like (134) and in "free floating" positions in contexts like (135).

(134) a. I resent *him* finishing ahead of me.

     b. *Him* being drunk, I had to find Joan.

     c. For *him* to win would be revolting.

(135) a. Who shouted that? Him.

     b. Harry may like applesauce, but not *me* (=but I don't).

Given this situation, though, there is no basis for choosing (133) over the view which would say the following:

(136) a. Pronouns have the nominative case as subjects of finite clauses.[38]

     b. Pronouns have the objective case otherwise (ignoring genitives).

But (136) offers no way to turn contrasts like (130) and (131) into an argument for Raising in B-verb infinitival complements. So that these contrasts seem to me to be irrelevant.

[38] This ignores special cases like the following:

(i) Melvin is taller than I.

(ii) Arthur wrote to Louise and I.

(iii) The only one who can do that is I myself.

7

Raising Operation into Superordinate Object Position: Summary

In Chapters 3 and 4 of this study I have described an alternative to the view that Raising operates to move elements into superordinate object positions as well as into superordinate subject positions, the latter not being controversial. I have (i) presented approximately twenty arguments against this alternative (see also Sections 12.6, 12.7, and 12.8 for later, additional arguments); (ii) shown the lack of validity of three purported arguments in favor of it; and (iii) discussed eight classes of facts that give some promise of ultimately providing additional arguments. I think that the weight of evidence on this matter already leaves no choice but to conclude that any alternative to Raising grammars like that recently advocated by Chomsky must be incorrect. Thus, although Chomsky (to appear: 36) claims that "As already noted, under the analysis proposed here, there is no necessity for a rule raising the subject of an embedded sentence to the object position of the matrix sentence (and, furthermore, it is questionable whether such a rule could even be added)," a wide range of facts of many different sorts reveals that just such a rule is a necessity.

What we have seen is that a myriad of different generalizations treat the underlying subject NPs of B-verb infinitival complements, W-verb complements, and N-verb complements as if they were derived objects, that is, derived constituents of the main clause. This structure is produced only in a grammar that recognizes the existence of Raising in the relevant derivations.

Of course, the last sentence, like almost all of this study, assumes that the only alternative analyses in question are Raising systems and systems like Chomsky's, in which underlying complement subject NPs are claimed to remain complement subjects throughout derivations. This ignores the possibility of "extra NP" analyses of the relevant cases of the form given in (1), that is, Equi analyses, or pseudo-Equi analyses, in which B-verbs, etc., are assumed to take not only underlying complements but object NPs in addition.

(1) a. Harry believes Bob to know Spanish.

  b. Harry believes Bob [$_S$ Bob to know Spanish $_S$].

In this case, the post-B-verb NP is taken to be a constituent of the main clause to be sure, but as a function of base rules rather than Raising operation.

In orienting this discussion toward a criticism of Chomsky's recent innovative proposals, I have provided arguments showing that the post-B-verb NP, such as *Bob* in (1)a, is a derived main clause constituent. Such arguments do not, of course, directly distinguish between Raising analyses and Equi or pseudo-Equi analyses like (1)b, since both would have the consequence that the post-B-verb NP is a derived main clause constituent.

I touched upon Equi and pseudo-Equi analyses as alternative to Raising systems in the case of A-verbs and N-verbs. And roughly the same considerations would argue against these analyses in the case of B-verbs and W-verbs. In particular, sentences like (2) provide immediate grounds of the sort already touched on in discussions of A-verbs and N-verbs favoring Raising analyses as against "extra NP" analyses like those in (1)b.

(2) a. I believe there to be trouble in Iraq.

  b. Jim wants there to be trouble in Iraq.

  c. Harry proved the cat to be out of the bag.

  d. Harry wants tabs to be kept on Joan's movements.

Sentences like (2) are the most obvious grounds for explaining why there are at present, so far as I know, no actual advocates of "extra NP" analyses for B-verb or W-verb infinitival complements. Thus, in terms of contemporary writings, at least, the only currently defended alternatives are Raising systems and the kind of analysis suggested by Chomsky. This is the reason why I devoted the bulk of my attention to supporting the former and disconfirming the latter. Sentences like (2) show, however, that the materials are at hand to reject "extra NP" analyses as well.

The view that Equi analyses for this range of cases are even a priori possible depends on the assumption that Equi can have a controller NP that is a derived object (at the point when control is determined).

This is a traditionally plausible assumption partly because of cases like (3), in which everyone agrees that Equi has applied, and the controller is a derived object (provable in the strictest terms by the possible passivization of *Bob* in such examples).

(3) I $\begin{Bmatrix} \text{persuaded} \\ \text{asked} \\ \text{compelled} \\ \text{forced} \end{Bmatrix}$ Bob to repudiate lexicalism.

However, under Predicate Raising analyses of such cases, in which surface verbs are derived from combinations of underlying elements, it seems that such cases can be reduced to a model in which the controller for Equi is a cyclic subject. Thus, if we take *persuade* for discussion, the underlying form for (3) might be something like (4)—ignoring a

(4)

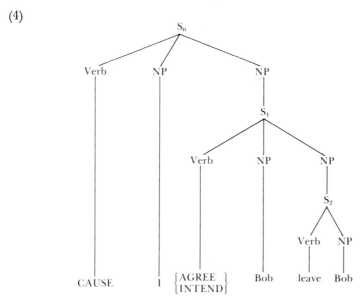

possible inchoative structure below the predicate CAUSE—in which the controller for Equi is the cyclical subject of the verb AGREE or INTEND, that is, the subject at the end of the cycle on the S headed by this predicate. Thus, Equi is determined in structures like (4) just as it is in sentences like the following, which are equivalent to cases in which the S_1 of (4) is not embedded:

(5) Bob $\left\{ \begin{array}{l} \text{agreed} \\ \text{intended} \end{array} \right\}$ to leave.

If structures like (4) can be maintained for all verbs like *persuade,* it seems that there is a basis for a restrictive conception of Equi embodying the following claim:

(6) The controller NP for Equi is always a cyclical subject at the point when control is checked, which is at the end of the lowest cycle covering the controller.

For an independent development of a similar idea, see Grosu (1971), who treats a variety of cases like those in (3). However, in order to maintain something like (6), it is not sufficient to reanalyze cases like (3) involving forward application of Equi. One must also deal with backward applications like those in (7):

(7) a. Finding the dinosaur egg excited Wilbur.

   b. Shooting myself seems unwise to me.

Analyses of such sentences which would meet the conditions of the principle in (6) have not, as far as I am aware, ever been proposed. One possible solution would involve distinguishing two different rules, Forward Equi and Backward Equi, with only the former subject to (6). There are, in fact, grounds for such a division. For instance, forward deletion is always obligatory, but backward application is often optional.

In any event, despite the obvious problems involved in justifying a constraint like (6), it deserves much further study because of its restrictive power. If something like (6) is correct, of course, then Equi analyses of the range of constructions for which I would propose Raising analyses are ruled out in principle. That is, a theory of grammar embodying (6) would provide a principled explanation for the fact that the derived objects after B-verbs, N-verbs, and W-verbs achieve that status through Raising application.

In the case of W-verbs at least, other empirical arguments against Equi analyses beyond those provided by sentences like (2) are also available. For instance, consider sentences like (8):

(8) a. I want to win.

   b. I want Joan to win.

In a Raising system like that advocated here, these sentences will have remote structures of roughly the form given in (9):

(9) a. I want [I to win].

   b. I want [Joan to win].

That is, they will be parallel underlying structures differing only in the reference of the complement subject, correlating correctly with the meaning difference between (8)a and (8)b. The derivations then differ in that Equi applies to the former structure, but Raising to the latter.[1]

   In an "extra NP" system, however, the underlying structure of (8)b is not (9)b but rather (10), which is not at all parallel to (9)a.

(10) I want Joan [Joan to win].

Special semantic principles are then required to indicate somehow

---

[1] I would not rule out the possibility that Raising also applies in the former, so that the NP is not deleted until it has been moved into the main clause. This would eliminate an otherwise peculiar asymmetry for the class of W-verbs, where Raising would apply only when the complement subject NP is *not* coreferential with the main clause subject, in contrast, say, to verbs like *believe*, where Raising is not so constrained. This would then mean that Equi actually deletes in these cases what would otherwise become a reflexive pronoun.

   There are, however, apparently troublesome consequences. Namely, it would seem that Equi would then work differently in cases like (9)a in the text, where the class of verbs otherwise triggers Raising, than in cases like *arrange, pray*, and *anxious* in sentences like (i), where Raising is never relevant and the deleted NP must always have remained in the lower clause.

(i) a. I arranged to leave.

   b. I prayed to be permitted to continue.

   c. I am anxious to retire.

Similarly, Equi in cases like (9)a would be distinct from *backward* applications of Equi, as in (ii), where also the deleted NP never could have gotten into the main clause.

(ii) Finding the jewels pleased me.

However, a solution to this asymmetry involving Equi is available in *global* terms, by having the rule specify that the deleted NP need only have once been an appropriate cyclic subject of a complement, coreferential with the proper main clause NP, it being irrelevant whether it is in the complement or in the main clause at the point when it is finally erased. This is consistent with other evidence (see Postal, 1970b) that Equi must be defined globally.

that the extra NP plays no role in the interpretation. See also footnote 11 of Chapter 1.

Next, I shall comment on an older argument, given originally in Rosenbaum (1967), which attempted to differentiate Raising from Equi derivations in terms of meaning contrasts related to passivization contrasts in complements. Thus it was pointed out that in cases like (11) the *a* and *b* pairs share meaning up to the point of truth value determination.

(11) a. John seems (to me) to have seduced Barbara.

b. Barbara seems (to me) to have been seduced by John.

That is, it was claimed that if (11)a is true, so is (11)b, and conversely. This would follow, in a Raising system, from the parallel truth value equivalence of pairs like (12), which in turn follows from the general fact that the choice of passivization or not in a clause normally yields no truth value contrast.

(12) a. It seems (to me) that John seduced Barbara.

b. It seems (to me) that Barbara was seduced by John.

In contrast, Rosenbaum noted that pairs superficially parallel to (11), such as (13), have no truth value equivalence at all.

(13) a. John longs to seduce Barbara.

b. Barbara longs to be seduced by John.

The contrast between elements like *seem* and *long* can then naturally be accounted for by recognizing the A-verb Raising analysis for the former type but an "extra" NP plus Equi analysis for the latter. Hence, where (11)a has the structure (14)a, (13)a has the structure (14)b, etc.:

(14) a. seem to me [seduce John Barbara]

b. longs John [seduce John Barbara]

Similarly, it was observed by Chomsky (1965: 22–23; 1967: 432) and by Rosenbaum that a verb like *persuade* yields truth value contrasts in cases like (15), while a B-verb like *believe* does not, as shown in (16).

(15) a. Jim persuaded the nurse to move the patient.

b. Jim persuaded the patient to be moved by the nurse.

(16) a. Jim believed the nurse to have moved the patient.

   b. Jim believed the patient to have been moved by the nurse.

This, then, can apparently be explained in a fashion parallel to the account in (14) by providing contrasting underlying structures of the kind shown in (17) for (15), but a single source, like (18), for (16).

(17) a. persuade Jim the nurse [move the nurse the patient]

   b. persuade Jim the patient [move the nurse the patient]

(18) believe Jim [move the nurse the patient]

That is, it can be explained by providing an "extra" NP analysis for verbs like *persuade (force, encourage,* etc.), but a Raising analysis for *believe,* etc.

   While I believe there is considerable merit in this argument, which applies as well to N-verbs[2] and W-verbs[3] as to B-verbs, since these contrast with verbs like *persuade* in the same way, the situation is really

---

[2] That is, to N-verbs like *prevent, keep,* and *stop,* for which sentences like (i) are truth-functionally equivalent.

(i) a. I $\left\{\begin{array}{l}\text{prevented}\\\text{kept}\\\text{stopped}\end{array}\right\}$ the nurse from moving the patient.

   b. I $\left\{\begin{array}{l}\text{prevented}\\\text{kept}\\\text{stopped}\end{array}\right\}$ the patient from being moved by the nurse.

However, N-verbs like *discourage* and *deter* behave like *persuade,* so that pairs like (ii) are not equivalent.

(ii) a. I $\left\{\begin{array}{l}\text{discouraged}\\\text{deterred}\end{array}\right\}$ the nurse from moving the patient.

   b. I $\left\{\begin{array}{l}\text{discouraged}\\\text{deterred}\end{array}\right\}$ the patient from being moved by the nurse.

[3] Thus the following pairs are equivalent in the sense in question:

(i) a. I $\left\{\begin{array}{l}\text{expect}\\\text{intend}\\\text{want}\end{array}\right\}$ the nurse to move the patient.

   b. I $\left\{\begin{array}{l}\text{expect}\\\text{intend}\\\text{want}\end{array}\right\}$ the patient to be moved by the nurse.

somewhat more complex in two different ways that do not ultimately affect the force of this argument, I think, but do indicate the need for further clarifications. The problems are briefly dealt with in Chapter 11.

In summary, then, the facts seem to show unequivocally that post-B-verb, W-verb, and N-verb NPs are derived constituents of main clauses, and the only viable account of this derivation involves Raising operation into superordinate object position. Nearly everyone who has worked on complements within the overall framework of generative grammar, including Chomsky and myself, are agreed on the need for a raising analysis of A-verb contexts and hence for the need to postulate a Raising rule in such cases. Given then the existence of a Raising rule in B-verb, W-verb, and N-verb contexts, it follows, as McCawley (1970a) showed, that these two rules can be trivially combined into one, as in Section 1.5, number (49), of Chapter 1. However, if it is true, as argued in Section 1.4, that Raising cannot operate on the output of Extraposition, as Rosenbaum (1967) had assumed, then the only way so far proposed to combine A-verb and B-verb raising rules requires verb-initial structures, as McCawley proposed. Chomsky (to appear: footnote 33) argues that "It is pointed out by McCawley (1970) that if English is a VSO language, then raising to subject and to object position can be formulated as a single rule. There is, however, no persuasive independent evidence for the assumption. If there is no rule of raising to object position, then there remains no substantial argument for the VSO analysis, so far as I can see." But at this juncture it is clear that there is no real possibility of avoiding recognition of a "rule of raising to object position." It follows that the relevant part of McCawley's argument stands up as originally given. That is, an important basis for the verb-initial analysis of English clauses is that it permits the unified statement of A-verb and B-verb (also W-verb and N-verb) Raising.

It should be stressed, though, that the argument for verb-initial order based on this combination of raising operations into a single rule Raising is no stronger, and can at best be no stronger, than the evidence, briefly discussed in Section 1.4, showing that Raising cannot operate on the output of Extraposition. The latter mode of derivation would also permit a unified statement of all kinds of subject raising as a movement to the left.

McCawley (1970a) argued that the possibility of combining A-verb and B-verb types of raisings into a single Raising rule provided an argument for the assumption that the underlying structures of English clauses are verb-initial. I have tried to support this argument in the present study by showing (i) that, despite Chomsky's recent conceptions, Raising actually operates into superordinate object positions; and (ii) that Raising in A-verb cases cannot be regarded as operating on the output of Extraposition. It thus seems that McCawley's argument has been strengthened. However, a number of people, particularly John Kimball, have pointed out that it is equally possible to combine the two types of raising into a single rule by assuming underlying verb-*final* structures for English clauses. This is certainly true. It thus follows that the line of argument in McCawley (1970a) does not provide a method for distinguishing between the claims of underlying verb-initial and those of verb-final conceptions on the basis of facts related to Raising.

This point is elaborated by G. Hudson (1972), who argues that underlying structures are, in fact, unordered. With reference to McCawley's verb-initial argument from Raising, Hudson claims that the two rules can be combined not only with either verb-initial or verb-final underlying structures but also with verb-intermediate structures. To quote Hudson (1972: 58–59):

> Since the simplification of Subject-raising, Passive, and THERE-insertion is the clearest achievement of the analyses of English as either a VSO or SOV language, fatal to the arguments is the fact that the same simplification of these three transformations, even along with the collapsing of the two cases of subject-raising, can readily be obtained not only with SOV ordered inputs, but with SVO order. This alternative will also employ the rule which puts the verb in second position. The effect of this rule is to restore SVO order after one operation of rules of THERE-insertion, Passive, and Subject-raising have applied. This rule moves the verb into position to the right of the clause initial NP.

> (10) $[\underline{NP\ X\ V\ Y}]$
> S
>
> $\overline{\ 1\ \ 2\ \ 3\ \ 4\ }\quad \Rightarrow\quad 1\ 3\ 2\ 4$

> A version of rule (10), recall, is independently required in the derivation of questions like (9a) and (c). Rule (10) applies to the strings resulting from the three transformations in question, which can therefore be stated as single operation rules applying to SVO ordered inputs.

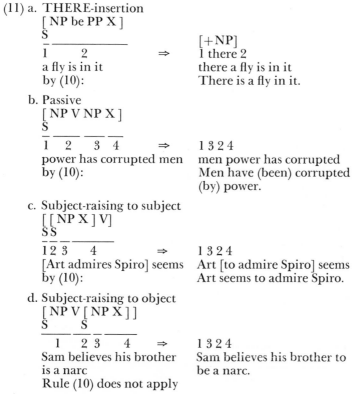

(11) a. THERE-insertion
   [NP be PP X]
   S
   ———————————   [+NP]
   1   2   ⇒   1 there 2
   a fly is in it   there a fly is in it
   by (10):   There is a fly in it.

   b. Passive
   [NP V NP X]
   S
   —— —— —— ——
   1   2   3   4   ⇒   1 3 2 4
   power has corrupted men   men power has corrupted
   by (10):   Men have (been) corrupted
                          (by) power.

   c. Subject-raising to subject
   [[NP X] V]
   S S
   —— —— ————
   1 2 3   4   ⇒   1 3 2 4
   [Art admires Spiro] seems   Art [to admire Spiro] seems
   by (10):   Art seems to admire Spiro.

   d. Subject-raising to object
   [NP V [NP X]]
   S   S
   —————— —— ——————
   1   2 3   4   ⇒   1 3 2 4
   Sam believes his brother   Sam believes his brother to
   is a narc   be a narc.
   Rule (10) does not apply

Notice that in this approach also both cases of Subject-raising are raising to the immediate left.

However, Hudson's claim that verb-intermediate order permits combination of the two rules without loss of generalization is not correct. Note that he himself does not so combine them, providing instead two distinct rules. While these have been formulated in such a way as to have the same number of terms and the same elementary transformational operation, they cannot be combined into a single natural rule because of the different positions of the symbols. I see no basis, therefore, for Hudson's claim that verb-intermediate structures are on a par with the other two types with respect to the phenomena in question. One seems to be left, then, with the choice between verb-initial or verb-final possibilities, under the assumption that underlying structures are indeed ordered.

One might think that, since English has a variety of transitive verb-initial clauses, as illustrated in (19), but no transitive verb-final clauses, the choice is obvious in favor of the verb-initial conception.

(19) a. Will Bob agree to it?

     b. Have you lost your senses?

     c. John is, whispered Arthur to his priest, no longer devout.

     d. "What is happening?" wondered Bill to himself.

     e. Were we to resign, chaos would ensue.

Moreover, McCawley's (1970a) typological considerations also seem to favor this decision. Finally, Bach (1971) has presented an argument for verb-initial structures that seems to support this proposal rather than the verb-final one.

Bach's argument is perhaps worth reiterating briefly. Bach assumes that the rule attracting *wh*-marked questioned NP to the left is a universal rule whose triggering element is a higher verb. This assumption serves as a basis for explaining the crucial typological fact adduced by Bach, namely, that in superficial verb-final languages the question movement rule is never found. This would follow, since if the elements must be attracted to a verb on the left, movement must fail when all verbs follow the (clausal) NP related to them. These considerations thus suggest that English and similar languages are, in fact, verb-initial since movement in interrogative clauses is found equally when these clauses are in subject or object positions:

(20) a. I asked who he loved.

     b. Who he loved is unknown.

The movement of the questioned word *who* in examples like (20)b is then taken as evidence that at the point of movement the subject clause followed the presumed movement trigger *unknown*. Thus it is basically clear how Bach's assumption provides an ingenious argument for the verb-initial character of English clauses.

However, while this argument is formally quite beautiful, it cannot be regarded as fully compelling even if all of Bach's explicit assumptions are validated. What is particularly troubling to me is the assumption that, in an example like (20)b, the movement is triggered by the element *unknown*. For note that, alongside such examples, one can find cases like (21), in which it seems that it is actually the embedded element *question* that triggers the movement.

(21) The answer to the question who he loved is unknown.

This is, I think, shown further by such examples as (22):

(22) a. The question who he loved does not interest me.

   b. The important question is the question (of) who he loved.

The possibility that it is something like *question* that triggers question movement in subordinate clauses greatly clouds the force of Bach's argument.

Moreover, recently Ross (to appear g) constructed an equally ingenious argument that English (and German) are verb-final in underlying clause structure. I thus regard the question of a choice between verb-initial and verb-final order as quite unsettled and shall take no position on the matter here. However, for convenience, I shall continue to assume that the verb-initial position is justified whenever it is relevant. For some further discussion of these questions in the context of comments about the surface verb-final language Japanese, see Section 12.2.

A further point must be made. Although I believe Hudson's line of argument, that verb-intermediate order provides as adequate a base as either of the extremity orderings of the verb, is incorrect, my objections are relevant only under certain presently accepted assumptions, which are not themselves unchallengeable by any means. His ultimate claim about underlying structures being unordered may well be correct. Most of the arguments relevant to underlying order, particularly that involving combination of rules into a general Raising rule, depend crucially on the assumption that rules are stated in terms of constituent configurations. It is quite possible, however, that *cyclic* rules are, in fact, essentially specified in terms of grammatical relations (for discussion of this possibility, see Section 8.4 and Perlmutter and Postal, to appear a, to appear b; Postal, to appear e). However, notions like "subject of" and "object of" are defined quite independently of the position of the verb in a clause. If, therefore, Raising were stated in terms of grammatical relations, the argument for either verb-initial or verb-final order as against verb-intermediate order would, I believe, certainly collapse.

The unsettled situation just discussed is thus relevant to Chomsky's remarks (to appear: 36–37) apropos of raising into superordinate object position: "One might then raise the question whether cyclic transformations should not be constrained so as to forbid operations that never change the terminal string of a phrase-marker, but only its structure, as in some formulations of subject-raising to object position (see, e.g. Kiparsky and Kiparsky (1970))." At best, this principle would be relevant only if the verb-initial view can be eliminated. For, with the verb in a clause in initial position, a cyclical rule of Raising (see Section 7.2), and a postcyclical rule of Subject Formation, the operation of Raising in all cases affects the terminal string, since the raised NP must at least hop over the main verb of the complement clause. Moreover, this discussion is somewhat inconsistent with other views of Chomsky's, in particular, with his view that every clause begins with a complementizer constituent. If this were true, then, barring appeals to constituents with no terminal elements and other bizarre devices, Raising would always change terminal strings regardless of verbal position. Furthermore, it is by no means clear independently of Raising, that always vacuous operations can be banned from the cycle. Hankamer (personal communication) suggests that the rule incorporating generic objects into the verb in Turkish has just this property. (See Aissen, to appear, for some discussion.) Finally, the evidence in favor of raising into superordinate object position in English is massive and, I believe, overwhelming. Therefore, if this operation turns out to be one that affects only constituent structure and not terminal strings, then the relevant facts suffice to show that the principle suggested by Chomsky is incorrect.

8
Remarks on Raising

8.1 Comments

The earlier chapters of this study have dealt mostly with a narrow range of questions involving the existence of a raising operation relevant for producing derived main clause objects as well as derived main clause subjects. Having concluded that such a rule exists and that in one way or another it can be combined with the rule producing derived subjects to yield a single natural Raising rule, I shall now devote a limited amount of attention to certain properties of this rule. Here I shall consider the cyclicity of the operation, its relation to extrinsic rule ordering, and, finally, the possibility of a general theory predicting some of those properties of Raising which have hitherto been implicitly regarded as brute facts having to be stated in the grammar of English.

8.2 The Cyclicity of Raising

I shall present here a brief empirical argument supporting the view that Raising is a cyclical rule. The argument will depend crucially on the following assumptions:

(1) a. Raising is a movement rule, rather than a combination of a "doubling" rule and a separate deletion rule.

    b. There exist generalizations about English grammar depending on the status of elements as *derived* Clause Mates. In particular, I shall assume, following Sections 3.2 and 3.4, that Ordinary Reflexivization and the Inclusion Constraint depend on the derived Clause Mate status of pairs of NPs.

Condition (1)b is, of course, rejected by Chomsky (to appear), but I have already dealt with these objections. Condition (1)a is, at least for purposes of argument, rejected by Grinder (1972), who considers the possibility of taking Raising to be a "doubling" rule, one that places the original NP in the superordinate sentence, leaving a pronominal "copy" behind, this being subsequently deleted by a further rule.

There is no independent evidence for this view,[1] and it requires a special deletion rule to remove the pronominal "copy."

Given (1)a, b, the cyclicity of Raising can be demonstrated on the basis of cases of multiple application of Raising. I shall give the argument first on the basis of reflexive facts, and then more briefly give the relevant Inclusion cases. Consider first this example:

(2) Melvin believes himself to be immortal.

---

[1] This was also contemplated in Postal (1971: 162–163). There is a rule operative, at least for perceptual verbs like *look* and *sound*, which has, as noted in Postal (1971: 163), this "doubling" property:

(i)   a. It looks like there is going to be a riot.
      b. There looks like there is going to be a riot.

In that study, I suggested that the existence of a "doubling" rule for these cases gave some support for the notion that Raising might have this character. I now reject this idea. Observe that the existence of sentences like (ii) shows that the deletion rule necessary to derive Raising sentences from underlying "doubled" structures like (iii) cannot be subsumed under the independently needed Equi, which is subject to conditions of coreference that structures like (iii) cannot meet:

(ii) a. I believe there to be gorillas in the zoo.
      b. I believe tabs to have been kept on his wife.

(iii) a. I believe there [there to be gorillas in the zoo].
      b. I believe tabs [tabs to have been kept on his wife].

Hence, as stated in the text, a "doubling" statement of Raising requires a special deletion rule.

Moreover, as noted by Rogers (1971), who discussed the rule that was given in (i) at some length, that operation can also affect nonsubjects:

(iv) a. It looks like Jane has been hassling Ted again.
      b. Ted looks like Jane has been hassling him again.

(v)   a. It sounds like Max has been hammering nails with this violin.
      b. This violin sounds like Max has been hammering nails with it.

An attempt to combine Raising with this rule would make it hard to state that Raising in all other cases is restricted to subjects. In these terms, then, the existence for the same class of perceptual verbs found in sentences like (iv) and (v) of sentences like (vi) raises a problem.

(vi) a. Melvin looks sick.
      b. Joan sounds tired.

Should these be derived by the "doubling" rule relevant for (iv), etc., or by Raising, if this is a separate rule? This and other problems involving this class of elements are being further investigated by Rogers, and I am happy to leave them to him.

Here the former complement subject takes on reflexive form because, after it has undergone Raising, it is a Clause Mate of its coreferential antecedent. Hence, if Ordinary Reflexivization is regarded as cyclical,[2]

[2] I shall argue ultimately that what I am calling Ordinary Reflexivization is not so much a rule that carries out some operation but rather a partial definition of the notion "member of the category Reflexive." What it says in effect is that a pronominal NP, N is assigned to the category Reflexive if there is some tree structure containing a clause T in which at least the following three conditions exist:

(i) In T
    a. N and some other (antecedent) NP, A are Clause Mates.
    b. A precedes N.

(ii) The correspondents of A, N in logical structure are marked as stipulated co-referents.

(iii) T is the final structure derived by the last cyclical rule application on the *lowest cycle that covers* (in the obvious sense) the sets of corresponding nodes of *both* A and N.

Conditions (i)a,b are the standard Clause Mate and precedence conditions for reflexive marking. Condition (ii) is the requirement of coreference underlying all pronominal linkages. Condition (iii), which is easy enough to make precise, but only in a context in which the underlying notions of global grammar have been made explicit, says roughly that an antecedent-pronoun pair becomes an antecedent-reflexive pronoun pair only if condition (i) holds at the end of the first cycle— defined by an S that dominates correspondents of both antecedent and pronoun. The importance of condition (iii) is that, although the point in derivations where Ordinary Reflexivization applies does not correspond to any of the normally distinguished levels of grammatical structure, it is not necessary (or, in fact, possible) to say that this rule holds at the ends of arbitrary cycles. That is, it is not necessary to pick out the appropriate point by quantifying over the set of all cycle-final structures. Rather, there is a function that picks out the appropriate cycle-final structure for any pair of antecedent-pronoun corresponding node sets, namely, that function informally indicated by the lowest covering cycle specification.

According to this approach, whose intimate connection with the notions of global grammar needs no stress, no ad hoc markers need be placed on NPs, that is, no features like [+Reflexive], as in the primitive accounts in Postal (1966a, 1970c), and no morphemic markers, Refl, etc. Rather, the rule informally specified in (i)–(iii) will assign certain nodes defining NP constituents to a certain category; this information, like all other categorical information, is recorded in a *table* of category memberships distinct from any of the trees in a derivation. Language-particular rules will then apply (possibly globally) to determine the morphemic properties of NPs assigned to the category Reflexive. Thus in English it will be necessary to say that such NPs take the stem shape *self* and that, like other definite, coreferential pronouns, they undergo an agreement rule linking their shape to properties of their antecedents.

The argument given later in the text that Raising is cyclic also simultaneously supports the view that Ordinary Reflexivization is cyclic, a traditional assumption, of course. See Lakoff (1967); Postal (1969a, 1970c, 1971); Ross (1967).

the point of reflexive marking in (2) is at the end of the second cycle,[3] after the pronoun has become the derived object of *believe* and a Clause Mate of its subject.

On the other hand, the reflexive marking in sentences like (3) takes place at the end of the first cycle, while *Joan* and the object of *critical* are still Clause Mate members of the lowest clause.

(3) Melvin believes Joan to be overly critical of herself.

Thus, so far, one sees that in some derivations, like (3), reflexive marking must occur *before* an application of Raising, and in others, like 2, *after* an application.

The really crucial examples are those involving multiple applications of Raising, as in (4):

(4) a. *Melvin* seems to have believed *himself* to be overly critical of himself.

   b. Melvin considers *himself* to have proved *himself* to be innocent.

The key point is that the pairs of italicized NPs neither start out in underlying structures as Clause Mates nor end up in surface structures as Clause Mates. Nonetheless, the leftmost of the pair regularly triggers the reflexive marking of the rightmost, indicating (given (1)b) that at one stage they were Clause Mates. But, strikingly, the existence of such an intermediate stage is a direct theorem of the cyclicity of Raising. For (4)b, the underlying structure, ignoring tense and other irrelevancies, would be that shown in (5). To derive (4)b from (5), Raising must apply to both of the italicized occurrences of he_i. However, a random application or, in particular, application to the leftmost first would destroy the principled basis for reflexive marking. That is, if the subject of *prove* is raised first, it will cease to be a constituent of S_1 before the subject of *innocent* becomes a constituent of S_1. Consequently, there will be no stage at which these two NPs are Clause Mates. If, however, in all cases, applications of Raising to more deeply

---

[3] In speaking of "second cycle" here, I ignore my view that auxiliaries like *be* and adjectives like *immortal* in (2) are each the underlying main verb of an independent clause, so that at the least (2) really involves three cycles. I shall continue to ignore auxiliaries, their associated cycles, etc., throughout the discussion of this argument, since they have no bearing on relevant questions.

(5)

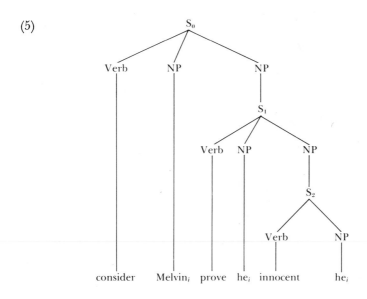

embedded structures must occur before application to less deeply embedded ones, then the subject of *innocent* must be raised before the
subject of *prove* can be. But it is just this sequence that the assumption
of a cyclical, bottom-to-top order for Raising guarantees, since it requires that in configurations like (5) a cyclical rule apply to S_{j+1} before
it applies to S_j, for all j.

The meaning of this argument can be clarified as follows. In a
cyclical theory like that being argued for here, Raising is checked for
application and obligatorily or optionally applied from bottom to
top in hierarchies of successively embedded clauses. At the end of each
cycle, Ordinary Reflexivization is checked, and NPs are assigned to
the category Reflexive if the appropriate conditions are met at that
point. In this sense, these two rules cycle on each other, and both are
applied in each relevant cycle. Consider, then, the alternatives to this
view. One would be what could be called "random application." Each
rule can be applied whenever a (subpart of) a tree meets its condition.
This view is disconfirmed under our assumptions as follows. Given a
structure like (5), random application permits, in particular, the subject of *prove* to be raised before the subject of *innocent* has been.
Therefore, there is no tree in which these two NPs are Clause Mates,

and Ordinary Reflexivization would never be triggered. Thus the grammar would predict falsely such structures as (6), in which all three NPs are coreferential but the final one is not reflexive.

(6) *Melvin$_i$ considers himself$_i$ to have proved him$_i$ innocent.

Hence random application must be rejected.

Another alternative to a cyclical theory in which the set of cyclical rules is applied on each cycle would be one in which each rule cycles on itself. That is, the grammar would apply each rule successively (possibly with some principles determining the order in which rules are chosen) to the most deeply embedded structures, to the next most, etc. Let us call this mode "individual cyclic application." This can also be easily disproved on the basis of structures like (5). For there would be two possibilities. Either one would first cycle on all levels with Raising, or first with Ordinary Reflexivization. In the former case, all raisings would be carried out before any applications of reflexive marking. Thus Ordinary Reflexivization would, in fact, have to operate on a structure essentially equivalent to the surface structure of (4)b with respect to clause memberships. In particular, it would have to apply to a structure in which the subjects of *prove* and *innocent* are not Clause Mates. Hence the principled basis for reflexive marking is lost. Or, on the contrary, it could be Ordinary Reflexivization that is cycled on first. In this case, the rule would have to apply directly to (5), that is, to structures totally independent of those derived by Raising. But in (5) none of the relevant NPs are Clause Mates, and again the basis for reflexive marking is lost. Thus individual cyclic application must also be wrong. In fact, then, the ordinary cyclical mode is the only known way to derive all the correct structures and none of the wrong ones in cases like these.

Hence, under assumptions (1)a, b, it is only the fact that Raising (and Ordinary Reflexivization) are cyclical that explains why reflexive marking takes place for antecedent-pronoun pairs that neither start out as Clause Mates nor end up as Clause Mates.[4] The cyclical character of these rules guarantees that all the relevant derivations will have intermediate stages in which the Clause Mate condition holds.

---

[4] T. Wasow (personal communication) has made the interesting observation that it might be possible to avoid the consequences of this argument by making use of *global* power. I shall discuss this question briefly at the end of this section.

This argument can be duplicated for Inclusion Constraint cases, where violations ensue basically when pairs of NPs both overlap in coreference and are derived Clause Mates. Given such assumptions, sentences such as the following provide the same argument for the cyclicity of Raising:

(7) a. *_I_ believe _us_ to know French.

   b. *Melvin believes _me_ to be overly critical of _us_.

   c. *_I_ seem to have believed _us_ to know French.

   d. *Melvin considers _me_ to have proved _us_ to be innocent.

Here (7)a corresponds to (2), (7)b to (3), (7)c to (4)a, and (7)d to (4)b. Thus (7)a is ill-formed because the italicized NPs become Clause Mates after Raising applies; (7)b is ill-formed because they were Clause Mates before Raising applied. In (7)c and (7)d, however, the violations ensue because the italicized NPs were Clause Mates after the first application of Raising (triggered, respectively, by the distinct occurrences of _believe_) but before the second application of Raising (triggered, respectively, by _seem_ and _consider_). Thus a cyclical rule Raising also guarantees that sentences with Inclusion Constraint violations but without either underlying or surface structure Clause Mate status for the relevant pairs of NPs will have the proper intermediate stages in which the pairs are Clause Mates.

It should be clear that the same line of argument could be constructed on the basis of any other phenomenon that could be argued to involve derived Clause Mate status for pairs of NPs.

It follows, then, that given (1)a, b, examples like (4) and (7)c, d provide arguments not only for the cyclic nature of Raising (as well as Ordinary Reflexivization and the Inclusion Constraint) but also more generally for the notion of a cycle and for the notions of intermediate stages in derivations distinct from either underlying structures or surface structures.

Consider now, though, the possibility raised by Wasow, mentioned in footnote 4, that these arguments can be circumvented if the Clause Mate condition on Ordinary Reflexivization is specified globally. Thus, let us take a structure like (5), repeated here as (8). Even if Raising applies to the higher occurrence of he_i first, that is, if it applies anticyclically, in global grammar it would be possible to make use of the

(8)

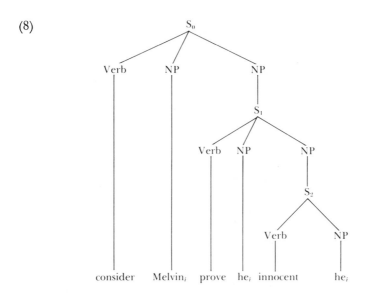

fact that it was *once* in S_1, and hence to define the category Reflexive partly in terms of joint membership of two NPs in the same S at different points in the derivation. However, I believe there may be objections to this suggestion.

First, there is the technical point that a node like S_1 in (8) occurs only in a single tree, so that the global equivalent of the Clause Mate condition on Ordinary Reflexivization (in context with noncyclic Raising) could not refer to membership of NPs at different stages in the same S, but only in a corresponding S. At best, then, the definition of Reflexive would be more complicated. Moreover, the complications would involve the restatement not only of (i)a but also of (i)b in footnote 2.

Second, a noncyclic account of Raising and Ordinary Reflexivization runs into empirical difficulties. There is a process of reducing answers to questions, appealed to earlier, in Section 6.2, yielding the *c* sentences in the following (see Morgan, to appear).

(9) a. Q: Who should Joan call?

   b. A: I think Joan should call Bob.

   c. A: I think Bob.

(10) a. Q: How much will he eat?

   b. A: I think he will eat very little.

   c. A: I think very little.

Observe, though, that the result of this answer-reduction process never induces reflexivization:

(11) a. Q: Who should Bob call?

   b. A: I think Bob should call me.

   c. A: I think me (*myself).

(12) a. Q: Who should Joan call?

   b. A: Bob$_i$ thinks Joan should call him$_i$.

   c. A: Bob$_i$ thinks him$_i$ (*himself).

In a theory with Ordinary Reflexivization specifying membership in the category Reflexive in terms of configurations existing at the ends of specified cycles, such facts follow naturally merely from the assumption that *the answer-producing process relevant for (9)c–(12)c is post-cyclical*. Observe that this is consistent with the assumptions needed for this rule with respect to its interaction with *Each* Shift, noted in Section 6.2. For then there would be no cycle-final structure meeting the conditions of (i) of footnote 2 in cases like (11)c and (12)c. At the end of the relevant cycle, (11)c, for example, would have a structure essentially like (11)b, which does not, of course, meet the conditions for Ordinary Reflexivization.

On the other hand, if reflexive marking is triggered *without* regard to cyclic contexts by joint membership in the correspondents of some simple clause, then reflexive marking is wrongly predicted for cases like (11)c and (12)c. What this point strongly suggests is that there is a real "level" break in the grammar with some processes (Raising, Passive, Ordinary Reflexivization, etc.) defined "before" it, and others, like the answer-reduction process, "after" it. And the only serious account of this break so far proposed is that it is defined by the end of the cycle.[5]

5 The following mysterious facts about the interaction of Ordinary Reflexivization and Complex NP Shift are worth noting:

(i) a. I talked to Bob about himself on the boat.

Moreover, there are other phenomena parallel to (11)c and (12)c. There is a rule that deletes pronoun heads of NPs with genitive modifiers:

(13) a.   Martha's large dog is healthy, but her small one is sick.

     b. *Martha's dog is healthy, but Sarah's one is sick. $\Rightarrow$

     c.   Martha's dog is healthy, but Sarah's is sick.

If membership in a simple clause is sufficient to trigger Ordinary Reflexivization independently of cyclical constraints, the grammar would predict (14)a instead of (14)b:

(14) a. Martha's$_i$ dog didn't fall on her$_i$, but *Sarah's$_j$ fell on herself$_j$.

     b. Martha's dog$_i$ didn't fall on her$_i$, but Sarah's$_j$ fell on her$_j$.

---

     b.*I talked about himself on the boat—to the man who had offered to sell me the rotten oats.

(ii) a. I believe Melvin to have talked about himself on the boat.

     b. I believe to have talked about himself on the boat—the man who offered to sell me the rotten oats.

It seems that Complex NP Shift can move the antecedent of a reflexive to the right of it only in those cases where, in our terms, the antecedent has undergone Raising, and thus ceased to be a Clause Mate of the reflexive.

Formally, this contrast would follow from our cycle-final account of Ordinary Reflexivization *if* Complex NP Shift were taken to be a cyclic rule. For in this case, in an example like (i)b, Complex NP Shift would apply *before* the end of the cycle in which Ordinary Reflexivization could apply, and (i)b would properly be underivable. However, in (ii)b, Complex NP Shift could not apply on the first cycle because the antecedent is a subject, and we recall from Section 4.1 that Complex NP Shift does not apply to subjects. Therefore, the antecedent remains in a position appropriate to trigger reflexive marking at the end of the first cycle. On the next cycle, in a Raising system, it is lifted up into the main clause, where it could undergo Complex NP Shift on the second cycle, without any violation of the subject condition.

It follows that if Complex NP Shift is cyclic, the contrast between (i) and (ii) provides an additional argument for Raising. However, I regard the cyclic character of this rule as extremely dubious. Intuitively, it seems to fall into the class of operations that are postcyclic. Its analogue in languages (like German) with rich case-marking systems in general operates after case assignment, that is, without affecting case assignment. And since it is natural to take case assignment to be universally defined on cycle-final structure, this means that the analogous rule is postcyclic in such languages. In Perlmutter and Postal (to appear b) a general theory of the cyclic-postcyclic contrast in rules is worked out according to which the properties of Complex NP Shift determine that it is postcyclical. However, if Complex NP Shift is postcyclical, then the contrasts in (i) and (ii) are unexplained. This strikes me as an interesting mystery.

On the other hand, in a cyclic theory, the facts in (14) follow again from having the deletion rule that produces the derived Clause Mate status (for example, of *Sarah's* and *her(self)* in (14)) postcyclic.

What both examples like (11)c, (12)c and those like (14) seem to show is that Ordinary Reflexivization cannot be a rule that applies anywhere its structural description is met; that is, it cannot be a so-called "anywhere rule."

The preceding discussion assumes that the answer-reduction process, whose existence is strongly supported in Morgan (to appear), is post-cyclical. In defense of this position we have so far said only that it is consistent with our earlier description of *Each* Shift and that it predicts the reflexive-marking facts properly. I think some independent evidence for it is available, however. It was observed in Section 4.11 that there is a strict ban on interpolating adverbials and other parenthetical material between a verb and a following sister NP. Hence, we have, for example,

(15) a. *I like very much Bob.

　　 b. *I understand very well you.

　　 c. *He believes very strongly that (to be true).

However, as pointed out to me by Kuno, such interpolation is entirely possible with reduced answers like (9)c, (10)c, and the following:

(16) a. Q: Who should we hire?

　　 b. A: I think very definitely (that) we should hire Bob.

　　 c. A: I think very definitely Bob.

(17) a. Q: Who do you think won?

　　 b. A: I would guess first that Harry won.

　　 c. A: I would guess first Harry.

This shows minimally that the interpolation ban, formulated earlier as principle (109) of Section 4.11, cannot be defined exclusively as a condition on surface structures. That is, facts like those noted by Kuno show that the restriction in question is not a simple output condition in the sense of Ross (1967) or Perlmutter (1971). This might suggest an account in which the ban is defined on cycle-final structures.

That this is insufficient, however, is shown by the fact that movement

of the offending NPs by presumably postcyclical rules like Topicalization, Complex NP Shift, and *Wh* Rel Movement yields acceptable sentences:

(18) a. *I believe very strongly Bob to be a Turkish spy.

    b. Bob, I believe very strongly to be a Turkish spy.

    c. I believe very strongly to be a Turkish spy—the doctor who
       you met yesterday in Ankara.

    d. *I hate very much my job.

    e. What I hate very much is my job.

We are left then with a constraint that has not been properly localized
at any level of structure.

    What is going on here, I believe, involves both the view, mentioned
in footnote 49 of Chapter 4, that the restriction under discussion inherently involves grammatical relations, and *global* notions. I shall develop this idea at length in Postal (to appear e). Here I shall say only
the following. The interpolation ban is defined on surface structures
to the extent that it blocks a sequence of the form, shown in (19), existing in surface structures. The surface structure reference, then, ac-

(19)

counts for the well-formedness of examples like (18)b, c, and e. However, the constraint is, in effect, global in that it must be the case that
the NP in question bears a grammatical relation to the verb. That is,
in most of the cases considered, the NP must be the direct object of the
verb. The globality arises from the fact that such relations are defined,
I claim, in the cycle, and postcyclical structures are generally not relevant. Hence the examples discovered by Kuno, (16)c, (17)c, etc., are
well-formed, in spite of the fact that they manifest structures isomorphic to (19), because the relevant configurations are generated postcyclically (by the answer-reduction process). Thus, in (16)c, despite the
fact that *Bob* is in roughly an object position, it is in no sense the direct
object of *think*. Hence interpolation is allowed.

    This global-relational account of principle (109) requires, of course, the assumption that the answer-reduction process is postcyclical, according to the view that grammatical relations are, in effect, fully defined by the end of the cycle. Moreover, the assumptions just made involving a limitation of grammatical relation assignment to the cycle, based on the answer-reduction process, are nicely supported by parallel facts brought to my attention by George Lakoff. He observes a quite analogous interaction between interpolation and the Sluicing rule, discovered by Ross (1969c). Thus, although one cannot interpolate adverbs in contexts like (20), such interpolation is all right if Sluicing applies, as in (21).

(20) *I remember pretty well $\left\{ \begin{array}{l} \text{John} \\ \text{that girl} \\ \text{your wife} \end{array} \right\}$.

(21) a. Someone hit me, and I remember pretty well who hit me.
$\underset{\Rightarrow}{\text{Sluicing}}$
   b. Someone hit me, and I remember pretty well who.

Here it is the contrast between (20) and (21)b that is crucial. These facts would be consistent with the account of the interpolation ban just given if one assumes, as seems quite natural, that Sluicing, like the question answer-reduction process, is postcyclical. For under this assumption, given our view about where grammatical relations are assigned, *who* in (21)b is not the direct object of *remember*. Thus, although (21)b violates the superficial part of the interpolation ban represented in (19), it does not fulfill the relational condition, and is hence well-formed.

Lakoff provides some evidence for the view that Sluicing is postcyclical. He observes that sluiced NPs like the *who* in (21)b can occur in raised positions:

(22) Someone stole Mary's jewels, but who is not likely to be discovered.

More important, such NPs do not determine the agreement in such positions:

(23) Harry killed some villagers, but which ones $\left\{ \begin{array}{l} \text{isn't} \\ \text{*aren't} \end{array} \right\}$ known by the police.

As Lakoff notes, this would follow from having Sluicing postcyclical, since then the agreement in (23) follows from that in (24):

(24) Harry killed some villagers, but which ones he killed $\begin{cases} \text{isn't} \\ \text{*aren't} \end{cases}$ known by the police.

All of this argument is based on the independently necessary assumption that subject-verb agreement is defined in terms of cyclic structures, either as a cyclical rule or as a global rule with a cyclic environment.

Although none of this account is conclusive by any means, it gives us some reason, I think, to suspect that ultimately the possibility raised by Wasow can be eliminated; that is, it will be possible to show that even global reference will not permit the interaction of Raising and phenomena like Ordinary Reflexivization to be stated properly without having these grammatical elements make reference to conditions definable only in terms of the assumption that a subset of rules, including Raising and Ordinary Reflexivization, apply cyclically.

8.3 A Note on Extrinsic Ordering

I now strongly suspect[6] that what Chomsky (1965: 223) called "extrinsic ordering" does not exist for syntactic rules. Hence, I believe that all putative cases of extrinsic ordering proposed for syntactic rules so

[6] I have had this view since early 1969. See Binnick et al. (1969: 138), Postal (1972d), the latter a paper written in September 1969. The incorrectness of extrinsic rule ordering is also foreshadowed by the discussion of "The Ordering Strain Condition" in Perlmutter (1971), a principle stating that the less ordering the better. Koutsoudas (1972) argues that there is no evidence for extrinsic syntactic rule ordering and quite rightly observes that many past arguments for such, including several of mine, involve the fallacy of arguing, from the fact that *if* two rules A, B are ordered, then A must precede B, to the conclusion that A precedes B, where all that is justified is a disjunction of this conclusion with the proposition that the rules are unordered. I am sure, however, that ultimately the appeal to extrinsic rule ordering can be eliminated totally only if *global* and possibly *transderivational* rules are available, a point not mentioned by Koutsoudas. Note finally that the cyclic-postcyclic distinction imposes a set of ordering constraints formally similar to those achieved by particular ordering statements. The greater generality involved in having a principled distinction will emerge further when and if it becomes possible to state principles that predict from the nature of individual rules whether they are cyclic or not. For an approach in this direction, see Perlmutter and Postal (to appear b). For further antiordering arguments in roughly the framework of Koutsoudas (1972), see Lehmann (1972), Ringen (1972).

far are artifacts of at least partially incorrect analyses or else unnecessary in that the needed ordering follows from independent principles
such as cyclic application, or the difference between cyclic and postcyclic rules. (For the latter, see the cases in the previous section involving answer reduction, Sluicing, etc.) It might seem that such a view
is incompatible with the analysis just given of the interaction of Raising and Ordinary Reflexivization. It may seem necessary to say, for
instance, that Ordinary Reflexivization must follow Raising.

This conclusion might be drawn since, without it, it is not obvious,
in cases like (25), what would prevent Ordinary Reflexivization from
applying first on the last cycle, before the subject of *to be faithful* had
undergone Raising on that cycle.

(25) Jim believes himself to be faithful to his principles.

This would yield the impossible case of (26), which could be prevented in traditional terms by specifying an extrinsic ordering between
the two rules such that on any cycle Raising had to apply first.

(26) *Jim_i believes him_i to be faithful to his principles.,

In fact, however, it is apparently possible to say something much
stronger and more interesting than this, to give a principle from which
the apparently ad hoc ordering of two rules of English follows as a
theorem. Namely, it can apparently be claimed that Ordinary Reflexivization, as a feature of universal grammar, is defined on the structures existing at the ends of a specified class of cycles, as already touched
on in footnote 2. In other words, given some clause in a derivation
that is the result of applying all relevant cyclical rules on some cycle,
the Ordinary Reflexivization condition will define a pronoun P in that
clause as a Reflexive if there is an antecedent A in that clause, and if
the Clause Mate condition (among others, of course) is met at that
stage, where the cycle in question is the lowest one covering both A
and P. Such a universal characterization eliminates the necessity for saying as an ad hoc fact that in English one of two rules must precede the
other, that is, the necessity for giving a special extrinsic ordering statement for this pair of rules.

Obviously, a theory that allows extrinsic rule-ordering statements, as
in traditional transformational grammar, permits in principle a vast

array of potential orderings, differing in unprincipled ways from idiolect to idiolect and from language to language. Thus, in such a theory, it would be only an accident that, for example, Ordinary Reflexivization did not *precede* Raising in English, so that the grammar would predict the well-formedness of (26) and the ill-formedness of (25); that is, Raising would never induce reflexive marking. I think this is a clearly impossible situation, yet one perfectly consistent with a theory claiming that, in general, rules are extrinsically ordered. For the explicit claim that a pair of rules, $R_1 R_2$, have to be extrinsically ordered in a particular way involves the implicit claim that they could be ordered in the opposite way.

It should be apparent now that other obvious interactions between Raising and well-known rules do not require ordering. For instance, the facts that subjects created by Passive are raised and that raised NPs are passivized, and so on, without limit, provide no argument for an extrinsic ordering of these rules. Thus, given an underlying structure like that shown in (27) and unordered Passive and Raising, one will

(27)

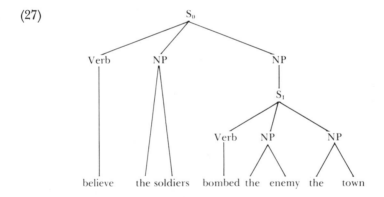

get (28)a if neither rule applies on either cycle; (28)b if Passive applies only on the first and Raising not at all; (28)c if Passive applies only on the second cycle and Raising not at all; (28)d if Passive applies on both cycles but Raising not at all; (28)e if Raising applies but not Passive on either cycle; (28)f if Passive applies on the lower cycle but only Raising on the higher cycle; (28)g if Passive applies on the lower cycle and both Passive and Raising on the higher; and (28)h if Passive does not apply on the lower but Raising and Passive apply on the higher cycle:

(28) a. The soldiers believe (that) the enemy bombed the town.

    b. The soldiers believe (that) the town was bombed by the enemy.

    c. (i) That the enemy bombed the town was believed by the soldiers.

       (ii) (via Extraposition) It was believed by the soldiers that the enemy bombed the town.

    d. (i) That the town was bombed by the enemy was believed by the soldiers.

       (ii) (via Extraposition) It was believed by the soldiers that the town was bombed by the enemy.

    e. The soldiers believe the enemy to have bombed the town.

    f. The soldiers believe the town to have been bombed by the enemy.

    g. The town was believed by the soldiers to have been bombed by the enemy.

    h. The enemy was believed by the soldiers to have bombed the town.

In no case can an erroneous sentence be derived by applying Raising after Passive, or by applying Raising before Passive, provided the principle of the cycle is observed and provided the grammar specifies, as noted in Section 1.3, that application of Raising triggers de-finitized (in these cases, infinitival) form for the remnant of the complement.

There is only one apparent exception to the claim that no erroneous sentence can be derived. Notice that, when a Raising-derived B-verb clause is passivized, there are, in general, at least two possible positions for the generated *by* phrase, before the infinitive or after the infinitival phrase, though various factors (like length and complexity) make one or the other preferable in particular cases, as in (29):

(29) a. The enemy was believed by the soldiers to have bombed the town.

    b. ?The enemy was believed to have bombed the town by the soldiers.

However, as pointed out by Warren Plath, if the subordinate clause has itself been passivized, the postinfinitival position of the main clause *by* phrase is impossible, not just less desirable.

(30) a. The town was believed by the soldiers to have been bombed
         by the enemy.

   b. *The town was believed to have been bombed by the enemy by
      the soldiers.

But there is no reason to think that the unacceptability of cases like
(30)b is related to rule ordering. What clearly seems crucial is the succession of *by* phrases. Note that an intervening adverb improves such
examples:

(31) ?*The town was believed to have been bombed by the enemy yes-
     terday by the soldiers.

I conclude that the deviance of (30)b is due to some sort of constraint
designed to prevent the confusion of the two *by* phrases. This can be
done without ruling out any useful derivations because of the possible
preinfinitival position of the main clause *by* phrase.

   Incidentally, the rough freedom of positioning relative to each other
of *by* phrases and infinitives in such sentences as these has never been
investigated, as far as I know. I believe that this freedom can be shown
to follow from a theory in which grammatical relations are destroyed
in part by the application of rules like Passive and Raising, that is, a
theory stating that the former subject of a clause ceases to bear any
relation when that clause is passivized (hence *by* phrases bear no relation to the main verb), and a theory also saying that, when an NP is
raised out of a subject or object NP clause C, this C ceases to bear any
relation. With this specified, then, neither *by* phrase nor infinitival
phrase in sentences like (29) and (30) bears any relation, and their relative freedom is a function of the fact that such phrases are generally
quite free within the clause in English. Consider the general permut-
ability of prepositional phrases, for example. See Perlmutter and
Postal (to appear a, to appear b) for further discussion of these relational ideas.

8.4 Toward a General Theory of Rules like Raising
It has been argued in this work that there is a grammatical rule of
English which, with a definite set of main clause verbal elements
(called "R-triggers" later in Chapter 9), operates to map complement
subject NPs into main clause subject NPs under certain conditions,

into main clause object NPs in others. Limiting ourselves to English and making use of the metatheoretical devices that are customary in transformational grammar, we can formulate this rule as (49) of Section 1.5, assuming underlying verb-initial structures or, equivalently, assuming verb-final structures (see Section 12.2). There are, however, good grounds for considering any such formulation extremely doubtful. Such statements assume implicitly that many of the various properties of Raising cluster together only accidently. Every feature of the rule which is explicitly specified in a grammar of English involves the implicit claim that that feature is accidental, that it could have turned out not to be present. It is natural to inquire, however, whether there are not, in fact, significant features of Raising (more generally, of every rule) which are not at all accidental but which rather follow from principles of universal grammar.

The following properties of Raising are notable:

(32) a. It is cyclical.

  b. It is bounded: the transported NPs are raised into the immediately higher clause.

  c. The raised NPs are complement subjects.

  d. In derived structure, the moved NPs are sisters of the main verb (the R-trigger) of the main clause that they enter.

  e. Under certain conditions C_1, the raised NPs become main clause subjects.

  f. Under other conditions C_2 (where $C_1 + C_2$ jointly exhaust the set of all conditions under which Raising operates), the raised NPs become main clause objects.

It is easy enough to imagine a rule possessing arbitrary proper subsets of the different properties in (32). For instance, one can conceive of a language otherwise like English except that its rule of Raising manifests only properties (32)b–e, that is, in which Raising is post-cyclical. In such a case, Raising would not feed such cyclic rules as Passive and Tough Movement; it would not be iterative, that is, each NP would be raised at most once, even when there are successively stacked R-trigger structures, etc. If such a situation is possible for a human language, then the fact that English Raising is actually cyclical is accidental in an obvious sense—that is, a contingent fact about this rule which must be stated in the grammar of English. And the case is similar with the other properties.

I see no reason to believe that the clustering of features in (32) is accidental, however. That is, I see no reason to believe that there are possible human languages having rules containing some but not all of the properties in (32). In Perlmutter and Postal (to appear a, to appear b) steps are taken toward constructing a general theory of rules and their organization into cyclical and postcyclical components according to which the clustering in (32) is seen as largely lawful. For instance, the cyclicity of Raising as well as its bounded character are considered principled functions of the property in (32)d. It is also argued that the fact that Raising operates on (complement) subject NPs is largely a predictable function of the fact that cyclic rules are inherently defined in terms of grammatical relations (of a specifiable, if not entirely customary, sort). From this point of view, it is claimed to be no accident that the NPs that undergo Raising are selected by a principle like (32)c rather than by some statement like (33):

(33) a. the first NP in a complement

    b. the second NP in a complement

    c. the first NP in a complement that contains a relative clause

    d. the first NP after the complementizer *that* (*for*, etc.)

Perhaps most surprisingly, it can be argued that the terminal status of the raised NPs, as either subjects or objects, is also governed by regularities statable in universal grammar. In particular, there is a correlation between the condition C_1 and the terminal status of subject and between condition C_2 and the terminal status of object. In Perlmutter and Postal (to appear a) it is argued that the regularity here is rather simple. Those NPs which are raised out of sentential subjects become subjects, and those raised out of sentential objects become objects. This is, at the lowest level, a true observation about English Raising. This state of affairs is not, however, a consequence of logic or of any hitherto accepted general principles of grammar. For instance, nothing proposed previously is known to block derivations yielding the *c* sentences in (34) and (35), in contrast to the actual Raising-derived *b* sentences:

(34) a. [$_S$ happen [$_{NP}$ [$_S$ know Blake Turkish $_S$] $_{NP}$]

   b. Blake happens to know Turkish.

   c. *To know Turkish happens Blake.

(35) a. [$_S$ believe I [$_{NP}$ [$_S$ understand Sally herself $_S$] $_{NP}$]

   b. I believe Sally to understand herself.

   c. *Sally believes me to understand herself.

Thus, in (34), where Raising actually turns the raised NP into a derived subject, there could logically be an otherwise identical rule that made it the derived object, leaving the complement (remnant) as subject, yielding (34)c. Similarly, in (35), where Raising, in fact, makes the raised NP a derived object, there could be a rule otherwise like Raising which made the raised NP a derived subject, yielding something like (35)c.

If the properties illustrated in (34) and (35) are accidental, one expects to find languages with derivations pairing structures like (34)a, c, (35)a, c. In Perlmutter and Postal (to appear a) it is argued that this is impossible and that the factual state of affairs in English is not contingent but rather a function of a principle. Moreover, it is claimed that the principle in question holds not just for Raising but for a whole class of partly similar cyclical rules, called "Promotion Rules," which have the effect of extracting one NP from a larger containing NP. The principle in question, called there the "Functional Succession Principle," says in effect that when a promotional rule extracts one NP, NP_a, from a containing NP, NP_c, in the output, NP_a takes on the grammatical function manifested by NP_c in the input. Such a principle makes it automatic that when Raising extracts an NP from a sentential subject, as in (34), it becomes a subject, and that when Raising extracts an NP from a sentential object, as in (35), it becomes an object. The principle in question claims that no promotion rule can extract an NP from a subject and make it an object, or conversely.

Naturally, in the present context, these remarks are little more than suggestive. Nonetheless, if something like the principles just suggested can be precisely formulated and justified, it becomes clear that any formation of a rule like Raising which specifies properties like those in (32) as contingent features of individual grammars is simply mistaken.

It seems rather that Raising is, in effect, essentially a feature of universal grammar, a rule that says something like (36), other features of the final rule being largely predictable.

(36) Promote the subject of a complement.

Language-particular features of derivations involving (36) then involve chiefly (i) the class of elements in a language which can function as R-triggers, whose complements are subject to (36); and (ii) the conditions on complements determining which can undergo (36), both in general and with particular R-triggers. One other matter of relevance here is the question of whether (36) has the function of de-finitizing clauses. On the basis of the facts in English and other European languages, one would like to claim that de-finitization is a lawful consequence of Raising application, as suggested earlier. However, this idea runs into difficulties in the case of Japanese, as discussed in Section 12.2. It is thus quite possible that in part at least de-finitization must also be a language-particular concomitant of the utilization of (36).

If anything along the lines of the account in this section is correct, it follows that in studying English Raising we have actually been studying Raising in every other language that contains it as well. In a framework like that suggested here, the properties in (32) not only are regarded as noncontingent for English but are necessarily claimed to characterize the analogous rule in any other language. For some discussion of Japanese relevant to such claims, see Section 12.2.

9
The Scope of Raising in Clause Domains

9.1 Comments

It seems necessary to conclude that the operation of Raising is controlled in some (to be sure, not well understood) way by the main verbal of the superordinate clause into which a complement subject NP may potentially be raised. Hence, from this point of view, the scope of the rule is largely, though not entirely (see footnotes 9 and 25 of Chapter 1),[1] a matter of the class of superordinate verbal elements which permit the operation of Raising. Let us refer to any such element as an "R-trigger."

So far, I have divided the set of R-triggers into four rough classes: A-verbs, B-verbs, N-verbs, and W-verbs. These fall naturally into two subtypes, A-verbs and all the others, with the difference lying in whether the raised NP becomes a superordinate derived subject (A-verbs) or a superordinate derived object (the others, unless Passive applies in the main clause). However, this is not entirely suitable terminology, since there are, among the class of R-triggers, unquestionably a subset that are surface adjectives. Therefore, let us replace the earlier terminology by one that is more neutral with respect to surface categories, and let us make the grouping explicit. I shall therefore speak of *type I* R-triggers, and *type II* R-triggers, the former containing the set of A-elements, the latter the sets of B-elements, N-elements, and W-elements. It will turn out, however, that all type II R-triggers are, in fact, surface verbs (ignoring nominalizations; see Chapter 10), with all of the adjectives lying in the type I category.

I have said that the basic difference between type I and type II R-triggers is that, in the case of Raising with the former, the raised NP becomes a superordinate subject without any application of Passive in the main clause, while in the latter the raised NP becomes a superordinate derived object. There are, however, two different sorts of A-elements in type I. With one sort, which are underlying pure *intransitives,* including *happen, turn out, likely,* etc., a raised NP clearly becomes a derived

---

1 I ignore here possible cases where the main verbal that triggers Raising ends up, through the operation of nominalization rules, as (part of) a noun. This matter is discussed in Chapter 10.

superordinate subject purely through the operation of Raising (sub-sequently determining preposing of the raised NP in most cases under Subject Formation). The other sort of A-element R-triggers are underlying *transitives,* including *seem, appear, strike,* etc. And here the situation is more obscure. If these are treated (as in footnote 34 of Chapter 6) in such a way that the underlying sentential complement is an underlying subject, then they are perfectly parallel to the intransitive A-verbs except for the presence of an underlying "experiencer" NP. But if these are treated in such a way that the sentential complement is an underlying object, with the surface word order being derived by a main clause application of the Psych Movement rule as well as Raising, then their presence in the A-element class is anomalous.[2] In fact, while I have maintained the Psych Movement analysis in the past (see Postal, 1970a, 1971) and still consider it correct, I have nonetheless persisted in grouping verbs like *seem* with those like *happen* for discursive purposes since

---

2 That is, if the underlying structure of a sentence like (i) is (ii), then the derivation of (i) proceeds by the application of Raising to (ii), yielding (iii):

(i) Melvin seems to me to love Lucy.

(ii) SEEM me $[_S$ LOVE Melvin Lucy$_S]$

(iii) SEEM me Melvin $[_S$ LOVE Lucy$_S]$

Here *Melvin* has become a derived superordinate clause *object,* in conflict with the supposed chief characteristic of A-verb Raising. Example (i) is then derived by the application of the rule Psych Movement to (iii), with subsequent application of Subject Formation. In these terms, which are, I believe, ultimately correct, *seem* is really more like a B-verb such as *believe* than an intransitive A-verb. Thus the underlying structure of a sentence like (iv) is (v), which is essentially like (ii).

(iv) I believe Melvin to love Lucy.

(v) BELIEVE I $[_S$ LOVE Melvin Lucy$_S]$

The difference between *believe* and *seem* is then chiefly that the latter obligatorily triggers application of Psych Movement. This rule is formally parallel to Passive in its effects on NPs. When optional Passive applies to the Raising output from (v), the result is (vi), which is unacceptable for reasons given in footnote 1 of Chapter 1.

(vi) ?Melvin is believed by me to love Lucy.

But the formal parallelism between (vi) and (i) should be apparent.

   Ultimately, then, verbs like *seem, appear, strike,* and *impress* belong in the class of type II R-triggers, not type I. There they form a special class obligatorily triggering Psych Movement, and not subject to Passive, in contrast to previously discussed type II R-triggers of the B-verb, N-verb, and W-verb varieties, which have the opposite properties.

(i) this is the grouping that has been traditionally made, (ii) it has one reasonable basis in that for both types of verb the raised NP becomes superordinate clause subject without any application of Passive in the main clause, and (iii) the operation or not of Psych Movement is irrelevant to almost all of the issues dealt with crucially in this study.

9.2 A-Element R-Triggers

Let us consider first the class of A-element R-triggers. Previously this class has generally been illustrated by a relatively small group of less than a dozen predicates. But it appears to me that something on the order of sixty or more elements serve as A-element R-triggers. I shall give what appear to me currently to be the likely members of this set in four alphabetical lists, divided according to a largely traditional surface category terminology.[3]

Given (1), two questions immediately arise. First, the logically prior one, what evidence is there that the elements in (1) are all in fact (A-element) R-triggers? Second, what principle or principles, if any, determine that these elements serve as A-element R-triggers and that others (*probable, obvious, true*) do not? Take the second question first, since it will require the least space. The answer is that I do not know. One near generalization, which holds not only for type I but also for type II R-triggers, is that the predicates in question are nonfactive (see Kiparsky and Kiparsky, 1970). But even this is not quite true, since elements like *stop* and *continue* appear to be factive. Consequently, I am not at all in a position to be able to specify necessary and sufficient conditions for membership in list (1) or even in its correct expansion. If such conditions exist, as in part they most likely do, their specification is a matter for future analysis, particularly of the semantics of the relevant predicates.

The answer to the logically prior question is that the elements in list (1) manifest subsets of the properties which can be shown (see Section 12.1) to support the claim of Raising operation in the A-element type of configurations. For example, more than half of the elements listed in (1) take existential *there* as derived subject.

[3] The status of *begin, start, continue, keep, stop,* and *threaten* as A-element R-triggers is briefly discussed by Perlmutter (1970). Jesperson (1969: 47) grouped *happen, fail, sure,* and *seem* together under his "split-subject" analysis, which amounted essentially to an informal treatment of these forms as A-element R-triggers.

(1) a. *Adjectives*
about
apt
bound
certain
going
liable
likely
set
supposed
sure
unlikely

b. *Verbs*
appear
become
begin
cease
chance
come
commence
continue
end up
fail
get
grow
happen
impress
keep (on)
need
persist
proceed
promise
prove
quit
remain

resume
seem
stand
start
start out
stay
stop
strike
tend
threaten[4]
turn
turn out
were[5]
wind up

c. *Mysteries*
had best
had better

d. *Auxiliaries*

(Modals)
can
could
ought
may
might
must
shall
should
will
would

(Nonmodals)
be
have
used[6]

[4] The use of both *threaten* and *promise* as A-element R-triggers, as in (i), in contrast to their more central uses, is the more remarkable because it is paralleled by the analogous extension of the French forms *menacer* and *promettre*.

Thus, concentrating on forms that have *not* been frequently used to illustrate A-element R-triggers, we can enumerate the following:

(2) a. There is about to be a fight in the kitchen.

    b. There is apt to be cholera in Turkey.

    c. There is bound to be a riot in Dacca.

    d. There is going to be trouble in Indiana.

    e. There is liable to be some trouble.

    f. There is (all) set to be a meeting at Bob's house.

    g. There is supposed to be a second chance for criminals.

    h. There chanced to be a deathray in his pocket.

    i. There came to be twenty-five families in the valley.

    j. There ended up being an orgy.

    k. There failed to be any evidence of his guilt.

    l. There grew to be opposition to the foam program.

    m. If there keep on being disturbances, we will have to use poison gas.

    n. There need be no further discussions.

    o. ?If there persists in being no evidence, we will have to hang the suspect.

    p. There proved to be toxins in the soap.

    q. There tends to be corrupion in government.

    r. There threatens to be famine in Bulgaria.

(i) a. It threatens to rain today.
    b. It promises to be sunny today.

See Ruwet (1972: Chapter 2).

5 The *were* here is that of conditional clauses:

(i) a. If there were ten honest men in the legislature, things would be different.
    b. Were it to rain tomorrow, our party would be a failure.
    c. If you were to learn Swahili, your mother would be surprised.

Despite the shape, I see no obvious relation between this element and the verb *be*.

6 The *used* in question is that of sentences like the following:

(i) a. There used to be a serious field of linguistics.
    b. It used to snow here every week.
    c. Tabs used to be kept on all of my movements.

    s.   There wound up being a riot.

    t.   There had better not be any flaws in your argument.

    u.   There cannot be a better peanut butter than that.

Similarly, many of these elements occur with derived subjects that are chunks of idioms; these chunks can become complement subjects only as a result of movement (passivization, etc.) and thus do not in general occur freely as subjects:

(3) a.   Tempers are about to flare.

    b.   Little headway is apt to be made on that problem.

    c.   Tabs are bound to be kept on leftists.

    d.   Tabs are going to be kept on leftists.

    e.   ?Tabs are liable to be kept on us.

    f.   —

    g.   Tabs were supposed to be kept on leftists.

    h.   If tempers chance to flare, . . .

    i.   —

    j.   Tabs ended up being kept on all the foreigners.

    k.   —

    l.   —

    m.   If tempers keep on flaring, . . .

    n.   Tabs need not be kept on him any longer.

    o.   —

    p.   —

    q.   Tabs tend to be kept on leftists.

    r.   Tempers are threatening to flare.

    s.   —

    t.   Tabs had better not be kept on him.

    u.   Tabs cannot be kept on him.

Furthermore, in many cases, the elements in (1) can occur with impersonal *it* as subjects with complements of the weather expression and other types that take only impersonal *it* as subject (such as *be a long way from a to b*). Thus we find patterns like the following which support the claim of R-trigger status:

(4) a. It is snowing.

   b. *X ($\neq it$) is snowing.

(5) a. It proved to be snowing in Manchuria.

   b. *X ($\neq it$) proved to be snowing in Manchuria.

We also find, as is typical of Raising cases (see the discussion in Chapter 10), that floating quantifiers in the complements of elements in (1) are understood to bind the subject NP. Thus in (6) *each* actually binds the occurring NP *they,* in contrast to Equi-derived cases like (7), where *each* does not bind *they,* but rather a deleted NP.

(6) They proved to each have left separately.

(7) They wish to each leave separately.

Finally, the truth-value equivalence argument under passivization proposed by Rosenbaum (discussed briefly in Chapters 3, 10, and 11) shows the A-element status of many of the forms in (1). Thus such pairs as (8) are truth-functionally equivalent, in contrast to Equi-derived pairs like (9), which are not.

(8) a. The king proved to have slapped the queen.

   b. The queen proved to have been slapped by the king.

(9) a. The king wished to slap the queen.

   b. The queen wished to be slapped by the king.

These facts, plus others, serve as the basis for arguments that all of the elements in (1) are indeed A-element R-triggers. The arguments are, however, not without problems. In particular, some of the distinctive properties of Raising elements do not show up with some of the elements, as the gaps in (3) already partially indicate. For one example, consider the element *strike,* as in (10):

(10) Melvin strikes me as (being) overworked.

I should like to claim that this element is an R-trigger. Nonetheless, it does not occur with existential *there,* with idiom chunk subjects, or with impersonal *it.*[7]

(11) a. *There strikes me as being a hole in that argument.

    b. *Tabs struck me as having been kept on Melvin.

    c. *It struck me as having $\begin{Bmatrix} \text{snowed} \\ \text{been foggy} \end{Bmatrix}$ in Vermont.

This is true, even though the corresponding extraposed *that*-clause complement sentences are well-formed:

(12) a. It strikes me that there is a hole in that argument.

    b. It struck me that tabs were kept on Melvin.

    c. It struck me that it $\begin{Bmatrix} \text{snowed} \\ \text{was foggy} \end{Bmatrix}$ in Vermont.

Nonetheless, there are arguments for claiming that *strike* does undergo Raising. These arguments go beyond the desire to use Raising to account for the obvious relations between sentences like (10) and those like (13):

(13) It strikes me that Melvin is overworked.

In particular, since the only alternative to a Raising analysis of sentences like (10) would be an Equi analysis, the fact that quantifiers in cases like (14) are understood to bind the occurring main clause subject NP, and not some deleted NP, argues for a Raising analysis.

(14) a. They strike me as having both violated the agreement.

    b. John and Bill strike me as each being unable to work alone.

My approach to cases like *strike,* which are not rare, is to claim that *strike* undergoes Raising and to assume that some special constraints exist to account for facts like (11). A similar approach is useful in other cases, like the gaps in (3) and in many other paradigms constructible out of the elements in (1). A full grammar of English will have to specify that many of the properties typical of Raising elements are not found in association with all of the A-element R-triggers, and in some

---

[7] The impossibility of *there* with *strike* was first noted, to my knowledge, by Cantrall (1970), who concluded—wrongly, I think—that *strike* was consequently not an R-trigger. See Chapter 11 for further discussion.

cases, at least, we can hope that an explanation as well as a description for these gaps can be found.

In Section 12.1, I present a sketch of some seventeen-odd arguments capable of showing that a putative A-element is a real A-element. They are presented by using the element *seem*, which is extremely free in manifesting all of the desired properties. The reader can then apply these arguments to the full list in (1), discovering that many of the properties hold for many of the elements but also that there is a large set of gaps. This fact can then provide considerable data for studying the nature of these restrictions. But, overall, the clustering of a significant number of properties with most of the elements in question leaves little doubt, I think, that Raising is operative for all of them. It is quite likely that many, and probably most, of the restrictions or gaps can be shown to follow either from the logical form of the A-element predicates involved or else from semantic assumptions associated with these elements, and that these assumptions, in effect, define the appropriate contexts for their use. This approach is described further in Chapter 11.

One final point is that A-element R-triggers differ along the parameter of whether or not they occur in sentences derived without Raising, that is, whether Raising is, in effect, obligatory for them or not. Thus for *happen, seem, likely,* etc., one can find extraposed sentences with no Raising. But for *apt, bound, threaten,* etc., this is impossible, a fact that a full grammar must also in some way specify.

9.3 B-Element R-Triggers

For the type II R-triggers, I have given as exhaustive lists as I can of N-elements and W-elements in earlier sections. It remains, therefore, to consider the class of B-elements. In general, I have designated by the quite imprecise term B-element (verb)[8] those transitive verbs like *believe* which occur in contexts of the form given in (15):

(15) a. NP _____ (that) + S

b. NP _____ NP infinitive

---

[8] In fact, obviously all of the terms B-element, N-element, etc., are imprecise and function more as discursive aids than as a serious categorization of grammatical elements. In particular, the terminology ignores many sharp differences among the members of these classes, although some have been noted here or there.

Following an implicit tradition in studies of these matters, I have utilized chiefly the verb *believe* as an illustration of this class, occasionally offering also *prove, find,* or *show.* Further characteristics of this class are that the NP before the infinitive is passivizable on the cycle of the main clause, is subject to reflexive marking, and in general behaves like a nonsubject or derived main clause object constituent in derived structures.

In spite of the fact that previous work suggests that the class of B-elements is miniscule, I shall suggest that there is reason to believe that in reality this class also contains on the order of fifty or more members. Nonetheless, it is not gratuitous that the class is generally illustrated by a tiny minority, for it turns out that most members of the super-class involve one or more mysterious, so far largely unstudied, restrictions that prevent them from manifesting the full distribution typical of *believe, find, prove,* and *show.*

For an initial example, consider the verb *estimate.* This occurs harmoniously with *that*-clause complements:

(16) I estimate that Tunisia has over 20,000 mosques.

Thus the question is whether it occurs in the proper infinitival cases. And, in fact, one finds both:

(17) a. I estimate that it is ten miles from here to there.

b. I estimate it to be ten miles from here to there.

Therefore, *estimate* seems to be behaving like a proper B-verb. Moreover, as expected, the putatively raised *it* in (17)b passivizes:

(18) It is estimated to be ten miles from here to there.

So far, then, *estimate* does not seem different in its relevant behavior from *believe.*

Contrasts arise, however, when one looks a little further:

(19) a.   I estimate that your sister weighs 250 pounds.

b. *I estimate your sister to weigh 250 pounds.

(20) a.   They estimated that Bill's dinosaur was 175 feet long.

b. *They estimated Bill's dinosaur to be 175 feet long.

Note that (19)b and (20)b involve putatively raised **nonpronouns**, while

(17)b involves a raised pronoun, and observe the well-formedness of examples like (21):

(21) a. I estimate there to be two million people in that valley.

    b. I estimate it to be raining about two inches per hour.

On this basis one might conclude that the constraint on *estimate* is that a raised NP with this trigger must be a pronoun, in some unclear sense of this term. However, the relevant constraint is much more complicated.

First, there are the following contrasts:

(22) a. *I estimate Bill's boat to be 36 feet long.

    b. I estimate the length of Bill's boat to be 36 feet.

(23) a. *I estimate that beam to weigh 47 tons.

    b. I estimate the weight of that beam to be 47 tons.

It seems, then, that the complement of *estimate* must contain a measuring phrase specifying a value along some parameter. Hence, contrast the following:

(24) a. *I estimate that Harry is tall.

    b. I estimate that Harry is six feet two inches tall.

Moreover, when *estimate* triggers Raising, the raised NP must apparently be either a pronoun *or* an NP whose head noun designates the dimension along which the required measuring is specified.

However, even this formulation is insufficient, as shown by (25):

(25) a. *I estimate it to be six inches long.

    b. *Joan estimated them to own 1000 cows each.

Evidently, there is some contrast between the pronouns in well-formed structures like (17)b, (21)a, b, on the one hand, and those in the ill-formed (25), on the other. Intuitively, this contrast is not so hard to grasp. The pronouns in (25) are ordinary coreferential anaphoric elements. The pronouns in (17)b and (21) are, however, not anaphoric at all. The *it* in (17)b seems to be generated from an underlying structure of the form, shown in (26), by extraposition of the locative sequences.

(26) [the one from here to there]

It is a regular fact that unmodified [the one] shows up as *it* (see Postal, 1966). The pronoun *there* in (21)a presumably arises simply from a rule that inserts it during the derivation of existential sentences. The pronoun *it* in (21)b is more obscure but probably has a similar derivation. For a speculation on this score see Postal (1966b).[9] One property that all three of these pronouns have in common is a lack of commutability. Replacing the pronoun by anything else yields an ill-formed structure. Thus the contexts in (27) uniquely predict the elements occurring as the terminals of the NPs in subject position:

(27) a. NP is ten miles from here to there.

b. NP are two million people in that valley.

c. NP is raining two inches per hour.

In this sense, the pronominal elements that can undergo Raising with *estimate* are in some sense very grammaticized. While I do not understand this phenomenon very well, let us refer to the grammaticized pronouns as *empty pronouns*. It seems that the constraint on *estimate*

[9] The plausibility of a derivation of sentences like (i) from underlying structures like (ii) increases when one surveys the relations in paradigms like (iii):

(i) It is $\begin{Bmatrix} \text{snowing} \\ \text{raining} \end{Bmatrix}$.

(ii) $[_S \text{ V }_{\text{weather}} + \text{ing} \begin{Bmatrix} \text{snow} \\ \text{rain} \end{Bmatrix} \text{s}]$

(iii) a. Five inches of snow is falling per hour.
b. It is snowing five inches per hour.

Here it is evident that the logical relation between *five inches* and *snow* is the same in both cases. Thus I suggest structures for both (iii)a, b of the form (ignoring the *be* of the progressive) given in (iv):

(iv) $[_S \text{ V }_{\text{weather}} + \text{ing } [_{\text{NP}} \text{ five inches of snow}_{\text{NP}}] \text{ per hour }_S]$

This would be converted to (v) by a "promotion Rule" (see Perlmutter and Postal to appear a), which extracts the embedded NP of the original complex subject and makes it the new derived subject.

(v) $[_S \text{ V }_{\text{weather}} + \text{ing } [_{\text{NP}} \text{ snow}_{\text{NP}}] [_{\text{NP}} \text{ five inches}_{\text{NP}}] \text{ per hour}_S]$

Structure (v) would, in turn, be converted to the structure directly underlying (iii)b by the incorporation operation suggested in Postal (1966b).

is that a raised NP must be either an empty pronoun or an NP whose head designates the dimension of estimation.[10]

The constraint as so far specified seems odd enough. The facts are, however, considerably more complicated. First, main clause passivization "rescues" all ill-formed structures like (19)b, (20)b, (22)b, (23)a, and (25)a, b:

(28) a. Your sister is estimated to weigh 250 pounds.

    b. Bill's dinosaur was estimated to be 175 feet long.

    c. Bill's boat was estimated to be 36 feet long.

    d. That beam was estimated to weigh 47 tons.

    e. It was estimated to be six inches long.

    f. They were estimated to own 1000 cows each.

Two possibilities thus seem to present themselves. Either the constraint on *estimate* mentions passivization directly in some way, or else the crucial property is whether or not the raised NP ends up in derived object position in the main clause. Support for the latter tack comes from the fact that other rules that cause raised NPs to cease to be derived objects also serve to rescue violations of the peculiar constraints on *estimate*. In particular, this is true of the operations Topicalization, *Wh*-Q Movement, and *Wh* Rel Movement:

(29) a. Your sister, I estimate to weigh 250 pounds.

    b. Bill's dinosaur, I estimate to be 175 feet long.

    c. Bill's boat, I estimate to be 36 feet long.

    d. That beam, I estimate to weigh 47 tons.

(30) a. Whose sister did he estimate to weigh 250 pounds?

    b. Which dinosaur did they estimate to be 175 feet long?

---

[10] Although my opinion wavers, I think that sentences such as (i) are passable.

(i) I estimate tabs to have been kept on over 800 leftists.

If so, then the "empty" NPs discussed in the text must include idiom chunks. Note also that the *it* of sentences like (17)b would survive even without appeal to any notion of "empty" pronoun, since this NP designates the estimated dimension, the distance.

    c. What boat did they estimate to be 36 feet long?

    d. Which beam did they estimate to weigh 47 tons?

(31) a. the girl who he estimated to weigh 250 pounds

    b. the dinosaur that they estimated to be 175 feet long

    c. the boat that I estimated to be 36 feet long

    d. the beam which they estimated to weigh 47 tons

Since all three of these rules, however, as well as Passive, guarantee that an affected raised NP comes to *precede* the occurrence of *estimate* that originally triggered the application of Raising, one might claim that an account in terms of preceding versus following *estimate* is equally as correct as one referring to derived object position. That something like the latter is correct is indicated by the fact that application of Complex NP Shift to the raised NP, as discussed in Section 4.1, also rescues structures that would otherwise yield violations with *estimate*:

(32) a. *I estimated all of the dinosaurs which we caught yesterday in Central Park to be over 175 feet long.

    b. I estimated to be over 175 feet long—all of the dinosaurs which we caught yesterday in Central Park.

(33) a. *They estimated the wrestler who Bill hired to protect his nieces to have a right bicep with a 68-inch diameter.

    b. They estimated to have a right bicep with a 68-inch diameter— the wrestler who Bill hired to protect his nieces.

It appears, then, that any rule that gets the offending NP out of the directly post-*estimate* position, that is, out of derived object position, regardless of whether to the left or right, rescues the potentially ill-formed structure.

While these facts do not uniquely indicate by any means how the constraint on *estimate* with infinitival complements should ultimately be stated, they do indicate a broad set of empirical conditions that must be met by the proper formulation. Space does not permit further pursuit of this question here. In this context, however, I think it is easy to see that *estimate* must be regarded as a B-element, albeit one subject to peculiar restrictions of a poorly understood sort. How else could one account for sentences like (28)–(33)? Note how (32)b and (33)b in particular indicate that the NPs in question cease to be subjects, since we know that Complex NP Shift does not operate on subjects. Other tests for derived object behavior also support this view—for example, that involving *not*-initial NPs:

(34) a. I estimate that not many people's weights are over 500 pounds.

   b. *I estimate not many people's weights to be over 500 pounds.

(35) a. I estimate that not many battleships carried less than 2000 quarts of beer.

   b. *I estimate not many battleships to have carried less than 2000 quarts of beer.

The adverb argument of Section 4.11 reveals the same point:

(36) a. Harry estimated on very poor evidence that the engine's rpm was averaging about 5000.

   b. *Harry estimated on very poor evidence the engine's rpm to be averaging about 5000.

It follows that *estimate* differs from *believe* essentially only in the peculiar constraints we have been discussing.[11]

It is, however, easy to see how a superficial look at *estimate* infinitival sentences, for example, one that noted (19)b, (20)b, (22)a, (23)a, etc., but not (28)–(33), could easily conclude that *estimate* is not a B-verb and does not trigger Raising. Further apparent support for this mistaken view could come from the fact that the constraints documented for *estimate* automatically block standard position reflexivization with this verb:

(37) a. *Bob estimated himself to be worth over 300,000 escudos.

   b. *Mary estimated herself to be five feet tall.

---

11 Unlike typical B-verbs, however, *estimate* can also occur with *as*-initial gerundive complements:

(i) a. I estimated Nixon's plurality as (being) less than Woodrow Wilson's.

   b. They estimated the plane's weight as (being) 600 tons in excess of specifications.

This fact will be of some importance in the discussion of Raising in nominalizations in Chapter 10.

Observe that there is a strong parallelism between sentences like (i) and infinitival complement structures with *estimate*, in that for (i) sentences the postverbal NPs must also designate the estimated dimension.

However, given our earlier discussion, Topicalization can predictably rescue examples like (37):

(38) a. Himself, Bob estimated to be worth over 300,000 escudos.

b. Herself, Mary estimated to be five feet tall.

It follows that (37) does not really argue against a Raising analysis of *estimate* infinitival complement sentences, although out of context it might easily be thought to do so.

I have considered *estimate* in some detail because I think it is more typical than atypical. There are many B-verbs whose true nature is partly disguised in one way or another by the existence of constraints somewhat like those seen to control the occurrence of *estimate.*

A particularly interesting class of such verbs involves a constraint quite like that manifested by *estimate,* except that there is no reference to the raised NP's designating a measured dimension. For this class, the facts seem to be simply that the raised NP cannot end up as a derived object unless it is an empty pronoun. An example is *allege.* Previously, it has usually been observed that *allege* occurs in contexts like (39):

(39) a. He alleged that Melvin was a pimp.

b. Melvin was alleged to be a pimp.

And, crucially, it has been observed that sentences of the form given in (40) are ill-formed:

(40) *He alleged Melvin to be a pimp.

Hence the basic, simple Raising sentences are not possible in general. However, as with *estimate,* such examples seem passable if the raised NP is an empty pronoun:

(41) He alleged there to be gambling going on in the back room.

Thus it might seem that taking *allege* to involve Raising would mean recognizing a constraint that the raised NP must, if it is a nonempty pronoun, undergo passivization. But this is not the case. For, again, any of the rules Topicalization, *Wh*-Q Movement, *Wh* Rel Movement, or Complex NP Shift, which destroy the derived object status of the raised NP, serve to rescue potentially offending structures like (40):

(42) a. Melvin, he alleged to be a pimp.

b. Who did they allege to be a pimp?

c. the Parisian who they alleged to be a pimp

d. They alleged to be pimps—all of the Parisians who the CIA had hired in Nice.

Let us call the constraint manifested by *allege* the "Derived Object Constraint" (henceforth: DOC). Thus DOC marks a derivation as ill-formed if it contains an R-trigger *allege*, which, except for empty pronouns, ends up with a raised NP as derived object.[12] In my speech, DOC holds not only for *allege*, however, but for a large class of verbs, more than two dozen in number:[13]

(43) *B-Element R-triggers Subject to DOC*[14]

acknowledge	feel
admit	gather
affirm	grant
allege	guarantee
assume	guess
certify	intuit
concede	know
decree	note
deduce	posit
demonstrate	reveal
determine	state
discern	surmise
disclose	think
discover	understand
establish	verify

There are, no doubt, others. All of these verbs occur naturally in passives, but in general simple Raising sentences of the form [NP Verb NP infinitive] are ill-formed. I shall provide, however, a well-formed

[12] It seems to me that DOC-violating structures are greatly improved if the derived object NP has extremely strong stress. But I have not investigated this question.

[13] The verb *estimate* can be regarded as essentially subject to DOC, with the proviso that an additional class of derived objects is permitted—those designating the measured dimension.

[14] I have greatly benefited from the lists in Alexander and Kunz (1964) in compiling this list and following classifications, although my groupings do not correspond exactly to any of theirs.

sentence for each in which the raised NP has undergone Topicalization, indicating that it is a constraint like DOC rather than some obligatory passivization requirement that rules out these simple Raising-derived forms:

(44) Rogers, I acknowledge to be superior to Acheson.

That, I admit to be incorrect.

That report, he affirmed to have been classified.

The brakes, he alleged to be defective.

Mary, I still assume to be innocent.

Tom, they certified to be totally insane.

That, I concede to be unlikely.

Bodily contact between adults, I hereby decree to be illegal.

That, I deduce to be false.

Any analysis like that, I will easily demonstrate to be inconsistent.

Those accusations, he determined to be based on prejudice.

That, he discerned to be the case.

That ring, they disclosed to have been stolen.

Marilyn, the detectives discovered to be living with Sydney.

That claim, I established to be incorrect two years ago.

That, I feel to be an overly harsh punishment.

That, I gather to be the case.

Melvin, I must grant to be a superior tennis player.

That, I can guarantee to be the case.

That, I just guessed to be the case.

That, he just intuited to be wrong.

Melvin, I know to be dishonest.

That, I noted to be incorrect at the time.

That rule, he posited to be universal.

That proposal, they finally revealed to be under consideration.

Bob, I surmise to be more interested in chemistry than girls.

That, I now think to be wrong.

Those premises, I understood to have been vacated.

That, I have verified personally to be the case.

Similar well-formedness results from parallel applications of the question and relative clause movement rules, which have the same derived-object-destroying effect. Complex NP Shift has the same consequences.

The existence of sentences like (44) and parallel forms produced by the other three rules leaves little doubt therefore that the verbs in (43) serve as B-element R-triggers, despite the general ill-formedness of sentences parallel to (40). It should be clear, however, that the ill-formedness of sentences such as (40) could easily lead to the erroneous conclusion that these verbs are not (B-element) R-triggers.

Moreover, this mistake could be induced further by the fact that many of the verbs in (43) appear to be subject to other constraints besides DOC. For instance, some do not permit the raised NP to be "animate," even in constructions that fail to violate DOC:

(45) a. I deduce that Melvin is a Venusian spy.

　　 b. *I deduce Melvin to be a Venusian spy.

　　 c. *Melvin, I deduce to be a Venusian spy.

　　 d. *Who did you deduce to be a Venusian spy?

　　 e. *the general who I deduced to be a Venusian spy

　　 f. *I deduced to be Venusian spies—all of the officers who were eating pickled grapes.

　　 g. *Melvin was deduced to be a Venusian spy.

Similarly:

(46) a. I intuit that Mary is pregnant.

　　 b. *I intuit Mary to be pregnant.

　　 c. *Mary, I intuit to be pregnant.

　　 d. *Who did you intuit to be pregnant?

　　 e. *the girl who I intuit to be pregnant

　　 f. *I intuit to be pregnant—all of the girls who Tom wanted to invite.

　　 g. *Mary was intuited to be pregnant.

As a consequence of this restriction, of course, Ordinary Reflexivization, which is blocked in derived object position for all of the verbs in (43) by DOC, is also blocked for these verbs in topicalized positions:

(47) a. *I deduced myself to be the victim of a plot.

b. *Myself, I deduced to be the victim of a plot.

(48) a. *I intuited myself to have pneumonia.

b. *Myself, I intuited to have pneumonia.

Of course, the *a* forms here are worse than the *b* forms, since they violate both DOC and the animacy constraint, while the latter violate only the animacy constraint.

Furthermore, observe that some members of the list in (43) do not seem to permit empty pronouns in derived object positions, although these judgments may be variable:

(49) a. *I concede there to be gambling in the back room.

b. *I deduce there to be no evidence for that.

Overall, then, it seems clear that there is some basic constraint like DOC operating for many B-element R-triggers, supplemented by other special constraints. In some cases, an extreme form of DOC may function, blocking all sentences that contain a raised NP as derived object. In others, a weaker form is manifest in which the raised NPs can be derived objects if they are empty pronouns or meet other special conditions (as with *estimate*). No doubt, other variations exist, since it is clear that the verbs in (43) are quite diverse. I have not studied them in anything like sufficient detail to make firm statements about them beyond the conclusion that they are B-element R-triggers subject to DOC.

The list in (43) does not by any means exhaust the class of B-element R-triggers. There is a further group that is not subject to DOC but that does appear to reveal a variety of other constraints blocking many of the expected sentences:

(50) declare   recognize
     figure   remember
     hold   report
     imagine   rule
     judge   specify
     presume   stipulate
     proclaim   suppose
     reckon   take

Sentences showing these verbs with derived object raised NPs include the following:

(51) a. The official declared the fight to be over.

b. I figure that to be the best course of action.

c. He holds certain principles to be absolute.

d. I had imagined him to be somewhat older.

e. I judged him to be lying.

f. I presumed that to be the case.

g. They proclaimed him to be an outlaw.

h. I reckon the money to be all gone by now.

i. I recognize him to be an authority on whining.

j. I remember him to have said very little.

k. They reported him to be missing.

l. They ruled that evidence to be inadmissible.

m. You should specify that to be the minimum acceptable amount.

n. The contract stipulated 1974 to be the earliest year the crypt could be opened.

o. I took him to be a priest.

For some speakers, though not for the present writer, verbs like *hypothesize, presuppose, recollect, suppose,* and *wager* may also be in this class. But despite attempts, I have been unable to convince myself that these verbs occur in any infinitival sentences describable in terms of B-element Raising. The reader can determine for himself, however, that Raising must be involved in sentences like (51) by applying the various arguments of Chapters 3 and 4 which indicate that the post-main-verb NPs are derived objects.

Despite (51), most of the verbs in (50) are subject to severe limitations on the possible infinitival constructions in which they occur. I have not been able to make a thorough study of this matter. But many restrictions are evident. For example, many of the verbs are subject to a constraint that the raised NP not be animate:

(52) a. *I figured Joan to be a spy.

    b. *He holds gorillas to be telepathic.

    c. *I presumed Tom to be there.

Note that the corresponding *that*-clause sentences are perfect. However, something like DOC may also be relevant here as well since, for example, sentences like (52) at the very least greatly improve if topicalized:

(53) a. Joan, I figured to be a spy.

    b. Gorillas, he holds to be telepathic.

    c. Tom, I presumed to be there.

Evidently, then, the verbs in (50), like those in (43), are in need of intensive study. But, taken together, they suggest further that the scope of B-element Raising is far wider than may have been suspected.

    There are various other verbs that, I think, turn out to be B-element R-triggers in disguise. Consider first *ascertain*. This certainly does not occur in simple infinitival cases:

(54) a.   I ascertained that Bill was a Greek.

    b. *I ascertained Bill to be a Greek.

Although, curiously, application of rules yielding structures that do not violate DOC certainly improves sentences like (54)b, they still seem imperfect:

(55) a. ?*Melvin, I ascertained to be a Greek.

    b. ?*Who did you ascertain to be a Greek?

    c. ?*The only person who I ascertained to be a Greek was Spiro.

    d. ?*I ascertained to be Greeks—all of the men who were working on Bob's yacht.

However, sentences that would be regarded as passives of structures like (54)b seem acceptable:

(56) a. Bill was ascertained (by the police) to be living with an Italian countess.

    b. The letter was ascertained to have been written by Lemmingsworth.

Thus, although I earlier rejected the view that verbs like *allege* were subject to a constraint making Passive obligatory when they serve as an R-trigger (noting that instead DOC was involved), such an account seems appropriate for *ascertain*.

In these terms, *ascertain* contrasts with *rumor*, discussed in footnote 3 of Chapter 1. I also regard *rumor* as a disguised B-element R-trigger, but, unlike *ascertain*, *rumor* cannot occur unpassivized, even with *that* clauses, while *ascertain* can, as (54)a shows.

(57) *Harry rumored that Bob was a pervert.

Moreover, *ascertain* in passives can cooccur with *by* phrases, while *rumor* cannot:

(58) a. Harry was rumored (* by the CIA) to be Mexican.

    b. Harry was ascertained (by the CIA) to be Mexican.

(59) a. It was rumored (*by the CIA) that Harry was Mexican.

    b. It was ascertained (by the CIA) that Harry was Mexican.

Thus apparently one must say for *rumor* that passivization is required by the very insertion of this verb, while for *ascertain* it is required only when the verb functions as an R-trigger.

I believe that two extremely common verbs, *think* and *say*, also function as R-triggers of a restricted sort. The latter has recently been discussed by Brame and Baker (1972: 66–68), who make the following interesting observations:

    . . . In this alternative analysis, the verb *say* is broken up into two distinct lexical entries, say_1 and say_2. Say_1 is that found in 47 above. Say_2 is that found in 51, and also in

(56) It is said that John is tall.

Say_2 occurs only in agentless passives, whether it takes the infinitival complementizer, as in 51 above, or the *that* complementizer, as in

(57) *It is said by Bill that John is tall.

(58) It is said that John is tall.

In addition, extraposition is obligatory for say_2:

(59) *That John is tall is said.

(60) It is said that John is tall.

Say_2, then, is parallel in syntactic behavior to the verb *rumor*:

(61) *John rumors that Bill is tall.

(62) *John rumors Bill to be tall.

(63) *Bill is rumored by John to be tall.

(64) Bill is rumored to be tall.

(65) It is rumored that Bill is tall.

(66) *It is rumored by John that Bill is tall.

(67) *That Bill is tall is rumored.

In this analysis of *say,* no significant difference is tied to the choice of complementizers. *Say₂* may take either *that* or *for-to* as complementizer, and in either case can appear only in agentless passives. . . .

It should be noted in conclusion that the analysis which we propose receives additional support from the fact that what we have referred to as *say₂* has a more narrowly restricted semantic range than *say₁*. Only *say₁* can be used in reporting a single speech act. In each of the following pairs of sentences, only the active voice with indefinite subject is grammatical; the passive voice without agent is not:

(79) All of a sudden, someone said that George was turning blue.

(80) *All of a sudden, George was said to be turning blue.

(81) Someone said in a loud voice that the carrots were overcooked.

(82) *It was said in a loud voice that the carrots were overcooked.

The sentences they refer to as 47 and 51 are, respectively:

(60) a. Sam said that John was tall.

   b. John was said to be tall.

However, although I agree with their factorization of *say* into distinct lexical items, not all of their claims are correct, at least for my idiolect. In particular, the claim that *say₂* occurs only in agentless passives is incorrect, but I agree that their (57) is ill-formed. The following, however, are not:

(61) a. It is said by everyone that the war will end in November.

   b. It was said by most authorities that cancer was caused by a virus.

Note that the examples become ill-formed if *rumored* replaces *said.* It seems that the constraint requires the *by*-phrase NPs to be "general," nonspecific, or possibly in some sense "generic." Contrasts between *rumor* and *say* are also found in cases involving Raising:

(62) a. Melvin was rumored (*by $\left\{\begin{array}{l}\text{everyone}\\\text{the authorities}\\\text{most people}\end{array}\right\}$) to be insane.

b. Melvin was said by $\left\{\begin{array}{l}\text{everyone}\\\text{the authorities}\\\text{most people}\end{array}\right\}$ to be insane.

It appears to me, then, that although say_2 is like *rumor* in requiring passivization of the clause of which it is the main verb, it differs from the former in permitting (some) surface *by* phrases. Similarly, say_2 contrasts partially with *ascertain* in that it does not occur with *that* clauses, and passivization is required independently of Raising.

Brame and Baker (1972: 67–68) go on to suggest that say_2 has similarities with verbs like *seem* and *appear* and that it should be derived as a passive by base rules, thus without any application of Passive. This proposal is linked to a suggestion of Emonds (1970), under which the subject of say_2 would be "empty." This idea is suggested to these authors by their belief in the impossibility of explicit *by* phrases with say_2, and it seems to me to collapse immediately in the face of sentences like (61) and (62)b, which show that this idea is wrong, quite independently of any general objections to "empty" constituents.

Brame and Baker do not consider *think*, but I suspect that a factorization similar to what they suggest for *say* is also in order:

(63) a. I think that Bob is insane.

b. It is thought (by most authorities) that monarchies are stable.

c. Monarchies are thought to be stable (by most authorities).

Here the division would be between (63)a and (63)b, c. But a meaning contrast like that unearthed by Brame and Baker for *say* is harder to see here. In any event, I take (63)c to involve Raising and hence to support the claim that at least one *think* is an R-trigger. Since Brame and Baker's suggestion to assimilate *say* to A-elements also seems impossible for *think*, I further suggest that both *think* and say_2 are B-element R-triggers.

Next, I shall comment on *consider*. This functions like an ordinary B-element R-trigger in most ways:

(64) a. I consider him (to be) incompetent.

    b. He is considered (by us) to be incompetent.

There is, however, the exception that it cannot take *that* clauses:

(65) a. *I consider that he is incompetent.

    b. *It is considered (by us) that he is incompetent.

But I see no reason to regard this other than as a case where Raising is obligatory.

    The verb *deem* is similar to *consider* in this regard:

(66) a. *They deemed that he was too old for the job.

    b. *They deemed him to be too old for the job.

    c. They deemed him too old for the job.

But, as (66)b indicates, this verb has the further peculiarity of requiring *to be* deletion. This means that it only can occur with *be* type complements. Again, though, I take these to be special constraints that disguise the B-element character of *deem* rather than facts that militate against it.

    The element *repute* is a difficult case. Like *rumor,* it can occur only in passives:

(67) a. Joan is reputed to be a countess.

    b. *They repute Joan to be a countess.

    c. *They reputed that Joan was a countess.

But, unlike *rumor,* it cannot take *that* complements even in passives, as shown in (68)a, and it cannot take even "general" *by* phrases, as shown in (68)b, c.

(68) a. *It is reputed that Joan is a countess.

    b. *Joan is reputed by most people to be a countess.

    c. *It is reputed by experts that Joan is a countess.

This means that we have no direct evidence that sentences like (67) are, in fact, to be regarded as passives of B-element Raising structures, rather than as simple A-element structures with an adjectival A-element *repute*. The latter seems intuitively wrong, no doubt, because of the semantic similarity between *repute* and true passives like those for *say₂*, *think*, *rumor*, etc. The one piece of evidence for passive status is that *reputed* occurs together with the adverb *widely*, which, as far as I know, otherwise occurs only with the passives of (mostly B-element) R-triggers:

(69) Jane was widely $\left\{ \begin{matrix} \left\{ \begin{matrix} \text{reputed} \\ \text{believed} \\ \text{thought} \\ \text{reported} \end{matrix} \right\} \text{to be} \\ \left\{ \begin{matrix} \text{recognized as} \\ \text{regarded as} \end{matrix} \right\} \text{being} \end{matrix} \right\}$ in line for the judgeship.

However, *widely*, which is in complementary distribution with *by* phrases,[15] does not go with all B-element R-triggers in passives.

(70) a.   Jack is believed by everyone to be into grave robbing.

   b.   Jack is widely believed to be into grave robbing.

   c. *Jack is widely believed by $\left\{ \begin{matrix} \text{everyone} \\ \text{most authorities} \\ \text{two out of three local officials} \end{matrix} \right\}$ to be

   into grave robbing.

For example, it does not go with *prove* or *show*:

(71) a. *Jack was widely proved to be insane.

   b. *Jack was widely shown to be insane.

This, however, may well be a function of the meaning of the elements involved. Note that *prove* and *show*, unlike *believe, think*, etc., are active verbs. But *report* is a problem, since it not only seems to be active but also takes *widely*. At any event, the cooccurrence of *reputed* with *widely* is suggestive, if hardly conclusive, since I know of no clear cases of adjectives distinct from passive participles that occur with *widely*:

15 Conceivably, then, *widely* should be derived from a *by* phrase, say along the lines of (i):

(i) [by a wide range of individuals] $\Rightarrow$ *widely*.

(72) a. *Jack is widely likely to leave.

   b. *Jack is widely certain to do that.

   c. *Jack is widely unhappy.

   d. *Jack is widely tough to please.

   I shall conclude this rambling survey of potential B-element R-trig-gers disguised by special factors,[16] by commenting further on cases in-

---

[16] Problems are raised by sentences like (i), which are, in all likelihood, passives of structures derived by Raising.

(i) a. Melvin was seen to enter the building.
   b. Melvin was heard to say he had cancer.

However, the unpassivized versions are impossible:

(ii) a. *Everyone saw Melvin to enter the building.
   b. *Everyone heard Melvin to say he had cancer.

Nor can rules like Topicalization or Complex NP Shift, which rescue DOC-violating configurations, help here:

(iii) a. *Melvin, everyone saw to enter the building.
   b. *Everyone heard to say he had cancer—the man who had just returned from the Papuan expedition.

An immediate question that arises is whether the unpassivized structures underlying (i), which would otherwise end up as (ii), are converted by some rule of *to* deletion to those like (iv):

(iv) a. Everyone saw Melvin enter the building.
   b. Everyone heard Melvin say he had cancer.

I have not investigated this point, but it is striking that sentences like (iv) have no direct passives:

(v) a. *Melvin was seen (by everyone) enter the building.
   b. *Melvin was heard (by everyone) say he had cancer.

However, to complicate things, whereas the lower verb in sentences like (iv) are quite free, the lower verb in sentences like (i)b must apparently represent a *verbal* event:

(vi) a. Everyone heard Melvin $\left\{ \begin{array}{l} \text{burp} \\ \text{scrape his ear on the nail} \\ \text{slide on the beam} \\ \text{crack his joints} \end{array} \right\}$.

   b. *Melvin was heard to $\left\{ \begin{array}{l} \text{burp} \\ \text{scrape his ear on the nail} \\ \text{slide on the beam} \\ \text{crack his joints} \end{array} \right\}$.

Moreover, there are verbs that enter into paradigms like (iv), but that do not form passive clauses such as (i). These include *watch* and *smell*.

volving *as*, briefly considered already in Section 6.7. I think there is a class of what are in fact B-elements, which have the property of permitting *as* and gerundive form for the complement instead of infinitival form, once Raising applies. This class probably includes the main verbs in the following sentences:

(73) a. He accepted her as (being) his equal.

    b. She acknowledged me as (*being) her equal.

    c. The movie depicted him as (being) an idiot.

    d. The bookies established him as (being) a two-to-one favorite.

    e. The film pictured him as (being) merciless.

    f. I recognized him as (being) the assailant.

    g. I remembered him as being shorter.

    h. They specified that as (being) the boundary.

It can be seen that some of the verbs occur in constructions of the sort normal for B-element R-triggers, for example:

(74) a.   I acknowledge that Joan is my superior.

    b. *I acknowledge Joan to be my superior. (because of DOC)

    c.   Joan, I acknowledge to be my superior.

    d.   I acknowledge Joan as my superior.

Consequently, I think we have reason to assume that when *as* cases are analyzed in detail, the class of cases falling under the rough rubric of B-element R-trigger will grow further.

In this section, I have attempted not so much to provide serious or detailed analyses as to suggest roughly the scope of cases that must be studied to gain some idea of the true range of B-element Raising, that is, taking note of the more restricted sets falling into the N-element and W-element classes, in order to get an idea of the true range of Raising into superordinate object position—Raising operation of just the sort whose existence has recently been denied by Chomsky.[17]

17 Earlier, in footnotes 55 and 68 of Chapter 4, I had occasion to criticize as unrealistic Chomsky's conception of rules as applying "blindly" to input phrase markers. The criticisms were formulated in terms of facts relating to Passive, the rule chosen by Chomsky to exemplify his claims. It should need little stress at this point in our account of the myriad restrictions on Raising application that Chomsky's account is equally inappropriate for Raising.

9.4 Other Possible Cases

Although it is not possible to consider this matter in any detail, I should not like to leave the impression that the rough classes of A-elements, B-elements, N-elements, and W-elements, even when accurately and fully specified sometime in the future, exhaust the set of English R-triggers. On the contrary, I am convinced that Raising plays a fundamental role in a wide variety of other derivations. In this section, I shall simply indicate my views about possible elements of this type, with little attempt to justify the decisions.

I think it is evident that Raising functions in cases like (75):

(75) a. I allowed there to be a riot.

   b. I permitted him to vaccinate the gerbils.

The various tests of Chapters 3 and 4 show that the postverbal NP in such cases is a derived object. For instance, observe the following:

(76) a.   I $\left\{ \begin{array}{l} \text{allowed} \\ \text{permitted} \end{array} \right\}$ to leave—all those students who had completed their exams.

   b. *I $\left\{ \begin{array}{l} \text{allowed} \\ \text{permitted} \end{array} \right\}$ not many people to leave.

   c. *I $\left\{ \begin{array}{l} \text{allowed} \\ \text{permitted} \end{array} \right\}$ us to leave.

   d. *I $\left\{ \begin{array}{l} \text{allowed} \\ \text{permitted} \end{array} \right\}$ without any qualms Bob to leave.

However, as insightfully observed by Huddleston (1971: 158), despite sentences like (75), this class of permission sentences seems to involve an ambiguity. Thus a sentence like (77) means either "I gave permission for Bob to leave" or "I gave Bob permission to leave."

(77) I allowed Bob to leave.

The former meaning is naturally consistent with a Raising analysis. On this line of interpretation, we find sentences like (78), which are semantically equivalent:

(78) a. I allowed the bomb to blow up the building.

   b. I allowed the building to be blown up by the bomb.

On the other line of interpretation, however, we find sentences like (79), which are *not* equivalent on one reading, in that the *a* example describes a situation where permission was given to John, the *b* example where it was given to the witness.

(79) a. I allowed John to interrogate the witness.

b. I allowed the witness to be interrogated by John.

In a manner consistent with past ideas about this sort of thing—for example, the past observations by Chomsky (1965: 22–23); Rosenbaum (1967); Stockwell, Schachter, and Partee (1968)—Huddleston suggests similar contrasts between sentences like (80) and (81):

(80) a. I expect Bob to interrogate the witness.

b. I expect the witness to be interrogated by Bob.

(81) a. I convinced Bob to interrogate the witness.

b. I convinced the witness to be interrogated by Bob.

He proposes that the two senses of *allow, permit* be structurally distinguished as follows. In the sense where passivization yields no semantic contrast, he would recognize a transitive analysis triggering Raising. In the other, parallel to *convince,* he would recognize a three-NP analysis, triggering Equi:

(82) a. I allowed [Bob to leave] $\overset{\text{Raising}}{\Rightarrow}$ I allowed Bob to leave.

b. I allowed Bob [Bob to leave] $\overset{\text{Equi}}{\Rightarrow}$ I allowed Bob to leave.

I am, however, not at all convinced that a structure like (82)b is the proper way to represent the second sense of verbs like *allow,* nor am I convinced that a parallel structure is appropriate to represent verbs like *convince.* I shall deal with this matter briefly in Chapter 11. In any event the problem is a real one, which has received too little attention, although the facts have been known at least since 1964.

Consider also the verb *order,* where we find such amazing contrasts as the following:

(83) a. I ordered that Bob be removed from the room.

b. *I ordered Bob to be removed from the room.

c. I ordered Bob removed from the room.

    d. I ordered the chair (to be) removed from the room.

    e. I ordered Bob to leave the room.

Here in (83)a, c the order is not given to Bob, while in (83)b and (83)e this is the only interpretation, a fact not clouded by the ill-formedness of (83)b. In fact, probably the ill-formedness of (83)b is a function of this semantic fact, in combination with the passive complement. The key sentence for present purposes is (83)c, which, I suggest, must involve Raising. That is, it is interpreted like (83)a, but various tests show that the postverbal NP is a main clause constituent:

(84) a. I ordered removed from the room—all those women who were making offensive remarks.

    b. *I ordered not many women removed from the room.

    c. *I ordered us removed from the list.

Since, however, sentences like (83)b do not correlate in interpretation with (83)a, it seems that *order* has the same dualistic structure as *allow* and *permit,* however this is ultimately to be described. But in the case of *order,* the situation is further obscured by interaction with some constraint relating Raising to obligatory loss of the infinitive marker, when the raised NP designates a mind-possessing entity.

    Finally, certain explicit causative verbs occur in structures that cannot, I believe, be properly described without Raising, for instance:

(85) a. Melvin had tabs kept on his wife.

    b. If he could, Melvin would have it snow on July Fourth.

    c. I will make it rain on your birthday.

    d. John caused there to be riots in Samoa.

If we take these sentences without empty NPs in the postverbal position, we shall again find situations like those with *allow, permit,* and *order*—that is, again a dualistic analysis. Thus, on one reading at least, the following are not semantically equivalent:

(86) a. Tom had Melvin interrogate the witness.

    b. Tom had the witness interrogated by Melvin.

So one sees further that this sort of meaning contrast is a pervasive problem in the analysis of English complement structures, one to which I shall return in the next chapter.

Finally, I should like to mention only that one must consider the role of Raising in derivations involving the Predicate Raising rule, suggested by McCawley, a rule that combines main verbs and the main verbs of their complements into complex derived verbals. One productive class of such derivations involves causatives. Hence, roughly, we have the following:

(87) a. CAUSE Melvin [BECOME [OPEN the door]] $\overset{\text{Predicate Raising}}{\Rightarrow}$

    b. CAUSE Melvin [BECOME + OPEN the door] $\overset{\text{Predicate Raising}}{\Rightarrow}$

    c. CAUSE + (BECOME + OPEN) Melvin the door =

    d. open Melvin the door = Melvin opened the door.

One might conjecture, however, that in such cases, Predicate Raising never applies to a complement clause verbal that still has its subject. Thus in these cases, it is possible that Raising has applied first. In other cases, I should say that Equi removes the complement subject. This amounts, then, to the claim that Predicate Raising applies only to complements that are what were earlier called quasi-clauses. If so, then Raising is intimately involved in a basic portion of the set of Predicate Raising derivations and has on these grounds alone a much wider range than might be thought. But space does not permit further exploration of this complex matter here. See Perlmutter and Postal (to appear b).

10
Raising in Nominalizations

10.1 Background

So far, every instance of Raising operation dealt with in this study has involved application within the domain of the clause, that is, where the R-trigger is realized as a verbal element heading a main clause. The question arises, however, as to whether Raising applies in any other cases, in particular, as to whether it applies within nominalizations, in which the R-trigger ends up, in effect, as (a part of) the head noun. Of course, this is a logical possibility.

Chomsky (1970: 189) made the interesting observation that a class of nominalizations that might well be expected are, in fact, impossible, particularly those given in (1), among others.

(1) a. *John's easiness (difficulty) to please

   b. *John's certainty (likelihood) to win the prize

Since *certain* and *likely* are A-element R-triggers, (1)b is evidently just the sort of case to be expected if Raising operation were involved in the derivation of nominalizations. Example (1)a is the sort of situation to be expected if Tough Movement were involved in the derivation of nominalizations.

Chomsky suggested that the facts in (1) follow from the so-called lexicalist hypothesis about nominalizations—the claim that these are derived directly by base rules rather than transformationally. In Chomsky's account of this conception, this is a consequence, since nominalizations must then correspond essentially to base structures rather than to transformed structures. Given, however, Tough Movement and Raising analyses, respectively, of sentences like (2), the nominalizations in (1) correspond to derived rather than base structures.

(2) a. John is easy (difficult) to please.

   b. John is certain (likely) to win the prize.

Chomsky (1970: 191) puts it as follows:

Consider next the examples *John's certainty to win the prize* [=(8b)], *John's certainty that Bill will win the prize* [=(9b)]. Again, the lexicalist hypothesis provides an explanation for this distinction between the two senses of *certain*. The sentence *John is certain to win the prize* is derived by extraposition and pronoun replacement from a deep structure in which *certain* is predicated of the proposition *John—to win the prize*, as is clear from the meaning. In this sense, *certain* does not permit a propositional complement; it therefore follows from the lexicalist hypothesis that there cannot be a derived nominal *certainty to win the prize*, in this sense. But *John is certain that Bill will win the prize* derives from *John is certain* [$_S$Bill will win the prize$_S$]. In the sense of *certain* in which it is predicated of a person, a propositional complement can be adjoined in the base. Consequently, the lexicalist hypothesis permits the associated derived nominal *John's certainty that Bill will win the prize*, generated by lexical insertion of *certain* in the noun position before a sentential complement.

And again Chomsky (1970: 204) states:

. . . if it were really the nominalization of a passive, this fact would refute the lexicalist hypothesis that transforms should not undergo the processes that give derived nominals. In fact, one major empirical justification offered for the lexicalist hypothesis was that, in a number of otherwise puzzling cases, it is precisely this state of affairs that we discover.

Of course, the great significance of Chomsky's discussion centers on the fact, if sustainable, that it reduces some otherwise accidental facts, the ill-formedness of structures like (1), to a rather deep principle of language, namely, that nominalizations correspond to base, not derived, structures. However, for this principle to work out, it must at least be the case that the situation illustrated in (1) is neither accidental nor atypical. In fact, it must be uniformly true that, among other things:

(3) There are *no* nominalizations whose derivations involve Raising.

I shall argue now, however, that (3) is false.

10.2 A-Element Nominalization Analogues

We saw in Section 9.2 (see also Section 12.1) that the verb *tend* is an A-element R-trigger. Thus there are such sentences as (4) that must have derivations from remote structures like (5):

(4) a. There tends to be corruption in city governments.

b. Unfair advantage tends to be taken of pretty nurses.

c. It tends to rain on weekends.

(5) a. tend [$_S$there be corruption in city governments$_S$]

    b. tend [$_S$unfair advantage be taken of pretty nurses$_S$]

    c. tend [$_S$it rain on weekends$_S$]

Consider now the following:

(6) a. Melvin tends to lie about his age.

    b. Melvin's tendency to lie about his age

Since we know the verb *tend* is an A-element R-trigger, there should be an immediate presumption of a parallel analysis for *tendency*. The meanings of (6)a and (6)b seem entirely parallel, and there is, moreover, the structure (7), which reveals the "intransitive" structure to be expected of an A-element.

(7) the tendency for Melvin to lie about his age

The significance of this is that the only serious alternative to a Raising analysis of cases like (6)b would seem to be an Equi analysis, in which underlying (6)b would be a structure like (8), which, on some readings at least, takes *tendency* to be a "transitive" noun.

(8) Melvin's tendency [$_S$for Melvin to lie about his age$_S$]

In this sense, then, forms like (6)b would be analyzed in a fashion parallel to those like (9):

(9) Melvin's wish to lie about his age

    Such an analysis is immediately suspicious, though. For nominalizations like (9) correspond to clear Equi-derived clauses like (10)a, where the coreference underlying Equi is not required by the construction in (10)b:

(10) a. Melvin wishes to lie about his age.

    b. Melvin wishes for Lucy to lie about his age.

This is in contrast to the situation with the A-element R-trigger *tend*:

(11) *Melvin tends for Lucy to lie about his age.

This contrast is equally manifest for the following nominalizations:

(12) a.   Melvin's wish for Lucy to lie about his age

   b. *Melvin's tendency for Lucy to lie about his age

Thus, on grounds of semantics, parallelism with verbal cases, and the need for an "intransitive" treatment of some occurrences (because of (8), etc.), the Equi analysis of *tendency* nominalizations like (6)b is quite without plausibility. Indeed, in the absence of a principle like (3), it is hard to imagine anyone adopting such an analysis, even on the basis of just the factors considered so far.

   However, given the strong claims made by (3), motivation for seeking to avoid a Raising analysis of *tendency* is not lacking. Moreover, it can be pointed out that the "empty" NPs found as subjects of the verb *tend,* which show so directly the need for a Raising analysis, are impossible with *tendency*:[1]

(13) a. *there's tendency to be riots on campuses

   b. *its tendency to rain on weekends

   c. *unfair advantage's tendency to be taken of pretty nurses

While such cases are no problem for a Raising analysis of *tendency,* since there is an obvious output condition blocking all cases where these "empty" NPs have the genitive, as in (14), the impossibility of nominals like (13) eliminates the most direct sort of argument for Raising.

(14) a. *There's being no riots on campuses worries us.

   b. *Its raining every weekend is depressing.

   c. *Unfair advantage's having been taken of you is rotten.

   Other arguments are available, though. Recall, for instance, the argument based on truth-value preservation under passivization, discussed in Chapters 7 and 9. And consider the following:

(15) a.   the servant's tendency to praise the queen

   b. ?the queen's tendency to be praised by the servant

---

[1] That is, in preposed position. They occur, of course, in sentence frames like (7):

(i) a.the tendency for there to be riots on campuses
   b.the tendency for it to rain on weekends
   c. the tendency for unfair advantage to be taken of pretty nurses

(16) a. the servant's wish to praise the queen

   b. the queen's wish to be praised by the servant

While (15)b is possibly a bit weird on semantic grounds, there is no difficulty in perceiving its truth-functional equivalence to (15)a. That is, if the tendency in (15)a exists, so must that in (15)b. In (16), however, the two wishes are completely independent. This is just what we have seen is to be expected from Raising and Equi structures, respectively. Note the correlation between the facts in (15) and those in (17):

(17) a. the tendency for the servant to praise the queen

   b. the tendency for the queen to be praised by the servant

Note also the similar correlation between the situation in (15) and that in (18):

(18) a. The servant tends to praise the queen.

   b. The queen tends to be praised by the servant.

I conclude that this argument eliminates any serious possibility of accepting an Equi analysis for *tendency* nominalizations with preposed genitive NPs.

   Consider also the following cases:

(19) a. Jack and Jill wish to each testify separately.

   b. Jack and Jill tend to each testify separately.

What is of relevance here is what NP the quantifier *each* binds. I claim that in (19)a, the *each* occurrence binds the NP deleted by Equi.[2] Thus (19)a refers to a common wish by X and Y that each of X and Y testify

2 This is not literally accurate. More precisely, I should argue that the *each* here binds an NP related by a partitive predicate to the NP deleted by Equi. Thus underlying (19)a might be something like this:

(i) $X + Y$ wish [for each A included in $X + Y$, A testify separately]

The NP corresponding to A here is then deleted by the sequence of operations that float the quantifier off, the same sequence that turns (ii)a into (ii)b:

(ii) a. For each A included in $X + Y$, A likes applesauce.
   b. $X + Y$ each like applesauce.

The partitive analysis, with *each* binding an index distinct from $X + Y$, avoids an incoherent logical structure of the form shown in (iii), where there is an occurrence

separately. In (19)b, however, the *each* actually binds the NP *Jack and Jill*, necessary since *tend* is a Raising verb and there is simply no other NP. Thus the properties of (19)b are also found with other A-element R-triggers like *seem, appear, likely*:

(20) a. Jack and Jill seemed to each tell slightly different stories.

    b. Jack and Jill appeared to each speak different dialects.

    c. Jack and Jill are likely to each come separately.

Similarly, the properties of (19)a are typical of other verbs like *want, expect, desire,* which trigger Equi:

(21) a. Jack and Jill want to each leave separately.

    b. Jack and Jill expect to each testify separately.

    c. Jack and Jill desire to each come at different times.

But now consider the following:

(22) a. Jack and Jill's wish to each testify separately

    b. Jack and Jill's tendency to each testify separately

The properties of these nominalization cases with respect to what is bound by *each* are exactly those of the sentential cases in (19). This shows further that one cannot maintain an Equi analysis for *tendency* nominalizations, which contrast in various properties with true "transitive" Equi nominalizations based on words like *wish*.[3]

---

of $X + Y$ not bound by a quantifier commanding the same index combination under the scope of a quantifier.

(iii) $X + Y$ wish [for each $X + Y, \ldots$

Another type of example that can be saved from the same unhappy fate by the partitive analysis of quantifier structures involves nonrestrictive relative clauses:

(iv) the marines, each of whom called Betty

[3] Another argument against an Equi analysis can be based on the properties of emphatic reflexives, briefly discussed earlier in Section 6.7 and in Chapter 7. It was noted that these float away from NPs that are raised, thus appearing in complements when the "antecedent" NP is in a higher clause, as in (i):

(i) John seems to have himself told several jokes.

But it was noted that they do not float away from NPs deleted under Equi:

The properties of *tendency* nominalizations, which have already been discussed, suggest that principle (3) cannot be sustained. Moreover, *tendency* is not an entirely isolated noun case. As noted by Chomsky (1970: 205), nominalizations with the head *likelihood* are, for some speakers, quite analogous to those based on *tendency*, although, for many other speakers, *likelihood* nominalizations with a preposed genitive NP are not acceptable:

(23) a. The likelihood of Nixon's being reelected is minimal.

  b. Nixon's likelihood of being reelected is minimal.

Thus, while everyone accepts examples like (23)a, some do not accept (23)b. However, even for such speakers, the degree of ill-formedness seems minimal. I find those like (23)b marginally acceptable.

We know, of course, that the adjective *likely* is an A-element R-trigger, and in general *likelihood* has the same properties that indicate that an Equi analysis is not possible for *tendency*. Example (23)a indicates the "intransitivity" of *likelihood*. Example (23)b has a meaning that seems entirely parallel to that in (24), which is known to involve Raising.

(24) Nixon is likely to be reelected.

And there is no truth-value contrast in pairs like (25):

(25) a. *Spock's likelihood of praising Nixon

  b. Nixon's likelihood of being praised by Spock

That is, if (25)a is 3 percent, so is (25)b, in spite of the fact that the

---

(ii) *John wants to himself tell several jokes.

However, note the contrast between (iii)a and (iii)b:

(iii) a. ?Melvin's tendency to himself tell the most outrageous lies
  b. *Melvin's wish to himself tell the most outrageous lies.

Example (iii)a is somewhat strained, to be sure, and may be rejected by many speakers. But it is far better than the impossible (iii)b. The facts with these nominalizations then correlate closely with those for the verbal cases, as a Raising analysis of *tend*, *tendency* and an Equi analysis of *wish*, *wish* predicts:

(iv) a. ?Melvin tends to himself tell the most outrageous lies.
  b. *Melvin wishes to himself tell the most outrageous lies.

former seems ungrammatical. This follows under a Raising analysis, of course. Note the parallel behavior in the following:

(26) a. the likelihood of Spock's praising Nixon

   b. the likelihood of Nixon's being praised by Spock

Finally, in cases like (27) we find for both that the quantifier binds the occurring conjoined NPs, in contrast to the behavior of *each* in Equi cases.

(27) a. Nixon and Agnew's likelihood of each getting public service awards

   b. Nixon and Agnew are likely to each get public service awards.

I conclude that *likelihood* is at worst a marginal example of the application of Raising within nominalizations.

Consider next the verb *continue*. It was noted earlier that this is an A-element R-trigger, taking either infinitival or gerundive complements. What was *not* mentioned in the brief discussion of *as* constructions in Section 6.7 was that *continue* also occurs with *as*:

(28) a. Melvin continues to study pornographic science.

   b. (If) Melvin continues having trouble with his spleen, . . .

   c. Murphy continues as police chief.

   d. Nationalist China continues as a Security Council member.

Of course, the *as* construction here is highly restricted; in fact, it is apparently limited to cases where the underlying complement was of the predicate nominal variety:

(29) a. *Murphy continues as fat.

   b. *Max continues as having the mumps.

Given that sentences like (30) are derived by Raising, there should be a presumption that sentences like (28)c, d are as well.

(30) a. Murphy continues to be police chief.

   b. Nationalist China continues to be a Security Council member.

This permits a uniform account of *continue* as an R-trigger taking sentential subjects (ignoring the causative, hence transitive *continue*). But there are nominalizations corresponding to (28)c, d, such as (31), which are, I suggest, derivable naturally only through a similar application of Raising.[4]

(31) a. Murphy's continuation as police chief

 b. Nationalist China's continuation as a Security Council member

The verb *persist*, seen earlier to be an A-element R-trigger, and the nominal *persistence* seem quite parallel in behavior to *continue* and *continuation*:

(32) a. Cancer persists in being in a frightening killer.

 b. Cancer persists as a frightening killer.

 c. cancer's persistance as a frightening killer

(33) a. Heroin usage persists in being the number one problem.

 b. Heroin usage persists as the number one problem.

 c. heroin usage's persistence as the number one problem

So I suggest that *persistence*, like *continuation*, is also a nominalization formed with the aid of Raising.

---

[4] The word *continuation* can also occur with prepositional phrases, including those beginning with *in*:

(i) a. Their continuation in power would be tragic.
 b. Our continuation under the yoke of the capitalist system is intolerable.

The weird contrasts in (ii) are worthy of note, since it seems an absolute mystery what principles assign the stars.

(ii) Max's continuation
$$\left\{ \begin{array}{l} \text{in power} \\ \text{in office} \\ \text{in the grip of mental paralysis} \\ *\text{in control of the situation} \\ *\text{in the Republican party} \\ *\text{in opposition to abortion} \\ *\text{in awe of her} \\ *\text{in the bathroom} \\ \text{in the role of king} \end{array} \right\}$$

Observe that, in each case of (ii), a sequence of the form *Max is in X* is well-formed. However, I believe some evidence for the view that *continuation* and *continue* must be grammatically related derives from the fact that replacement of *Max's continuation* in (ii) by *Max continues* yields a grammaticality array that is almost identical, differing for me only in the case of the third example.

I have argued that an Equi analysis is inappropriate for nominalizations involving *tendency, likelihood, continuation,* and *persistence.* I have suggested, therefore, that these nominalizations must be analyzed in terms of Raising, like their verbal counterparts *tend, likely, continue,* and *persist.* However, it should be stressed, of course, that the impossibility of an Equi analysis does not in itself fully justify a Raising analysis. There are alternatives, one of which is hinted at by Chomsky (1970: 205) himself: "Some speakers apparently accept expressions such as *John's likelihood of leaving,* though to me these are entirely unacceptable. Perhaps such expressions can be derived, by an extension of NP-preposing, from *the likelihood of John leaving.* Such expressions as **John's likelihood to leave* apparently are acceptable to no one, exactly as is predicted by the lexicalist hypothesis." Let us consider the last sentence first. The facts appear right, and Chomsky stresses that they are a consequence of the lexical hypothesis. But, of course, the analogous sentences are fine with *tendency*:

(34) John's tendency to leave

Thus the hypothesis in question is apparently in some difficulty.

More generally, though, one might try to avoid this consequence by claiming that (34) is derived by "an extension of NP-preposing," the latter being the rule that, in Chomsky's system, turns objects into derived subjects in passive clauses, and also functions to derive nominals like (35)a from those like (35)b:

(35) a. the city's destruction by the enemy

b. the destruction of the city by the enemy

In particular, it could be claimed that (34) is derived by this rule from (36):

(36) the tendency for John to leave

Thus cases like (34) would not involve an appeal to Raising, but neither would one adopt anything like the unsuitable Equi analysis rejected earlier. Such an approach would then offer hope of saving principle (3) and the more general theory that has (3) as a theorem. Cases like (37)a, b would be analogously derivable from (37)c, d:

(37) a. Murphy's continuation as Prime Minister

b. cancer's persistence as a serious health threat

c. the continuation of Murphy as Prime Minister

d. the persistence of cancer as a serious health threat

I agree that it is quite plausible to derive the preposed genitive cases from those in which the NP follows the nominalization head, and to this extent I do not reject Chomsky's proposal (although it is another matter whether the same rule is involved in passive clauses). I think, though, that postulating this derivation does not save cases like *tendency* from having to be analyzed in terms of the operation of Raising. For, alongside cases like (38)a, there are those like (38)b:

(38) a. the tendency for Bob to lie to the authorities

b. $\left\{\begin{array}{c}\text{that}\\ \text{a}\end{array}\right\}$ tendency of Bob's to lie to the authorities

That is, with *tendency* there are following structures that, like (38)a, have the form of full infinitival clauses, and there are also those like (38)b, in which there is an *of*-marked NP, which can take the genitive. What is crucial is the relation between them. I think it is clear, given the ordinary operation of Chomsky's rule of NP preposing, that the preposed cases would have to be derived from those like (38)b, and not, as I first assumed for argument, from those like (38)a.[5]

Moreover, there are strong grounds for rejecting any attempt to take pairs like (38)a, b to be mere trivial variants, differing, say, only in preposition shape and genitive distribution. Rather, it can be shown that the NP in the *a* class of cases is a (derived) subject, while that in the *b* cases is not. In particular, this is most clearly indicated by reference to the arguments of Sections 4.2 and 4.3.

[5] This argument is supported by a kind of complementary distribution typical of genitive cases. Thus note the relation between (i) and (ii):

(i) a. a book of Jim's

b. $\left\{\begin{array}{c}\text{that}\\ \text{this}\end{array}\right\}$ book of Jim's

c. *the book of Jim's ⟹ Jim's book

(ii) a. a tendency of Melvin's to tell outrageous stories

b. $\left\{\begin{array}{c}\text{that}\\ \text{this}\end{array}\right\}$ tendency of Melvin's to tell outrageous stories

c. *the tendency of Melvin's to tell outrageous stories ⟹ Melvin's tendency to tell outrageous stories

Recall that both *not*-initial and *alone*-final NPs are restricted to occurrence in surface *subject* positions. See footnote 9 of Chapter 4. Strikingly, though, these types of NPs can occur after *for* in contexts like (38)a, but not after *of* in contexts like (38)b.

(39) a. The (continuing) tendency for not many children to learn Chinese is regrettable.

   b. *That (continuing) tendency of not many children('s) to learn Chinese is regrettable.

(40) a. The tendency for not much money to be spent on hospitals is unfortunate.

   b. *That tendency of not much money('s) to be spent on hospitals is unfortunate.

(41) a. The tendency for Kronzheim alone to make all the decisions is frightening.

   b. *That tendency of Kronzheim alone('s) to make all the decisions is frightening.

Compare (39)b, (40)b, and (41)b with (42):

(42) a. That tendency of many children to learn Chinese poorly is regrettable.

   b. *That tendency of much money to be spent on hospitals is unfortunate.[6]

   c. That tendency of Kronzheim's to make all the decisions is frightening.

Given the principle that *not*-initial and *alone*-final NPs are restricted to superficial subject positions, these facts would seem to support the notion that *a* cases in (38)–(41) have the NPs in subject position, but that the *b* cases do not.

Of course, there is no particular problem in understanding why

[6] The unexplained ill-formedness of (42)b is, I suspect, a function of semantic assumptions linked to the operation of Raising with nominalizations like *tendency* (for such linkages, see Chapter 11). In particular, Raising with *tendency* seems linked to the assumption that the tendency in question is attributable to, or localized in, the entity designated by the raised NP. This would probably also account for the problem with examples like (15)b in the text. This aspect of Raising nominalizations requires detailed investigation, but I have not been able so far to look into it.

NPs after the *for* in examples like (38)a and (39)a should be superficial subjects. If one assumes, as indicated in footnote 9 of Chapter 4, that the subject NP of a clause *C* is the leftmost immediate constituent NP of *C*, then subject status follows directly for these cases, given the need to ignore prepositions and their associated structure, if any. Moreover, it might be unnecessary to ignore this if, as Kuno (personal communication) suggests, the *for* of infinitival clauses is associated, not with the subject NP, but with the entire complement NP. Hence, we have (43)a or, more likely (43)b.[7] It is perhaps not obvious, however, given a Raising analysis of nominalizations involving *tendency*, why the post-*of* NP

(43) a.

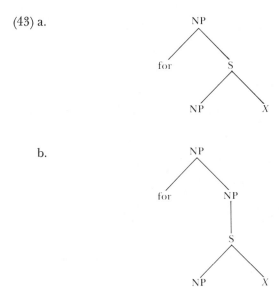

b.

<hr />

[7] In favor of this view, Kuno points out that in multiple-question cases like (i), *who* is preferable to *whom* after *for*:

(i) Who arranged for who to die?

(ii) *Who arranged for whom to die?

However, a preposition can normally determine *whom* if it is in construction with a *wh*-NP, even if *who* is also an option:

(iii) a. Who works for whom?
      b. Who works for who?

Moreover, a stronger argument for the claim that the *for* of infinitival clauses is not

in cases like (38)b and (39)b should *not* have the status of a superficial subject. I shall now indicate why this is an automatic consequence.

Under a Raising analysis of nominalizations, Raising actually applies in the clause underlying the nominalization. Thus, for (44)a, b

(44) a. that tendency for Melvin to insult people

  b. that tendency of Melvin's to insult people

  c.

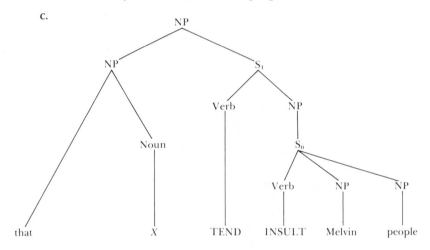

in construction with the following subject NP is available. As far as I know, the word *only* can never occur in the structural configuration shown in (iv), at least where the NP is "short," as in (v):

(iv)

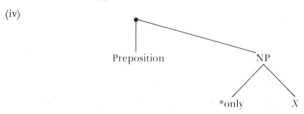

(v) a. *I talked to only Bob.
  b. *I decided on only the boat.
  c. *We voted for only him.
  d. *A picture of only him is on the table.
  e. *I gave the book to only Bob.

But the following cases are grammatical:

we might posit, extremely sketchily,[8] an underlying structure like (44)c. Here, *Melvin* is the subject of the clause S_0 throughout the cycle on S_0, and is raised only on the cycle of S_1, to derive (44)b, (44)a involving no application of Raising. The problem is, then, given contrasts like those in (38) and (39), that application of Raising on S_1, which is supposed to be a crucial part of the derivation of structures like (44)b, in which the post-*of* NP is claimed not to be a superficial subject, makes the raised NP the derived subject of S_1. Moreover, there is no way around this difficulty because, in those cases where structures like S_1 function as simple clauses rather than as components of a nominalization, the derived subject status is absolutely required, as examples like (45) show quite clearly:

(45) a. Not many people tend to like rotten grapes.

   b. Bob alone tended to like their rotten grapes.

Despite the fact that *Melvin* in (44)b must have gone through a stage in which it became the derived subject of S_1 in the output of Raising to (44)c, there is no real problem in accounting for its lack of ultimate surface subject status. For, in order to convert (44)c to (44)b, it is necessary for some nominalization rule to take away the main verb of S_1 and make it part of the head NP, generating the underlying structure of

---

(vi) a. For only Bob to come would be unfortunate.

   b. It would not be possible for only me to speak.

   c. I arranged for only him to have to take part.

I mentioned the property "short" because examples like the following seem acceptable:

(vii) I will speak to only those men who have passed their examinations.

[8] I should like to stress here that at no point am I committed, for either *tendency* or any other nominalization, to the view that the underlying structure includes a subassembly completely identical to that for the corresponding verbal, which is here *tend*. It is for this reason, among others, that I have written the main verbal element in S_1 of (44)c as TEND, rather than *tend*. No doubt, the relation is very close, and I do not wish to preclude identity in some cases, including this one. But the analysis does not depend on it. In other words, to say that *tendency* is derived from an underlying verbal structure like that in (44)c is not to say necessarily that it is derived from a cognate verbal. And I think this point generalizes to all nominalizations, and even to all cases of derivation.

the noun *tendency*. But, as indicated in footnote 21 of Chapter 6, the removal of the main verb of an *embedded*[9] clause causes the pruning of the S node defining that clause. Therefore, the structures in (46) are derived as shown in the diagrams. Furthermore, given our assumptions so far, it is a direct consequence that the NP *Melvin* is not a superficial subject in (44)b (=(46)d), since this requires that the NP be the leftmost immediate constituent NP of some clause. However, the NP *Melvin* in (46)d is neither the leftmost immediate constituent of any

(46) a. (44)c $\xRightarrow{\text{Raising}}$

(46) b.

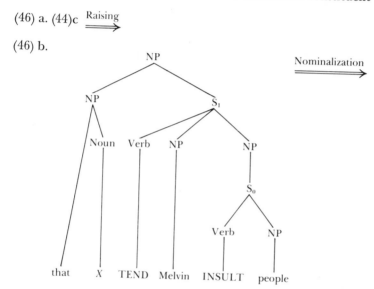

Nominalization
$\Longrightarrow$

[9] Reference to *embedded* clauses is crucial here. For instance, Gapping eliminates the main verb of clauses, but I do not want to say that this has the effect of pruning the S nodes of such clauses. Such pruning would yield very strange derived structures and, more importantly, interfere with other regularities. For example, we saw that *not*-initial NPs can be the subjects of gapped clauses, but the definition of surface subject would not apply to such clauses if they had lost their defining S nodes under pruning triggered by Gapping application. Such pruning would, however, be automatically avoided if verb-loss pruning of S nodes applied only to subordinate clauses. For then the clauses operated on by Gapping would not be subordinate. This is true even in cases like (i), suggested by Ross.

(i) That she loves him and he her is obvious.

For in (i), only the entire subject clause is a subordinate clause. Its two conjuncts are coordinate constituents of that clause. Hence, Gapping would not, under our assumptions, prune the S node over *he her*.

(46) c.

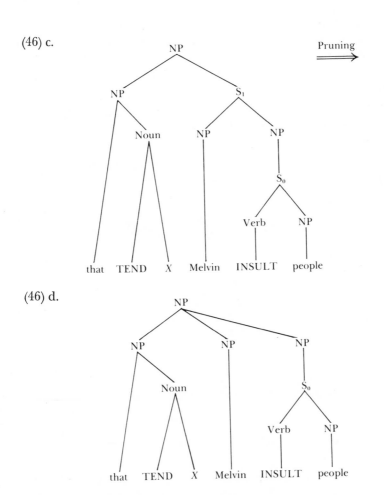

(46) d.

constituent nor an immediate constituent of any S. It thus totally fails to meet the conditions for subjecthood.

In contrast, the structure of (44)a, derived from (44)c with *no* application of Raising, and hence only through the relevant application of Nominalization and the pruning it triggers, would be as shown in (47), if Kuno's suggestion about the status of *for* is adopted. And in such a structure, *Melvin* meets the conditions for (surface) subjecthood. It follows that a Raising analysis of nominalizations does provide appropriately contrasting derived structures for cases like (44)a, b. It might be noted that the presence of the preposition *of* in examples like (44)b requires no special statement, since *of* is clearly the unmarked

(47)

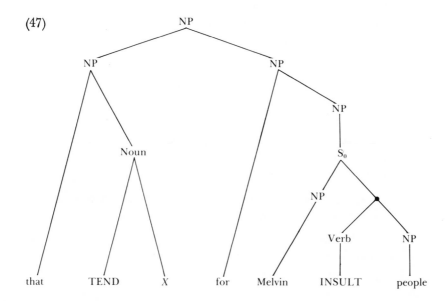

preposition occurring on the directly post-noun NP of a complex nominal.[10]

According to the Raising analysis just given, *for Melvin to insult people* in (44)a is a derived constituent, but *of Melvin's to insult people* in (44)b is not. There is independent evidence of various sorts for this contrast. Thus adverbial elements can be inserted between *tendency* and *for,* but not between *tendency* and *of.* On the other hand, adverbials are allowed after the *of* phrase, but not after the *for*:

(48) a.   The tendency at the turn of the century for men to beat their wives has been widely noted.

   b. * $\begin{Bmatrix} \text{A} \\ \text{That} \\ \text{The} \end{Bmatrix}$ tendency at the turn of the century of men('s) to beat

their wives has been widely noted.

[10] My rejection of the view that the italicized sequence in examples like (i) is a (derived) subject of the complement avoids the problem of having to recognize, in this unique class of cases, *of*-marked infinitival subjects, otherwise unknown.

(i) That tendency *of Jack's* to lie is shameless.

That is, given structures like those suggested by Kuno for infinitival *for,* the regularity is that infinitival subjects are never marked with prepositions. This, then, provides a further argument for denying the subject status of *of*-NPs like those in (i).

c. *The tendency for men at the turn of the century to beat their wives has been widely noted.

d. $\begin{Bmatrix} \text{A} \\ \text{That} \\ \text{The} \end{Bmatrix}$ tendency of men at the turn of the century to beat their wives has been widely noted.

These facts are consistent, under the proposed analysis, with a principle limiting such adverbials to points that are the boundaries of (derived) clauses. The following contrasts are also relevant:

(49) a. The tendency at the turn of the century was for men to beat their wives.

b. *The tendency at the turn of the century was of men('s) to beat their wives.

c. The tendency, which Bill noticed, for men to beat their wives is distressing.

d. *The tendency, which Bill noticed, of men('s) to beat their wives is distressing.

Examples (49)b, d also argue against any claim of constituent status for *of* + NP + infinitive sequences.

Next, note that the rule RNR, discussed in Section 4.8, treats the sequences beginning with *for* as constituents, but not those beginning with *of*:

(50) a. Bill is aware of the tendency for Melvin to lie but does not approve of the tendency for Melvin (him) to lie.

b. Bill is aware of the tendency but does not approve of the tendency—for Melvin to lie.

c. Bill is aware of that tendency of Melvin's to lie but does not approve of that tendency of Melvin's to lie.

d. *Bill is aware of that tendency but does not approve of that tendency—of Melvin's to lie.

While sentences like (50)b are strained and clumsy, to be sure, probably because they do not make maximum use of the possibilities of reduction under RNR, they have nothing like the impossible status of those such as (50)d, which supports a constituent structure contrast, given our knowledge that RNR operates only on constituents.

Furthermore, there are contrasts in extraposability:

(51) a. The tendency for the government to lie has developed only recently.

    b. That tendency of the government's to lie has developed only recently.

    c. The tendency has developed only recently for the government to lie.

    d.*The tendency has developed only recently of the government's to lie.

This view argues that the *of* . . . sequence is not a constituent, under the well-supported assumption that the extraposition rule in question operates only on (actual NP) constituents. It is interesting and significant, I believe, to contrast the behavior of *of* sequences with *tendency* with those following *possibility*:

(52) a. The possibility of our being arrested still exists.

    b. The possibility still exists of our being arrested.

The difference would follow naturally from an analysis that noted that *possibility,* like *possible,* is *not* an R-trigger, so that *of* . . . is a constituent in (52)a, in contrast to the raised structure of (51)b.

Finally, there are contrasts with respect to coordinate structures:

(53) a. The tendency for Melvin to come late and for Joan to leave early is shocking.

    b. *That tendency of Melvin's to come late and of Joan's to leave early is shocking.

This difference follows naturally from the assumption that the sequences that begin with *for* are constituents, hence conjoinable, but that those that begin with *of* are not, and are hence not conjoinable.

All in all, then, I think there is ample evidence that the status of the *for* sequences and *of* sequences in post-*tendency* position is different, and that this difference is attributable to the contrast between subject phrases and nonsubject phrases. It follows that the proposal to derive cases like (34) and (36) by NP preposing has little bearing on the question of whether Raising functions for these nominalizations. This rule would operate on the *of* phrases, which are not (derived) constituents of the complement clause.

One is driven then to the question of how the *of* phrases are derived and, in particular, how they are related derivationally to the NPs that are subjects in the *for* sequences. The difference is that, in the latter, one finds NPs that are surface complement subjects, in the former, NPs that are immediate constituents of constituents dominating the complement. But we know already that there is a rule that has essentially the effect of making this kind of change, namely, Raising. It should follow, as I have already indicated in sketching the derivation in (46), that the *of* phrases are related to the post-*for* NPs exactly as raised NPs are related to unraised NPs.

Given the differences in constituent structure and subject status between post-*of* NPs and post-*for* NPs, the only alternative to a Raising analysis would seem to be a new appeal to an Equi analysis of the *of* cases, thus to a claim that the underlying structure of (54)a is something like (54)b:

(54) a. that tendency of Melvin's to complain constantly

b. that tendency of Melvin's [$_S$for Melvin to complain constantly$_S$]

Earlier I rejected such an analysis for preposed genitive cases like (55):

(55) Melvin's tendency to complain constantly

Now it can be added that the same considerations show the inappropriateness of such a "transitive" analysis for cases like (54)a. *First,* there is the expected truth-functional equivalence between (56)a and (56)b, where the existence of one tendency guarantees the existence of the other.[11]

(56) a. that tendency of Melvin's to ignore Barbara

b. ?that tendency of Barbara's to get ignored by Melvin

Second, in quantifier cases like (57), the *each* is understood to bind the occurring NP.

11 Because of assumption linkages and other semantic constraints like that mentioned in footnote 6, the truth-functional equivalence does not guarantee full meaning equivalence. In fact, (56)a and (56)b quite clearly contrast in meaning, with the difference being the localization of the basis of the tendency (in Melvin in (56)a, in Barbara in (56)b).

(57) that tendency of John and Bill's to each claim the other has the
     money

Third, emphatic reflexives in such cases have the properties associated
with Raising, and not Equi:

(58) a. ? $\left\{ \begin{array}{l} \text{that} \\ \text{a} \end{array} \right\}$ tendency of Melvin's to himself tell outrageous stories

    b. *that wish of Melvin's to himself tell outrageous stories

Finally, it naturally strains credulity to invoke an Equi analysis for
examples like (54)a, but not for those like (55), as such diversity only
complicates the grammar. I conclude that Raising functions in the
derivation of *tendency* nominalizations.

    The situation with *likelihood* is confusing in certain respects. For,
despite the presence of a postposed *of*, I think that the structure of
likelihood examples is not superficially parallel to the *tendency of*
cases, but rather to the *tendency for* cases. Thus in (59) I should assign
contrasting derived structures.

(59) a. the likelihood of Bob's leaving early

    b. that tendency of Bob's to leave early

The phrase *of Bob's leaving* is a constituent, so that (59)a contains a
full gerundive nominal like those in (60):

(60) a. your discussion of Bob's leaving early

    b. your insistence on Bob's leaving early

And *Bob's* in this position is a subject, proved by the *not*-initial and
alone-final arguments:

(61) a. the likelihood of not many people(*'s) coming[12]

    b. the likelihood of Bob alone(?*'s) coming

Thus, while I claim that Raising has operated in (59)b, I deny its
operation in (59)a. But since I claim that Raising has operated in (62),

---

[12] A survey of examples with *likelihood, tendency,* etc., will indicate that the principles determining the need, possibility, or optionality of the genitive on the NP
following *of* are very complicated and poorly understood. Moreover, in many cases,
judgments are highly uncertain, a factor that the reader should take into account in
interpreting such examples.

it follows that I am committed to having the rule of NP preposing obligatory with *likelihood,* though optional with *tendency.*

(62) Bob's likelihood of leaving early

This claim is based on the assumption that this rule operates on (derived) constituents of the nominalization itself, and not on (subject) constituents of the complement within the nominalization (hence not on (59)a). In fact, as in the parallel discussion of Passive in Section 2.4, and the discussion of other rules at the end of Chapter 2, I think that a rule that could operate in a manner internal to nominalizations (as in (35)a, for example) and could also work down into a complement is not a possible rule for a human language. Under the analysis I suggest, this is unnecessary, because an application of Raising will intervene here, as in the passivization and other cases, to make the former complement (subject) constituent a constituent of a dominating phrase so that some purely internal operation can then apply.

For *continuation* and *persistence,* the facts seem to indicate again that the post-*of* phrases function as derived nonsubjects:

(63) a. The continuation of (*not) many Turks as members is regrettable.

b. The continuation of Bob (*alone) as a participant would be unfortunate.

(64) a. The persistence of (*not) many companies as members is frightening.

b. The persistence of Jack (*alone) as a reserve is worrisome.

Thus Raising is presumably to be regarded as obligatory for these examples.

10.3 B-Element, N-Element, and W-Element Nominalization Analogues

It is apparent, then, that there are, in conflict with principle (3), a number of cases of Raising-derived nominalizations corresponding to R-triggers of the A-element type. What of Raising-derived nominalizations corresponding to type II R-triggers, that is, those analogous to cases involving B-elements, N-elements, and W-elements?

In Chomsky's (1970) original discussion of the lexicalist hypothesis and nominalizations, there was no mention of any cases involving B-verb and other analogues. In Chomsky (1972: 90), he made the following claim:

First, derived nominals correspond only to forms that exist prior to syntactically motivated transformations. Thus we have such forms as (37) but not (38):
(37) (i) —
     (ii) —
     (iii) —
     (iv) the belief that John was killed
     (v) —
(38) (i) —
     (ii) —
     (iii) —
     (iv) the belief of John to have been killed
     (v) —
Notice that the proper generalization concerning admissible derived nominals is expressed in terms of deep structure—i.e., the level prior to application of syntactically motivated transformations— . . .[13]

But, in Chomsky (to appear: footnote 56), this claim is withdrawn:

In Chomsky (forthcoming) I suggested that the impossibility of "John's belief of Bill to win" was a consequence of the lexicalist hypothesis regarding derived nominals. The considerations just mentioned, however, indicate that the example was irrelevant to that issue, since "John's belief for Bill to win" is also impossible.

However, as we shall see, in general, a claim of irrelevance is too strong. What really follows is only that the nonoccurrence of such nominals in particular cases can provide no evidence in favor of the lexicalist view. But the occurrence, if any, of such nominals definitely would count against it, given a Raising grammar for B-verbs, etc.

The facts seem to be these. In the case of N-verb R-triggers, I can find no nominalization analogues:

(65) a. *your prevention of Bob from leaving

   b. *your stop(page) of Bob from leaving

   c. *your keep of Bob from leaving

---

[13] The term "syntactically motivated" is used by Chomsky again and again in this paper (twice in the present quotation alone), often in very forceful ways. Despite this, no hint of a definition has ever been offered. For me, moreover, it is difficult to imagine a definition that does not beg the presently much discussed and controversial question of whether there is any nonnull domain of syntax totally distinct from semantics.

   d. *your prohibition of Bob from leaving

   e. *your dissuasion of Bob from leaving

   f. *your deterrence of Bob from leaving

   g. *your discouragement of Bob from leaving

The same seems initially to be true of B-verbs, regardless of whether they are subject to DOC or related constraints:[14]

(66) a. *your belief of Bob to be dishonest

   b. *your proof of Bob to be dishonest

   c. *your finding of Bob to be dishonest

   d. *your demonstration of Bob to be dishonest

   e. *your admission of Bob to be dishonest

   f. *your disclosure of Bob to be dishonest

But, of course, many of these nominalizations can occur with *that* complements:

(67) a.   your belief that Bob is dishonest

   b.   your proof that Bob is dishonest

   c. *your finding that Bob was dishonest[15]

   d.   your demonstration that Bob was dishonest

   e.   your admission that Bob was dishonest

   f.   your disclosure that Bob was dishonest

These facts would thus apparently support principle (3), given a Rais-

---

[14] Baker and Ross have independently suggested to me that there exists an output condition blocking all nominals of this form:

(i) *[X Noun of NP infinitive]

If so, it is this constraint that blocks examples like those in (65) and (66), and these forms yield no support for the lexicalist hypothesis even with a rule of Raising operating into superordinate object position.

[15] This sequence of words is, of course, well-formed in certain contexts, but, when it is, it has the structure of a gerundive verbal complement, indicated by the impossibility of a preceding adjective:

(i) your foolish$\left\{ \begin{matrix} \text{admission} \\ \text{*finding} \end{matrix} \right\}$that Bob was dishonest

ing analysis of the verbal analogues. However, given Chomsky's (to appear) present non-Raising system, they would be irrelevant.

The situation with W-verbs is a little more complicated, but basically the same:

(68) a. *your desire of Bob to win

    b. *your expectation of Bob to win

    c. *your hatred of Bob to win

    d. *your intention of Bob to win

    e. *your liking of Bob to win

    f. *your meaning of Bob to win

    g. *your need of Bob to win

    h. *your preference of Bob to win

    i. *your want of Bob to win

    j. *your wish of Bob to win

The complication arises from the fact that, as in the verbal situation, some of these nominalizations can occur not only with *that* clauses but also with full *for*-initial infinitival clauses:

(69) a. your desire for Bob to win

    b. ?your intention for Bob to win

    c. your need for Bob to win

    d. your wish for Bob to win

However, it is easy to see, on grounds of adverbial insertability, conjoinability, and the distribution of *not*-initial and *alone*-final NPs, that the post-*for* NPs are derived constituents of the complement clauses, that is, unraised:

(70) a. your desire for Bob alone to win

    b. your wish for not many people to be present

    c. your need, during this period, for people to be with you

    d. *your need for people, during this period, to be with you

    e. your desire for Bob to win and for Sally to lose

    f. *your desire for Bob and for Sally to win

Hence these cases are not candidates for recognition of Raising within nominalizations.

It might appear, then, that the entire class of cases involving Raising operation into superordinate object position, that is, the entire class of type II R-triggers, is without nominalization analogues. This is not true, however. Recall that the verb *estimate* was argued at some length to be a B-element R-trigger and was also noted to take gerundive complements with *as*. But one finds the following cases:

(71) a. your estimate that Bob's weight is 200 pounds

　　 b. ?your estimate of Bob's weight to be 200 pounds

　　 c. your estimate of Bob's weight as (being) 200 pounds.

That is, the *as* type of complements have perfect analogues, while the infinitival ones seem slightly strained. The following shows that the *of* phrases are not surface subjects, that is, not part of the complement:

(72) a. *Your estimate of Bob's weight alone $\left\{ \begin{matrix} \text{as (being)} \\ \text{to be} \end{matrix} \right\}$ 200 pounds was incorrect.[16]

　　 b. *Your estimate of not many people's weights $\left\{ \begin{matrix} \text{as (being)} \\ \text{to be} \end{matrix} \right\}$ 300 pounds was wrong.

　　 c. *Your estimate, without even using a scale, of Bob's weight $\left\{ \begin{matrix} \text{as (being)} \\ \text{to be} \end{matrix} \right\}$ over 200 pounds was incorrect.

　　 d. Your estimate of Bob's weight, without even using a scale, $\left\{ \begin{matrix} \text{as (being)} \\ \text{?to be} \end{matrix} \right\}$ over 200 pounds was incorrect.

　　 e. *Your estimate of Bob's weight $\left\{ \begin{matrix} \text{as (being)} \\ \text{to be} \end{matrix} \right\}$ 300 pounds and of Mary's weight $\left\{ \begin{matrix} \text{as (being)} \\ \text{to be} \end{matrix} \right\}$ 200 pounds was incorrect.

　　 f. I didn't want to criticize your estimate of Bob's weight as

---

[16] Example (72)a has a grammatical reading, I think, but this is irrelevant, since according to that reading *alone* does not mean 'only', but it means rather something like 'not in combination with others'.

(being) 300 pounds, but I had to take issue with your estimate of his weight as (being) 300 pounds.

g. *I didn't want to criticize your estimate—but I had to take issue with your estimate—of Bob's weight as (being) 300 pounds.

Thus, if a Raising analysis of nominal *estimate* is rejected, the alternative would have to be one in which the post-*of* NPs here start out as noncomplement constituents, presumably an Equi analysis. While it is difficult to apply the argument about truth-value equivalences under passivization,[17] the quantifier argument indicates the inappro-

[17] It is nevertheless possible to utilize what is, I think, essentially a variant of this argument, based on non-Passive-related pairs like (i), which have a truth-functional equivalence.

(i) a. John is superior to Max.
     b. Max is inferior to John.

Observe the difference between Equi cases like (ii) and Raising cases like (iii):

(ii) a. John hopes to be superior to Max.
      b. Max hopes to be inferior to John.

(iii) a. John is certain to be superior to Max.
      b. Max is certain to be inferior to John.

Here, the truth values of (ii)a, b are fully independent, but those of (iii)a, b are not. A Raising analysis of *estimate* nominalizations is then supported by the extensional equivalence of pairs like (iv):

(iv) a. your estimate of John's weight as being greater than Max's by ten pounds
     b. your estimate of Max's weight as being less than John's by ten pounds

Thus, in any world where the nominals in (iv)a and (iv)b both have referents, they have the same referent. So if the estimate in (iv)a is off by six pounds, so is that in (iv)b. This is not to make the (false) claim that (iv)a and (iv)b have the same meaning. On the contrary, they differ in meaning in just the way that the following cases differ, which is, roughly, that (v)a assumes that Max's weight is the standard, while (v)b assumes that John's is:

(v) a. John's weight is greater than Max's by ten pounds.
     b. Max's weight is less than John's by ten pounds.

Observe, though, that in clear cases of nominalizations involving Equi, there are not only meaning differences but sharp truth value or extensional differences as well:

(vi) a. your wish to be superior to the king
     b. the king's wish to be inferior to you

Clearly, there can exist some world in which the referent of (vi)a is distinct from that of (vi)b. In fact, if both have referents, no other situation is imaginable. I suggest, then, that pairs like *greater/less* and *superior/inferior* provide a test like passivi-

priateness of an Equi analysis, which is a priori evident anyway, given the R-trigger status of the verbal analogue *estimate* and the extremely close semantic relations between verbal and nominal *estimate*:[18]

(73) your estimate of Bob and Tom's weights as each being over 300 pounds

Here *each* binds the occurring NP, and not some deleted one, as in typical Raising cases. Moreover, emphatic reflexives can float away from the post-*of* NP to positions internal to the complement, consistent with a Raising treatment, but not with an Equi derivation:

(74) your estimate of Bob's weight as being (in) itself more than Bill and Tom's combined

I suggest, then, that nominal *estimate* must be regarded as the nominalization of a B-verb R-trigger, with structures like (75) formed on the sketchy analogue of (46), from a common underlying structure like (76)a:

(75) a. $\left\{ \begin{array}{l} \text{the estimate by you} \\ \text{your estimate} \end{array} \right\}$ of Bill's weight $\left\{ \begin{array}{l} \text{as being} \\ \text{?to be} \end{array} \right\}$ 300 pounds
    b.

---

zation for the difference between "extra" NP underlying structures operated on by Equi and simple complement structures without an "extra" NP, operated on by Raising.

[18] Both verbal and nominal *estimate* are equally subject to the constraint that the complement specify a precise measure:

(i) a. *I estimated the weight of that boat to be enormous.
     b. *my estimate of the weight of that boat as (being) enormous

Similarly, they both require that a raised NP that is not an "empty" pronoun designate the thing that is estimated:

(ii) a. *I estimated Bob to weigh 200 pounds.
     b. *my estimate of Bob as weighing 200 pounds

However, while verbal *estimate* permits the raising of "empty" elements, as already noted, nominal *estimate* does not:

(iii) a. I estimate there to be 200 people in this blimp.
      b. *my estimate of there as being 200 people in this blimp

(iv) a. I estimate it to be snowing six inches per hour.
     b. *my estimate of it to be snowing six inches per hour

But possibly this is attributable to independent constraints. See Ross (to appear a, to appear b).

Here again, the operation of Nominalization prunes the S node defining the clause headed by S_1, according to the principle that the S node defining a subordinate clause is pruned if that clause loses its head verbal. Later rules will then turn (76)c into (75), by de-finitizing the complement, making it either infinitival or gerundive with *as*, by adding *of* before *Bob's weight*, and by either optionally preposing *you* with the genitive or adding *by*.

(76) a.

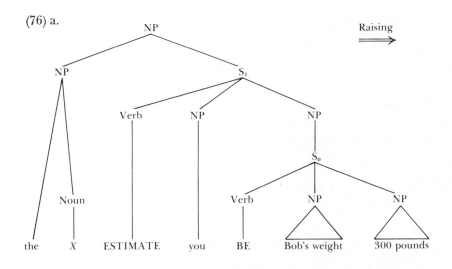

b.

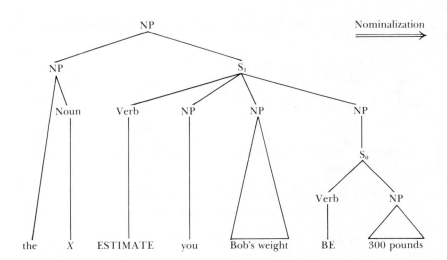

c.

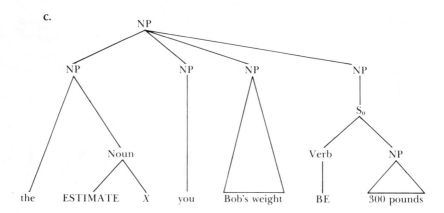

Recall also that the verb *recognize* was suggested to be the kind of type II R-trigger whose complement ends up in *as* + gerundive form. But there are nominalization correlates for *recognize*:

(77) a. I recognize him as (being) the outstanding living malingerer.

b. $\left\{ \begin{array}{l} \text{the} \\ \text{my} \end{array} \right\}$ recognition of him as (being) the outstanding living malingerer

Again, the facts indicate that the post-*of* NP is not a surface subject:

(78) a. the recognition of many officials as (being) criminals

b. *the recognition of not many officials as (being) criminals

(79) *the recognition of Bob alone as (being) a suitable candidate for dogcatcher

Moreover, the inappropriateness of an Equi analysis is indicated by a variety of factors, including the truth-value equivalence in (80):

(80) a. your recognition of the queen as superior to the king

b. your recognition of the king as inferior to the queen.

Compare the following, where there is a lack of equivalence, and a justified Equi analysis:

(81) a. your request to the queen to be superior to the king

b. your request to the king to be inferior to the queen

Similarly, in (82) the quantifier binds the occurring NP.

(82) your recognition of Bob and Tom as each being capable of speaking alone

Finally, floating emphatic reflexives are possible:

(83) the recognition of Mary's participation as being by itself a guarantee of victory

I conclude that Raising is involved in the derivation of *recognition* nominalizations.

Although nominalization analogues to type II R-triggers are rare, to be sure, cases exist. Thus they combine with the A-element type of nominalizations to show the falsehood of principle (3). But, if (3) is incorrect, then any (lexicalist) theory that has (3) as a consequence is also empirically disconfirmed.

10.4 Other Cases

In spite of these conclusions, the original observations that motivated Chomsky's formulations about the relation between nominalizations and clausal structures derived by rules like Raising remain *approximately* correct—they indicate a real tendency, if not an absolute law. This requires some explanation. A possible explanation is offered by Ross (1972b) in terms of a categorization of rule domains according to the part of speech type of their head (verb, adjective, noun). Ross argues that for all sorts of operations, there is a hierarchy of productivity in which rules apply with maximum freedom for constituent domains with verbal heads, with less freedom for those with adjectival heads, and with the least of all for those with noun heads. If such an account can be sustained, of course, the relative rarity of Raising-derived nominalizations as against Raising-derived clauses takes its place as one expected tendency among many. This account also simultaneously explains why adjective-headed clauses involving Raising— that is, those headed by *likely, certain, sure,* etc.—are much rarer than those whose heads are pure verbs. It may also ultimately offer hope of explaining why there are *no* known adjective cases of the type II R-trigger variety.[19]

19 This cannot be a purely semantic fact, since, alongside the W-verbs *desire, wish, want,* for example, there are adjectives like *anxious, eager,* which could logically trigger Raising, yielding such actually impossible clauses as (i), in contrast to such non-Raising examples as (ii):

In conclusion, there is no reason to think I have exhausted the list of Raising-derived nominalizations in this section, any more than there is to think that I have exhausted the lists of verbal and adjectival R-triggers in earlier sections. For example, I agree with Jespersen (1969: 47) that *fail* serves as an R-trigger, and this sense has a nominalization analogue:

(84) a. The bomb failed to go off.

    b. the bomb's failure to go off

    c. the failure of the bomb to go off

Again, it is easy to see that the post-*of* NP is not a derived subject, hence not a constituent of the complement in surface structure:

(85) a.   the failure of (*not) many bombs to go off

    b.   the failure of your bomb (*alone) to go off

    c. *the failure of Bob to speak and of Max to stop speaking

The relevant sense of *fail* is essentially 'not',[20] or possibly 'not occur', where the more common meaning is 'not succeed', consistent with the "intransitive" analysis of an A-element R-trigger. No doubt, then, *failure* is another Raising-derived nominalization.

Other cases suggested by late observation include *opportunity* and *chance*:

(i) a. *I am anxious of Bob [$_S$ to go$_S$].

    b. *I am eager of there [$_S$ to be a conference$_S$].

(ii) a. I am anxious [$_S$ for Bob to go$_S$].

    b. I am eager [$_S$ for there to be a conference$_S$].

20 By saying "essentially" here, I refer to the fact that, although the core meaning of this sense of *fail* is 'not,' there is an associated assumption about the complement of the predicate being expected, appropriate, or the like. In this sense, the division of meaning of *fail* into 'not' + some assumption is similar to the division needed for *lack,* which has a core meaning 'not have' but an associated assumption about appropriateness or something of the sort. In both cases, explicit negation, questioning, etc., affect only the core meaning of these cases. What is required but not yet available is a theory of how core meanings, which are naturally specifiable in tree forms representing the strict logical form of sentences, are related formally to assumptions like those associated with *fail* and *lack,* which do not seem capable of being naturally associated with the underlying tree structures. We shall see later that such assumptions are also associated with rules like Raising, so perhaps it is better to say technically that in cases like *fail, lack,* the assumptions are associated with the rules that introduce these lexical items into trees rather than with the items themselves.

(86) a. my opportunity to date Louise

    b. your chance to escape

Note that these are quite parallel to *tendency* in that they occur in superficially "intransitive" structures, rendering an Equi analysis immediately suspect:

(87) a. the opportunity for me to date Louise

    b. the chance for you to escape

   Finally, one should investigate the possibility that the nouns in the following phrases are Raising-derived nominals:

(88) a. his air of honesty

    b. his position of indifference

    c. his reputation $\left\{ \begin{array}{l} \text{for cruelty} \\ \text{as a fink} \end{array} \right\}$

    d. his look of surprise

    e. his tone of regret

    f. his manner of replying

I have no doubt that further research will reveal many additional cases of Raising-derived nominals, although Ross's principle suggests that these will always be considerably less numerous than verbal or adjectival examples.

11

Raising and Meaning

As early as 1969, Partee (1971) and others pointed out examples like the following:

(1) a. Nobody is certain to pass the test.

　 b. It is certain that nobody will pass the test.

Examples (1)a and (1)b differ both in truth conditions and in meaning, despite the fact that *certain* is an A-element R-trigger, but they seem to differ syntactically only in that in (1)a Raising has actually applied. However, contrasts like those in (1), though quite interesting and significant from many points of view, do not provide a serious problem for an account of Raising. For there are general principles governing the scope of quantifiers that account for the differences between such pairs, quite independently of Raising. The difference in (1) involves the relative scopes of the predicate corresponding to *certain*, on the one hand, and the negative and quantifier underlying *nobody*, on the other. But the facts follow from the general principle, no matter how it is ultimately formalized,[1] that left-to-right precedence in grammatical structure[2] correlates with wider scope in logical structure. Observe the somewhat parallel difference between pairs related by Tough Movement, which follows from the same sort of principles:

(2) a. Nothing is hard for Melvin to lift.

　 b. It is hard for Melvin to lift nothing.

I shall have nothing more to say about such cases.
Now consider sentences like (3):

(3) a. Melvin struck me as honest.

　 b. It struck me that Melvin was honest.

Given our claim that *strike* is an A-element R-trigger, these sentences seem to differ syntactically only in that Raising has applied in (3)a, but

---

[1] I favor a formulation along the lines of Lakoff (1969).
[2] A key point that has never been determined satisfactorily is exactly what levels of grammatical structure are relevant for such constraints.

not in (3)b. Here there is no question of quantifier scope. And yet there is a difference in meaning between such pairs. This was apparently first noted by Cantrall (1970: 2), who observed:

. . . but as far as I can see, strike does not undergo RAISING in the manner described, if transformations are seen as meaning preserving:

9.   It just now struck me that my wife has been dead two years to-morrow

10. *My wife (has) just now struck me as having been dead two years tomorrow

11. *It strikes Mary that Max has a larger liver than he has

12. Max strikes Mary as having a larger liver than he has

The difference in meaning between such pairs is often subtle but is brought out by the proper choice of example, as Cantrall's 9 and 10. Thus consider (4):

(4) a. Julius Caesar struck me as honest.

    b. It struck me that Julius Caesar was honest.

If we assume that the term *Julius Caesar* designates the well-known Roman figure, there is no context in which I, for example, can really use (4)a. Example (4)b, on the other hand, could naturally be utilized in a discussion of Rome, famous Romans, etc.

These contextual contrasts are, I claim, a function of differences in meaning. I cannot use (4)a, because to do so implies (i) that I have, in fact, had some kind of perceptual experience of Julius Caesar, and (ii) that the judgment expressed is a function of this experience. Since (i) is false, (ii) is also. Note that (4)a would become natural in a context of time travel, etc. On the other hand, (4)b is normal in ordinary discourse, because it makes no assumption about the speaker's experiences vis-à-vis Julius Caesar. Observe also that (i) and (ii) explain what is wrong with Cantrall's example 10, since the judgment expressed could not have been based on perceptual experience of the entity designated by the raised NP (under normal assumptions about dead people being buried, etc.). Let us refer to the feature of meaning that characterizes sentences like 4(a), that is, (i) and (ii), as *P*.

It seems that *P* correlates with Raising application in clauses whose R-trigger is *strike*. That is, to apply Raising with *strike* commits the user to the assumption *P* about the entity designated by the NP that is raised. I should like to argue that, in fact, *P* is more properly regarded as linked with Raising than as a part of the meaning of the item *strike*. In particular, negation, questioning, etc., of *strike* clauses do not relate to *P*:

(5) a. Julius Caesar didn't strike me as honest.

b. Did Julius Caesar strike you as honest?

In (5)a, *P* is not at all negated. Example (5)a can be honestly used by a speaker only with the experience represented by *P* to negate the honesty of the individual. Similarly, in using (5)b, the speaker assumes that the addressee has had the experience represented by *P* and that his judgment will be determined by this. Thus *P* cannot be questioned or negated, as it is not under the scope of negation or questioning in the main clause. Similarly, if one embeds *strike* sentences, one finds that *P* is not under the scope of the main verbs.

(6) a. I believe that Julius Caesar struck me as honest.

b. I forgot that Julius Caesar struck me as honest.

Thus (6)a does not say I believe *P*, nor does (6)b imply I forgot *P*. In these respects, *P* behaves with respect to the core meaning of *strike*, just as that aspect of meaning which distinguishes *lack* from *not have* does and just as that which distinguishes *fail* from *not*.

I suggest, then, that we are dealing here with a special feature of natural languages, namely, the linkage of certain *assumptions* (like *P*) with certain rules (applications). These assumptions are not part of the core meanings of sentences and are not under the scope of explicit negations, questionings, higher predicates, etc. It is thus an important,[3]

---

[3] The solution must be able to handle cases like (i), that is, examples in which the raised NP corresponds to an existential quantifier under the scope of negation, such that, in an obvious sense, there is no referent.

(i) No one there struck me as intelligent.

The question arises whether such sentences can be treated in accord with the claim in the text that the assumption linked to Raising with *strike* is not under the scope of explicit negations, etc. Baker suggests that they can be, along the following lines:

(ii) Assumption: There exists a set *X* (denoted by the NP undergoing Raising) such that for all *a* in *X*, *a* satisfies condition *C*.

(iii) Assertion: There does not exist an *a* in *X* such that it struck me that *a* was intelligent.

technical problem as to how their relation with core meanings and grammatical structure should be described. I have no serious proposal to make[4] beyond the view that we must, for example, say that a derivation in which *strike* actually serves as an R-trigger is necessarily linked to *P*. Further, this linkage involves coreference between the experiencer NP of *strike* and the element (variable) in *P* which designates the individual who has had the perceptual experience in question.

I have suggested that *P* is linked to Raising application with the A-element R-trigger *strike*. Some support for the view that Raising is relevant comes from the fact that a similar pattern seems to exist for the B-element R-trigger *find*. Thus contrast the following:

(7) a. I found Julius Caesar (to be) boring.

    b. I found (that) Julius Caesar was boring.

These cases seem to differ just as such *strike* pairs as (8) do:

(8) a. Julius Caesar struck me as boring.

    b. It struck me that Julius Caesar was boring.

Example (7)a is also unusable by me or my contemporaries outside a time machine context, and it involves either *P* or an assumption very much like it. There is, however, an important difference between *find* and *strike* in this regard, to which I shall return later. The similarity between the semantic characteristics of pairs of derivations like (7) and (8) might, however, ultimately be usable to construct a further argument for Raising in such derivations, for otherwise it is difficult to see what grammatical property binds the two sets together.

Recall now the argument utilized on several occasions earlier to help distinguish Raising structures from those generated by Equi, the argument about truth-functional equivalence with passivization. This argument took it to be support for Raising that pairs like (9)a and (9)b are truth-functionally equivalent.

(9) a. Jim is likely to call Joan.

    b. Joan is likely to be called by Jim.

---

[4] But I suggest an investigation of the notion of regarding such linkages as described by transderivational rules that link one derivation (that in which Raising applies) to (the logical structure of) another derivation (providing the meaning of the assumption).

But now examine (10):

(10) a. Jim struck me as having outplayed Ted.

    b. Ted struck me as having been outplayed by Jim.

One's initial impression may be that these are not truth-functionally equivalent since, for example, (10)a might be false if I had never met Jim, while (10)b might be true if I had met Ted. I think, though, that this is a confusing way of describing such sentences. Rather, I claim that one must always consider sentences that are linked to some assumption like P first in terms of whether P is true. If P is, in fact, false, then the sentence is inappropriate, weird, contextually anomalous, or something of the sort. Moreover, pairs like (10)a, b, with different raised NPs, involve different tokens of P, since P refers to perceptual experience of the entity designated by the raised NP. Thus the truth conditions for the different tokens of P are different in the two cases. However, once the claims involving the tokens of P are separated out, I think (10)a, b are truth-functionally equivalent. That is, if I express the judgment that Jim outplayed Ted, then I express the judgment that Ted was outplayed by Jim, regardless of whether I arrived at this judgment on the basis of experience of either Jim or Ted or both or neither. It follows that, at best, to apply the truth-functionality argument, one must take care to distinguish core meanings from linked assumptions like P and to hold the truth values of related assumptions like P constant to avoid confusion. I think, then, that this argument does support a Raising analysis of *strike* sentences if applied in these terms. The problem of linked assumptions is the first of those clouding factors relating to this argument mentioned in Chapter 7.

Suppose it is true, then, although I do not claim to have done much more than suggest the plausibility of this, that certain rule applications, particularly certain applications of Raising, are linked formally in some as yet technically unspecified way to assumptions like P. This gives a quite different way of looking at certain contrasts that have previously been treated in terms of contrasting underlying tree structures.

Thus, recall the cases discovered by Huddleston, mentioned in Section 9.4, in which *allow* sentences such as (11) are ambiguous, according to whether the permission is understood to have been given directly to Bob, or not.

(11) I allowed Bob to leave.

According to Huddleston's quite traditional analysis, similar to that given by Chomsky (1965: 22–23), Rosenbaum (1967), and Stockwell, Schachter, and Partee (1968) for parallel cases, this difference would be represented by the presence or not of a third NP in the contrasting cases, an NP designating Bob. But, an assumption linkage analysis like that suggested for *strike* and *find* offers, I believe, another possibility. The act designated by *allow* can be regarded logically as binary for both readings of sentences like (11). In all cases, *allow* must relate an individual with power to some potential state of affairs. It states that such an individual did not prevent that state of affairs. Suppose, then, one claims that the core meaning of *allow* is neutral with respect to how the "permission" is expressed. But suppose one says further that there is some assumption, called Q, which is *optionally* associated with Raising application triggered by *allow*, an assumption that the power-possessing individual expressed his permission to the individual designated by the raised NP. Presumably Q could be formulated in such a way that it was an automatic consequence that this individual be mind-possessing, accounting for the fact that the reading in question is found only when the raised NPs are "animate" in the traditional sense. In this way, the meaning difference between the two senses of sentences like (11) would be treated in a way parallel to the differences associated with Raising application or not with *strike* and *find*, that is, without underlying tree-structural differences.

If such a parallel is right, one expects that the positive assumption that distinguishes the two senses of *allow* cannot be under the scope of negation, questioning, and higher predicates, just like P. And consider (12):

(12) a. I didn't allow Bob to leave.

    b. Did you allow Bob to leave?

    c. I forgot that I allowed Bob to leave.

Surely, (12)a does not negate giving the permission to Bob; it simply negates giving permission for the leaving. Similarly, (12)b questions the giving of permission, not to whom this was expressed. And (12)c talks about forgetting giving permission, not forgetting giving it to Bob.

Thus, it seems to me that the aspect of the meaning of *allow* that I have designated as Q follows a pattern like P with *strike*.

The meaning of predicates like *allow* and *permit* is rather complicated. The situation seems much clearer to me in the case of causatives like (13), where the underlying structure clearly involves a predicate of causation in binary relation to an individual[5] and a state of affairs.

(13) a. I made Sylvia kiss John.

    b. ?I made John be kissed by Sylvia.

The sentences then differ in meaning because of an assumption that the causation is brought to bear through action aimed at the entity designated by the raised NP. Thus, if such assumptions are disregarded, the underlying tree structures of the sentences will be the same, even though the meanings differ, because they differ in linked assumptions, rather than in core properties.

An immediate difficulty with an assumption-linkage analysis of the kind of meaning contrasts under discussion is implicit in the facts already dealt with. As pointed out by Cantrall (1970: 18), *strike* does not permit existential *there* to be raised, and the same is true of other "empty" NPs like weather *it* and idiom chunks. An approach involving an assumption P can provide, I believe, a natural explanation for this problem. Namely, if P says that there must be perceptual experience of the entity designated by the logical correspondent of the raised NP, then the condition cannot possibly be met if the raised NP has no correspondent in logical structure, as in the case of the "empty" NP. Such an account would thus induce violations in all sentences that have *strike* as an R-trigger and an "empty" NP raised. So far, so good.

But what of cases like *find* and *make*, for which I have also suggested an assumption-linkage analysis, but where at least some "empty" NPs can be raised?

(14) a. I made it rain.

    b. I made there (appear to) be two people present.

(15) a. I found there to be no beer in the boat.

    b. I found tabs to have been kept on Melvin.

---

[5] This is, no doubt, an oversimplification, since more likely, as McCawley (to appear a) has argued, CAUSE relates two events. I shall ignore this in what follows.

Clearly, the assumptions associated with *make* and *find* also cannot be met in these cases. The only solution that has occurred to me is that whereas *P*, in association with *strike*, is stated in absolute terms, the assumptions associated with *make, find,* and similar cases would be *conditional.* That is, it would say that *if* the raised NP has a correspondent in logical structure, then it must have the properties described in the assumption. Thus absolute assumption linkages would impose one class of what have traditionally been called "selectional restrictions," while conditional linkages would not.[6, 7]

[6] The situation may be even more complicated, however. Thus, in general, there is no visible assumption associated with Raising application for a verb like *believe.* But note the contrasts in the following cases:

(i) a. I believe that I am of Turkish ancestry.
b. ?I believe myself to be of Turkish ancestry.

(ii) a. I believe that I am drunk.
b. ?I believe myself to be drunk.

(iii) a. I believe that I am flying over Patagonia.
b. ?I believe myself to be flying over Patagonia.

(iv) a. I believe that I am talking to Melvin Kronzmeyer.
b. ?I believe myself to be talking to Melvin Kronzmeyer.

All of the *b* examples seem to involve some violation, which, no doubt, has to do with the fact that there is a subtle assumption associated with Raising in these cases involving reflexivization. But what that assumption is I do not know. The following strange contrast may also be related to assumptions:

(v) a. That leads me to believe (that) Joan is dead.
b. *That leads me to believe Joan to be dead.

[7] An interesting set of cases relevant to assumption linkage involves a set of verbal elements with the form Verb + *on*, including *bet on, depend on, bank on, count on, rely on.* Consider *depend on.* This occurs with both gerundive and infinitival complements:

(i) a. You can depend on him to do something decent.
b. You can depend on $\begin{Bmatrix} him \\ his \end{Bmatrix}$ doing something decent.

I should like to argue that sentences like (i)a are, in fact, derived by Raising. However, examples like (i)a and (i)b are not strict paraphrases. Compare the following:

(ii) a. ?You can depend on that corpse to remain here for another hour.
b. You can depend on that corpse's remaining here for another hour.

It seems clear again that the putative Raising examples entail the analogous unraised examples, but not conversely. That is, there seems to be an assumption linked

However, even this degree of technical flexibility is not sufficient for *allow* cases, where, if Huddleston is correct, even NPs with logical correspondents are in some cases assumption-linked if raised but not in other cases. We must then possibly countenance as well cases of optional linkage with rule applications for fixed lexical items.

I have suggested that assumptions linked to rule applications offer a possible alternative in certain cases to the "extra" NP analyses that have often been assumed in the past for types of semantic contrast. A complication arises, however, from the fact that for different cases there appears to be a partially distinct sort of alternative, one involving an "extra" predicate and Predicate Raising. This problem was touched on in Section 4.13, Chapter 7, Section 9.4, and Chapter 10 as well as in footnote 53 of Chapter 4, footnote 37 of Chapter 6, and footnote 11 of Chapter 10.

Let us consider first sentences with a verb like *persuade*:

(16) I persuaded Bob to marry Gladys.

The traditional analysis of this (see Chomsky, 1965: 22–23; Rosenbaum, 1967; Stockwell, Schachter, and Partee, 1968) would be as in (17), triggering Equi, which ultimately removes the complement subject.

(17) I persuaded Bob [Bob to examine Gladys]

But since these are causative sentences, an alternative to regarding *persuade* as a primitive element taking three NPs is one with logical motivation that factors *persuade* into a predicate CAUSE and a predicate like AGREE, and that assigns a structure for (16) like (18):

(18) CAUSE I [AGREE Bob [EXAMINE Bob Gladys]

In such an analysis (see Lakoff, 1970b), Equi would indeed apply, but as determined on the second cycle. The verb *persuade* would be inserted

with Raising application for *depend on*. Roughly this is that the dependable state of affairs is so because of the will(s) of the entities designated by the raised NPs. Hence (ii)a is anomalous because corpses have no wills, etc. Since it is easy to show that the post-*on* NP with infinitival complements in such cases is a main clause constituent, the alternative to a Raising analysis would involve distinct underlying structure types for the *a* and *b* examples in such pairs, a highly unsatisfactory account. I think that these verbal examples with *on* should thus provide a fruitful domain for studying the interaction between Raising application and particular linked semantic assumptions.

for the combination of CAUSE + AGREE generated by an application of Predicate Raising, which is subsequent, if an earlier conjecture was correct, to Raising application (affecting the underlying subject of AGREE), and which turns the complement of CAUSE into a quasi-clause. This analysis, as opposed to one for the simple transitives like *believe* and *expect* has an "extra" NP, to be sure, but it has it as the subject of an "extra" predicate, AGREE, which forms an additional level of structure and defines an intermediate cycle between the ultimate main verb level and the level of the surface complement verb, *examine* for (17).

In these terms, the semantically nonequivalent (17) and (19) differ as (18) and (20), that is, in terms of the subjects of AGREE.

(19) I persuaded Gladys to be examined by Bob.

(20) CAUSE I [AGREE Gladys [EXAMINE Bob Gladys]]

This analysis is formally isomorphic with the traditional "extra" NP analysis in one sense, though it differs in the greater degree of structure assigned, all of which is nevertheless logically motivated.

I think that "extra" predicate analyses are highly motivated for many cases like *persuade,* among which I would include those N-verbs found to yield semantic contrasts under complement passivization. Thus, I would suggest "extra" predicate analyses for such pairs as (21), with a complex dominating structure CAUSE I [NOT [   ]] in each case.

(21) a. I $\begin{Bmatrix} \text{discouraged} \\ \text{restrained} \\ \text{prohibited} \end{Bmatrix}$ Bob from kissing Gladys.

b. I $\begin{Bmatrix} \text{discouraged} \\ \text{restrained} \\ \text{prohibited} \end{Bmatrix}$ Gladys from being kissed by Bob.

Problems lie in determining the correct nature of the main predicate of the subordinate structure. Very roughly these seem to be for *discourage, restrain,* and *prohibit,* something like WISH, ABLE, and LEGAL, respectively. The other class of N-verbs, like *prevent* and *keep,* would differ from these verbs in not having this intermediate level of structure. Thus a pair like (22) would have the same underlying form, as shown in (23):

(22) a. I prevented Bob from kissing Gladys.

  b. I prevented Gladys from being kissed by Bob.

(23) CAUSE I [NOT [KISS Bob Gladys]]

This accounts for their truth-functional equivalence.

The existence of "extra" predicate analyses is the second factor mentioned in Chapter 7 as clouding the application of the truth-functional equivalence argument for Raising. For, clearly, if "extra" NP analyses like those suggested are correct, the lack of truth-functional equivalence does not disconfirm Raising analyses for complex cases in which some main verbs have been combined with others and in which Raising and Equi *both* apply.

Let us assume, then, that assumption-linkage analyses are motivated for some cases, and "extra" predicate analyses for others. A general problem is thus raised, of course. Namely, for some cases there would be a choice between these two sorts of analyses for representing semantic contrasts, with simple "extra" NP analyses providing a still further possibility. For example, how shall one analyze sentences like (24), noting that there are forms like (25)?

(24) I $\begin{Bmatrix} \text{chose} \\ \text{selected} \\ \text{picked} \end{Bmatrix}$ Larry to be my assistant.

(25) I $\begin{Bmatrix} \text{chose} \\ \text{*selected} \\ \text{*picked} \end{Bmatrix}$ that Larry be my assistant.

The alternatives include a Raising analysis. But this would have to be assumption-linked since examples like (26) have different meanings, with an extra component beyond the neutral (25), as in (27):

(26) a. I chose Bob to kiss Sylvia.

  b. I chose Sylvia to be kissed by Bob.

(27) a. I chose that Bob kiss Sylvia.

  b. I chose that Sylvia be kissed by Bob.

But it is at least conceivable that an "extra" predicate analysis could be suggested, such that (26)a, b would differ in underlying form as in (28):

(28) a. CHOOSE I [PR Bob [KISS BOB SYLVIA]]

　　b. CHOOSE I [PR Sylvia [KISS Bob Sylvia]]

One trouble with this analysis is that it is difficult to say what the predicate PR would be. For this and other reasons, I happen to think a Raising, assumption-linked analysis is correct here. But I am more interested at this point in clarifying the general problem of these alternatives.

Questions of assumption linkage to Raising versus other analyses are also raised by adjectival constructions like those in (29):

(29) a. It was cruel for Bob to hit the bird.

　　b. It was cruel of Bob to hit the bird.

These were briefly touched on in Section 4.12. Sentences (29)a and (29)b differ in meaning. Example (29)a does not really attribute the cruelty to Bob but attributes it to some unspecified individual(s), not excluding Bob. However, (29)b definitely attributes it to Bob. The difference is brought out by such pairs as the following:

(30) a.　It was cruel for the ship to abandon the survivors.

　　b. *It was cruel of the ship to abandon the survivors.

Here (30)a is perfectly normal, but (30)b involves personification of the ship, because it attributes cruelty to the entity designated by the post-*of* NP. The facts are even clearer with the following pairs suggested by Baker and McCawley, respectively:

(31) a. It was cruel $\left\{ \begin{array}{c} \text{for} \\ \text{*of} \end{array} \right\}$ the survivors to be abandoned.

　　b. It was cruel $\left\{ \begin{array}{c} \text{for} \\ \text{*of} \end{array} \right\}$ pot smoking to be punishable by death.

Two immediate alternatives suggest themselves for sentences like (29)a, b—a Raising analysis, linked to an assumption that the cruelty is attributed to the entity designated by the raised NP, or an "extra" NP + Equi analysis. The former would assign identical underlying tree structures to pairs like (29)a, b, the latter contrasting pairs. The most obvious virtue of the former is just that it would provide uniform underlying structures for such adjectival elements, specifying that in all cases a predicate *cruel* (*nice, mean,* and dozens of others) relates some un-specified individual to a state of affairs. The obvious drawback of such an analysis,[8] stressed by Kuno, is that it does not relate sentences like (29)b to those like *Bob was cruel.* Nor is it obvious what to say about those like (32):

(32) Bob was cruel to hit the bird.

I have no solutions to offer here, and it is obvious that these construc-tions provide a challenge to any approach to complement structures.

I shall not pursue this discussion of the relation between proposals about Raising and meaning. I think it is clear that the ultimate status of Raising for many constructions depends on questions about assump-tion linkage, "extra" predicate analyses, and Predicate Raising, matters that have only begun to be considered recently and remain mostly terra incognita. I shall end this section by simply giving a representa-tive, though quite incomplete, list of the more obvious verbs that must be considered from the point of view of the various alternatives just gone over:

(33) accuse, allow, appoint, beg, choose, command, consider, convince, designate, deter, discourage, dissuade, drive, elect, encourage, feel, force, get, have, hear, implore, lead, let, make, name, nominate, order, permit, persuade, promise, restrain, see, select, smell, tell, urge, watch

[8] Another, very serious drawback would be the fact that a Raising analysis here would make these the only adjectives outside of the A-element class which function as R-triggers.

12
Varia

12.1 A-Element Raising Arguments

In this section, I shall present very tersely a brief sketch of arguments that support the view that some potential R-trigger is actually an A-element R-trigger. Each argument is intended to disconfirm the position that the relevant sentences are derived by Equi, with no application of Raising and with the relevant NPs having an underlying origin in the main clause. As noted earlier, the arguments will all be given with *seem*.

12.1.1 Existential *There*

In simple clauses, existential *there* is found only with a restricted class of verb structures containing an indefinite NP and either a form of *be* or one of a handful of other existential items (*arise, develop, exist, remain*, etc.):

(1) a. There is a man in your bed.

   b. *There groans a man in your bed.

But just these selections exist "across" *seem*:

(2) a. There seems to be a man in your bed.

   b. *There seems to groan a man in your bed.

A Raising analysis explains the correlation without any special statement about *seem*, without expanding the rule to introduce *there*, and without any special deletion rule distinct from Equi, to delete *there*, if a pseudo-Equi analysis is chosen.

12.1.2 Weather *It*

Verbs like *rain, snow,* and *sleet* occur only with the subject NP *it*:

(3) a. It is $\left\{\begin{array}{l}\text{snowing}\\\text{sleeting}\end{array}\right\}$.

   b. *Ice is $\left\{\begin{array}{l}\text{snowing}\\\text{sleeting}\end{array}\right\}$.

The same restriction exists for *seem*, which follows from a Raising analysis without special statement:

(4) a. It seems to be $\left\{\begin{array}{l}\text{snowing}\\\text{sleeting}\end{array}\right\}$.

   b. *Ice seems to be $\left\{\begin{array}{l}\text{snowing}\\\text{sleeting}\end{array}\right\}$.

12.1.3 Subject Idiom Chunk (due to David Perlmutter)
There are idioms like *the cat has his tongue,* so that some rule must associate a clause of this type with a special meaning. Yet the meaning is also found in cases like (5), which follows automatically from a Raising analysis, but which would require an ad hoc statement under any different analysis.

(5) The cat seems to have his tongue.

12.1.4 Predicate Idiom Chunks
There are many idioms like *keep tabs on,* where there is some NP that occurs only with a particular verb, as here *tabs* occurs only with *keep.* Such NPs become subjects only through passivization:

(6) Tabs were kept on all of them.

Such NPs occur also with *seem,* though, of course, only where the complement verb is *keep.*

(7) Tabs seem to have been kept on all of them.

Without a Raising analysis, *tabs* must be introduced not only in the idiom *keep tabs on* but by some otherwise unneeded statement as subject of *seem.*

12.1.5 Adjectival Subjects
There are phrases like *the important* (or *crucial*) *thing to me* that, for many speakers, can occur in simple clauses only as the subject of *be* with a predicate nominal as in (8):

(8) The important thing to me $\left\{\begin{array}{l}\text{is beer}\\\text{*worries Selma}\\\text{*lay on the table}\\\text{*was discussed by the committee}\end{array}\right\}$.

But the same selections exist across *seem*:

$$
\text{(9) The important thing to me seems to}
\begin{Bmatrix}
\text{be beer} \\
\text{*worry Selma} \\
\text{*lie on the table} \\
\text{*have been discussed by} \\
\text{be the committee}
\end{Bmatrix}.
$$

12.1.6 Generics with Adjectives

Consider the following examples:

(10) a. Swedes are nice, fat, healthy, immoral.

    b. *A Swede is nice, fat, healthy, immoral.

The same selections exist across *seem*:

(11) a. Swedes seem to be nice, fat, healthy, immoral.

    b. *A Swede seems to be nice, fat, healthy, immoral.

12.1.7 *So-Called*

So-called seems to require a subject NP that is a name, or a generic:

(12) a. Meathead is so-called because of X.

    b. Mothers are so-called because of Y.

    c. *That man is so-called because of Z.

    d. *Your mother is so-called because of W.

The same selections exist across *seem*:

(13) a. Meathead seems to be so-called because of X.

    b. Mothers seem to be so-called because of Y.

    c. *That man seems to be so-called because of Z.

    d. *Your mother seems to be so-called because of W.

From this point on, I shall give the arguments in even more terse form, unless some special remarks are required:

12.1.8 The Inclusion Constraint (see Section 3.4)

(14) a. *I understand us.

b. *It seemed to Bob that I understood us.

c. *I seemed to Bob to understand us.

12.1.9 Truth-Functional Equivalence

(15) a. Max is likely to visit Ken. = Ken is likely to be visited by Max.

b. Max is anxious to visit Ken. ≠ Ken is anxious to be visited by Max.

12.1.10 *Anyone* Selection

(16) a. Anyone $\begin{Bmatrix} \text{is} \\ \text{seems to be} \end{Bmatrix}$ able to see that.

b. *Anyone $\begin{Bmatrix} \text{is} \\ \text{seems to be} \end{Bmatrix}$ unable to see that.

12.1.11 Extraposition from Noun Heads[1]

(17) a. The suggestion that Bill was a necrophile $\begin{Bmatrix} \text{was} \\ \text{seems to have been} \end{Bmatrix}$ $\begin{Bmatrix} \text{made} \\ \text{discussed} \end{Bmatrix}$.

b. The suggestion $\begin{Bmatrix} \text{was} \\ \text{seems to have been} \end{Bmatrix}\begin{Bmatrix} \text{made} \\ \text{*discussed} \end{Bmatrix}$ that Bill was a necrophile.

---

[1] The facts are quite clear in the case of the head *possibility*, from which extraposition is highly restricted:

(i) The possibility that he is not going to recover $\begin{Bmatrix} \text{exists} \\ \text{remains} \\ \text{worries me} \\ \text{was discussed} \end{Bmatrix}$.

(ii) The possibility (seems to) $\begin{Bmatrix} \text{exist(s)} \\ \text{remain(s)} \\ \begin{Bmatrix} \text{*worries} \\ \text{*worry} \end{Bmatrix}\text{me} \\ \begin{Bmatrix} \text{*was} \\ \text{*have been} \end{Bmatrix}\text{discussed} \end{Bmatrix}$ that he is not going to recover.

As Ross observes, the phenomenon here is evidently global since the extraposition must take place at the top level (proved by the derived constituent structure), but the restrictions in (ii) are statable only in terms of the simple clauses existing before Raising applies.

12.1.12 Extraposition with *Follow*

(18) a. It $\left\{ \begin{array}{l} \text{follows} \\ \text{seems to follow} \end{array} \right\}$ from this that God exists.

b. That God exists $\left\{ \begin{array}{l} \text{follows} \\ \text{seems to follow} \end{array} \right\}$ from this.

c. It $\left\{ \begin{array}{l} \text{follows} \\ \text{seems to follow} \end{array} \right\}$ that God exists.

d. *That God exists $\left\{ \begin{array}{l} \text{follows} \\ \text{seems to follow} \end{array} \right\}$.

12.1.13 Backward Equi

(19) a. Praising himself$_i$ (*him$_i$) (seems to me to have) annoyed Bill$_i$.

b. Praising me (*myself) (seems to me to have) annoyed Bill$_i$.

The point here is that the deleted pronoun must be commanded by its antecedent (controller). See Section 4.7.

12.1.14 Backward *Any*

(20) That anyone came $\left\{ \begin{array}{l} \text{seems to have been} \\ \text{was} \end{array} \right\} \left\{ \begin{array}{l} \text{denied} \\ \text{*asserted} \end{array} \right\}$ by most of the witnesses.

The point here is that an *any* that precedes its triggering element must be commanded by that element. Thus note the following:

(21) a. *That anyone came proves that no one was guilty.

b. *That anyone came annoyed the boy who wasn't there.

c. *Because anyone came, I am not leaving.

12.1.15 Nominal Deletion

(22) a. It seems to me that a relative $\left\{ \begin{array}{l} (\;\text{of hers}_i) \\ (\text{*of mine}) \end{array} \right\}$ kissed Gladys$_i$.

$$\Downarrow$$
$$\emptyset$$

b. A relative $\left\{ \begin{array}{l} (\;\text{of hers}_i) \\ (\text{*of mine}) \end{array} \right\}$ seems to me to have kissed Gladys$_i$.

$$\Downarrow$$
$$\emptyset$$

In cases like (22)b, an NP of the form *a relative of NP* behaves with respect to the principles governing the coreference required for deletion just like a complement subject. Contrast (22) with (23):

(23) A relative (of mine) talked to me.
$$\Downarrow$$
$$\varnothing$$

12.1.16 Negative Polarity Items with *No* Subjects

(24) a. $\left\{ \begin{array}{l} \text{Nobody} \\ \text{*Melvin} \end{array} \right\}$ budged.

    b. $\left\{ \begin{array}{l} \text{Nobody} \\ \text{*Melvin} \end{array} \right\}$ seems to have budged.

    c. *Nobody wanted to budge.

    d. *Nobody refused to budge.

    e. *Nobody expected to budge.

    f. *Nobody was anxious to budge.

12.1.17 Backward Super-Equi

(25) a. John$_i$ claimed that criticizing himself$_i$ was like torturing himself$_i$.

    b. Criticizing himself$_i$ was claimed by John$_i$ to be like torturing himself$_i$.

    c. Criticizing $\left\{ \begin{array}{l} \text{himself}_i \\ \text{*him}_i \\ \text{me} \\ \text{*myself} \end{array} \right\}$ seems to me to have been claimed by John$_i$ to be like torturing himself$_i$.

This argument is like 12.1.13, in that the deleted NPs must be commanded by their controller.

No doubt, someone with the required diligence and interest could expand this list of arguments, but I see little point in attempting that.

12.2 Raising in Japanese and Universal Grammar

Except for a few hints at the end of Chapter 2 the discussion has dealt exclusively with the facts of English. Important perspectives on the

English rule Raising can, however, be obtained by a consideration of parallel phenomena in other languages. In the present section, which depends entirely on information kindly provided by Kuno, for whose gracious and extensive help I am deeply grateful, I shall briefly consider some data from Japanese, with the ultimate goal of drawing some significant if highly tentative conclusions about the place of Raising in universal grammar, and some of the implications of this status. See Kuno (1972b).

Japanese contains apparently quite similar sentence pairs of the following sort:

(26) a. John *wa* Mary *ga* baka da to omotte ita.

   b. John *wa* Mary *o* baka da to omotte   ita.
               fool   is   thinking was
       'John thought that Mary was a fool.'

These sentences, with the same glosses, differ morphemically only in the choice of case marker postposition on the NP *Mary, ga* versus *o.* Japanese is, of course, a classic case of the strict verb-final language type, in the sense of Greenberg (1963a); see also McCawley (1970a); Bach (1971); Kuno (to appear b). In Japanese the verb in a surface clause is final, there are postpositions, relative clauses precede their heads, etc. Thus a sentence like (1)a with a sentential object for the verb *omotte*[2] *(-ita)* would have a superficial structure something like that shown in (27). In (27), the sequence *Mary ga baka da* is a (clause) constituent, with *Mary ga* its subject. From this point of view, the presence of the case marker *ga* on *Mary* is perfectly regular, since *ga* is a typical case marker for embedded subjects. If, however, sentence (26)b is supplied a structure exactly like (27), except for the replacement of *ga* by *o*, the structure would be anomalous. For, in fact, *o* is otherwise exclusively an object NP case marker.

---

[2] Other verbs with the relevant properties of *omou* 'think' in (26) include the following:
danteisuru 'conclude'
suiteisuru 'guess'
sinziru 'believe'
kantigaisuru 'think erroneously'
kateisuru 'hypothesize'
omoikomu 'believe erroneously'

(27)

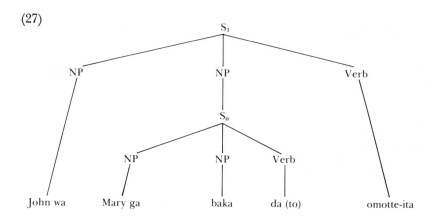

(28) a. John ga Mary o nagutte-iru.
          hitting is
   'John is hitting Mary'

 b. John ga Mary o hoomonsita.
            visited
   'John visited Mary.'

But *Mary* in (27) is in subject position with respect to its immediate clause, not in object position. This fact alone suggests that the structure of (26)b at the point relevant for case marking should be, not (27), but rather something like (29). Here *Mary o* is in the object position of the clause defined by the node S_1. A structure like (29) would then auto-

(29)

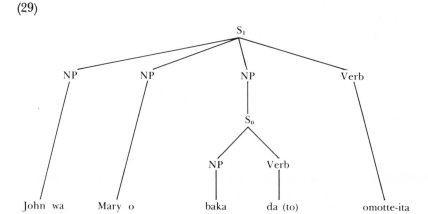

matically predict the occurrence of the postposition *o*, given the independently needed regularity of Japanese that *o* is assigned to objects.[3, 4]

Now, the difference between structures like (27) and (29) is immediately more than reminiscent of formal structural differences of the
sort that one finds, for example, between English B-verb *that*-clause
complement structures and B-verb infinitival complement structures,
the sort of difference that has been argued to be a function of the
English rule Raising. That is, in (27) the NP *Mary ga* is the subject of a
complement clause, but in (29) *Mary o* is the object of the superordinate
clause. Formally, the difference between (27) and (29) can be directly
described in terms of a subject-raising operation for complement clauses,
given identical underlying structures, an operation parallel to those sub-
cases of Raising operation in English which involve moving the complement subject into derived superordinate object position.

Is there any evidence for contrasting structures like (27) and (29),
beyond the facts of case marking? Kuno observes that there is. In particular, there is an argument quite parallel to that involving adverb
placement for English, discussed earlier, in Section 4.12. Thus there are
such contrasts as the following:

(30) a.　John wa Mary o *orokanimo* hannin da to 　omotte-ita.
　　　　　　　　　　 stupidly 　 culprit is that thinking was
　　　 'John stupidly thought that Mary was the culprit.'

　　 b. *John wa Mary ga *orokanimo* hannin da to omotte-ita.

That is, the adverb *orokanimo*, which "modifies" *omotte* 'thinking',
can follow *Mary o*, but not *Mary ga*. Given structures like (27) and (29),
this follows naturally from the same principle utilized in the discussion
of English in Section 4.12. Namely, a main clause adverb cannot be
inserted into a complement clause. Sentence (30)a remains well-formed,

---

[3] I ignore here the question of which object NPs are assigned *o*, and which *ni*, the
dative case postposition.
[4] The situation here is a model of the sort of case anticipated earlier, in the discussion
at the very end of Chapter 2. Another such model is provided by Aissen (to appear),
who provides such Turkish examples as (i), where the NP *Ahmet* has the specific accusative case marker.

(i) Mehmet　Ahmed-i　kendin-i　yika-dɨ　　zannediyor.
　　 Mehmet　 Ahmet 　 self 　　 wash past　 supposes.
　　 'Mehmet supposes Ahmet to have washed himself (Ahmet).'

even with this principle, since *Mary o* is a derived constituent of the superordinate clause whose verb is *omotte*; hence *orokanimo* can follow it and still be a constituent of that clause. But since, according to structures like (27), *Mary ga* is not a constituent of the *omotte* clause, word order like that in (30)b could result only if *orokanimo* were actually a part of the complement of *omotte*, which the general principle about adverb placement precludes, as in English. On the contrary, note that the adverb can occur before *Mary* with either case marker, since this word order does not violate the principle of placement for either the (27) or the (29) type of structure:

(31) John wa orokanimo Mary $\begin{Bmatrix} ga \\ o \end{Bmatrix}$ hannin da to omotte-ita.

    'John stupidly thought that Mary was the culprit.'

A parallel example is (32):

(32) a. John wa Mary o hukoonimo   kono ziken no giseisya da to
                       unfortunately this   event's victim   is that
       omotte   iru.
       thinking is

    b. John wa Mary ga hukoonimo kono ziken no giseisya da to omotte
       iru.

Sentence (32)a is ambiguous between these two readings:

(33) a. 'Unfortunately, John thinks that Mary is a victim of this incident.'

    b. 'John thinks that Mary is, unfortunately, a victim of this incident.'

But (32)b can mean only (33)b. Again, the facts follow from the principle that precludes a main clause "modifier" from being inserted into a complement, if (32)a, b contrast formally along the lines of (29) versus (27).

Another factor that may be relevant to the claim that *o*-marked NPs in the class of sentences under consideration are actually derived main clause constituents follows from the fact that in pairs like (26) the *o*-marked NP is preposable, but the *ga*-marked NP is not:

(34) a.   Mary o, John wa hannin da to omotte-ita.

    b. *Mary ga, John wa hannin da to omotte-ita.

      'Mary John thought to be the culprit.'

But, in general, complement subject NPs are not preposable under this rule, so that a subject-raising analysis accounts for the preposability of *Mary o* by assigning it a derived nonsubject status.

    Finally, there are facts of quantifier scope which are similar to those discussed for English in Section 6.3. A sentence like (35) means primarily that there is someone who loves all.

(35) Dareka ga minna o aisite   iru.

    someone   all   loving is

However, it is not impossible to get for (35) the interpretation that 'For each person X, there is someone who loves X.' A quantifier sentence parallel to (26)a, such as (36), can mean only that there is someone who thinks that everyone is a fool.

(36) Dareka   ga minna ga baka da to omotte   iru

    someone   all   fool are   thinking is

But there is a contrast between (36) and the putative subject-raised case (37):

(37) Dareka ga minna o baka da to omotte iru.

Although the predominant reading of (37) is that of (36), sentence (37) can also mean weakly that 'For each person X, there is someone who thinks X is a fool.'

    Thus in (37), where a raised structure would change the asymmetrical command relation between *dareka* and *minna* of (36) into a symmetrical command relation, a reading with *minna* having superior scope is possible, just as it is in (35), where these two forms are clearly Clause Mates, and hence not asymmetrically connected by the command relation.

    While obviously the arguments given are far from conclusive, they definitely suggest that NPs like *Mary o* and *minna o*, in such sentences as (26)b, (30)a, (32)a, and (37) are derived constituents of the superordinate clauses. Given the obvious relations with parallel *ga* sentences, the natural conclusion is the need for a subject-raising analysis. That is, an Equi type of analysis of the *o* sentences with underlying structures containing an "extra" NP is implausible. Kuno observes, moreover, that there are some arguments against such a proposal. Particularly, in sentences where a third NP is needed in underlying structures, as in (38), the "extra" NP is marked with the dative case, *ni*, and not the *o* of the potential subject-raising cases.

(38) a. John wa Mary ni (kanozyo ga) sore o suru koto o meizita.
                to she   it   do   that   ordered
     'John ordered Mary that she do it.'

   b. John wa Mary ni (kanozyo ga) sore o suru koto o settokusita.
                                                  persuaded
     'John persuaded Mary to do it.'

Furthermore, as the parenthesization of *kanozyo ga* in (38) indicates, pronoun deletion in such cases is optional in Japanese. But putative subject-raising cases in which the pronoun is left in are completely ungrammatical:

(39) *John wa Mary o kanozyo ga baka da to omotte ita.
    'John thought Mary that she was a fool.'

Thus an Equi-like analysis of the *o* cases seems to raise empirical difficulties, correlating with its semantic and intuitive implausibility.

The likely conclusion is, then, that Japanese has a class of constructions in which complement subjects are raised into the superordinate clause, to yield the NP-*o* cases we have discussed. Let us call the rule required for these constructions J-Raising, and let us temporarily rename the English rule E-Raising. We must now ask what the relation is between J-Raising and E-Raising and, further, what the relation of both is to the principles of universal grammar. In purely formal terms, there are obvious similarities between J-Raising and E-Raising. Both operate on the subject NP of complement clauses, and both detach this NP and make it the derived object of the next most superordinate clause. Less obviously, but ultimately perhaps no less significant, if one compares the meanings of the items that trigger J-Raising, mentioned in footnote 2, with the class of B-element R-triggers of English discussed in Section 9.3, one can see nonrandom parallels. Both sets seem to involve nonfactive verbs of thinking.

If one thinks of the situation in terms of sheer logical possibilities, these similarities are mysterious. Given all the possible rules that two languages could have, why should two unrelated languages have rules that are so similar? It is one of the jobs of universal grammar to answer such questions. The most direct, natural, and ultimately most interesting answer to this kind of question would be that the similarities are a function of the fact that, in effect, both languages *have the same rule*, this being an element of universal grammar, characterized in general linguistic theory. Such a view depends on, and is one element of, a general view according to which universal grammar is regarded as containing, essentially, not only general constraints on types of rules and their interactions but also a nontrivial set of actual universal rules.[5] Assuming this, let us consider in greater detail the possibility that J-Raising and E-Raising are simply variant manifestations of a single element of universal grammar: the Raising rule.

There is an immediate major obstacle to this identification, easily seen by comparing the formulation given earlier, in Section 1.5, for E-Raising, repeated here as (40), with the formulation that would apparently be needed for J-Raising in the cases considered, namely, something like (41):

(40) E-Raising

$$X, \quad \text{Verb}, \quad (NP) \quad [_{NP} [_{S} \quad \text{Verb}, \quad NP, \quad Y \quad _{S}] _{NP}], \quad Z$$
$$1 \qquad 2 \qquad 3 \qquad\qquad 4 \qquad 5 \qquad 6 \qquad\qquad 7$$

(41) J-Raising

$$X \quad (NP), \quad [_{NP} [_{S} \quad NP, \quad Y, \quad \text{Verb} \quad _{S}] _{NP}] \quad \text{Verb}, \quad Z$$
$$1 \qquad 2 \qquad\qquad 3 \qquad 4 \qquad 5 \qquad\qquad 6 \qquad 7$$

---

[5] Chomsky (1968: 57) says the following:

Notice that we are interpreting 'universal grammar' as a system of conditions on grammars. It may involve a skeletal substructure of rules that any human language must contain, but it also incorporates conditions that must be met by such grammars and principles that determine how they are interpreted. This formulation is something of a departure from a traditional view that took universal grammar to be simply a substructure of each particular grammar, a system of rules at the very core of each grammar. This traditional view has also received expression in recent work. It seems to me to have little merit.

While hard to interpret in some respects, this statement seems to indicate some doubt about the role of universal rules. In any event, my own view is that such rules play a crucial part in universal grammar, though one that is in no way inconsistent with other aspects of universal grammar, like the conditions on grammars which Chomsky has quite properly stressed.

While (40) and (41) mention the same constituent types, they are organized rather differently. Thus, where (40) specifies the extraction of the NP of term 5 and its reattachment to the main clause at a point closer to the Verb of term 2, (41) specifies the extraction of the NP of term 3, and its reattachment in the main clause at a point farther away from the main verb of that clause specified in term 6. Thus, although (40) and (41) bring out further similarities between E-Raising and J-Raising, namely, the similarity of constituent types in the structural indices and the fact the both rules *reorder constituents to the left*, they also bring out a major difference, namely, the way the given constituent types are organized in the rule description.

If (40) and (41) were accurate portrayals of the existing rules for the two languages, I think this would count as some evidence against the view that there is a single Raising rule characterized in universal grammar. For, because of their configurational contrasts, there is no real way to regard (40) and (41) as manifestations of a single universal mapping. It is worth asking, then, what factors determine this contrast. The answer is surprisingly simple. All of the difference between (40) and (41) is due to the fact that (40) assumes E-Raising operates on verb-initial clauses, while (41) assumes that J-Raising operates on verb-final clauses. In other words, the contrast between (40) and (41) is fully a function of the contrast between verb-initial and verb-final clause structures. The formulations of (40) and (41) could be trivially reduced to a single homogeneous mapping if one assumed *either* that both rules operate on verb-initial structures or that both operate on verb-final structures. The former would mean that Japanese (and presumably other verb-final languages) had a rule shifting verbs to final position, the latter that English (and presumably other verb-initial languages) had a rule shifting verbs to initial position. Under the former view, there is a point in underlying structures where all languages have verb-initial structures; under the latter, a point where all languages have verb-final structures. Under either of these conditions,[6] E-Raising and J-Raising combine in a single rule, Raising. Unfortunately, the present considerations do not allow any choice between these incompatible alternatives. However, I believe they do suggest that verb-initial and

---

[6] I am ignoring here the possibility, briefly touched on in Chapter 7, that underlying structures might be *unordered*, in which case verb-initial or verb-final stages would be induced by early rules, with essentially the same problems arising.

verb-final clause structures are not primitive, contrasting types, but rather that at least one type should be regarded as arising within the course of derivations. For only this alternative would appear to permit the maximum generalization involved in specifying Raising as an element of universal grammar, manifested in various languages as E-Raising, J-Raising, etc.

Can one choose between (40) and (41) on the basis of considerations available today? The discussion in Chapter 7, showing that even the choice between verb-initial and verb-final order for English alone was by no means clear, already suggests a negative answer. Suppose one were to try to justify the universal verb-initial assumption, and hence the formulation in (40), as follows.

First, it could be claimed that there are no independently attested cases of a rule that moves verbs to clause-initial position. On the other hand, there seem to be cases of rules that move verbs to clause-final position, in particular, the rule operative in subordinate clauses in German (see Bach, 1971). Thus we might conclude on independent grounds that a verb-final rule is a possible feature of a human language. It would then be necessary to say only that languages like Japanese have a generalized form of this rule compared to German, that is, one valid for main as well as subordinate clauses.

However, this argument is extremely weak. It depends totally on the assumption that German has underlying verb-initial clauses, with a verb-final rule in subordinate clauses. Despite the argument in Bach (1971), this conclusion is far from secure (note that it goes against much previous generative work such as Bach, 1962; Bierwisch, 1963). Moreover, as noted in Chapter 7, Ross (to appear g) has constructed an important argument for the verb-final character of both German and English. The argument is based on the generalization, which seems otherwise valid, that while grammatical rules can be restricted to main clauses, they cannot apply to subordinate clauses without also applying to main clauses. But a German rule of verb-final positioning would violate this condition. A rule of verb-initial placement would not violate it, because, given underlying verb-final structures, this rule would apply in nonsubordinate clauses only, as is permitted.

Second, one might argue as follows. Not only is Japanese a verb-final language, it is a strict verb-final language. Nothing can follow the verb within a clause. However, setting up underlying structures with the verb in final position does not guarantee this strict verb-final property, which is a feature of surface structures. It would also be necessary to guarantee that none of the transformational rules of the grammar affect this verb-final structure. But if verb-final position is generated in languages like Japanese by a verb-final rule, this guarantee is not too difficult to provide in a global system of grammar. What is necessary, basically, is to stipulate that the output configuration produced by the verb-final rule must also apply to the correspondents of that structure in surface structure, or, in other words, to specify that the output configuration be "Surface True." This notion of having the outputs of certain rules necessarily persist into surface structure is, I believe, needed for other cases.[7] If so, the notions involved are part of linguistic theory, and it would require little to make the necessary stipulation for a verb-final rule in a language like Japanese.[8] However, this argument favoring verb-initial structures is obviously quite weak.

We have been led to inquire into the possibility of uniform underlying structures for languages like Japanese and English on the basis of considerations having to do with Raising, in particular, the apparent impossibility of combining E-Raising and J-Raising into a single rule,

[7] One such case involves the ban on adverb interpolation, described initially as an output condition, (109), in Section 4.11, and then more fully as a global rule involving grammatical relations in Section 8.2. The latter account can be given in terms of the notion Surface True. Namely, if the sisterhood condition (which is fundamental for defining the object relation between verb and NP) is Surface True, so must be the condition that the verb directly precede the NP.

Another case might be the *that*-deletion phenomenon in complement clauses as discussed in footnote 35 of Chapter 4 and in later sections. Here the claim would be that the *input* configuration to the deletion rule, namely (i), must be Surface True.

(i) [Verb [$_S$ $_S$] $\cdots$]

A third case would involve the rule of Particle Movement, which is discussed in Section 12.6. Here the facts are that when this rule moves a particle to the right of an NP, as in (ii), the sequence NP + Particle is from that point on immutable.

(ii) Harry turned the offer down.

Thus nothing can be inserted between them. This can be stated by specifying that the output configuration must be Surface True.

[8] Apparently, the verb-final rule for German subordinate clauses, if there is one, cannot be regarded as strictly Surface True, for certain extraposed elements can sometimes be postverbal in such clauses. This also seems to be the case for main clauses in Turkish, but not for subordinate clauses, where the verb-final property is strictly Surface True. See Hankamer (1971). These matters and their relations to the facts in Japanese should be investigated in greater detail. See also Ross (to appear g).

given that one must operate on verb-initial and the other on verb-final structures. Note, however, that the problem of combination is entirely dependent on the assumption that the relevant raising rules are to be stated in terms of constituent configurations, that is, as in (40) and (41). But this basic assumption has already been challenged in Section 8.4. There it was suggested that Raising was, in fact, inherently to be stated in terms of grammatical relations, in terms making crucial utilization of the Functional Succession Principle. If it is true that Raising is reducible to a statement of the form indicated in (42), with the output structure determined by the Functional Succession Principle, then under the assumption that the relevant grammatical relations can be defined independently of the position of the main verb of a clause, it would not matter whether a universal rule of Raising operated on verb-initial or verb-final structures.

(42) Promote the subject of a complement.

In short, the problem of combining (40) and (41) into a single rule, which seems to require that either English be an underlying verb-final language or that Japanese be an underlying verb-initial language may be a pseudoproblem arising only from the incorrect view that rules like Raising are to be stated configurationally, as in (40) and (41), rather than in terms of grammatical relations linked to universal principles like the Functional Succession Principle.

The present discussion is, of course, completely inconclusive along several different lines. Generative grammarians have generally been operating in a framework requiring rules to be stated as in (40) and (41). This clearly raises fundamental problems with respect to underlying verb position. But if rules are stated as in (42), then, at least in the case of Raising, the problems do not arise. That is, given terms like (42), it is easy to formulate a universal account of Raising, which is as valid for English as for Japanese, independently of assumptions about the underlying position of the verb. It should be clear, then, that the study of subject raising in diverse languages is linked to many quite profound questions about the structures of particular languages and about the basic features of universal grammar itself.

Several other features of J-Raising require comment. *First*, it was pointed out at the end of Chapter 2 that those cases in French susceptible to a subject-raising analysis parallel to that for English B-verbs involved raising out of subordinate clauses of the copula (*être*) type. Kuno observes, interestingly enough, that just this sort of constraint holds for the J-Raising cases generating *o*-marked NPs in Japanese. This type of strange correlation between unrelated languages suggests also that we are dealing with a single rule of universal grammar. But it suggests something more: namely, that some of the apparently ad hoc limitations on the classes of derivations generated by language-particular manifestations of the universal rule are themselves in part a function of universally characterizable constraints.

Second, every language known to me which has constructions plausibly analyzed as involving subject raising into superordinate object positions also has constructions involving subject raising into superordinate subject positions, that is, parallels to English A-element R-triggers. Moreover, general "primacy" considerations of the sort discussed in Ross (to appear c) suggest that this should be the case. But Kuno has been unable to find any clear examples of such cases in Japanese. Perhaps this is because those predicates which would serve as A-element R-triggers end up attached to other verbs as suffixes. This is a matter that requires considerable further study.

Third, I conjectured earlier that it is a universal that Raising operation triggers de-finitization of the complement clause that loses its subject—in other words, that quasi-clauses of this type are always de-finitized. However, Kuno stresses that, although Japanese has nonfinite clauses, the complements left behind when J-Raising yields the raised *o*-marked NPs are finite, on many grounds.[9] Therefore, the generalization must either be restricted in some way or be abandoned. I am unable to offer at this time any plausible restriction. I note only that the known cases of de-finitization are in superficially verb-initial/verb-medial languages.

Fourth, I suggested earlier (see footnote 16 of Chapter 2) that verb-final languages may not contain rules that extract constituents leaving truncated clauses behind. But J-Raising violates this proposal as well, and again I do not know how to formulate a proper statement not inconsistent with this fact. Possibly the difference between bounded and unbounded rules is relevant, or, more likely, the whole idea was just wrong.

[9] Therefore, J-Raising violates Chomsky's (to appear) tensed clause condition, if this is interpreted as a universal.

12.3 An Argument against the Verb-Initial Hypothesis

As noted several times earlier, it is not at all clear that the verb-initial hypothesis about English clause structure can be chosen over a verb-final account, or over one that would have underlying clause elements unordered. It is important, however, to distinguish real objections to any of these proposals from those which are founded on untenable assumptions or partial accounts of the relevant data.

Newmeyer (1971) argues that the verb-initial analysis of English is suspect, because he does not accept an important feature of that analysis. Namely, he rejects my claim, adopted by McCawley, that the inversion rule required in a verb-initial system for generating the typical subject + verb declarative clause order, which I have been calling Subject Formation, is not a new or extra rule, but simply, in effect, the rule of Subject-Auxiliary Inversion found in past NP-initial systems for generating the order of most interrogative clauses (and many other clause types as well).[10] To quote Newmeyer (1971: 390): "If English is an underlying *VSO* language, we need at least two inversion rules to do the work that one rule can do under the more traditional verb-second hypothesis."

However, at least with respect to the class of facts brought up, only one rule of verb-NP inversion suffices in a verb-initial system. Newmeyer's opposite conclusion is based on a failure to recognize the role that Raising plays in the constructions of relevance.

Newmeyer's discussion is, I believe, unnecessarily burdened by his initial adoption of essentially the *Syntactic Structures* analysis of auxiliaries and tenses. This analysis is quite arbitrary and unmotivated. It is strange to see it assumed in an analysis of McCawley's arguments,

---

[10] An extensive, though still only partial, survey of clause types in which auxiliary verbs precede their subject NP is to be found in Live (1967). One such type seldom if ever discussed involves emphatic negative imperatives:

(i) a. Don't you do that.
 b. Don't you dare call her.

A complete and accurate specification of the conditions blocking Subject Formation and hence yielding verb-initial order has, of course, never been worked out. In part, moreover, these conditions are subject to some idiolectal variation. For example, where standard English has (ii)a, there are dialects, including the Harlem dialect, which have things like (ii)b:

(ii) a. I want to know where he put it.
 b. I want to know where did he put it.

since, of course, McCawley totally rejects this analysis and has devoted much of a (1971) paper to the topic. Furthermore, over the years many linguists, including myself (see, for instance, footnote 42 of Chapter 4 and Postal, to appear e) but most notably Ross, have provided counter-arguments to the view that there is an auxiliary constituent distinct from verb, as well as to other aspects of the *Syntactic Structures* conception. Ross (1972a) provides what, I believe, is quite strong evidence showing that the auxiliary *be* must be treated as a main verb.

This is not very important for present purposes, since Newmeyer argues finally that his point is equally valid for the main verb analysis of auxiliaries. It is this claim that I shall here argue is false.

Newmeyer is concerned with these two sentences:

(43) a. John sees Bill.

b. What does John want?

In the first there is subject + verb order, in the second verb + subject order. He provides these sentences with trees in which the auxiliary functions as a higher verb of the forms shown, respectively, in (44)a and (44)b.[11] He grants that the derivation of (43)b from (44)b is straightforward. He says that "The presence of *what* in the higher sentence blocks the application of Inversion there; this rule applies only in the lower sentence, (9) results which is transformed into (5) [my (43)b] by

(44) a.

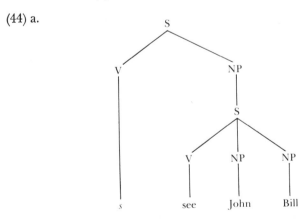

---

11 Newmeyer's tree (44)b is, of course, not an underlying structure but rather the output of the rule that moves *wh*-marked NPs in questions. Newmeyer assumes that this rule daughter-adjoins the moved NP to the front of the S that contained it, but

b.

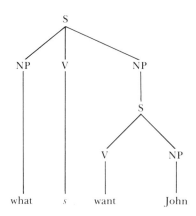

Do-Support." I shall return to this derivation shortly. According to New-meyer, however, a problem arises in attempting to derive (43)a from (44)a. Namely, he claims that nothing blocks inversion from applying to both subordinate and superordinate clauses in (44)a, yielding the ill-formed (45). He then concludes (1971: 392): "The only way to solve this problem would be to *invent* [emphasis mine] a special rule whose only function would be to invert the higher tense verb around the *lower* sub-ject. Therefore, whether auxiliaries are main verbs or not at the time of

I argue that the rule actually involves Chomsky adjunction, so that properly (44)b should be as shown in (i). But I shall follow Newmeyer's practice in this regard.

(i)

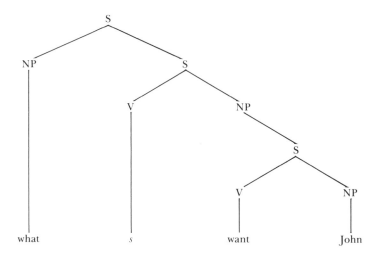

(45)

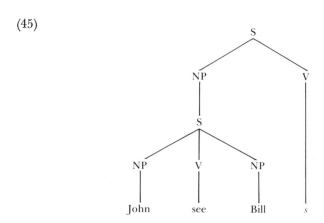

V-NP inversion, a verb-initial analysis of English leads to serious complications in the statement of this rule."

However, Newmeyer's entire argument and conclusion, insofar as systems taking auxiliaries as main verbs are concerned, depends on examples like (45) and the claim that in a verb-initial system these require some newly invented rule to block them.

Unquestionably, if the rule that creates verb-second order in declarative clauses, etc., applies to trees like (44)a, it will indeed produce trees like the ill-formed (45). Newmeyer's argument depends, however, not only on this fact but on the additional claim that no independently motivated feature of the grammar of English prohibits such application. It is the latter assumption that does not stand.

We can approach this matter by replacing Newmeyer's tree (44)b with a more natural and motivated one, in which instead of an isolated

(46)

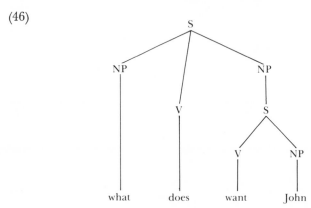

tense marker as verb we represent the actual verb that shows up if it is not deleted, as shown in (46). As previously seen, according to Newmeyer, Subject Formation (his V-NP Inversion) occurs only in the lower S, yielding a structure like (47) for (43)b. However, assigning sentences like (43)b structures like (47) raises a fundamental problem, one that Newmeyer ignores. Observe that in (43)b the verb *does* agrees with the NP *John*. Hence, if *John* is replaced by *the two thieves*, *does* must be replaced by the plural form *do*:

(47)

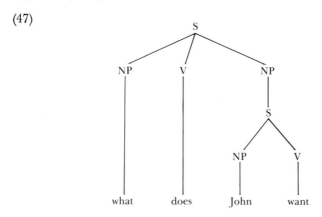

(48) What do (*does) the two thieves want?

This is hardly a new observation. Moreover, it is surely not an isolated fact about inverted questions. Clearly, the agreement in such sentences is simply a special case of the general fact that finite verbs in English agree with their subject NP. But now the difficulty in (47) is clear. There is no sense in which (47), or its underlying structure (46), or in fact any structure assigned in Newmeyer's terms would make the NP *John* the subject of the finite verb *does*. In (46) and (47), the NP *John* is not even in the same simple clause with *does*. Thus, in the terms adopted for Newmeyer's argument, the existing agreement in sentences like (43)b could not be a function of the general subject–finite verb agreement rule. Some totally new agreement rule would be needed.[12]

Naïvely, one might take this to be an argument against the main verb

---

[12] Moreover, there is every reason to believe that the needed rule is theoretically impossible. That is, I know of no agreement rule in any language whereby a verb in one clause agrees with an NP in a different clause, and I suggest that verbal agreement must involve Clause Mates, as in principle (40) of Chapter 2.

conception of auxiliaries like *do/does*. But this conclusion is unwarranted, since there is an independently motivated operation in the grammar, namely, Raising, which will map trees like (46) into those like (49). But in (49) *John* is the subject of *want* according to the general principles sketched in footnote 9 of Chapter 4. Roughly, the subject of a verb is the leftmost NP sister of that verb. Note that here the remark in footnote 11 of Chapter 12 is relevant, however. Hence, the general

(49)

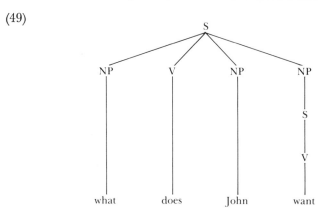

agreement rule can operate. Moreover, the blockage of Subject Formation by the preposed NP (*what*) yields the correct word order for (43)b as before.

Now, if we turn to (44)a, which yields the ill-formed (45) when Subject Formation applies to it, we can see that the same stipulation that

(50)

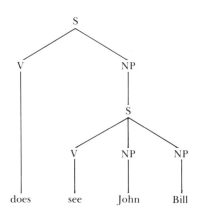

(51)

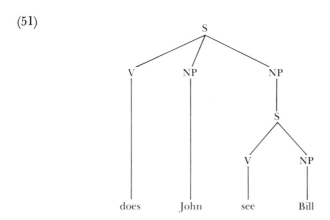

solves the agreement problem in (44)b solves this problem. Namely, if we once more replace *s* by *does* and turn (44)a into (50), we shall get (51) when Raising applies. But when Subject Formation applies to this type of structure, it is not the ill-formed (45) that results, nor the ill-formed (52)a, but rather (52)b:

(52) a. *John see Bill does.

    b. [John does see Bill]

This presentence structure will be converted into either (53), if in some way the *does* is assigned contrastive stress, or else into (54) by the rule of *Do* Deletion.[13]

(53) John dóes see Bill.

(54) John sees Bill.[14]

This rule is the analogue in this system of the rule of *Do* Support in the *Syntactic Structures* type of analysis.[15]

[13] The relevant rule would appear to say that unstressed *do/does* is deleted directly before a verb. Alternatively, it may be that instead of a special deletion rule, the effect of deletion is accomplished by the rule McCawley (1970a) refers to as Predicate Raising.
[14] There is one further matter, namely, the occurrence of the tense affix on *see* in (54) but on the form of *do* in the following:

(i) Does John see Bill; who does John see?

I think the proper way to express this is to assume that all verbs are tensed, with the tense affix being suppressed in infinitival phrases. The loss of *do* then prevents the next verb down from being marked as infinitival.
[15] The deletion approach to *do* is superior to the insertion approach introduced in

The fact that a verb-initial system of grammar automatically generates structures like (52)a or, more strictly, like (55) if Raising does not apply is exactly what would be expected.

(55) a. *That John see(s) Bill does.

 b. *It does that John see(s) Bill.

For ultimately, Subject Formation operates on whatever is the cyclic subject of the relevant verb. If Raising does not operate, the cyclic subject will be the underlying subject (assuming no application of Passive, etc.). But if Raising does operate, it will be the complement subject that becomes the main clause subject which is inverted. Thus, the situation with *do/does* is essentially parallel to that with *happen*, where one finds the following:

Chomsky (1957), since it permits assignment of the verb status required by many rules and particularly the subject-verb relation (required for the agreement facts and operation of Subject Formation) in a non-ad-hoc way through the use of the apparatus operative for other underlying verbs. As Perlmutter observes, the *Do* Support system fails to give any motivated explanation for the following:

(i) a. Why the inserted element is a verb.
   b. Why the inserted element bears tense.
   c. Why the tense affix follows *do*.

That is, an insertion system would be equally compatible with the negations of (i) a–c.
  Moreover, Perlmutter points out that the *Do* Support system is factually untenable because it runs into an ordering paradox:

(ii) a. Haven't they been there?
    b. Have they not been there?
    c. *Have theyn't been there?
    d. *Have not they been there?

These facts would fall out if Negative Contraction preceded Subject Formation, the rule that inverts subject NPs and part of the Aux in the *Do* Support system.
  Subject Formation must precede *Do* Support because of (iii):

(iii) Does he believe them?

That is, it is the application of Subject Formation which creates the environment for *Do* Support. But *Do* Support must precede Negative Contraction, because of the following:

(iv) Don't you believe them?

(v) We don't believe them.

Thus altogether there is the system in which Negative Contraction precedes Subject Formation, Subject Formation precedes *Do* Support, but *Do* support precedes Negative Contraction, an inconsistent system under the assumption that rule ordering is transitive.

(56) a. *That John sees Bill happens.

   b. It happens that John sees Bill.

   c. John happens to see Bill.

The difference lies precisely in this. Whereas the item *happen* only *optionally* triggers Raising, with (56)a resulting when the option is not taken,[16] *do/does* obligatorily triggers Raising, so that both of the sentences in (55) are ill-formed. And it is, in fact, this *obligatory* application of Raising which ultimately blocks the equivalents of Newmeyer's (45) or, better, my (52)a. Since Raising is cyclical but the inversion of verb and NP is postcyclical, having Raising obligatory automatically prevents structures like (44)a from being input to Subject Formation.

Finally, saying that *do/does* obligatorily triggers Raising is neither an ad hoc remark about these words nor an ad hoc *type* of remark. Thus, it seems, in general, that all of the so-called auxiliaries, modal or not, must be treated as main verbs, and in these terms they all must be regarded as obligatorily triggering Raising, since we also do not find things like (57):

(57) a. *It will that John visits Turkey.

   b. *It must that you are happy.

   c. *That John visits Turkey will.

Hence, the fact that *do/does* obligatorily triggers Raising follows from the fact that it is an auxiliary (whatever that means exactly) and the fact that auxiliaries obligatorily trigger Raising.

Furthermore, it is not an ad hoc feature of the analysis of auxiliaries as main verbs to require specification that certain elements obligatorily trigger Raising. There are other terms that can easily be shown to involve Raising which also do not occur unless this operation applies. Among these are the adjective *about*, and the sequence *had better*, previously seen to be A-element R-triggers. Thus the obligatory Raising feature of auxiliaries is part of a wider pattern in English, whereby certain elements occur only in structures formed by Raising. This just shows further the main verbal character of auxiliaries.

In conclusion, Newmeyer's claim that a verb-initial system requires

---

16 As with many other verbs (*seem, appear, strike, turn out*, etc.), *happen* structures like (56)a are then subject obligatorily to Extraposition, yielding outputs like (56)b.

an extra rule of inversion, not just the equivalent of the older Subject-Auxiliary Inversion rule, to block sentences like (45) or (52)a is incorrect. There is no flaw in the verb-initial assumption here. All that seems necessary is to spell out further the way in which this analysis interacts with Raising and with the peculiar, though not unique, feature of auxiliaries of obligatorily triggering the application of Raising.

12.4 Emonds's Rejection of Extraposition

Rosenbaum (1967) established an analysis of sentences like (58) and (59) according to which the *that* and infinitival complements in the *b* examples achieve their clause-final position by the operation of the rule Extraposition on structures essentially like those of the *a* examples:

(58) a. That we must surrender becomes more and more obvious.

   b. It becomes more and more obvious that we must surrender.

(59) a. For you to lie would annoy Lewis.

   b. It would annoy Lewis for you to lie.

This analysis has since been widely accepted. I have adopted it myself in all places where it is relevant. Emonds (1970: especially Chapter III) has, however, rejected the existence of any rule like Extraposition and has proposed a quite different analysis. Emonds's treatment of this matter has been closely analyzed by Higgins (1971), in a work that I hope will be published. He shows that Emonds's treatment is untenable from several points of view. Here, although space does not permit extensive discussion, I should like to give a few largely complementary criticisms.

What Emonds is most concerned about denying is the NP status of infinitival and *that* complements (in contrast to gerundive complements), which, he claims, they never have. Rather, he claims that extraposed clauses like those in (58)b and (59)b are directly generated in that position in the base, as expansions of the Verb Phrase and Adjective Phrase nodes. The *a* examples are then derived by a new rule posited by Emonds, called Intraposition. This rule has the property, unique as far as I know, of carrying out a substitution operation in which the inserted phrase does not take on the constituent structure (NP) of the replaced element. Thus Intraposition substitutes clauses for subject NPs, but without these clauses becoming NPs. This unique property is one

(60)

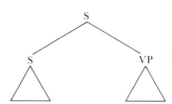

immediate reason to reject this analysis, apart from objections that could be made to derived structures like (60) for sentences like (58)a and (59)a.

As for the latter, Emonds does not explain how such structures are compatible with the distribution of emphatic reflexives normally restricted to NPs:

(61) a. That we must surrender in itself means dishonor.

b. That in itself means dishonor.

c. For us to lie in itself would be immoral.

d. That in itself would be immoral.

Observe the incompatibility of these with the *it* of the extraposed sentences, or with the extraposed sentences themselves:

(62) a. That Bob is insane in itself is enough to worry me.

b. That Bob is insane is in itself enough to worry me.

c. It is enough to worry me that Bob is insane.

d. *It in itself is enough to worry me that Bob is insane.

e. *It is enough to worry me that Bob is insane in itself.

f. *It is in itself enough to worry me that Bob is insane.

Thus attributing (61)a, (61)b to the properties of the underlying *it* does not seem promising.

Next, extraposed sentences are, of course, interpreted in such a way that the extraposed complement functions like an element in the position of *it*. Thus in (63) *that Bob is a Mongolian* functions semantically just as *that claim* does in (64):

(63) It is obvious that Bob is a Mongolian.

(64) That claim is obvious.

That is, it functions as the argument on which *obvious* is predicated. This is an automatic consequence in an Extraposition analysis, where the extraposed clause starts out in the same functional position as *that claim*. In Emonds's terms, however, it requires some special "interpretive" devices invented for just this purpose. Emonds's chief device, which he hardly discusses, is to claim that S nodes can be "coreferential" with other elements and to represent sentences like (63) as (65). Some

(65)

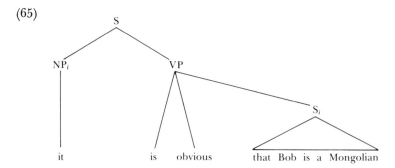

kind of "interpretive" rule will then have to say that this kind of symbolic configuration is to be understood essentially as if the logical correspondents of S_i were the correspondents of NP_i. In other words, these unique, otherwise unmotivated theoretical extensions, which so far are really not worked out, will somehow reconstitute the unity of the *it* and the complements that the underlying syntactic analysis fails to assign, since this unity is a semantic fact.[17] An analysis like Emonds's would therefore be impossible in natural grammar, where underlying structures are determined by logical properties.

[17] The treatment of this unity in Extraposition systems is quite parallel to that which must be adopted in the description of cases like the following, where everyone would presumably agree that (i)b is derived by an extraposition rule from structures like (i)a.

(i) a. The suggestion that we disband was made by Melvin.
    b. The suggestion was made by Melvin that we disband.

By adopting the Intraposition analysis, with its necessary semantic supplements, Emonds thus allows a theory of grammar in which the parallelism between (i) and cases like (ii) is lost:

(ii) a. That we disband immediately was proposed by Melvin.
    b. It was proposed by Melvin that we disband immediately.

Of course, there are sentences like (66), in which there are two complements within a single containing clause.

(66) That Bob would do that $\left\{\begin{array}{l}\text{proves}\\\text{shows}\\\text{indicates}\\\text{means}\end{array}\right\}$ that he is dishonest.

Given that such clauses are generated in NP positions, as in the system underlying the Extraposition analysis,[18] this is an automatic consequence, since there are sentences like (67):

(67) This $\left\{\begin{array}{l}\text{proves}\\\text{shows}\\\text{indicates}\\\text{means}\end{array}\right\}$ that.

But in Emonds's Intraposition system, where complements are generated at the right extremity of VPs, how are sentences like (66) to be generated? Emonds's answer is a further unique, again undeveloped extension of grammatical theory, already touched on (in footnote 5 of Chapter 3), called the "doubly filled node," which is supposed in some way to allow both complements to hang off the VP "in a single position," later to undergo separate applications of Intraposition. Why this consequence is not regarded by Emonds as a complete refutation of the Intraposition analysis and its underlying assumptions is a mystery to me.

Let us turn to more technical criticisms, a variety of which are con-

---

[18] Extraposition is inapplicable to either *that* clause in cases like (66). This fact requires a special statement in such a system. But it has no bearing on the choice between Intraposition and Extraposition grammars, since the former needs the parallel special statement making Intraposition obligatory. Neither system has provided any explanation of the impossibility of having the complements in (66) appear in extraposed positions. An explanation of the limitations on Extraposition with the verbs in (66) should also indicate why *that*-clause objects are also not subject to Topicalization with them:

(i) That he is honest, I can no longer believe.

(ii) a. *That Bob is honest, this proves.
    b. *That Bob is honest, (the fact) that he returned the beer indicates.

sidered by Higgins, and observe such sentences as (68) and (69), already considered in Section 4.14.

(68) a. I resent it being possible for Bob to leave.

   b. I believe it to be possible for Bob to leave.

(69) a. I resent it being publicized that I am divorced.

   b. I found it to have been publicized that I am divorced.

As described there, under an Extraposition analysis combined with a B-verb Raising system, it is possible to explain the differences between *resent,* on the one hand, and *believe* and *find,* on the other. Since *resent* does not trigger Raising, but B-verbs like *believe* and *find* do, under an Extraposition analysis, the complement is extraposed from the higher

(70) a.

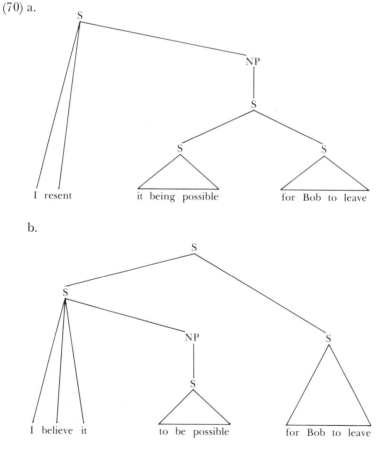

b.

clause in (68)b, (69)b, and hence adjoined ultimately as a sister of that clause, while in (68)a, (69)a, the Extraposition application is complement internal. Thus such an analysis predicts contrasting surface bracketings like (70)a and (70)b, which correspond correctly to intuitions about such matters. Moreover, as earlier noted, the difference in assigned structures explains differences in extractability from the complements of the two types of cases under weak extraction rules like Adverb Preposing. Hence, consider (71):

(71) a. ?On Thursday, I resent it being possible for Bob to leave.

b. On Thursday, I believe it to be possible for Bob to leave.

Only in (71)b can *on Thursday* "modify" *leave,* since weak rules cannot extract elements from the complement of *resent,* indicating that the complement of *possible* remains internal to the complement of *resent.*

But Emonds's Intraposition analysis would necessarily assign the same structures to both types here, a structure formally more like (70)a, with the infinitival complement internal to the complement of the main verb (but a VP constituent). Thus, although extraposed complements are generally bracketed as main clause constituents, Emonds's analysis systematically assigns them incorrect VP bracketings. Thus, for example, Emonds's system assigns to (72)a the structure (72)b instead of the correct (72)c:

(72) a. It worries me that Bob is late.

b. it [worries me (that Bob is late)]

c. [[it (worries me)] (that Bob is late)]

Of course, Emond's analysis can be patched up to deal with this matter by adding a "readjustment" rule to take out the complement from the VP and attach it higher up, that is, by adding to his Intraposition analysis a rule much like Extraposition. The redundancy of such a system becomes thereby clearer. But the situation is even worse than it appears. For an Extraposition analysis distinguishes pairs like (70)a, b naturally by operating differently on structures that either have or have not undergone Raising, that is, by operating on structures of the form shown in (73), which remain complement internal or which have been lifted into a higher clause:[19]

---

[19] In support of this point, recall such previously discussed contrasts as the following:

(73)   NP

        S

But, in Emonds's system, *for Bob to leave* in such cases is generated identically as the right extremity of the phrase whose head is *possible*. Therefore, since infinitival clauses wrongly have the same structure in both cases, any "readjustment" rule added to an Intraposition grammar would treat these two cases in the same way, again giving the wrong answers. To handle the facts, such a system needs two different "readjustment" rules at best. Thus, unlike an Extraposition analysis, an Intraposition system cannot interact correctly with the differentiation provided by Raising contrasts. Consequently, an Intraposition system misses the generalizations existing for this range of phenomena.

A final point must be made. According to Emonds, Intraposition is what he calls a "root transformation," which means, among other things, that it cannot apply within embedded structures. This is supposed to explain facts that Ross (1967) handled by means of an output condition blocking cases where infinitival or *that* complements were "internal." This range of phenomena still has not been satisfactorily dealt with, as Ross would be among the first to admit. By making Intraposition a root transformation, Emonds thus sought to explain such facts as the following:

(74) a.   I find it difficult to believe that Bob is a werewolf.

     b. *I find that Bob is a werewolf difficult to believe.

Example (74)b is supposedly blocked because Intraposition would here apply in an embedded structure, the complement of *find*. However, although there is certainly motivation for seeking to explain facts like (74)b in terms of some general principle, Emonds's account is far from satisfactory here. What must be regarded, under an Extraposition an-

---

(i) a.   What I resent is it being possible for him to avoid taxes.
    b. *What I believe is it to be possible for him to avoid taxes.

(ii) a.   Bill resents—but Sarah doesn't resent—it being possible for him to avoid taxes.
     b. *Bill believes—but Sarah doesn't believe—it to be possible for him to avoid taxes.

alysis, as the topicalized version of (74)b is, in fact, well-formed (similar sentences were independently discovered by Higgins):

(75) That Bob is a werewolf I find (*it) difficult to believe.

Topicalization in general operates on NPs, not on S. Therefore, the underlying structure of (75) must include an intermediate stage like (74)b, which must thus be generated, in contradiction to Emonds's claim that Intraposition does not function within embeddings.

The only alternative for Emonds would be to claim that the grammar generates (75), not by having Topicalization operate on the supposedly underived (74)b, but rather by having Topicalization operate on the *it* of (74)a, with some extension of Intraposition then later substituting the complement for the *it* in topicalized position. (For the reason why this is an extension of Emonds's rule, see Higgins, 1971.) The most obvious difficulty with this tack is, of course, that there is no reason to think that Topicalization can operate on elements like the *it* of these constructions:

(76) a. *It I find it difficult to believe.

  b. *It I found to have rained.

  c. *It I find to be far from Paris to Montreal.

  d. *It I find obvious that Melvin is a werewolf.

Thus sentences like (75) seem to condemn an Intraposition analysis to the need for further ad hoc repairs.[20]

---

[20] The restriction noted in footnote 45 of Chapter 4 may ultimately provide an argument against an Intraposition analysis. The point was that, in the terms adopted here, Complex NP Shift can operate neither on *that* clauses nor on gerundive clauses in contexts of the form [B-verb *NP* infinitival]:

(i) a. *I believe to be obvious—that Bob does not know French.
  b. *I believe to be disgusting—Bob's not knowing French.

This is also true of infinitivals:

(ii) *I believe to have been wrong—for Bob to come late.

In Emonds's system, the correlation between (i)a, b and (ii) is fortuitous, since (i)a and (ii) would, in his system, be explained by the fact that *that* clauses and infinitivals are never NPs, hence not subject to Complex NP Shift from the post-B-verb (or any other) position. Moreover, they cannot even attain this position because of the principle that Intraposition, as a root transformation, does not work in embeddings. On the other hand, since gerundives are taken to be NPs by Emonds, example (i)b must be regarded

In summary, not only do I see no way to consider Emonds's rejection of Extraposition correct, but I find at this point no reason why his alternative Intraposition analysis should be regarded as a serious competitor. It seems to me on every ground to be a largely unmotivated, mechanical artifact requiring unclear and otherwise unneeded extensions of both grammatical theory and the principles of English. Most important of all perhaps, his analysis is directly incompatible with the view that underlying grammatical structures are not arbitrary configurations of unconstrained symbols but rather structures determined by the semantic properties of the sentences they represent.

12.5 A Constraint on Complex NP Shift

The purpose of this section is to expand somewhat and clarify the discussion of footnote 3 of Chapter 4. In Section 4.1, I considered the rule Complex NP Shift, which I assume to function roughly as indicated

(77)

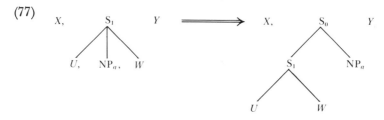

---

as due to a constraint on Complex NP Shift. But in an Extraposition system, examples (i)a, b and (ii) can all be explained uniformly as resulting from a constraint on Complex NP Shift's ability to postpose sentential NPs.

It is worth stressing that correlations like those in (i) and (ii) exist not only in post-B-verb positions. Compare also the following:

(iii) a. I kept that a secret.
    b. I kept John's having visited Mary a secret.
    c. I kept a secret—the fact that Melvin was insane.
    d. *I kept a secret—John's having visited Mary.
    e. *I kept a secret—that Melvin was insane.
    f. I kept it a secret that Melvin was insane.

(iv) a. I took that for granted.
    b. I took John's being willing to attend for granted.
    c. I took for granted—the analysis which we had earlier discussed.
    d. *I took for granted—John's being willing to attend.
    e. *I took for granted—that Melvin was insane.
    f. I took it for granted that Melvin was insane.

in (77). This rule, in conformity with Ross's (1967) discovery that right-ward-moving rules are upward bounded, can never cross higher clause boundaries. Thus it derives such sentences as (78)b and (78)d:

(78) a. They elected Bob president of United Death Ray Industries.

   b. They elected president of United Death Ray Industries—the leading liberal advocate of lobotomy on demand.

   c. I consider George to be intelligent.

   d. I consider to be intelligent—all of those who agree with my ideas about the cosmos.

It was argued in Section 4.1 that Complex NP Shift is subject to the constraint given in (79), accounting for the examples of (80):

(79) Complex NP Shift does not operate on subjects.

(80) a. *That was weird—the man who I met in Bloomingdale's is clear.

   b. *Instead of visiting Washington—the former monarch of Petrovia, I suggested that he acquaint himself with Baltimore.

   c. *The elephants will cross first, to follow them—the purple zebras, green ocelots, and the first thirty-three red lions.

   d. *Having run out—all of the noncarbohydrate beer we had stolen in Milwaukee, Jack was forced to drink Dr. Pepper.

Given this no-subject constraint on Complex NP Shift, the fact that the rule can operate in cases like (81) indicates that the post-B-verb NPs in such cases are derived objects at the point of application of Complex NP Shift:

(81) a. I believe Bob to be intolerant.

   b. I believe to be intolerant—all those who disagree with my fountain theory of language.

This is a direct consequence of having previously undergone Raising, which destroys their previous subject status, found in the corresponding *that* clauses of (82):

(82) a. I believe (that) Bob is intolerant.

   b. *I believe (that) are intolerant—all those who disagree with my fountain theory of language.

So far, then, the properties of Complex NP Shift seem reasonably comprehensible in terms of fairly well behaved types of constraints.

Consider now, however, the extremely interesting fact, pointed out by Howard Lasnik (personal communication), that Complex NP Shift is *not* generally applicable to the directly postverbal NPs with verbs like *want* or *wish*:

(83) a.   I want him to leave now.

   b.   I wish him to succeed in that venture.

   c.   *I want to leave now—all of those men who are tracking mud on my carpet.

   d.   *I wish to succeed in that venture—all of my friends who have just returned from the Venezuelan Highlands.

Given the knowledge that Complex NP Shift is controlled by the no-subject constraint, a natural first approach to ill-formed examples like (83)c, d would be to try to explain them in terms of that constraint. This would mean claiming that, in contrast to B-verbs, verbs such as *want* and *wish* are not R-triggers. Hence, their complement subjects would remain subjects, and application of Complex NP Shift would be impeded by the no-subject constraint. Such an approach has been suggested by Lasnik (personal communication). However, I have already argued at some length in Section 4.16 that *want, wish,* and other W-verbs are R-triggers, on many grounds, so that Lasnik's proposal about sentences like (83)c, d is not really viable.

I suggest that what is going on in (83)c, d involves a certain constraint on "ambiguity," in a certain sense of this term. There is a contrast in Complex NP Shift behavior between B-verbs and W-verbs. One of the most obvious independent contrasts between these two types is that whereas W-verbs trigger application of Equi, so that their complement subject NPs are deleted when coreferential with the main verb subject, B-verbs do not trigger Equi, and under parallel circumstances the original complement subject NP is reflexivized:

(84) a. I want [I be famous] $\implies$ I want to be famous.

   b. I believe [I to be famous] $\implies$ I believe myself to be famous.

Observe then what happens when Complex NP Shift applies to the NP directly following a W-verb, say, to a structure like (85):

(85) [I don't want those men who have committed war crimes to be elected to high office]

The result would be the ill-formed (86):

(86) *I don't want to be elected to high office—those men who have committed war crimes.

This would have the derived structure shown in (87). The key point to observe here is that, with *want* or other W-verbs, the derived S_1 constituent produced by Complex NP Shift looks essentially like a clause derived by Equi. Hence, S_1 of (87) is identical to the Equi-derived independent clause of (88):

(87)

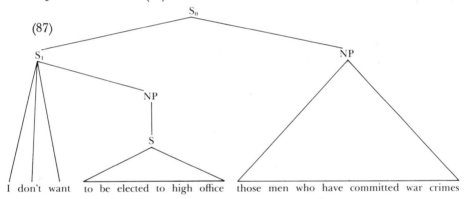

I don't want   to be elected to high office   those men who have committed war crimes

(88) I don't want to be elected to high office.

Thus, in the case of W-verbs, Complex NP Shift operation has the effect of producing a kind of "garden path" situation in which, for example, the perception mechanism involved in speech recognition and analysis could hear all of S_1 in (87) and be led to a perfectly determinate and completely wrong dead-end analysis of S_1 as having been Equi-derived. I suggest that it is this false-path property of such derivations which underlies the general unacceptability of Complex NP Shift application to post-W-verb NPs before infinitivals.

The immediate virtue of the proposal just made, which may be called the No Dead End Constraint (NODEC) to contrast it with Lasnik's suggestion, is that it accounts for the interaction of W-verbs like *want* with Complex NP Shift without eliminating the possibility of taking these to be R-triggers, which is necessitated by a wide variety of facts, as shown, for example, in Section 4.16. Moreover, there are other more direct pieces of evidence that support an approach like NODEC and further disconfirm the view that facts like (83)c, d are a function of the no-subject constraint on Complex NP Shift in concert with the view that *want*, etc., are not R-triggers.

First, Lasnik's explanation (which may be called Anti-Raising) makes a prediction about one possible class of verbs with Complex NP Shift which is inconsistent with that made by NODEC. Namely, if there are verbs that fall into *both* the reflexivization and Equi patterns, NODEC predicts that these will behave like W-verbs with respect to Complex NP Shift, while Anti-Raising predicts that they will behave like B-verbs. But, in fact, as we have seen, there is at least one such verb, namely, *expect*:[21]

(89) a. I expect to win.

b. I expect myself to win.

And, strikingly, *expect* behaves like *want* with respect to Complex NP Shift operation:

[21] Lasnik's Anti-Raising theory, which assumes that such verbs as *want* are not R-triggers, in contrast to B-verbs, whose R-trigger status he accepts, is based in part on passivization contrasts:

(i)   a. I want Bob to know French.
      b. I believe Bob to know French.

(ii) a. *Bob is wanted to know French (by everyone).
     b. Bob is believed to know French (by everyone).

Thus it seems that passivization constraints correlate with constraints on Complex NP Shift, both apparently explainable under the assumption that *believe* is an R-trigger and *want* is not. This lends Lasnik's proposal considerable initial plausibility. But this also disintegrates when it is noted that not only *expect* but also *intend* and *mean* behave like B-verbs with respect to passivization but like *want* with respect to Complex NP Shift:

(iii) a. I intend Bob to die peacefully.
      b. Bob was intended to die peacefully.
      c. *I intended to die peacefully—everyone who agreed to vote for that proposal.

(iv) a. I meant Bob to arrive too late.
     b. Bob was meant to arrive too late.
     c. *I meant to arrive too late—the man who saved her from the rapids.

Thus the passivization + Complex NP Shift correlation with *want* and *wish* is fortuitous. The facts in (iii) and (iv) follow, of course, from NODEC, given the view that *intend* and *mean* are (W-element) R-triggers.

(90) a. I expect Bob to win.

   b. *I expect to win—all of those candidates who told the truth at least once.

(91) a. They expect Joan to be reelected.

   b. *They expect to be reelected—all of those candidates who supported the president.

NODEC predicts the facts in (90)b and (91)b because the resulting sentences have derived S_1 clauses that are models of the Equi-overlap situation in (87). However, Anti-Raising predicts that sentences like (90)b and (91)b should be well-formed since, as a Raising trigger (proved by (89)b and the passive facts noted in footnote 21, etc.), *expect* occurs with postverbal derived objects at the point of Complex NP Shift, just like a B-verb.

Second, Anti-Raising, in contrast to NODEC, is incompatible with the well-formedness of Complex NP Shift application to the NP after *want* and *wish,* in such reduced cases as these:

(92) a. I want Bob fired now.

   b. I want fired now—everyone who failed to heed my fifty-first edict.

(93) a. I wish them removed from this property.

   b. I wish removed from this property—all those squatters who are polluting the stream.

NODEC predicts this well-formedness because the S_1 structures derived by Complex NP Shift in these cases are not matched with Equi-derived clauses:

(94) a. *I want fired now

   b. *I wish removed from this property

For Anti-Raising, however, such examples either are direct disconfirmations or force the claim, intolerable to me, that sentences like (92)a and (93)a have quite different derivations from (95), that is, one either with Raising or with an "extra" NP + Equi analysis:

(95) a. I want Bob to be fired now.

   b. I wish them to be removed from this property.

There are other, similar examples. Thus only NODEC can explain the differences in (97) because of (98):

(96) a. I reported Bob to be late for work.

  b. I reported Bob (to be drunk).

(97) a. I reported to be late for work—the new employee who arrived at 9:01.

  b. I reported to be drunk—the new employee who arrived at 9:01.

  c. *I reported drunk—the new employee who arrived at 9:01.

(98) a. *I reported to be late for work

  b. *I reported to be drunk

  c. I reported drunk

Third, evidence in favor of NODEC and against Anti-Raising is provided by certain cases with W-verbs themselves, where the application of Complex NP Shift does *not* yield a derived S_1 clause that is identical in shape to some Equi-derived clause. The Anti-Raising theory of W-verbs like *want* claims that such cases will be equally as ill-formed as those where there is a perfect match, while NODEC predicts that they will be well-formed. But consider the following:

(99) a. $\left\{ \begin{array}{c} I \\ *They \end{array} \right\}$ only want to become doctors—those students who have a genuine interest in alleviating human suffering.

  b. $\left\{ \begin{array}{c} I \\ *They \end{array} \right\}$ only want to criticize themselves—those of you who feel capable of undergoing deep probing.

  c. $\left\{ \begin{array}{c} I \\ *They \end{array} \right\}$ wish to look like fools—all those who are trying to discredit my interplanetary sailboat.

While the sentences with *I* are hardly models of stylistic felicity, it seems clear that they contrast in acceptability with examples like (83)c, d, as well as those with *they.* But this is just what NODEC predicts on the basis of cases like (100):

(100) a. $\left\{ \begin{array}{c} *I \\ They \end{array} \right\}$ only want to become doctors.

b. $\left\{\begin{array}{l} \text{*I} \\ \text{They} \end{array}\right\}$ only want to criticize themselves.

c. $\left\{\begin{array}{l} \text{*I} \\ \text{They} \end{array}\right\}$ wish to look like fools.

Anti-Raising, on the other hand, predicts no difference between (83)c, d and (99).

I think that the evidence is therefore decisive in indicating that the original constraints on Complex NP Shift with verbs like *want*, insightfully noted by Lasnik, cannot be attributed to a failure of Raising to apply with these verbs. The conclusion stands that W-verbs are R-triggers; consequently, the restrictions noted by Lasnik must be due to a principle along the lines of NODEC.

Of course, I have not formulated NODEC precisely, and most questions about it have not even been raised, to say nothing of having been answered. It seems clear that NODEC must be transderivational, since what it says, extremely roughly, is that a derivation D containing the mapping shown in (101) is ill-formed if S_1 is independently derivable in the grammar.[22] And such a statement determines the acceptability of a

(101)

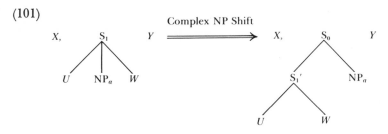

[22] An immediate problem with (101) as it stands is provided by facts like (i):

(i) a. Jack believes to be insane—anyone who voted for George Wallace more than once.
   b. Who did you say *Jack believed to be insane*?

As (i)b shows, the S_1 clause of (i)a is independently derivable in the grammar, yet (i)a is perfectly well-formed. Thus (101) inadequately makes no distinction between independent derivability by a rule like Equi and independent derivability by a leftward-moving unbounded movement rule like *Wh*-Question Movement (note that any other unbounded rule to the left will work the same way).

Ultimately, I have no doubt that the contrast here is a function of the fact that a rule like *Wh*-Question Movement, by placing the moved constituent to the left of its original position, in effect warns the listener to be on the lookout for a truncated clause, while Equi has no such characteristic. The point is, then, that the existence

derivation involving Complex NP Shift application by matching (part of) that derivation with other derivations. I hope that serious studies of NODEC and similar constraints can be carried out in the future, but space does not permit any deeper treatment here.

12.6 A Late Argument for Raising into Superordinate Object Positions

There is a rule in English normally called Particle Movement (see Fraser, 1965; Ross, 1967, for discussion) that maps a sequence of the form (102)a into (102)b:

(102) a. Verb Particle NP

     b. Verb NP Particle

Examples follow:

(103) a. I looked up the number.

     b. I looked the number up.

(104) a. He wore out the valve.

     b. He wore the valve out.

In accord with the principle discovered by Ross (1967), namely, that rightward-moving rules are clause-internal (see footnote 15 of Chapter 2),[23] every hitherto known case of Particle Movement application is purely clause-internal, as in (103) and (104).

---

of clauses like those in (i)b can cause no confusion in the perception of those like (i)a, while the existence of those like (ii)b can cause confusion in the perception of those like (ii)a:

(ii) a. I want to leave immediately—the truck loaded with pregnant zebras.
    b. I want to leave immediately.

[23] Actually, there is (independent of the matters discussed in footnote 15 of Chapter 2 and footnote 8 of Chapter 4) at least one further complication. Namely, some rightward movements are "clause-internal" in that they operate as in (i), while others are "clause-internal" in that they operate as in (ii):

(i)

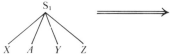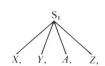

Consider now the following sentences:

(105) a. I figured it out to be more than 300 miles from here to Tulsa.

   b. I figured it out to be impossible for us to get there by 11:00.

   c. *I figured it out is more than 300 miles from here to Tulsa.

   d. *I figured it out is impossible for us to get there by 11:00.

What explains the possible word order of *it* and *out* in (105)a, b? Part of the answer must lie with Particle Movement, since it can be shown independently that *figure out* is subject to this rule:

(106) a. I figured out the answer.

   b. I figured the answer out.

It follows that underlying (105)a must be the following structure:

(107) I figured out [$_S$ it to be more than 300 miles from here to Tulsa $_S$]

In a non-Raising grammar, like that advocated by Chomsky, Particle Movement must operate directly on such a structure. This means, given that this rule moves a particle to the right, that the rule must in this case insert the particle into the complement clause. Therefore, in a non-Raising grammar, a rightward-operating rule of Particle Movement violates the condition of clause-internality on rightward-reordering rules.

In a Raising grammar, on the other hand, one need say only that *figure out* is an R-trigger. Then, Raising will operate on the structure in (107) to yield (108), which can be converted to (105)a by Particle Movement with no violation of the restrictive condition on rightward-movement rules.

(ii)

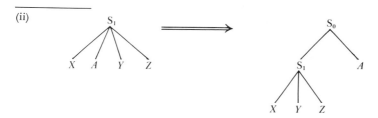

The sense of "internal" in (ii) is that while A gets out of S_1 it does not become attached to any nodes dominating or dominated by S_1, but only to some new node S_0, created by the operation for just that purpose.

(108) I figured out [$_{NP}$ it $_{NP}$] [$_S$ to be more than 300 miles from here to
   Tulsa$_S$]

Moreover, a derivation with a rightward-moving particle and no
Raising entails that, in (105)a, a sequence like *it out . . . Tulsa* is a
derived (S) constituent. This conclusion is grossly unintuitive, and the
test involving the rule RNR shows it to be quite incorrect:

(109) a. I didn't expect to figure it out to be impossible to do that, but
       I did figure it out to be impossible to do that.

   b. *I didn't expect to figure—but I did figure—it out to be im-
       possible to do that.

It is clear, then, that the existence of a rule of Particle Movement reordering particles to the right combines with the facts in (105) to yield
another argument for a rule raising NPs into superordinate object positions. It might be suggested, though, that there is an alternative to
describing Particle Movement as a rule that moves particles to the right:
namely, to consider it a rule that moves NPs to the left. If this was done,
then Particle Movement so understood could operate directly on (107),
obviously violating no constraints on rightward movements and also
generating the correct derived constituent structure, with both *it* and
out constituents of the main clause. In this approach the operation of
Particle Movement to structures like (107) in effect mimics in part the
operation of Raising.

   I think, however, that such an account of Particle Movement cannot
stand, and hence can offer no defense against the argument based on the
traditional view that it is the particle that is moved (to the right). *First*,
this account requires that Particle Movement be a rule that sometimes
operates purely clause-internally, but in other cases as a raising rule.
That is, it would have to be a rule of type (33)b (iii) of Section 2.4 and
would require the same weakening of linguistic theory discussed there
for the parallel treatment of Passive. There is no reason to think that
such rules exist. One of the arguments for Raising is that it permits
maintenance of the view that they do not.

   Second, the attempt to claim that Particle Movement operates directly
on (107) to generate (105)a requires that the rule be made obligatory in
this case, because of (110):

(110) *I figured out it to be more than 300 miles from here to Tulsa.

Moreover, although one also finds (111), in a non-Raising grammar in which Particle Movement is construed as a rule moving NPs to the left, the ill-formedness of (110) cannot be attributed to the constraint on Particle Movement illustrated in (111):

(111) *I figured out it.

That is, it cannot be said that Particle Movement is obligatory when the particle directly precedes a weak pronoun. The reason for this is shown in (112):

(112) I figured out it was more than 300 miles from here to Tulsa.

Thus the constraint on Particle Movement will have to involve the strange statement that this rule, typically optional, and typically optional even with *figure out*, is obligatory in just that case where *figure out* has an untensed complement. In a Raising grammar, on the contrary, (110) follows simply from the constraint underlying (111), which can be described as a constraint on the sequence particle + weak pronoun in cases where these are Clause Mates. Thus a Raising grammar in on sense explains facts like (110) on the basis of those like (111), whereas a non-Raising grammar cannot. A Raising grammar makes it clear why a speaker who has the experience underlying facts like (111) would automatically come to the judgment in (110).[24] In a non-Raising grammar, there is no basis for this projection, and descriptive adequacy requires the ad hoc statement about obligatoriness described earlier.[25]

---

[24] Observe that, from the point of view of this argument, the extreme marginality of examples like (105)a, b is a crucial factor strengthening the support for the Raising analysis, along the lines discussed in Section 4.6. That is, since it is very unlikely that the linguistic experience of speakers would include examples like (105)a, b, there is no reason to think they would ever be motivated to add to their grammars the ad hoc condition on obligatoriness apparently needed in a non-Raising system. What is required is an account that permits one to explain how the core linguistic experience of speakers is naturally projected to a grammar that automatically makes the judgment in (110) on the basis of facts like (111), even in the face of those like (112).

[25] Of course, this argument could be circumvented if there were, as Chomsky (to appear) claims, a principle barring elements in general from being extracted from tensed clauses. For this principle could explain the failure of Particle Movement to apply to structures like (112). However, I have been unable to find a single rule whose behavior is properly determined by such a principle. Its sole motivation seems to be based on a failure to recognize the existence of Raising into superordinate object positions. See footnote 1 of Chapter 5 and footnote 9 of Chapter 12.

Third, there is an argument that sentences like (105)a can*not* be derived by an NP to the left version of Particle Movement, an argument based on selections. It seems that the only NP that can occur as the subject of infinitival complements with *figure out* is *it*:

(113) a. *I figured there out to be no money in that box.

    b. *I figured Barbara out to be pregnant.

    c. *I figured that out to be wrong.

As we have seen in our discussion of R-triggers in Chapter 9, however, such restrictions are quite typical for R-triggers. Recall, for instance, the facts with the verb *estimate.* But if sentences like (105)a are derived exclusively by Particle Movement, then there is no natural locus in the grammar for the selections. Note that they cannot be attributed either to Particle Movement in general or to Particle Movement with *figure out* in particular:

(114) a. I figured Barbara out.

    b. I figured that out.

    c. I figured everything out.

Thus it would seem that a non-Raising grammar of *figure out* would have to attribute facts like (113) to constraints on underlying structures —it would have to say that *figure out* can take untensed complements, but only when the subjects of these are *it*. This is a peculiar, perhaps unprecedented type of restriction in itself. But the important point is that it fails to bring out the similarity of the restrictions on *figure out* with those typical of raised NPs in general, with respect to both type I and type II R-triggers. I conclude that the traditional view of Particle Movement as a rightward particle reordering is correct. Hence, the argument from examples like (105)a for Raising into superordinate object position with *figure out* stands.

12.7 The Next-to-Last Argument

The argument of this section was suggested by some of Maurice Gross's observations about French.

In a Raising system, the italicized sequences in (115) are not derived constituents, as we have seen, in contrast to those in (116):

(115) a. I believe *Bob to know French.*

　　b. I wish *Bob to know French.*

　　c. I prevented *Bob from knowing French.*

(116) a. 　I believe *(that) Bob knows French.*

　　b. 　I wish *(that) Bob knew French.*

　　c. ?*I prevented *Bob's knowing French.*

In general, we expect that constituents of the same type can be co-ordinated, while nonconstituents cannot be. If so, then the difference in constituent structure between (115) and (116) should show up in contrasting conjunction possibilities, in such a way as to support a Raising analysis of sentences like (115) and the derived nonconstituent status of the italicized sequences which such an analysis directly imposes.

However, initially the expectation of a contrast is frustrated, apparently providing some difficulty for a Raising treatment:

(117) a. I believe Bob to know French and Sally to know Spanish.

　　b. I wish Bob to know French and Sally to know Spanish.

　　c. I prevented Bob from knowing French and Sally from knowing Spanish.

(118) a. 　I believe that Bob knows French and that Sally knows Spanish.

　　b. 　I wish that Bob knew French and that Sally knew Spanish.

　　c. ?*I prevented Bob's knowing French and Sally's knowing Spanish.

The raised cases seem as conjoinable as the unraised cases, at first sight, inexplicably so in Raising terms. I suggest, however, that the parallelism between (117) and (118) is spurious. In (118)a, b we actually have conjoined *that* clauses and thus structures of the form indicated in (119). I claim, however, that this is not the case in (117), where the coordination is actually at the level of the main clause, as shown in (120). Thus what we have in (117) are truncated conjoined main clauses, not conjoined subordinate clauses. This is really the phenomenon discussed at the end of footnote 39 of Chapter 4, where it was suggested that the truncation involved Gapping. If so, then a rule is also needed to delete

(119)

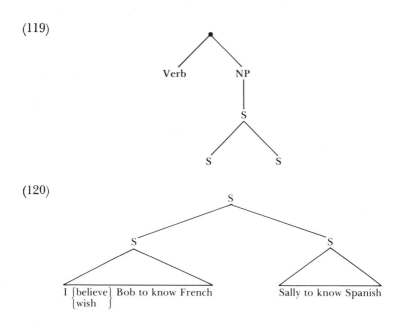

(120)

the coreferential subject, so that such derivations proceed as follows, taking *believe* for illustration:

(121) a. I believe Bob to know French, and I believe Sally to know Spanish. Gapping ⇒

b. I believe Bob to know French and I Sally to know Spanish. Coordinate Subject Deletion ⇒

c. I believe Bob to know French and Sally to know Spanish.

What is significant is that, in this analysis,[26] the deletion of the subject

[26] In this treatment, Gapping must operate in cases even where there are noncontrasting NPs, as in (121)a. Thus it would also operate in cases like (i), yielding (ii):

(i)   I like apples and I like peaches.

(ii) *I like apples and I peaches.

I conclude that what blocks such sentences is not a constraint on the inputs to Gapping but one on the outputs, which must in some sense contain contrasting elements in corresponding positions. However, this is not strictly correct if the analysis of (121) is right, since the deletion rule eliminates the condition that (121)b would violate if it were a surface structure. Therefore, the constraint is sensitive, not to the output of Gapping, but rather to surface structure. The restriction seems, then, to be, not that surface gapped clauses must contain contrasting elements in corresponding positions, but rather that they must not contain noncontrasting elements in corresponding positions.

of the following coordinate clause can be accomplished by the independently needed rule operative in (122):[27]

(122) Bob$_i$ entered the room, and (then) he$_i$ turned off the light.

Ø

As previously indicated (in footnote 39 of Chapter 4), an analysis like this seems necessary because of the possibilities with *promise* in example (123), where taking *Bob to go* and *Sally to stay* to be conjoined complement clauses is out of the question.

(123) I promised Bob to go and Sally to stay.

It seems to me that the intonational breaks of sentences like (117) and (122) support the analysis. That is, the main break is after the first infinitive and not after the main verb, in accord with a structure like (120). It is not like (119), which provides the correct bracketing for examples like (118).

So far, then, the facts have no sharp bearing on questions of the existence of Raising into superordinate objection positions, because we have not found structures that force an interpretation of conjunction at the level of complements in the case of those phrases for which a Raising analysis is in dispute. However, I claim such structures can be found, namely, those containing the markers *either . . . or*, *neither . . . nor*,

[27] However, this analysis does not extend to cases like (i), where the subject *there* has been deleted in the second clause.

(i) There are pears in the sink and apples on the table.

Clearly, this could not be accomplished by the rule relevant for (122), since there is no possible sense in which occurrences of *there* can be coreferents. It is conceivable that the deletion of *there* in such cases is carried out by the rule that deletes the verb *be*. Note that, unlike true coreferential cases, in which the relevant subject deletion can strand *be*, as in (ii), this is impossible in cases like (i), as shown in (iii):

(ii) Melvin is intelligent and (thus) (is) willing to compromise.

(iii) *There are pears in the sink and (thus) are apples on the table.

Possibly the joint loss of both auxiliary *be* and *there* can be attributed to a rule that attaches these forms, yielding a single phonological word:

(iv) a. [thǣːr] pears in the sink.
     b. [thǣːrz] a pear in the sink.

Such an approach is suggested by observations of Kayne concerning the deletion of auxiliaries with cliticized *on* in French. See Kayne (to appear: especially footnote 38).

both . . . and, and *not only . . . but also.* Expectably, we find the cases in (124) and analogously with the other three cases:

(124) a.   He believes either that Melvin is insane or that Joan has been giving him drugs.

b.   He wishes either that we would hire him or that Martha would support him.

c.   ?*He prevented either Bob's quitting or Martha's retiring.

But, strikingly, we also have the following:

(125) a.   *He believes either Melvin to be insane or Joan to have been giving him drugs.

b.   *He wishes either us to hire him or Martha to support him.

c.   *He prevented either Bob from quitting or Martha from retiring.

(126) a.   *He believes neither Nixon to be honorable nor Agnew to be decent.

b.   *He wishes neither the serum to be distributed nor the vaccine to be tested.

c.   *He prevented neither Bob from leaving nor Sally from staying.

(127) a.   *He believes both Bob to be immoral and Joan to be promiscuous.

b.   *He wishes both Larry to be discrete and Tom to be cautious.

c.   *He prevented both Joan from confessing and Sally from squealing.

(128) a.   *He believes not only Bob to be Turkish but also Martha to be Persian.

b.   *He wishes not only Joan to help him but also Max to appoint him.

c.   *He prevented not only Tom from calling but also Martha from leaving.

This sharp contrast follows simply, I suggest, from the fact that *either* ... *or*, etc., must be in construction with *constituents*. That is, in structures of the form *either A or B*, etc., *A* and *B* must be constituents.

But constituent status is destroyed by the operation of Raising in the B-verb, W-verb, and N-verb cases with non-*that* clauses. Note that all questions of tensed clauses are irrelevant here. Structures like *either* ... *or* are fine with untensed clauses that are not the result of Raising operation and hence maintain a derived constituent status:

(129) a. I arranged either for Bob to come late or for Sally to leave early.

   b. I resent neither Joan's marrying Lou nor Bob's dating Sally.

   c. I approve of both Tom's inviting Greta and Melvin's inviting Betty.

   d. I favor not only the president being allowed to do that but also the vice president's being allowed to do it.

I conclude that the contrasts between (125)–(128), on the one hand, and (123) and (129), on the other, provide a clear instance of factual differences naturally explained in a system that has Raising operating into superordinate object positions, but otherwise mysterious. Therefore, these facts of coordination support a Raising analysis and disconfirm non-Raising systems.

12.8 The Last Argument

As the following examples show, the more typical phrase type *the + Number + of + pronoun* has, in first and second person plural cases, a paraphrase of the form *pronoun + Number*:

(130) a. We three are happy.

   b. We four were arrested by the police.

   c. You two are difficult to contact.

   d. *They three are totally insane.

   e. *They two are hard to deal with.

All of the cases of (130)[28] have the latter construction in derived subject position, in fact, in finite clauses. In the speech of many people, there is no requirement of subject position. But for some speakers, including myself, while *you* + *Number* occurs freely, regardless of functional status, most of the positions in which *us* + *Number* would be expected are blocked. The following examples with *us* all have a definite substandard quality:

(131) a.   Harry wrote to you two.

b.   *Harry wrote to us two.

c.   They criticized you three.

d.   *They criticized us three.

e.   You two, they will never agree to rehire.

f.   *Us three, they will never agree to rehire.

It might be concluded, then,[29] that there simply is no well-formed NP phrase of the form *us* + *Number* in this idiolect type. But this is incorrect:

(132) a.   For us two to do that would be immoral.

b.   They would prefer for us three to remain here.

c.   It would be wise for us two to stay at home.

d.   The chief arranged for us three to be released.

28 One very strange property of the construction in (130) is that it exists only with small numbers and worsens as the number increases:

(i) We { two / three / four / five / ?six / ?seven / ?eight / ?nine / ?ten / *eleven / **eighty-eight / ***eight hundred thirty-four } are happy.

Possibly the number of syllables is relevant.

29 Amazingly, one gets a much better sentence than (131)f by substituting *we* for *us*. In fact, the result is probably well-formed. But this is not the case in (131)b, d, although the results are improved.

I suggest, then, that the appropriate constraint is that *us + Number* can occur in this idiolect type only in derived subject position,[30] as in (132). If so, the facts provide an argument for Raising because of such distributions as the following:

(133) a. He tried to show us (*three) the erotic postcards.

   b. He tried to show us (*three) to be spies.

   c. He wants to believe us (*three).

   d. He doesn't want to believe us (*three) to be spies.

That is, with respect to the suggested constraint, the NPs after B-verbs before infinitives behave as if they were in nonsubject position, in accord with a Raising grammar.

Note such W-Verb contrasts as those in (134), where, in a Raising grammar of the *for*-less cases, there are simple contrasts between derived subject positions and derived object positions.

(134) a. They would prefer for us (three) to resign.

   b. They would prefer us (*three) to resign.

   c. They intended for us (three) to be implicated.

   d. They intended us (*three) to be implicated.

N-Verb contexts also work as expected in a Raising system:

(135) a. They prevented us (*two) from boarding.

   b. That deterred us (*three) from continuing.

   c. They restrained us (*two) from grappling with each other.

It should be stressed that all the starred examples involving *us + Number* in (131)–(135) become well-formed if *the + Number + of + us*

---

30 This is a necessary, not a sufficient, condition. Such phrases are hopeless in contexts where derived subjects need the genitive, for example:

(i) a. *Us three's going late would be unfortunate.
   b. *Our three going late would be unfortunate.
   c. *Our three's going late would be unfortunate.

This is also the case, however, with the *the* variants:

(ii) a. *The three of us's going late would be unfortunate.
   b. *The three of our going late would be unfortunate.

is substituted. This indicates, I believe, that there is no independent reason for the ill-formedness.[31]

I conclude that the distribution of *us* + *Number* in the idiolect type under discussion provides a further argument for a rule raising the subject NPs of object complements into derived object position in the main clause. With this argument, the case for Raising rests.

[31] A further peculiarity of both constructions with numbers is that they have no relative pronoun analogues:

(i) a. *Max and Dorothy, the two of whom are living together, . . .
  b. *Max and Dorothy, who(m) two are living together, . . .

References

Adams, Douglas, Mary Ann Campbell, Victor Cohen, Julie Lovins, Edward Maxwell, Carolyn Nygren, and John Reighard, eds. (1971) *Papers from the Seventh Regional Meeting of the Chicago Linguistic Society*, Chicago.

Aissen, Judith (to appear) "Precyclic Rules."

Alexander, D., and W. J. Kunz (1964) *Some Classes of Verbs in English*, Linguistics Research Project, Indiana University, Bloomington.

Anderson, Stephen R., and Paul Kiparsky, eds. (to appear) *Studies in Honor of Morris Halle*, Holt, Rinehart and Winston, New York.

Andrews, Avery D. (1971) "Case Agreement of Predicate Modifiers in Ancient Greek," *Linguistic Inquiry* 2, Number 2.

Bach, Emmon (1962) "The Order of Elements in a Transformational Grammar of German," *Language* 38, Number 3.

———— (1970) "Anaphoric Pronouns and the Theory of Binding," presented at the Seminar on the Construction of Complex Grammars, sponsored by the Mathematical Social Sciences Board, Center for Advanced Study in the Behavioral Sciences, held at Harvard University, Cambridge, Mass.

———— (1971) "Questions," *Linguistic Inquiry* 2, Number 2.

Bach, Emmon, and Robert T. Harms, eds. (1968) *Universals in Linguistic Theory*, Holt, Rinehart and Winston, New York.

Baker, C. L. (1970a) "Notes on the Description of English Questions: The Role of an Abstract Question Morpheme," *Foundations of Language* 6: 197–219.

———— (1970b) "Double Negatives," *Linguistic Inquiry* 1, Number 2.

Bever, T. G., and W. Weksel, eds. (to appear) *The Structure and Psychology of Language*.

Bierwisch, Manfred (1963) *Grammatik des Deutschen Verbs*, Studia Grammatica II, Akademie-Verlag, Berlin.

Bierwisch, Manfred, and Karl E. Heidolph, eds. (1970) *Progress in Linguistics*, Mouton and Co., The Hague.

Binnick, Robert I., A. Davidson, G. Green, and J. Morgan, eds. (1969) *Papers from the Fifth Regional Meeting of the Chicago Linguistic Society*, Chicago.

Brame, Michael, and C. L. Baker (1972) "'Global Rules': A Rejoinder," *Language* 48, Number 1.

Bresnan, Joan (1970) "On Complementizers: Towards a Syntactic Theory of Complement Types," *Foundations of Language* 6: 297–321.

——— (1971) "Contraction and the Transformational Cycle in English," unpublished paper, M.I.T., Cambridge, Mass.

Browne, Wales (1968) "Srpskohrvatske enklitike i teorija transformacione gramatike," *Zbornik za filologiju i lingvistiku 11*, Yugoslavia.

Campbell, Mary Ann, James Lindholm, Alice Davison, William Fisher, Louanna Furbee, Julie Lovins, Edward Maxwell, John Reighard, and Stephen Straight, eds. (1970) *Papers from the Sixth Regional Meeting of the Chicago Linguistic Society,* Chicago.

Cantrall, William R. (1969) "On the Nature of the Reflexive in English," University of Illinois Doctoral Dissertation, Urbana.

——— (1970) "Why Do Trains Remind Me of Throwing Up?" unpublished paper.

Casagrande, J., and B. Saciuk, eds. (to appear) *Generative Studies in Romance Languages,* Newbury House, Rowley, Mass.

Chomsky, Noam (1957) *Syntactic Structures,* Mouton and Co., The Hague.

——— (1965) *Aspects of the Theory of Syntax,* M.I.T. Press, Cambridge, Mass.

——— (1967) "The Formal Nature of Language," in E. H. Lenneberg, *Biological Foundations of Language,* John Wiley and Sons, New York.

——— (1968) *Language and Mind,* Harcourt, Brace and World, New York.

——— (1970) "Remarks on Nominalization," in Jacobs and Rosenbaum, eds. (1970).

——— (1971) *Problems of Knowledge and Freedom,* Vintage Books, New York.

——— (1972) "Some Empirical Issues in the Theory of Transformational Grammar," in Peters, ed. (1972).

——— (to appear) "Conditions on Transformations," in Anderson and Kiparsky, eds. (to appear).

Darden, Bill J., Charles-James N. Bailey, Alice Davison, eds. (1968) *Papers from the Fourth Regional Meeting of the Chicago Linguistic Society,* Chicago.

Davidson, D., and G. Harman, eds. (1970) *Semantics of Natural Language,* D. Reidel, Dordrecht, Netherlands.

Dinneen, Francis, ed. (1966) *Nineteenth Monograph on Languages and Linguistics,* Georgetown University Press, Washington, D.C.

Dougherty, Ray C. (1969) "A Transformational Grammar of Coordinate Conjoined Structures," M.I.T. Doctoral Dissertation, Cambridge, Mass.

—— (1970) "A Grammar of Coordinate Conjoined Structures: I," *Language* 46, Number 4.

—— (1971) "A Grammar of Coordinate Conjoined Structures: II," *Language* 47, Number 2.

Emonds, Joseph E. (1969) "A Structure-Preserving Constraint on NP Movement Transformations," in Binnick et al., eds. (1969).

—— (1970) "Root and Structure-Preserving Transformations," M.I.T. Doctoral Dissertation, Cambridge, Mass.

Fauconnier, Gilles Raymond (1971) "Theoretical Implications of Some Global Phenomena in Syntax," University of California at San Diego Doctoral Dissertation, La Jolla.

Fillmore, Charles J. (1963) "The Position of Embedding Transformations in a Grammar," *Word* 19, Number 2.

—— (1968) "The Case for Case," in Bach and Harms, eds. (1968).

Fillmore, Charles J., and D. T. Langendoen, eds. (1971) *Studies in Linguistic Semantics*, Holt, Rinehart and Winston, New York.

Fodor, Jerry A., and Jerrold J. Katz, eds., (1964) *The Structure of Language*, Prentice-Hall, Englewood Cliffs, N.J.

Fraser, J. Bruce (1965) "An Examination of the Verb-Particle Construction in English," M.I.T. Doctoral Dissertation, Cambridge, Mass.

Garvin, Paul, ed. (1970a) *Cognition: A Multiple View*, Spartan Books, New York.

—— (1970b) *Method and Theory in Linguistics*, Mouton and Co., The Hague.

Greenberg, Joseph H. (1963a) "Some Universals of Grammar with Particular Reference to the Order of Meaningful Elements," in Greenberg, ed. (1963b).

——, ed. (1963b) *Universals of Language*, M.I.T. Press, Cambridge, Mass.

Grinder, John (1970) "Super Equi-NP Deletion," in Campbell et al., eds. (1970).

—— (1972) "On the Cycle in Syntax," in Kimball, ed. (1972).

Grinder, John, and Paul M. Postal (1971) "Missing Antecedents," *Linguistic Inquiry* 2, Number 3.

Grosu, Alexander (1971) "On Coreferentiality Constraints and Equi-NP-Deletion in English," in *Working Papers in Linguistics No. 7*, Computer and Information Science Research Center, The Ohio State University, Columbus.

Gruber, Jeffrey (1967) *Functions of the Lexicon in Formal Descriptive Grammars*, TM 3770/000/00, System Development Corporation, Santa Monica, Calif.

Hall, R. M. R., Beatrice L. Hall, and Martin D. Pam (1971) "Complementation in Tigrinya: Rules and Perceptual Strategies," paper read at Summer Meeting of the Linguistic Society of America, State University of New York, Buffalo.

Hankamer, Jorge (1971) "Constraints on Deletion in Syntax" Yale University Doctoral Dissertation, New Haven, Conn.

——— (to appear) "Unacceptable Ambiguity," *Linguistic Inquiry*.

Helke, M. (1971) "The Grammar of English Reflexives" M.I.T. Doctoral Dissertation, Cambridge, Mass.

Higgins, F. R. (1971) "A Squib on J. Emonds's Analysis of Extraposition" unpublished paper, M.I.T., Cambridge, Mass.

Huddleston, Rodney (1971) *The Sentence in Written English*, Cambridge University Press, Cambridge, England.

Hudson, Grover (1972) "Is Deep Structure Linear?" in *UCLA Papers in Syntax*, Number 2, Los Angeles, Calif.

Hudson, R. A. (1970) "On Clauses Containing Conjoined and Plural Noun-Phrases in English," *Lingua* 24, Number 2.

——— (1972) "Why It Is That That That That That Follows the Subject Is Impossible," *Linguistic Inquiry* 3, Number 1.

Jackendoff, Ray (1969) "Some Rules of Semantic Interpretation for English," M.I.T. Doctoral Dissertation, Cambridge, Mass. (revised and published under title *Semantic Interpretation in Generative Grammar*, M.I.T. Press, 1972).

——— (1971) "Gapping and Related Rules," *Linguistic Inquiry* 2, Number 1.

Jacobs, Roderick A., and Peter S. Rosenbaum, eds. (1970) *Readings in English Transformational Grammar*, Ginn and Company, Waltham, Mass.

Jakobson, Roman, and Shigeo Kawamoto, eds. (1970) *Studies in General and Oriental Linguistics*, TEC Corp., Tokyo.

Jespersen, Otto (1969) *Analytic Syntax*, Holt, Rinehart and Winston, New York.

Kachru, Braj, et al. (to appear) *Issues in Linguistics: Papers in Honor of Henry and Renée Kahane*, University of Illinois Press, Urbana.

Katz, Jerrold J., and Paul M. Postal (1964) *An Integrated Theory of Linguistic Descriptions,* M.I.T. Press, Cambridge, Mass.

Kayne, Richard (1969) *The Transformational Cycle in French Syntax,* M.I.T. Doctoral Dissertation, Cambridge, Mass.

———— (to appear) "Subject Inversion in French Interrogatives," in Casagrande and Saciuk, eds. (to appear).

Kimball, John, ed. (1972) *Syntax and Semantics,* Volume I, Seminar Press, New York.

Kiparsky, Carol, and Paul Kiparsky (1970) "Fact," in Bierwisch and Heidolph, eds. (1970).

Klima, Edward S. (1964) "Negation in English," in Fodor and Katz, eds. (1964).

Koutsoudas, Andreas (1972) "The Strict Order Fallacy," *Language* 48, Number 1.

Kuno, Susumu (1970) "Some Properties of Non-Referential Noun Phrases," in Jakobson and Kawamoto, eds. (1970).

———— (1972a) "Pronominalization, Reflexivization, and Direct Discourse," in *Linguistic Inquiry* 3, Number 2.

———— (1972b) "Subject Raising in Japanese," *Papers in Japanese Linguistics* 1, Number 1.

———— (to appear a) "Constraints on Internal Clauses and Sentential Subjects."

———— (to appear b) "Natural Explanations for Some Language Universals in Syntax."

Kuno, Susumu, and Jane Robinson (to appear) "Multiple Wh Questions," *Linguistic Inquiry.*

Lakoff, George (1967) "Deep and Surface Grammar," unpublished manuscript, Harvard University, Cambridge, Mass.

———— (1969) "On Derivational Constraints," in Binnick et al., eds. (1969).

———— (1970a) "Global Rules," *Language* 46, Number 3.

———— (1970b) "Linguistics and Natural Logic," *Synthese* 22, Numbers 1–2.

———— (1972a) "The Arbitrary Basis of Transformational Grammar," *Language* 48, Number 1.

———— (1972b) "The Global Nature of the Nuclear Stress Rule," *Language* 48, Number 2.

Lakoff, Robin (1968) *Abstract Syntax and Latin Complementation*, M.I.T. Press, Cambridge, Mass.

Langacker, Ronald W. (1969) "On Pronominalization and the Chain of Command," in Reibel and Schane, eds. (1969).

Langendoen, D. T. (1969) "Modal Auxiliaries in Infinitive Clauses in English," in *Working Papers in Linguistics No. 3*, Computer and Information Science Research Center, The Ohio State University, Columbus.

―――― (1970) "The 'Can't Seem to' Construction," *Linguistic Inquiry* 1, Number 1.

Lees, R. B. (1960) *The Grammar of English Nominalizations*, Mouton and Co., The Hague.

Lees, R. B., and E. S. Klima (1963) "Rules for English Pronominalization," *Language* 39, Number 1.

Lehmann, Twila (1972) "Some Arguments Against Ordered Rules," *Language* 48, Number 3.

Live, Anna H. (1967) "Subject-Verb Inversion (in English)," *General Linguistics* 7, Number 1.

McCawley, James D. (1967) "Meaning and the Description of Languages," *Kotoba No Uchu* 2, Numbers 9–11.

―――― (1968) "A Note on Multiple Negations," unpublished paper, University of Chicago.

―――― (1970a) "English as a VSO Language," *Language* 46, Number 2.

―――― (1970b) "Semantic Representation," in Garvin, ed. (1970a).

―――― (1970c) "Where Do Noun Phrases Come From?" in Jacobs and Rosenbaum, eds. (1970).

―――― (1970d) "A Program for Logic," in Davidson and Harman, eds. (1970).

―――― (1971) "Tense and Time Reference in English," in Fillmore and Langendoen, eds. (1971).

―――― (to appear a) *Syntactic and Logical Arguments for Semantic Structures*, TEC Corp., Tokyo.

―――― (to appear b) *Grammar and Meaning*, Taishukan, Tokyo.

Maling, Joan (1972) "On 'Gapping and the Order of Constituents,'" *Linguistic Inquiry* 3, Number 1.

Morgan, Jerry L. (1968) "Some Strange Aspects of *It*," in Darden et al., eds. (1968).

———— (to appear) "Sentence Fragments and the Notion 'Sentence,' " in Kachru et al., eds. (to appear).

Newmeyer, Frederick (1971) "A Problem with the Verb-Initial Hypothesis," *Papers in Linguistics* 4, Number 2.

Pam, Martin D. (1971) "Word Order in Tigrinya," unpublished paper, City University of New York, New York.

Partee, Barbara H. (1971) "On the Requirement that Transformations Preserve Meaning," in Fillmore and Langendoen, eds. (1971).

Peranteau, Paul M., Judith N. Levi, and Gloria C. Phares, eds. (1972) *Papers from the Eighth Regional Meeting of the Chicago Linguistic Society*, Chicago.

Perlmutter, David M. (1970) "The Two Verbs *Begin*," in Jacobs and Rosenbaum, eds. (1970).

———— (1971) *Deep and Surface Structure Constraints in Syntax*, Holt, Rinehart and Winston, New York.

———— (to appear) "The Globality of Object Raising in Portuguese," *Linguistic Inquiry*.

Perlmutter, David M., and Paul M. Postal (to appear a) "The Functional Succession Principle," *Linguistic Inquiry*.

———— (to appear b) *Relational Grammar*.

Peters, Paul Stanley, ed. (1972) *Goals of Linguistic Theory*, Prentice-Hall, Englewood Cliffs, N.J.

Postal, Paul M. (1966a) "On So-Called Pronouns in English," in Dinneen, ed. (1966).

———— (1966b) Review of R. Longacre, *Grammar Discovery Procedures*, in *International Journal of American Linguistics* 32.

———— (1966c) "A Note on 'Understood Transitively,' " *International Journal of American Linguistics* 32.

———— (1969a) Review of A. McIntosh and M. A. K. Halliday, *Papers in General, Descriptive and Applied Linguistics*, in *Foundations of Language* 5, Number 3.

———— (1969b) "Anaphoric Islands," in Binnick et al., eds. (1969).

———— (1970a) "On the Surface Verb *Remind*," *Linguistic Inquiry* 1, Number 1.

Postal, Paul M. (1970b) "On Coreferential Complement Subject Deletion," *Linguistic Inquiry* 1, Number 4.

——— (1970c) "The Method of Universal Grammar," in Garvin, ed. (1970b).

——— (1971) *Cross-Over Phenomena*, Holt, Rinehart and Winston, New York.

——— (1972a) "A Global Constraint on Pronominalization," *Linguistic Inquiry* 3, Number 1.

——— (1972b) "Two Remarks on Dragging," *Linguistic Inquiry* 3, Number 1.

——— (1972c) "On Some Rules That Are Not Successive Cyclic," *Linguistic Inquiry* 3, Number 2.

——— (1972d) "The Best Theory," in Peters, ed. (1972).

——— (to appear a) "Scopes and Islands."

——— (to appear b) "A Remark on the Verb-Initial Hypothesis," *Papers in Linguistics.*

——— (to appear c) "Floating Quantifiers."

——— (to appear d) "A Fundamental Pronominalization Constraint."

——— (to appear e) "A Non-Nich."

Reibel, David A., and Sanford A. Schane, eds. (1969) *Modern Studies in English,* Prentice-Hall, Englewood Cliffs, N. J.

Ringen, Catherine (1972) "On Arguments for Rule Ordering," *Foundations of Language* 8, Number 2: 266–273.

Rivero, María-Luisa (1970) "A Surface Structure Constraint on Negation in Spanish," *Language* 46, Number 3.

Rogers, Andy (1971) "Three Kinds of Physical Perception Verbs," in Adams et al., eds. (1971).

Rosenbaum, Peter S. (1967) *The Grammar of English Predicate Complement Constructions*, M.I.T. Press, Cambridge, Mass.

Ross, John R. (1967) "Constraints on Variables in Syntax," M.I.T. Doctoral Dissertation, Cambridge, Mass.

——— (1969a) "A Proposed Rule of Tree Pruning," in Reibel and Schane, eds. (1969).

Ross, John R. (1969b) "The Cyclic Nature of English Pronominalization," in Reibel and Schane, eds. (1969).

―――― (1969c) "Guess Who," in Binnick et al., eds. (1969).

―――― (1970a) "On Declarative Sentences," in Jacobs and Rosenbaum, eds. (1970).

―――― (1970b) "Gapping and the Order of Constituents," in Bierwisch and Heidolph, eds. (1970).

―――― (1971) "Mirror Image Rules and VSO Order," *Linguistic Inquiry* 2, Number 4.

―――― (1972a) "Doubl-ing," *Linguistic Inquiry* 3, Number 1.

―――― (1972b) "The Category Squish: Endstation Hauptwort," in Peranteau et al., eds. (1972).

―――― (to appear a) "Fake NP's."

―――― (to appear b) "Nouniness."

―――― (to appear c) "Primacy."

―――― (to appear d) "Niching."

―――― (to appear e) "Variable Strength."

―――― (to appear f) "Auxiliaries as Main Verbs," in Bever and Weksel, eds. (to appear).

―――― (to appear g) "Treetops and the Order of Constituents," read at Third Meeting, Northeastern Linguistic Society.

Ruwet, Nicolas (1972) *Théorie Syntaxique et Syntaxe du Français*, aux Éditions du Seuil, Paris.

Stockwell, Robert P., Paul Schachter, and Barbara Hall Partee (1968) *Integration of Transformational Theories on English Syntax*, Command Systems Division, Electronic Systems Division, Air Force Systems Command, United States Air Force, EDS-TR-68-419, Bedford, Mass.

Witten, Edward (1972) "Centrality," in *Report No. NSF-28 to The National Science Foundation*, The Computation Laboratory of Harvard University, Cambridge, Mass.

Index